Advance Praise:

"For anyone who has gone through their own in-an-instant moment when life is reconfigured in seconds, *Crash* so beautifully articulates the pain, struggle, and long road to recovery and acceptance in the aftermath of injury and loss. Roy-Bornstein reminds us, with heart-breaking prose, that life is a journey and a mother's heart is a powerful weapon."

> —Lee Woodruff, author of *Perfectly Imperfect* and
> co-author with Bob Woodruff of *In an Instant*

"*Crash* is a powerful book. It speaks to us on the most human and humane levels about love, family, healing, and renewal. Written by a physician mother, it puts the horror of a roadside accident into the contexts of familial terror and doctorly wisdom. It is a consequential book, one I read in two straight nights and which resonated with me for a long time afterward. Read it—I was blown away."

> —Caitlin Flanagan, author of *Girl Land* and *To Hell with All That*

"A true testament of the unique love, dedication, and human spirit of a family shattered by an unthinkable accident. Beautifully written . . . heartbreakingly intimate . . . unwaveringly honest."

> —Julia Fox Garrison, author of *Don't Leave Me This Way*

"This powerful memoir is both heart-wrenching and heart-warming. Every parent's nightmare and the amazing journey of a son and the family who loved him."

> —Julie Silver, MD, author of *You Can Heal Yourself*

"All of us, when passing the scene of a bad accident, know the flash of dread: 'That could have been one of mine.' For Carolyn Roy-Bornstein that flash was her fate. As a doctor herself, Roy-Bornstein knows too much and, at the same time, not enough when suddenly thrust into the chaos of caring for a son broken, quite literally, in mind and spirit."

> —Linda Keenan, author of *Suburgatory*

CRASH

A Mother, a Son, and the Journey from Grief to Gratitude

CAROLYN ROY-BORNSTEIN, MD

Guilford, Connecticut
An imprint of Globe Pequot Press

skirt!® is an attitude . . . spirited, independent, outspoken, serious, playful and irreverent, sometimes controversial, always passionate.

Project editor: Meredith Dias
Layout artist: Sue Murray

Library of Congress Cataloging-in-Publication Data

Roy-Bornstein, Carolyn.
  Crash : a mother, a son, and the journey from grief to gratitude /
Carolyn Roy-Bornstein.
    p. cm.
  ISBN 978-0-7627-8045-7
  1. Bornstein, Neil—Mental health. 2. Traffic accident victims—Biography. 3. Traffic accidents—Psychological aspects. 4. Drinking and traffic accidents. I. Title.
  RC1045.P78R69 2012
  363.12'514092—dc23
  [B]

                                                                    2012008388

Printed in the United States of America

10 9 8 7 6 5 4 3 2 1

For Neil and Trista

"No amount of doctoring can prepare you for being a patient."
—ERIC D. MANHEIMER

A Crack in the Glass

THERE IS THIS POINT that divides my life into two unequal parts. A line, like a crack in the glass, that carves time and events in two: those that occurred before the crash and those that tumble and falter in its wake. There is this one moment after which nothing is the same. It occurs in a heartbeat—a squeeze of the ventricles. A throb in which blood is pushed out of the heart and up into the brain. Here, in that moment, blood that should be contained within the intimal walls of the brain's blood vessels instead seeps beyond them through a rent, pooling in the arachnoids space, separating the thin layers of meninges and transforming a potential space into a gooey hemorrhage. In this moment the skull has careened through space and collided with glass, forming the crack that now divides my life in two.

"Two Kids Were Hit on Ferry Road"

JANUARY 7, 2003, WAS AN ORDINARY EVENING in our home. My son Neil and his girlfriend, Trista, were upstairs studying. My husband, Saul, and I were grilling hamburgers on the stove. When Neil wandered into the kitchen and picked a few cucumbers out of the salad bowl, I swatted his fingers and asked him whether Trista would want cheese on her burger. He shrugged.

"I dunno. Ask her."

I stepped past him to call upstairs and do just that when he suddenly grabbed my arm. A knowing smile spread over his face.

"Wait. She'll want cheese. Lots and lots of cheese."

I had wondered when they would start to know these little things about each other. Trista was Neil's first serious girlfriend. They were eight months into their young relationship. Everything was new and compelling. And Neil had learned this about Trista: that she liked a little burger with her cheese.

We all chatted over dinner about our evening plans. Saul was headed off to the Salvation Army gym for his Tuesday-night volleyball game. I usually played too, but tonight I was planning on meeting a friend at the Screening Room to see *Bowling for Columbine*. Neil and his older brother, Dan, played volleyball too, and tonight Saul tried to entice Neil and Trista to join him.

"C'mon Trista. It'll be fun. You'll get to see Neil in gym shorts," my husband cajoled.

Trista laughed at the image, her bright peals filling our small kitchen. Neil just grinned. I loved when Trista ate with us. Our son, who could be a typically monosyllabic, morose teenager, brightened in her presence. The whole mood of the house changed with her there.

The kids considered his invitation but ultimately turned him down. They were hoping Trista's mother, Mary, would let Neil spend the rest of the evening at the Zincks' home, doubtful on a school night. Mary was a strict disciplinarian with rigid rules for her only daughter.

"I'm afraid of her," Neil once told me about Mary.

I'd only met her a few times, dropping Neil off at her house or picking him up; at her semiformal, his prom. I could see what Neil meant. Mary projected a no-nonsense, tough-as-nails facade. But she was also quick with a laugh. She was the type of person who said what she meant and meant what she said. With Mary you always knew where you stood.

After dinner Trista sat on the footstool by the wood stove pulling on her boots. She stood and shrugged herself into her winter coat. Neil was making no move to get ready.

"Aren't you walking Trista home?" I asked. He always did. But tonight they looked at each other and smiled. They were concocting a scheme to convince Mary to let Neil come over. They reasoned that she would be most amenable to the idea if Trista showed up at home alone and before curfew. I disagreed.

"You guys have it all wrong," I told them. I held Neil's coat out for him, reaching my arms up over his almost six-foot frame that now towered over me. "You have to walk her home, Neil, the chivalrous gentleman delivering the lady to her doorstep safe and sound. Then Mary will *have* to let you stay."

The pair considered this for a moment. Then Trista winked and nodded, a twinkle in her eye. She gunned a finger in my direction.

"Better plan," she concurred.

With that they were off into a clear, cold January night. I cleared supper dishes and rinsed them at the kitchen sink. Then I did what I often did when Neil walked Trista home. I dimmed the kitchen lights so the couple wouldn't see me watching them walk down our street. I always gave them their privacy when they were in my home, making sure they heard me coming into a room they were in. In my presence they gazed at each other with obvious budding affection, but physical demonstrations of their tenderness were rare. This window surveillance was the only time I let myself watch them unobserved.

I tracked them as they turned left up Spofford Street, then crossed over to Plant Street, which would take them on to Ferry Road. The Zincks lived on Laurel Road, off Ferry. The whole route was less than a half mile and usually took the kids just fifteen minutes to get from one house to the other. They passed under the yellow glow of a street lamp, which outlined their silhouettes: two shadows holding hands.

I finished the dishes, wiped down the table and counters, and turned off the lights. The house was quiet. Logs shifted and crackled in the wood stove. In a sudden change of mind, I

3

decided to forgo the movies in favor of a quiet evening alone. I fixed myself a cup of tea then settled at the computer to write.

Half an hour later the phone rang. Mary did not even wait for me to say hello.

"Where are the kids?" she breathed. I looked at my watch. Almost forty minutes had passed since Neil and Trista had set out.

"They should have gotten to your house by now," I reported quietly, dully, the significance of my words only slowly sinking in even as I said them.

"Two kids were hit on Ferry Road." And with that Mary hung up. She didn't give me time to ask, "What kids? *Our* kids?" I stood there with the receiver in my hand, the line gone dead. I tried calling my husband at the Salvation Army. The Toastmasters met in a room down the hall from the gym. Maybe someone would pick up. But it just rang and rang. I pictured the phone ringing on the counter in the little kitchen, out of earshot of the players and the Toastmasters. I tried calling the police.

"We have no report of an accident on Ferry Road, Ma'am," the officer told me. I fantasized that maybe there was no accident. Maybe Neil and Trista had stopped at a friend's house, or stepped into the woods to kiss. Maybe it was a dog that was hit on Ferry Road, and Mary had just misunderstood.

Time was ticking by. I slipped my bare feet into open-backed clogs and threw on a coat. My black lab, Lucky, was pacing behind me. Perhaps she thought she was in for a bonus walk. Or more likely she sensed my anxiety and fear. I briefly considered taking her with me. I truly did not want to be alone, and canine company was better than no company at all. But I knew that if

I got to Ferry Road and it *was* our kids, I couldn't take Lucky with me to the hospital. Part of me wanted to take her anyway. I even reasoned that by taking her with me I would be defying the inevitable reality. It couldn't be Neil and Trista as long as I had my dog with me. By putting her leash down and not taking her, I was giving up, resigning myself to the fact that the two kids hit on Ferry Road *were* our two kids. I laid Lucky's leash on the arm of the loveseat by the front door and stepped out into the frigid January night alone.

2

The Crash Scene

TWO THINGS BECAME IMMEDIATELY CLEAR. I should have worn socks, and I should have brought my inhaler. I am not a runner but I am an asthmatic, and those two truths now combined to make breathing very difficult. I ran along the same route Neil and Trista had just traveled. The air was dry and cold; it hurt to breathe and made my nostrils stick together each time I inhaled. My eyes stung and watered in the bitter cold so I squinted, trying to see far ahead of me, listening for sirens and scanning the landscape for flashing lights but found neither. I crossed Spofford and ran up Plant Street. I wanted to slow, to stop, to catch my breath. But I forced myself on.

Farther ahead, at the end of Plant Street, I caught a glimpse of blue flashing lights. I quickened my step, but there were no ambulances. Six cruisers with their lights flashing were arranged haphazardly along the road. Officers in uniforms talked among themselves, but nobody talked to me. I didn't understand what they were all doing there.

I bent over, hands on my knees, my breath coming in short gulps and long painful exhalations. I knew the smooth muscles around my airways were constricting, trapping air inside my lungs, daring me to find a way to push it out. I pursed my lips and forced my breath out slowly, trying to stent my airways open. It was no use. I couldn't breathe. I could hear myself wheezing, tinkling strains, musical, rhythmic. A little cat sigh with every breath.

I felt a hand on my shoulder.

"C'mon. We'll drive you to the hospital." It was Maureen, her son, Kaes, by her side. They lived on this street. On Ferry Road. Maureen's daughter, Jess, was Trista's best friend. Kaes hung out with both my boys. At first I didn't comprehend what Maureen was saying to me. I thought she could see me struggling to breathe, thought I might need emergency attention. I waved her away.

"No . . . I'm . . . all right," I said. Then I saw the look. The subtlest exchange between her and her son. And I knew. They weren't talking about me at all.

"Did you see them?" I demanded of Kaes. He looked down at his shuffling feet.

"No," he admitted.

"Then . . . you don't . . . know . . . that it was . . . them," I cog-wheeled. "Maybe . . . it wasn't . . . them." I knew I sounded ridiculous. I could barely choke out a sentence, and I was denying what was clearly everyone else's reality. I could tell from the looks on their faces, from Mary's panicked voice on the phone, and from the cops' stringent avoidance of me. It was them.

Maureen's gentle, plump fingers found their way to my waist, edging me across the street.

"C'mon."

She opened the door of her car and ushered me inside then climbed into the driver's seat. Kaes sat silently in back. I did not fasten my seat belt. I remember feeling reckless and wild and unsafe. I was starting to let my mind grasp the fact that my child had been hit on Ferry Road. And if it had happened to him, I wanted it to be able to happen to me, too. I wanted to be there with him, vulnerable. Panic was now mixing with the cold and the exertion to make breathing a concentrated effort. Trying to prolong expiration by pursing my lips just wasn't cutting it any more.

I gradually became aware of a sound. A low groan. An animal noise. Something wild and raw, on edge, not human. But it had a rhythm to it. I gradually became aware that its rhythm matched my own respirations. That's when I realized that *I* was the sound.

3

The Bad Mother

MAUREEN DROPPED ME OFF at the entrance to the emergency room and went to park the car. I don't remember seeing her again that night. I gave my name to the triage nurse who sat behind a tiny square glass window.

"My boy was hit on Ferry Road," I told her, noticing that my breathing was starting to ease. Still tight, but I could get out a sentence in one breath now. The nurse looked awkwardly down at her feet. I was becoming familiar with that look, and I didn't like it.

"Wait right there," she said to the floor as she backed out of her cubicle and disappeared into the belly of the ER. I looked around the waiting room. An old man with stained pants sat in a chair framed by his walker. The heel of his foot tapped the floor at superhuman speed as he stared blankly in front of him. A child with a loud croupy cough was on the floor exploring the contents of his mother's purse while she watched a TV set mounted on the opposite wall. Torn copies of *People* magazine lay randomly on chairs. I stood frozen in front of the triage booth, waiting for permission to see my son.

I don't know what kept me cemented to the ground like that. Part of it, I'm sure, is genetic. I am my mother's daughter. My mother was a true Southern belle, demure and deferential. I have inherited her shell of calm, and it has stood me in good stead through the years. My fellow residents, even my attendings, were always glad to see their names next to mine on the on-call roster, making assumptions about what an outward veneer of quietude said about inner confidence. Even today, many parents I have dealt with have been grateful for that composure when we have faced fear and trauma and bad news together.

Maybe the reason I just stood there was because I'm a doctor. I know the rules. I expect people to follow the rules in my ER, and here I was, in someone else's ER, conforming to theirs.

Maybe it was just residual denial and fantasy. Maybe I was playing a game. As long as I didn't lose my cool, as long as I kept it together, it couldn't possibly be my child in there.

That's when Mary blew in.

"Where's my daughter?" she screamed. Then she flew by me, past the triage booth, out of the waiting room, and down the hall into the ER. She did not stop at the little glass window. She did not give her name to the nurse at the triage booth. She did not wait right there.

I followed her into the ER, feeling like a bad mother for following the rules.

4

The Other Side of the Stretcher

WHEN NEIL WAS A SOPHOMORE in high school, he played Tybalt in *Romeo and Juliet*. He had few lines but a formidable stage presence, with his fierce anger and menacing bluster. He learned the complicated fight choreography, expertly clashing sword against sword, first with Mercutio then Romeo. Advancing. Retreating. Slicing. Thrusting. A rhythmic dance. The theater was silent except for the soft shuffle of gliding feet, boots landing on stage in perfect balestra, swords clanking, first high then low.

And then the death scene. Romeo plunged his dagger deep into Tybalt's chest. Neil's chest. My son. He fell to the ground. Juliet dropped to her knees and cried over him.

"'Tybalt, my cousin! O my brother's only child!'"

"Doesn't that make me your nephew?" Neil would joke during rehearsals, cracking Juliet up every time. But on opening night he wasn't joking. And Juliet wasn't laughing. She was weeping, and so was I.

His fellow actors came on stage and lifted Neil reverently onto a slab of wood and then covered him with a pure white shroud. They walked slowly, as if marching to a silent dirge. They placed him carefully onto a makeshift bier, two foot-high blocks of wood pushed together at the back of the stage.

And there he lay for the rest of Act III. Scene after scene played out. Romeo. Friar Lawrence. Lady Capulet. Nurse. Their lines were silent to me, their movements unseen: My eyes were glued to the body at stage rear. Neil's shroud was made of a gauzy fabric. I could see his facial features beneath its flimsy folds. I tried to detect some movement. A breath. A twitch. But there was none.

It filled me with sorrow and dread watching my son, dead on stage. The rest of the audience was at a play. But I was at a wake, staring into a coffin and waiting for the victim to rise.

"I'm sorry my son keeps killing your son," Hal's mother joked after the performance. We chuckled together, but for months I could not shake the feeling of doom that enveloped me since Neil's onstage demise.

—◆—

Now, three years later, an ER nurse was taking me to my boy. And there he was again, my son. Behind a curtain. Under a shroud. On a bier. But now the stage was an ER cubicle, and the curtain here was stark white, not velvet red. His shroud was a sheet pulled up to his neck; his bier, a hospital stretcher. His clothes were lying in piles on the floor around him, cut from his body in haste. I tried to detect some movement. A breath. A twitch. His head was wedged between two big Styrofoam blocks secured by thick white adhesive tape to protect his neck. I laid my hand across his forehead and his eyes fluttered open.

"Hi, Mom."

He knew me. I felt a rush of relief. But he drifted immediately back into unconsciousness, and my brief elation gave way to a gathering knot of fear. A doctor came in and gave me the rundown on my son. I did not know this woman. I didn't know any of the medical personnel here at Anna Jaques Hospital. My admitting privileges were at a different community hospital twenty miles away, Lawrence General.

"What happened?" I asked her.

"The police are still trying to piece it together," she told me. "It looks like a hit-and-run."

I tried to follow her message, to stay focused on what she was telling me. But those words—hit-and-run—seemed to take over the part of my brain that paid attention. At first she told me his only injury was a broken leg. I lifted the sheet between my thumb and forefinger and peeked underneath while the doctor continued her update. Neil's lower leg was badly deformed; his fractured shinbone strained against his skin at an unnatural angle. Dark blood pooled just beneath the surface. My stomach turned in response. Though I have scrubbed in on dozens of strangers' surgeries over the years and patched together many patients' gashes and scrapes, I have always been totally squeamish when it came to the slightest wound on one of my own.

The doctor's words drifted back to me. "CAT scan . . . Just a precaution . . . Out at the scene."

I tried to follow the gist. Neil would be okay. He had a broken leg. They were CT'ing his head as a precaution because he had lost consciousness right after the crash.

I've talked to hundreds of parents in emergency rooms and ICUs. I've been the bearer of bad news or at least uncertainty more times than I care to remember. I know people shut down. I know they can only take in so much. I've learned to slow my pace, to read the signs in patients' eyes and faces that this is enough. The well is full and I should stop dumping information into it. And now here I was on the other side of the stretcher, trying to comprehend what was happening. My son recognized me—that was good. But he slept if you let him—that was bad. He was not asking what happened. He was not asking for his father or his girlfriend.

I could not be alone. I had to reach Saul. But I couldn't leave Neil alone either. I stepped out into the hall, clinging to the curtain that hung from the ceiling and separated Neil's cubicle from the bustling corridor as if it were some kind of mooring that anchored me to my son. As if by holding onto the curtain I was protecting myself from being swept away from him. I recognized the fire chief, Steve Cutter, pacing nearby. Our kids played soccer together years ago (a lifetime ago!). His hand rested lightly on his two-way radio.

"Steve, can you get a message to my husband? He's playing volleyball at the Salvation Army."

"I'll see what I can do," he said and strode off, happy to be on a mission.

I returned to my son's side. There was no chair in his cubicle so I stood over his stretcher, looking down on his sleeping face. I ran my hand through his long brown waves. His eyes opened sleepily.

"Hi, Mom," he said again. But it was as if he were seeing me for the first time. I shivered.

A nurse entered and deftly released the brakes on Neil's gurney with her foot while simultaneously swinging the bed around

14

and wheeling him out the door and down the hall. She called to me over her shoulder, "You can follow us to CAT scan." I fell in line behind the speeding procession.

We passed Trista's cubicle, next to Neil's. It was humming with activity. Monitors beeped. Doctors barked orders. Someone was crying. Mary was wailing in the hall outside her daughter's room. I kept my focus on my son. The nurse wheeled him into the radiology suite, motioning toward a couple of lonely plastic chairs in the bare hallway. I took a seat and waited.

A faraway jangling sound drew my attention down the long corridor. A uniformed police officer was striding up the hall, his heavy keys bouncing against his leg as he walked. He was escorting my husband to us. Saul broke away from the officer when he spotted me and I rushed to meet him. My husband is a big man with strong, broad shoulders. He owns his own restaurant supply store, and he is accustomed to moving industrial refrigerators and wrestling two-ton walk-in coolers into place. But as he raced down the hall to me, his arms open to gather me up, his frame was heavy and bent.

"He's okay," I blurted out, more because I could see how panicked Saul was than because I believed it was the truth. We fell into each other's arms.

"I thought he was dead, Cal." Saul's voice cracked. His face was buried in my neck, muting his words. I tried to console him as best I could.

"He's okay. He's okay," I repeated, trying to convince myself of the truth of the words as I spoke them. Saul's shoulders shuddered with small sobs. I had rarely seen my husband cry. I had never seen him this wracked. We held each other. I was relieved to see him. I was glad to have someone to talk to, to be scared with, to hold onto.

But I realized that no one was going to relieve me of the burden of duty here. I would be the interpreter, the bridge. This was my world: ambulances, hospitals, ERs. If there were medical decisions to be made, I would need to gather all the necessary information and make them. With the facts and on my own. I could not let my guard down. I did not feel strong enough for this.

As we withdrew from our embrace, I locked eyes with the police officer who had escorted Saul to me. He quickly looked away, perhaps discomfited by the raw display of emotion. He slowly turned and headed down the hall, his mission here over. I tried to fill Saul in on what I knew. The broken leg was a definite, but after that I was on shaky ground. The CAT scan had been presented to me as a mere precaution. Probably over-kill—doctors just being thorough. But the more Neil slept and the more he repeated himself every time he saw me, the more I worried about his brain.

The scanner door opened, and the nurse pushed Neil's stretcher back down the hall toward his room. Saul bit his lip and touched Neil's head as they moved.

"Hi, Dad," Neil said, monotone, then closed his eyes again. Saul looked at me with a smile and a sigh of relief. My heart cracked. I felt almost nostalgic for that sense of relief that I too had experienced just moments ago when I realized Neil was alive and knew me. But even though Saul was only minutes after me in responding to our son's accident, I felt like I was light years ahead of him in understanding the magnitude of what was happening. Not just because of my medical training but because Neil was repeating himself. His recognitions were without emotion. He seemed a shell. The blanker he was, the more I worried about damage to his brain.

Saul and I sat together waiting for the doctors to tell us the results of the scan. Saul caught me up on how he was informed of the accident. A uniformed police officer had walked into the Salvation Army gym and interrupted their volleyball game, asking for Saul by name. There were a couple of jokes among the players.

"Uh-oh, what'd ya do, Saul?"

"How many parking tickets do you have anyway?"

But it soon became clear that something was very wrong.

"Your daughter's been in an accident, sir."

"He just kept saying it, Cal, over and over. I told him I didn't have a daughter. Did he mean my son? But he just kept saying, 'I can't give you any more information than that, sir.'"

Saul's head dropped into his hands again.

"I thought he was dead," he said again, his voice a whisper.

I rubbed his neck, kissed his shoulder. But I knew none of it was a comfort to him. The only thing that would comfort him would be a piece of good news about Neil. Our chairs were close to where a group of scrubs huddled in front of the light box and murmured over someone's films. I wanted to join them, to render my own interpretation of the images. I strained to hear their words over the ambient bustle. "Brain." "Fracture." "Bleed." I knew they were talking about Neil. When they turned and walked toward us like one organism, I squeezed Saul's hand hard.

"Your son has a fractured skull," one of the scrubs explained. "There's a tiny bit of bleeding at the site," another added. "Nothing big really, but we'd like to transfer him to Boston. In case."

In case he needs a Richmond bolt, I thought. *An intracranial pressure monitor.* Anna Jaques was not equipped to do brain surgery on a child. I tried to push visions of Neil's shaved and bandaged head out of my mind. While I was glad he was being transferred to a tertiary trauma center with the best neurosurgeons in the world, I was terrified that he might actually need one of them. I squeezed Saul's hand, trying to interpret the situation for him.

"It's just a precaution, honey," I said, hoping this was true.

They led us back to Neil's cubicle. He was more agitated now. His leg was hurting him. He thought he was in a gym. After each arousal he fell back into a deep sleep. Saul and I stood over him, our hands on his shoulders, feeling helpless and scared.

The noise level outside our cubicle rose. I could hear Mary wailing. Police walkie-talkies crackled. Trista's brother, Bud, was pounding his fist into the arm of a metal chair in the hall, sputtering over and over, "I'll kill him. I'll kill him."

"I have to go say good-bye," I told Saul and stepped into the hall. I followed the sounds of Mary's cries and found her outside Trista's cubicle. I put my hands around her shoulders, trying to console the inconsolable.

"Have you seen her?" I asked. I had only seen Mary in the hall outside Trista's room.

"I can't; I can't," she sobbed.

But what if Trista didn't make it? What if this was Mary's last chance to see her daughter alive? I had helped countless

18

distraught parents see their intubated and unconscious children for the first time. I had done it as a nurse, a resident, and an attending. I explained the machines, the tubes. I held their hands and answered their questions. I was good at it.

"C'mon with me. You have to see her." I gently led this mother, this woman I was just beginning to know, to her daughter's side. A crowd surrounded Trista's stretcher. Her head was taped between two Styrofoam blocks, like Neil's. She was intubated. A respiratory therapist knelt against her, pressing air into her lungs rhythmically with an Ambu bag. A nurse was securing her heart monitor to the stretcher's side rails with Velcro straps.

"I can't," Mary screamed again and collapsed on the floor next to the stretcher. Mary's husband, David, lifted her gently, and together they moved into the hall. I stepped closer to Trista. I'm not sure why the local ER crew made room for me. They didn't know I was a doctor, but maybe they let me in because Trista was stabilized or because they thought of me as a surrogate mother, given Mary's inability to see her child this way.

Someone had put ointment into Trista's eyes to keep them moist. Despite the bright glare of the ER's fluorescent lights, her pupils yawned widely open. I swallowed hard, knowing what that meant: fixed and dilated. I kissed her forehead.

"Good-bye, sweetheart," I whispered. Then the helicopter crew arrived and whisked Trista out the door. I never saw her again.

5

Transport

When I was a resident at the University of Massachusetts Medical Center, one of the most stressful rotations was the neonatal intensive care unit. And in the NICU rotation, one of the most stressful calls we could get was a request to go out on transport. Calls came into our tertiary care center whenever a baby at an outlying community hospital was born prematurely or was too sick for the local hospital to care for.

Our catchment area spanned a fifty-mile radius, which made for some pretty long rides bouncing around in the back of an exhaust-filled ambulance. Usually a resident, a nurse, and a respiratory therapist made up the transport team. On the way there we checked equipment and reviewed emergency algorithms in our heads. Our biggest side effect then was nausea and motion sickness. On the return trip, with a tiny life hooked up to high technology, every bump in the road threatened to dislodge a hard-won breathing tube or IV line. If one of those lifelines needed to be replaced, our options were to continue our pellmell journey and risk failure or injury as the moving targets of miniscule veins and vocal cords hurtled down the highway or to stop the ambulance to have a bump-free shot at a do-over, losing precious minutes in the gambit. Either way, it was our call. The driver would forge on full speed ahead or screech to a stop at the side of the road at our request. We were in charge.

One sunny Sunday morning, after a particularly harrowing transport, I brought my sons out to my parents' house for a visit. I was reliving the drama over coffee with my dad.

"So I was on this transport the other night, Dad," I started. My father chewed his English muffin and asked from behind his *Telegram & Gazette*, "What do you mean, a transport?"

I poured milk and buttered toast for my sons and answered, "Well, if there's a sick newborn, we have to go out in the ambulance and pick the baby up."

My father lowered his newspaper and stopped chewing.

"You mean *you* drive an ambulance?" he asked, clearly impressed.

"Well no, Dad, actually I'm in the back, working on the baby."

My father swallowed a mouthful of coffee, muffin crumbs gathering at the corners of his mouth.

"Oh, I thought you *drove* the ambulance," he said, before disappearing back behind the paper.

<hr />

And now here I was in unfamiliar territory, in the cab of an ambulance, thinking of my dad, long since gone. I was peering through a small square of glass into the back, where the action was; where I belonged. An EMT watched over my child; he held Neil's wrist, checking his pulse, recording the blood pressure on his metal clipboard. He beamed his flashlight into Neil's eyes and noted their response.

It was like watching TV with the sound muted. I couldn't hear anything; I could only watch. Through the tiny glass square I saw the EMT asking Neil questions, recording his answers. I knew the drill. What's your name? Where are you right now? Who's the president? Determining if the patient was oriented to person, place, and time. If all three questions were answered appropriately, the patient was proclaimed "oriented times three."

Neil certainly wasn't alert. He slept when not stimulated. When we left the local hospital, he thought he was in a gym. I wondered where he thought he was now.

I glanced over at the driver of the ambulance. She was a young woman, no more than twenty-five years old, with closely cropped dark brown hair. She was deftly weaving through traffic on Interstate 95, lights flashing, sounding the siren in short, as-needed bursts to get past the occasional oblivious driver. She kept a watchful eye in her rearview mirror, waiting for instructions to either pull over or hit the siren and go full speed. She had my boy's life in her hands. At that moment I was filled with my father's love for her.

6

"He's Gonna Be Just Fine"

JUST AFTER WE REACHED THE AMBULANCE BAY at the Brigham and Women's emergency room, Neil's blood pressure dropped and he complained of belly pain. A liver laceration, my doctor mind told me. A ruptured spleen. They yanked his stretcher out of the back, its collapsible legs smashing to the pavement. They pushed him through the glass doors, using his gurney like a battering ram. Neil never opened his eyes. I followed close behind, my own eyes glued to my son the whole time.

Inside his new city cubicle, a team stripped him of his transport heart monitor leads and replaced them with their own. They got to work with stethoscopes, flashlights, and reflex hammers, poking and prodding, asking questions and recording responses. A resident young enough to be my son asked, "Do you mind stepping out, Mom?" *(Mom!)* I took my chances.

"Well actually I do mind. I'm a pediatrician. I'll stay out of the way." With that, he laid his hands gently on my shoulders and guided me through the curtain and out into the hall. Apparently it was a rhetorical question.

I stood there alone and adrift. Back at Anna Jaques, Saul and I had agreed that I would ride in the ambulance with Neil. Saul would stop at the house and pick up a few essentials (my asthma inhaler for one) and then meet us at the Brigham. I hoped he'd get there soon.

Now a burly bearded doctor in an attending-length white coat strode over and offered me a meaty hand. He pumped it twice, introducing himself as Chuck, or Mitch, or something equally short and informal.

"I just looked at your boy," he boomed jovially. "Don't worry. He's gonna be just fine." He then took off down the hall, calling over his shoulder, "They'll come get you once he's all settled in."

I watched him disappear. Even though he couldn't have done much more than literally "just look" at Neil, I felt oddly reassured by his words, as if years of experience at this sort of thing made his brief glance as sharp a predictor as any CT scan or thorough neurological evaluation. I imagined him popping into other cubicles, making pronouncements along the way. "Fine." "Not fine." "Well." "Not well."

I found the waiting room; capacious yet teeming with patients. Babies crying. Pregnant women carrying plastic containers of urine, trying to disguise the cups by wrapping them in paper towels. (I knew that trick.) A television mounted above the fray flashed silent images. I kept a wary eye on the scrolling headlines at the bottom of the screen. It was almost eleven, just over three hours since the crash. I knew it would be just a matter of time before we would become one of those banners.

By this time, I had a few things pieced together. One of the first responders was the fire chief and a neighbor of ours. He told us how he had been at home when the call came in. He'd heard it on his police-band radio, always on. A drunk driver, out of control. Some of the nurses at the local hospital had also filled us in. The kids were victims of a hit-and-run accident, but they had caught the driver, drunk, a teenager not so many years older than Neil and Trista. He left the scene in his SUV but flipped it on the Interstate 95 overpass a few hundred feet down the road. He had taken off on foot but was quickly apprehended. He had thirty empties in his car.

Oh, this would make the news all right.

As I watched the headlines, Saul came through the waiting room door. Just seeing him, I breathed easier, even before taking a hit of the inhaler he had brought. He carried a paper bag full of the "essentials" I had sent him home for: clothes Neil would never wear, books we would never read, and knitting I would never touch.

When they finally let us in to see our son, he still lay on the hard plastic board used to transfer patients from stretcher to bed. His head was still pinned between two Styrofoam blocks, but now his wrists were tethered as well. I knew what those straps meant. I had used them as a nurse many times to restrain confused old men or to keep belligerent drunks in the ER from injuring the staff. We used thick leather ones with metal buckles for the occasional inmate we treated, a security officer planted next to him. Then there were the thin cloth varieties padded with soft lamb's wool to gently remind the elderly woman not to get up to use the bathroom alone. Neil's were white Velcro straps slipped around each wrist and lashed to the side rails. The ends were tucked under his mattress, a maneuver I knew was to discourage escape.

My heart broke seeing my boy's fingers picking at the sheets and testing the limits of his restraints with short jerks. Those fingers had petted gerbils, iced cupcakes, moved chess pieces, turned book pages, tuned guitar strings, and played Beethoven. Those hands had never hurt anyone and did not need to be restrained.

I gently removed the straps and shoved them under the mattress. Neil's eyes opened.

"Hi, Mom," he whispered then drifted back to sleep, his fingers still working the sheets in constant motion, a frenetic Braille known only to him. I tried holding his hand, but it continued worming in mine.

He was shivering under his one thin sheet. Saul and I took off our coats and laid them over our son. He woke to complain about his head being trapped and the hardness of the backboard. I tried to explain that both would be gone once his spinal films have been cleared, but he wasn't comprehending. He was agitated, irritated. He thought he was in a gym. He yelled for us to bring him things that didn't make sense, and when we tried to clarify what he wanted, it only made him worse.

I tried to think about Chuck/Mitch and his reassuring words about my son. But this was a trauma center, and I was slowly realizing that by "He's gonna be just fine" the doctor really meant Neil's going to survive, to walk out of the hospital alive. And I wanted so much more for my boy. I was worried about his IQ and his personality. Would he still be smart? Would he still be Neil? I glanced over at my husband, who was looking uncharacteristically helpless.

"But honey, he's alive," he told me, as if reading my thoughts. It's no wonder Saul reacted so differently to our son's accident. Unlike Saul, I had found out about the crash gradually, with time at first to deny reality, to disbelieve:

"Where are the kids?"

"They should have gotten to your house by now."

"Two kids were hit on Ferry Road."

I had had time, running through the freezing cold, to postulate alternative scenarios. Two other kids were hit. Not our kids. Not Neil.

For Saul the news came all at once, with stomach-churning clarity.

"Your daughter's been in an accident, sir. I can't give you any more information than that."

And he was alive. And I was grateful. I thought of Mary somewhere else in the city, about Trista's unseeing eyes and how they were probably having a very different conversation with their doctors—and I felt guilty for my thoughts. I swallowed my grief and stroked my boy's hair. There was no dried blood, no broken glass, no evidence of the trauma he'd just been through. I thought, *How can he have brain damage when he doesn't even have dirt in his hair?* He opened his eyes.

"Hi, Mom."

7

"There Was a Crooked Man Who Had a Crooked Smile"

IT WAS AFTER MIDNIGHT when the doctors came in to update us on Neil's condition. His CAT scan was unchanged from the one back home. The bleed in his brain was still small. They had CT'ed his belly too. No lacerations of the liver or spleen. My husband and I squeezed hands at each piece of good news. He did have a fractured shinbone that would need an operation to repair; the orthopods would tell us more about that in the morning. His C-spines had been cleared. They'd be taking him out of his collar soon.

Eventually they took us up to the trauma ICU and deposited us in the waiting room. They showed us the phone on the wall and told us they'd call when Neil was settled in and we could see him. I protested briefly, but my husband led me over to the couch and sat down next to me to wait.

"This isn't right," I grumbled. "They've got it backwards. He's *our* kid. *We* should be giving *them* permission to see him. Not the other way around."

"We're going to need to start calling people," Saul commented, perhaps trying to distract me from my irritation. I thought of Saul's elderly mother. I wanted to get to her before the TV news did. We'd managed to avoid the eleven o'clock broadcast, but it was just a matter of time. We also didn't want to wake her with scary news at this time of night. Our oldest son, Dan, was studying Spanish in Mexico. But the only number we had for Dan was the Study Abroad Coordinator at Goucher College. That would also have to wait until morning. There were other calls to make as well. Friends, family, work. I was employed at a large community health center and had patients scheduled. Someone else would have to see them. Saul ran his own business, and his staff would have to be told that the boss wouldn't be in. But we decided all the phone calls would have to wait until morning. Right now we just needed to be with our son. Besides, maybe we would have more information by dawn.

Finally the phone on the wall rang and we were granted permission to come inside the ICU and see our son. The nurse brought in an office chair on wheels for me, and I sat down and lowered the side rail on Neil's bed to be closer to my boy. When Saul asked for a chair for himself, the nurse told him we couldn't "just camp out here" and left him standing. He went back to the waiting room to sleep on the couch. We made a plan to switch places every few hours, but I found I couldn't leave Neil's side. I was afraid that if I walked through those glass doors, the nurses would never let me back in. They'd tell me visiting hours were over and keep me from my son. I laid my head on Neil's belly, but I couldn't close my eyes. I was afraid if I were caught sleeping, they'd send me away. I didn't even go to the bathroom, afraid I wouldn't get buzzed back in.

The hours ticked by. Neil's blood pressure was low. I pressed my hand into my son's belly and squeezed his thighs, searching all the places where blood could hide. It was discomfiting for me. Neil is modest by nature. He closes his bedroom door just to change his shirt. I felt I was somehow violating him now, but I needed to know he wasn't bleeding out. I needed an answer to his low blood pressure. The nurse kept calling the resident with the numbers, and he kept ordering fluid boluses. But it didn't make sense. Neil's pulse was rock stable, and plenty of clear urine filled the bag hooked to the side of his bed. Bleeding just wasn't the cause of his pressure drop. Perhaps it was the whopping dose of antiseizure medicine he had been given in the ER.

I was trying hard to stay awake. The ICU was a surreal setting, hallucinogenic at times. At one point I thought I saw Neil's eyes open wide, but when I rubbed my own and looked again, he was sleeping peacefully. Later, the numbers on a wall calendar seemed to wriggle off the page and dance along the ceiling. But once I shook my head, the numbers had marched back into their orderly 2-D row.

A neurosurgeon came in the middle of the night. He took a tiny penlight out of the breast pocket of his white coat, pinned Neil's eyelids open with his fingertips like they were butterfly wings, and shined his light in them one at a time. PERRL: Pupils equal round and reactive to light. A good sign. He put Neil through all the moves. Squeeze my fingers. Raise your eyebrows. Smile. Wait. Smile again. I looked over the neurosurgeon's shoulder as he asked Neil to smile over and over. Something was wrong. The doctor didn't like the asymmetry he saw in Neil's face.

I thought of the nursery rhyme:
There was a crooked man.
He had a crooked smile.
How did the rest of that go?

Over and over my son contorted his face into an expression normally linked to cheer. But for Neil it was just a ticket back to sleep. It was a mask that said "Leave me alone." More snarl than smile. When I was a nurse on the eleven-to-seven shift in the pediatric intensive care unit, I often had to do hourly neuro checks on my patients. I knew how difficult it could be. After the sixth time of answering questions like "Where are you?" and "Who's the president?" folks get cranky. They want to go to sleep. They grunt and don't answer. Then it was up to us nurses to determine if this was a diminishing level of consciousness or just grouchiness. When do you call the resident?

Now the neurosurgeon was asking me if Neil's smile normally looked like that. I thought back to a case I had recently of a little boy with headaches and a positive Lyme titer. On exam one of his pupils was bigger than the other. We were trying to figure out if this anisocoria was a result of the Lyme disease, which would be very unusual. The mom swore it was new; otherwise she would have noticed it long ago. We asked her to bring in pictures of him as a baby and toddler so we could sort it all out. When she brought in the photos, sure enough, his pupils had been asymmetric right along. Could I be like that mother? Could I not have noticed all of my son's life that he smiled like Ellen Barkin? I flipped through a mental photo album. Neil at Horseneck Beach. Neil dressed as an alien for Halloween. Neil with his head in the stockades at Old Sturbridge Village.

"No," I answered. "This is new."

Another member of the neuro team tested Neil's hearing. I knew then that they were thinking he might have a basilar skull fracture. The resident rubbed several of Neil's hairs together between his fingers just in front of Neil's ears.

"What do you hear?" he asked gently.

"Beating off," Neil replied, eyes closed. We all looked at each other.

"What'd he say?" the team asked one another.

"Beating off," Neil asserted, more loudly. I searched my son's face for signs that he was making a joke. His sense of humor was notoriously dry. But I knew this was no joke. Though he had passed the bedside hearing test, my modest son's immodest response was one more sign of his injured brain, his usual inhibitions temporarily off duty.

The ICU attending ordered another CT scan for the morning to check for evidence of the fracture Neil's asymmetric smile suggested.

I thought again of those reassuring words. "He's gonna be just fine. Don't worry." I looked down at my boy and worried.

8

Pre-Op

INSIDE AN ICU CUBICLE, there are no windows. There is no clock. Time is measured not by the sun or any timepiece but by subtler changes in routine and personnel.

At the Brigham, the residents rounded early, moving from bed to bed like a many-legged organism. Clipboards in hand, their ranking was given away by the length of their white coats. Medical students wore short jackets. Residents' coats reached to their knees. Attendings could be distinguished by their names stitched in red cursive above their white breast pockets. Later the residents would be in scrubs of green and blue. But for morning rounds, they were all in their best civvies. The men sported pressed shirts and neat ties. The women wore skirts and blouses, nylons and pumps. Shifts changed. Seven-to-three nurses replaced their eleven-to-seven counterparts. Then there were the people who only worked the day shift: housekeeping, dietary services, social workers, ward secretaries. Lights at the nurses' station that were dimmed for the night shift now gleamed brightly in all their white fluorescence. The long dark hours of my nighttime vigil gradually gave way to morning's bustling routine.

A nurse came in and cranked the head of Neil's bed so that he was sitting more or less straight up. She handed him a glass of water and a toothbrush and laid a kidney-shaped emesis basin on his bedside table to spit in. He looked at them. I waited. Finally he took a sip of water and began to brush his teeth. I exhaled; Thank God. He knew what to do with a toothbrush. At that moment I was again sadly aware of the terrible burden of knowing too much as a physician. What other mother would sigh with relief when her son put his toothbrush in his mouth? He doesn't have apraxia! Yay!

The nurse and I continued getting Neil ready for the OR. We took turns wrestling with his long curls: combing, brushing, detangling. When the rounding team walked in, we gave up, stuffing the unruly mop under his paper operating room cap.

The doctors on the team included an orthopedic surgeon, an anesthesiologist, and a neurologist. Each came with several fellows, residents and medical students. Each team had its own list of risks they needed to warn us about in the name of informed consent. The orthopod's plan was to insert a titanium rod into Neil's lower leg and hold it all together with plates and screws. He warned us of the possibility of bleeding or infection. The anesthesiologist talked about the possibility of more invasive monitoring. Neil was going to the operating room with just a simple intravenous but may need an arterial line or a central venous pressure line, a CVP. The neurologist had his own worst-case scenarios to describe: intracranial pressure monitoring, a Richmond bolt. I listened to them all, understanding the lingo even as I had trouble acknowledging that the body they would be working on was my own son's. But I was waiting to hear from the trauma surgeon, the ICU attending, who had ordered one more CAT scan, which Neil had had around 4:00 a.m. He wanted to be sure the asymmetry he had seen in Neil's face hadn't been a harbinger of a basilar skull fracture. The results of that scan would determine if he should be having surgery on his leg or his head. So when they handed me the consent form to sign, I did something very much against my nature: I refused.

The team was outraged.

"You'll lose your OR slot," one threatened.

"Give it away," I dared them back. "I'm not signing anything until I see the CAT scan."

Maybe I was turning into that pain-in-the-ass mother everyone hates. But I didn't care. This was my kid. Meanwhile, Anesthesia was pacing around the room, fuming about their precious OR time. Tough. I wasn't signing until I was satisfied.

Finally the trauma surgeon came in, examined Neil, and gave us the CAT scan results. Unchanged. I signed the consent form, still wary and worried that with his blood pressure so low, anesthesia would make it worse. There's something called the watershed area of the brain, which is where the very ends of two blood supplies meet. That precious area can be at risk of having its oxygen supply cut off during times of low perfusion. The result could be devastating; Neil could essentially have a stroke.

They let Saul and me accompany Neil only so far. We kissed his forehead and said good-bye. My fingers reluctantly released their grip on the side rails of Neil's stretcher as they wheeled him into the elevator. As the doors closed, they told us he'd be gone for a few hours.

"Go to the cafeteria," they suggested. "Grab a bite."

We tried. I salted my soup with tears. Saul pushed little bites of burger around on his plate, rearranging lettuce and tomatoes but not eating any of it.

We finally gave up and went back to the ICU waiting room, where we felt more comfortable, even just waiting. We made phone calls, updating friends and family. We worried.

9

The Waiting Room

THERE IS A COMMUNITY that grows up around tragedy—an unlikely camaraderie forged among victims of similar, or at least similarly tragic, fates. Forced to wait long hours together for our loved ones, we gradually became aware of each other's personal stories. Whether through observation, overheard conversations, or direct mutual disclosure, we came to know one another. Or at least that small, vital piece of ourselves that led us to this place where our lives intersected.

Alice's husband, Frank, had prostate cancer. This was his second operation. The cancer had spread to his lymph nodes, and the doctors were going after it. He would be starting radiation once he got his strength back. Frank was seventy-two. Alice carried herself with a quiet inner strength. Her voice hinted of the South, a genteel lilt to match her regal frame. She didn't own a cell phone. I never heard her speak to anyone outside of the nurses who rang us on the waiting room phone to update us on our loved ones or let us in to see them. She spent long stretches of time with her knitting in her lap, but often her hands fell quiet, her mind seemingly deep in thought.

Maura, on the other hand, had a vast network of support. Her partner, Julie, was trying to survive a bone marrow transplant, and her course was perhaps the rockiest of all the ICU patients whose families I met during my stay there at the Brigham. In the waiting room large flocks of women held hands, lit candles, and prayed together. Their community was not restricted to the confines of the ICU walls either. They had designed a web page to update their circle as to Julie's condition. Friends and family could post photos and share memories about Julie, all of which gave Maura great comfort. She would read long passages aloud, laughing or crying in turns.

Not all the waiting room activity was maudlin. At one point a young hockey player was admitted next door to Neil: another head injury. He had brought a cheering college ice-skating rink to silence when he fell to the ice after a body check and did not rise or even move. He was collared and stretchered like Neil and brought here to the ICU, where now his friends in the waiting room gathered in terrified hugging packs. But the next day the danger was over—he had opened his eyes. He knew his mom. His spine wasn't broken—and the tears turned to cheers; the hugs turned to chest and fist bumps.

One time a handful of brawny boys, friends of another accident victim, decided to rearrange the waiting room furniture. They stacked end tables on top of one another to make more room and turned a couch to face kitty-corner instead of against the long wall. I watched Alice and Maura for signs of irritation or impatience, but there was none. That's the other thing tragedy does: puts things in perspective. None of us were sweating the small stuff anymore. I even found the boys' youthful cheeriness an uplifting distraction from my own constant worry.

While Maura used her turn at the computer to update friends about her partner's progress and gather family support, Saul and I used ours to keep updated about Trista's condition and the charges facing the drunk driver. By now we were all over the news, with names and photos. No one knows how the news outlets got hold of the photo that ran everywhere. It was taken at Trista's semiformal. Trista wore a shimmering blue gown and an even brighter smile. Neil's haystack of unruly hair sprang out from under his favorite top hat as he grinned into the camera. At first the local newspaper listed both kids' conditions as "extremely serious," leaving me some scant hope that Trista would make it. But her eyes with their fixed and dilated pupils had told me differently.

Mary called us often during that first night and the following day, checking on Neil's condition, updating us on Trista's. I was so impressed with and grateful for her tremendous generosity of spirit. For her to think of my child as hers lay dying was benevolent beyond words.

The Zincks ultimately made the terrible, beautiful decision to take their daughter off life support and donate her organs. It was the day after the crash. It was the day of Neil's surgery. I thought about it often: Neil was being intubated for his surgery as Trista was being extubated for hers. We were being told Neil was "gonna be just fine." Trista was being declared dead. Neil's surgeons were opening his leg to repair his broken bones. Trista's surgeons were opening her so that others might live. Each was lying on an operating room table in the same city. Two different Boston hospitals. Two different teams of doctors. Two very different fates. I imagined their two souls mixing in that sweet unconscious space. It gave me some measure of comfort over the following days and weeks to think about that: Neil and Trista, somewhere together, in spirit and unconsciousness.

The phone in the waiting room should have been our lifeline. It was, after all, how the nurses taking care of our son communicated with us. But from day one I disliked that thing. Even though I had been a nurse and was now a doctor and knew the rules of the ICU very well, I always resented the barrier, those rules placed between mother and son, husband and wife, partner and partner. Maybe it was different for me, being a pediatrician. On the children's ward we recognized the role comforting parents could play in their children's recovery, or even their reaction to a painful procedure. There have been many articles written in the medical literature over recent years about the positive effects parents report when allowed to remain at the bedside of their children, even during code situations. Apparently no one here at the Brigham had read that literature.

The time we spent listening for that waiting room phone to ring was stretched out, tense. Whenever it did ring, we all looked to one another, wondering who would answer it. There were no rules. If I answered the phone and it turned out the call was for me, allowing me to see my son, I felt vaguely guilty leaving all the others stranded out there, still blocked from their loved ones. If the call wasn't for me, if it was for Alice or Maura, I would make silent eye contact and lift the receiver in their direction. But if the name was new, if I didn't yet know who their family was, I would be forced to say their names out loud, then hand off the call. It felt so awkward and impersonal, giving over a phone so casually when the news could be so grave. What was the proper look? A slight smile? Pursed lips and worried eye contact?

Sometimes we learned what happened to people. Sometimes we didn't. Regal Alice just one day stopped appearing. The hockey player was discharged to his family, a bad concussion but no brain bleed.

Maura's partner did not survive her transplant. Small crowds hugged and cried in the waiting room. Maura still drew comfort from her web page. She read fitting tributes aloud through tears. Family and friends again lit candles and prayed, this time not for Julie's survival but for her peace. Sitting on the corner of the couch, waiting for Neil to return from the operating room, I tried to make myself small, to give the room over to Maura in her grief. Part of it was out of respect, but part of it was also out of fear. Being part of the waiting room community was one thing, but I did not want to be a part of this new group: the grieving community. I felt a great gratitude in that moment. Neil was alive. He was coming home. We didn't know what awaited us. But we knew it wasn't this.

The surgeon finally came in to say that everything had gone well. He showed us the X-rays, smiling. So proud of his work. None of my fears had come true. Neil's blood pressure had remained stable, his heart strong. No bandaged head. No ventilator. Nothing more invasive than a simple IV. He came back to us just the way he left us: sleepy and confused.

IO

A Bad Dream

IF HAVING MY YOUNGEST SON in an ICU in Boston with a head injury after being struck down by a drunk driver was a nightmare, then trying to reach my oldest son in Mexico to give him the news about his brother was a real bad dream. Dan was in between semesters of his freshman year at Goucher College in Maryland and was spending three weeks in Cuernavaca living with a Mexican family and learning to speak Spanish. He had been sending us short, newsy e-mails from a cybercafe in town every day or two: descriptions of the countryside, the food, and his host family. Funny stories of linguistic missteps—like the time he tried to tell a cab driver he was hot, meaning the environment was warm; only it came out "I'm hot," as in "hot for you." I tried not to be jealous when he told us how much he liked his *madre* there.

When Dan left, he had given us an emergency contact number for the language program coordinator at his school. We gave him a phone card he could use in an emergency. We thought we had our bases covered. We hadn't counted on this.

We thought about sending Dan an e-mail, but we couldn't count on him checking it right away. Besides, striking the right tone in an e-mail can be difficult. How would we convey the seriousness of the situation without throwing him into a total panic? We called the program director and explained our situation. Dan's brother was in an accident. We needed to get word to him. She promised she would try.

Since all we could do now was wait, Saul decided to book us a room in the hotel for hospital patients' families across the street. We figured we could take turns getting some sleep. Shortly after Saul left to bed down, the Goucher College study abroad director called me on my cell phone. She told us she had left word with her Mexican counterpart at the language school. She also gave me the number of the family that was hosting my son. From Dan's description of the area, it sounded pretty rural and quite indigent. So I was glad to learn they had a phone.

My Spanish is limited and informal. I never took it in high school or college but have learned on the job from my patients over the years. Saul's Spanish is nonexistent. So once again, I was on. I tried dialing the number from Neil's room, but the nurse told me cell phones weren't allowed in the ICU. She said they would interfere with patients' monitors. I knew that with newer cell phones this just wasn't true, an urban legend perpetuated, but I wasn't going to argue with the woman who had control over when I got to see my kid. I went out to the waiting room to make the call. That's when I learned that we don't have international calling on our plan and it would take four days to get it. And no, she couldn't connect the call, even if it was an emergency. I tried going through the hospital operator, but she couldn't connect me either. I tried charging the call to my home phone, but there was no one physically there to accept the charges, so the operator said her hands were tied. I finally got a supervisor at the phone company to place the call for me. The line crackled and rang with an unfamiliar tone. A woman answered. I used my best Spanish to ask for my son. The woman replied with an energetic round of rapid-fire Spanish I did not understand. Then the line went dead. I didn't know if I had been understood or not.

I felt lost and alone. I thought if only Saul were in charge, everything would be better. He was the rock of the family, the decision maker, the doer. I was thrust into this position of family leader first because of my medical background, now because of my Spanish. But I felt anything but in charge. I slammed the dead receiver into its cradle several times in an unusual display of frustration. I was glad there were no other families in the waiting room to witness my outburst. I just sat there, my face wet with tears and snot, not knowing what to do.

Then my cell phone rang.

"Hello?"

There was no sound. No reply.

"Dan?"

"Hey, Mom, what's up?" He sounded so upbeat I knew he couldn't have gotten the entire message from the language school or from his *madre*. His voice was crackly and time-delayed. It made me feel far away from him, but it was beautiful just the same. I hated giving Dan this news during what should have been the trip of a lifetime. I didn't know how to begin.

"Your brother's been in an accident," I said, quickly adding Dr. Chuck/Mitch's reassuring words. "He's gonna be just fine though. Don't worry."

But I was worried, and Dan knew it. I filled him in as best I could. The broken leg, the crooked smile. I told him about Trista. I didn't tell him yet that she had died, just that she was in worse shape than Neil. I didn't know how much he could take in over the phone. I paused, waiting for his response. It came in three words.

"Get me home."

A Nurse First

WHEN I WAS A LITTLE GIRL, I didn't know exactly what I wanted to be when I grew up, but I knew I would be in one of the helping professions. I thought about becoming a social worker or a teacher of the deaf. In high school I finally settled on being an operating room technician. The idea of being a witness to the drama of surgery was very enticing. A guidance counselor at the time suggested I go to nursing school instead. I could still become an OR nurse, she reasoned, but I would have many more options available to me. I followed her advice and started out at a hospital-based diploma program, an endangered species nowadays. Ultimately I graduated from Quinsigamond Community College with an associate's degree in nursing.

My first job as a graduate nurse was at a tiny community hospital in rural central Massachusetts where I rotated between the labor and delivery suite, the postpartum floor, and the normal newborn nursery. I loved the joy and drama of L&D and ministering to new mothers on postpartum. But it was in the normal newborn nursery where I first fell in love with caring for children.

Saul and I owned a wholesale doughnut business at the time. We would get up somewhere between two and three o'clock in the morning to mix, roll, and cut the dough, then fry, glaze, and package the doughnuts. We had a radio going all night; Dire Straits and the Cars, as well as debates and news from the National Press Club. After a breakfast, often fresh corn on the cob from our garden (never doughnuts!), Saul would load up the truck and head off to deliver our product to stores and restaurants and I would head to the hospital for my seven-to-three shift.

After I passed my boards and became a registered nurse, we moved to the city of Worcester. Saul opened a bakery, and I took a job in the pediatric intensive care unit of a large private hospital. My first patient was LiliBeth, a lovely four-month-old baby who was brought in not breathing by her distraught father, who had fallen asleep with her on the couch. He must have rolled onto her. I took care of her for days, suctioning her breathing tube, placing ointment in her eyes so they wouldn't dry out, sponge-bathing her tiny body. We all understood that she was brain dead, being kept alive only by her ventilator, but her parents took some time to accept that diagnosis.

In the meantime I changed the dressings at her IV sites and put clean sheets on her crib every day. We did all the tests to gently show her parents she was not alive: Her EEG showed no electrical activity in her brain; her eyes did not move when we irrigated her ears with water (called the caloric test) or turned her head from side to side (called the doll's-eye maneuver). When her parents ultimately agreed to take LiliBeth off life support, I turned off her ventilator and heart monitor. I gently slipped the breathing tube from her throat, unclipped the leads from her chest, wrapped her in a blanket, and laid her in her mother's arms while her father sobbed.

As a nurse I was not generally the one to give parents bad news—that was the job of the residents or the attendings—but I was there for the before and after. I answered their questions. I hugged them when they cried. I handed them tissues. And I took their babies from them when there were no more tears left to cry.

I got to know my patients intimately. There were children who came in regularly. Kids with cystic fibrosis had weeklong stays for pulmonary "clean-outs." Children with sickle cell disease had recurrent painful crises where their little blood vessels closed shut, causing them pain similar to a heart attack but in their limbs and backs. Children with leukemia came in for evaluation of their fevers when their white blood cell counts were low and their immune systems compromised. I cupped my hands on their backs for chest physiotherapy. I held their hands during painful procedures. I cut their meat, measured their urine, cleaned up their vomit, dabbed their sweaty foreheads with washcloths, and spooned ice chips into their mouths. I knew their bodies inside and out. I knew their parents by first names, and they knew me.

"Hey, Carolyn. Brought you a coffee. Black. Just the way you like it."

Every day, Jerel's mom came to the hospital to see her son, a quadriplegic after a tragic diving accident. She amazed me. In all her family tragedy, she not only thought of me at Dunkin's drive-through but also took the time to learn how I liked my coffee. Now that I was on the other side of the stretcher, I was not nearly so generous. I never once brought a nurse at the Brigham a cup of coffee.

I liked the technical aspects of my nursing job as well. I loved calibrating the machines at the beginning and end of my shifts: the ventilators, the CVP lines, the intracranial pressure monitors. I was good at starting IVs, dropping nasogastric tubes into little stomachs, inserting catheters into bladders. Some procedures, like lumbar punctures, were done by the doctors, but a steady nurse who knew how to hold a child, bending his or her spine out toward the needle, opening the vertebrae just so, could make the difference between a successful procedure and a bloody tap.

My last nursing job before I went to medical school was on the pediatric ward at City Hospital, then a teaching hospital. It was a very small unit, and I sometimes had to float to other floors when its beds were unoccupied. The pediatric residents from St. Vincent Hospital rotated through our unit regularly, and observing them as they wrote orders on new admissions, I would think, *I could do that.* I could anticipate everything. I knew that asthmatics would need bronchodilators and steroids. I knew that children with gastroenteritis and dehydration were going to need IV fluids. I knew that the child with leukemia who came in with fever and low blood counts would have blood cultures drawn and receive antibiotics to cover for possible infection.

But what fascinated me was what I didn't know. What did one do with the child whose diagnosis wasn't obvious? How did one approach a mysterious set of symptoms? How did one even go about thinking about the problem? Where did one start? That is what attracted me—the medical mystery, the diagnostic dilemma. I loved the intimacy of nursing: the laying on of hands. I considered it a sacred honor to enter another human being's personal space in the way that was required to be a good nurse.

But the thrill of actually making a diagnosis pulled me toward medicine. Nursing had its intellectual challenges of course—there was always something new to learn—but the idea that I could solve a puzzle, diagnose a case, was irresistible.

Making the diagnosis is still a very rewarding part of what I do. It is especially satisfying when I am able to figure out a child whose diagnosis has stumped or evaded even the specialists. There was the child with pertussis who presented to several Boston emergency rooms with a cough. They diagnosed him first with a cold, then with pneumonia. (His mother had forgotten to inform them that her son had not had all of his DTP shots due to a seizure when he was little—information that I, as his primary care physician, had at my fingertips.) There was the baby who came to me for his first visit after spending more than a month in a neonatal intensive care unit having his duodenal atresia repaired. One quick Ortolani and Barlow maneuver revealed an undiagnosed hip dysplasia. Then there's my patient with multiple symptoms and seeing multiple specialists whom I diagnosed with an unusual brain abnormality called a Chiari malformation. The specialists are still trying to decide if this is the cause of his problems or just an incidental finding.

Being a nurse first helped tremendously in medical school. While my classmates had to get used to talking to someone in a johnny, I had been the one to dress the patient in one. While they had butterflies in their stomachs, I held 23-guage butterflies in my hands, as familiar as silverware.

As a nurse I spent many more hours at patients' bedsides than any intern or resident or attending ever had time to. I saw transient events like absence seizures or abnormal heart rhythms that the doctors, with their once-a-day bedside rounds were unlikely to catch. I learned things about my patients that I could pass on at their discharge planning meetings.

"Better choose a medicine that doesn't need refrigeration. The Boulangers are in a shelter right now."

Now, as a doctor, I rely on nurses completely. They are my eyes and ears. I teach my residents to respect nurses' judgments and contributions too.

"If a nurse is worried, you should be too," I tell them when they roll their eyes at being awakened by a nurse at 4:00 a.m. to come check on an ill child.

Now Neil was that child. I respected the nurses who ministered to him. I related to the residents who cared for him. I hoped they'd all had enough sleep to make good decisions about his care. My child was now in their hands.

12

Temporal Lobe Agitation

NEIL'S DAYS IN THE ICU are a blur to me. To him they don't exist at all. He has no memory of them. It's just as well. He's haunted enough already without remembering days of pain and confusion. His leg, which the doctors had told him would feel better after the surgery, still ached, and nothing we did seemed to make him more comfortable. He'd yell at us to put it on a pillow and then scream at us to move it: up, down, left, right, higher, lower. It was never correct.

I bore the brunt of Neil's rants. Partly, I'm sure, because I was his mom but also because I was a physician and was supposed to be able to make patients feel better.

"Mom, you're a doctor. Do something," he'd rail. I'd try, feeling inadequate, like I was letting him down. I'd fluff his pillow, rearrange his leg. None of it was ever right.

"Mom, you're a terrible doctor," he'd snarl. "You can't even make my pain go away."

He'd order me out of the room.

"If you're not going to do anything, Mom, just get out." And when I tried to soothe him or busy myself arranging flowers or nightstand toiletries, he'd insist.

"I mean it, Mom. Get out!"

One of his nurses even told me I was making things worse. With me around, he "escalated." On her shifts I spent a lot of my time crying in the waiting room. I had always prided myself on being a good nurse, able to minister capably to my patients' needs. Now I couldn't give adequate care to the one patient who meant more to me than anything.

They ordered injections of the painkiller fentanyl for Neil, first administered by the staff then via a system called patient-controlled analgesia, or PCA. A plastic bag of the drug was hung from an IV pole. Its tubing was threaded through a machine that counted out incremental doses. There was a lock on the system so that patients could not overdose themselves. Neil was given a handheld device much like a nurse's call light. He was taught how to push the button whenever he felt pain to deliver himself a dose of the medicine.

But Neil never got the hang of using the PCA. He'd forget he had the button. He'd forget how to use it. He'd call for the nurses. He'd yell at me. We ended up having to push the button for him. We could never leave him alone.

Saul's brother, Louis, came to see Neil in those early days. He is an acupuncturist and tried using his needles and acupressure to stop the pain. But he got yelled at too.

"Louis, you're making things worse. Stop it."

All of this was so not my son. Neil is a quiet kid with a wide smile. He has enormous patience. Once he tried to teach me how to play the guitar. I am not very musical, and things weren't going well. I was discouraged and embarrassed that I couldn't seem to understand this one concept Neil was trying to get across to me. I wanted to give up.

"Never mind, Neil. I'm just not good at this."

"No, Mom. It's not you; it's me. Let me try another way."

He never lost patience with me. No rolling eyes. No sighs of exasperation. No muttering under his breath. He just tried different approaches with me until things eventually clicked.

Neil always took frustration and disappointment in stride. Before his junior prom he was supposed to meet up with some friends and then drive to the event in a limousine. I drove him to the address his friends had given him. No one was there. We drove slowly up and down the street. We tried one block over. We tried another close-by street with a similar name. But we couldn't find them. No gowned and tuxedo-clad students. And no limo. It was past seven o'clock, the time they were supposed to meet. I was afraid he'd miss out on half the fun of his junior prom: a ride in a real limousine.

"I'm sorry Neil. I can't find it," I apologized.

"That's okay, Mom. I'll just meet them there."

I thought back to my own teenage years. There'd be no end to the tears and drama if I were in Neil's shoes, unable to find my friends and about to miss out on my first limo ride. But here was Neil, looking handsome, holding his date's corsage in his lap, and maintaining his cool. We eventually located the house and he climbed into the limo, smiling and waving.

And now here was my sweet boy demanding, cursing, raising his voice. They call it temporal lobe agitation, and it happens to many brain-injured patients. It can cause disinhibition, excitation, irritation, and aggression—all the behaviors Neil was now exhibiting. He picked at his bed sheets, tore off his johnny, and tried to climb over the guardrails, all the while loudly admonishing his family for not making his pain go away.

But understanding the cause of his behavior, having a name for it, didn't make it any easier to watch. In fact, like so many other times during Neil's hospital stay and recovery, having an understanding of his brain's anatomy and function only left me guilt-ridden at noticing its workings.

During his numerous bedside neurological tests, Neil tried hard to comply with what was being asked of him. If he was asked where he was, he looked around the room for clues. Though he was unable to process what he saw into a correct response, he knew he was being asked for a place.

"I'm in a gym," he answered one time.

"I'm on a boat," another.

If asked what year it was, again he'd strain to think, to remember. His brain told him he was being asked for a number. He always gave them one.

"Ninety-nine."

"Six hundred and ten."

Though it wasn't a year, it was a number. It wasn't a correct response, but it showed thought and process as he tried to retrieve information from the various compartments of his injured mind. (He was definitely *not* "oriented times three.")

On one particularly foggy occasion, Neil kept plying us with the same request.

"Six little yellow pills. Get me my six little yellow pills."

Over and over. At first we weren't even sure we'd heard the words correctly.

"What'd you say Neil?"

"Six little yellow pills!" he shouted.

Then I remembered. Saul's brother, Louis, the acupuncturist was also a Chinese herbalist. Whenever one of us started experiencing cold symptoms—runny nose, scratchy throat—we'd start taking Gan Mao Ling to ward off a full-blown flu. Gan Mao Ling comes in doses of six little yellow pills.

"He must want a dose of fentanyl," I surmised, recognizing the pattern. He needed a medicine but didn't know how to name the PCA. So his brain simply substituted one medicinal product for another.

It scared me that he was so confused. It heartened me that he was working so hard to recognize patterns and provide answers. And it horrified me that I even thought about the workings of his brain lobes at all.

13

Dan

Dan's plane from Mexico landed in Boston at 11:15 the night of Neil's first surgery. Saul picked him up at Logan Airport and brought him right to Neil's hospital room. He laid his small duffel bag of clothes next to the bed. He would later use it as a pillow, sleeping next to his brother on the floor of the ICU. I hugged Dan tight. It was so good to see him, to feel him. He seemed so grown up. College was agreeing with him.

I gently jostled Neil's shoulder.

"Neil, wake up."

He slowly opened his eyes, saw Dan, and closed them again.

"Neil, do you know who this is?"

"Dan," he said without opening his eyes.

"And who's Dan?"

"Brother," he said and went back to sleep.

Dan smiled and gave us a thumb's-up sign, already seeming to grasp the significance of that recognition.

Saul and I quickly brought Dan up to speed on Neil's injuries. Then, with Neil sleeping peacefully, Dan pulled up a chair and quietly started telling us about his trip to Mexico. He flipped through the pictures on his digital camera, narrating the show.

He seemed so worldly. He was a traveler. He had been somewhere his parents had not and had stories to share.

After the travelogue, Dan told me to close my eyes and hold out my hand. Instead of placing the surprise in my palm as I expected, he clasped something around my wrist. I opened my eyes. There was a silver bracelet with a pressed flower encased in an acrylic oval. I collect pressed flowers, so the gift was perfect. He dug around in his duffel bag some more and pulled out an onyx chess set for Saul and a beaded belt for Neil.

"It reminded me of his hacky sack," Dan said.

I felt a stab of fear, wondering if Neil would be able to return to the foot bag game he was so good at.

"He'll love it," I promised.

All the while, Neil slept. Then, out of the blue, he called, "Dan, cut it out." We all laughed because of course Dan hadn't done anything at all.

"You're not in the country five minutes and already you're being blamed for stuff," Saul observed. We all laughed. It was the first time we had laughed since learning of the crash more than twenty-four hours ago, and it felt good.

—◦—

When the kids were little, Dan was always getting into trouble for beating up on Neil. Often he deserved it, starting fights and picking on his little brother. (Dan even managed to take some measure of credit for his brother's survival, telling him days after the crash, "I made your ass durable.") But years later, Neil would admit that sometimes they would be sitting together on the couch watching TV and out of the blue Neil would yell, "Ow!"

knowing I would come in and punish Dan, who all the while protested his innocence.

But while it may have been okay for Dan to beat up on his kid brother, it was not okay for anyone else to mess with him. One day after school, a group of kids started harassing Neil. The boys must have been in the second and third grade at this time. Dan came up behind his brother and quietly told him to drop his backpack and run home as fast as he could. Neil took off. Dan scooped up the pack, distracted the head bully with a kick to the shins to give Neil a head start, and then took off after him. The two arrived at home breathless but unharmed. We had a little talk about bullies and fighting, but I was secretly proud of Dan for sticking up for Neil.

Dan was a tremendous help to us those first days in the hospital. He carried Neil to the bathroom and helped him in the shower. He brought him smoothies from the cafeteria and fed him with a straw.

At one point Neil's nurse Sean wanted to get him out of bed. He told us he was going to go get another nurse to help with the transfer from bed to chair.

"I'll help you," Dan offered.

Sean looked wary.

"Don't worry," I assured him. "He worked at a camp for disabled youth. He knows how to transfer patients."

Sean brightened. Now each young man draped one of Neil's arms across his shoulders. Sean counted to three and they lifted Neil to his feet. Neil teetered weakly but regained his balance with their support. As they were getting ready to pivot him over to the chair, an older nurse passing by the room came running in, waving her arms.

"Family can't lift patients," she warned.

At that point, Neil released Sean, wrapped both of his arms around his brother's neck and said, "But I trust him."

He then laid his head on Dan's shoulder and added, "He lifts weights."

The boys were always close, but the accident served to bond the brothers in a way no other experience could. After Neil left the hospital and friends would gather around his makeshift bed, a pullout couch in the living room, I'd often overhear him telling them, "My brother came all the way from Mexico to be with me." And Dan's love and affection for Neil has deepened in a new and lasting way, precious now for almost having lost him.

14

Trista

THEY MET AT SCHOOL, on the set of the comedy *On the Razzle*. Neil played the constable; Trista played one of the townspeople and sang in the chorus. It was her first foray into the performing arts, and, though her role was small, she lit up the stage with her endearing smile. You hear that said a lot about people who have passed away. "She was always smiling" sounds like such a cliché, but with Trista it was true.

Her mother, Mary, gives Neil most of the credit for that smile. Neil was her daughter's first boyfriend, and Mary has often told me that Trista believed he was "the one." She is grateful to Neil for bringing Trista out of her shell, giving her confidence and poise. Apparently prior to Neil, her daughter was self-conscious and shy. But having a boyfriend made her glow.

They had a lot in common. They were both very smart and liked school. Trista was on the honor roll. Neil got a perfect eight hundred on his math SATs. They both planned to be teachers— Trista in history, Neil in mathematics. They had engaging senses of humor and enjoyed teasing each other. For such a young couple, they had a lot of chemistry.

They had only been dating for seven or eight months when she died. They were starting to talk seriously about the future. Neil would be heading off to college that fall and was in the throes of the application process at the time of the crash. But they had come to the decision that they would continue their relationship after he left.

Neil doesn't remember much from the night of the accident, but he told me once, months later, about the last conversation he had with Trista as he walked her home that evening. He asked her if she had noticed that now, when they talked about their future, they had stopped saying "if'" and started saying "when."

"Should I be afraid?" she had asked him.

"No," he told her.

That was the last thing he remembers.

⌒

I dreamed about Trista a few nights after she died. I was seeing patients at my clinic, and when I opened the door to an exam room, there she was, sitting on the exam table, smiling at me sweetly. Her wavy brown hair tumbled around her freckled face. She was dressed in her typical funky fashion: layered red skirt, chunky boots, woolen tights. The beaded red bracelet I had given her for Christmas jangled softly around her wrist. She waved to me without speaking. It was as if she was telling me it was okay. She looked happy and at home.

15

POV

Neil had been in the hospital for four days, and he still did not know what happened to him. He never asked. He knew he had a broken leg, but he never asked how he got it. He also never asked about Trista. But we knew it was just a matter of time. So we made a plan as a family as to how we would tell him. We met with the hospital social worker. She agreed to help us break the news to him when the time came. We made up rules. We would only give him information as he asked for it. We would wait until he was ready to hear it.

We also never left him alone. The accident was all over the Boston news, and we did not want him finding out haphazardly, from the janitor, say.

"Hey, man. Sorry about your girlfriend."

We made sure the doctors and nurses all knew that he wasn't aware of Trista's death so that they wouldn't accidentally let something slip. We wanted it to come from us. We had the social worker's phone number in case we needed her.

On the fourth day in the ICU, Neil uttered his first spontaneous words. He asked for a book.

"Mom, they say I'm going to be here for two weeks. Can you bring me my books?"

It was astonishing. His request reflected thought. Someone had given him information. He was going to be here two weeks. He had processed that information. *What am I going to do for two weeks?* He had come up with a solution. *I'll read.* And he had formulated a request to bring about that solution. "Mom, can you bring me my books?" It was amazing.

But as overjoyed as I was to hear this true conversation, my heart also grew cold with the realization that, number one, I didn't think there was any way he could actually read a book and, number two, if he could ask for books, it was just a matter of time before he asked for Trista.

Sure enough, that night, just before seven, just as he was drifting off to sleep, he asked, "Mom, can you bring Trista to visit me tomorrow?" Saul had just left for the hotel room. It was just Dan and I. I stared at Dan, panic-stricken. He motioned for me to go ahead. Tell him. We pulled our chairs up close to Neil, one on either side of him. Neil kept his eyes closed.

"Neil, I have to tell you about Trista."

"Okay."

"You two were both in a car accident."

"We were?"

"Yes."

"And?"

"And her injuries were more serious than yours."

No response. Eyes closed.

"They took her to a different hospital."

I used past tense. I didn't lie. But I didn't push either. I really didn't want to feed him this information at night as he was drifting off to sleep. This awful news that could only invade his slumber and give him nightmares.

"In that case, Mom, can you keep me updated?"

That was the other part of our family strategy for telling Neil. Only give him what he asked for. A bit at a time. Only what he could handle.

"Sure Neil. Just ask." Dan nodded at me like I'd done a good job. Like that was enough. We sat there in the darkened room for a while, listening to Neil breathe, waiting for him to wake up and ask more questions. But he seemed to be out for the night.

I stepped outside Neil's room and called the social worker. I just wanted to update her, see if there was anything else she recommended.

"I'm here but I'm not here," she told me, explaining that her shift ended at seven. It was 7:05. She gave me the name of her evening counterpart, but I didn't want to start all over with someone new. I felt abandoned. Let down. How many times had I stayed beyond my shift to see a family through a crisis?

Dan and I kept our vigil at Neil's bedside. We were both so tired. Neither one of us wanted to leave Neil, but there was another bed at the hotel room, and we had one more key. We argued briefly over who would stay with Neil, but there was really no contest.

"I'll call you if he wakes up," Dan told me with a wink, then rolled his sleeping bag out on the floor.

I crossed the frigid wind tunnel between the hospital and the hotel, my collar pulled up around my ears. I used the toothpaste and toothbrush the hotel provided and washed my face at the sink. I looked down at Saul, sleeping on top of the bedspread, fully clothed except for his shoes. Crow's feet and worry lines had cropped up overnight. Our carefree existence before the accident—professional careers growing, one son in college, another close behind—seemed a million miles away.

I kissed Saul's cheek and lay down next to him. It seemed like I had just shut my eyes when my cell phone rang. Saul and I both were fully upright before the first ring ended.

"Hello?"

"He's asking again."

Saul and I crossed the frigid street, the two buildings forming a wind tunnel to be forged each time.

In the hospital room Neil lay still, Dan at his side. I pulled up a chair next to Neil's right side. Dan was holding his hand on his left. Saul sat gingerly on the edge of the bed.

"So, Mom. Tell me about Trista," Neil said without opening his eyes, just sensing I was there. Something about the way he said it told me he already knew. He didn't ask how she was doing. He didn't ask for an update. Just "tell me about Trista." Like he knew there was a story there. Something he had to hear. The story I needed to finish. Dan held his hand. I put the side rail down and moved in close. I started with a recap.

"Do you remember me telling you that Trista was in the accident with you?" He nodded.

"And that she was taken to a different hospital in Boston?" Another nod.

"And that her injuries were more serious than yours?" A silent yes. He still had his eyes closed, so I wasn't sure if he had fallen back to sleep. I waited. He didn't say anything or even open his eyes, but he moved his hand in a circle, motioning for me to go on. I was crying now. I put my hand on his shoulder and spoke quietly.

"Trista tried very hard to stay alive, Neil. And the doctors and nurses did everything they could. But in the end, she didn't make it." My voice broke.

"I'm so sorry." Dan kept rubbing Neil's other shoulder. Neil didn't yell or scream or deny the reality. He didn't even open his eyes. He just turned over and said, "Then I don't want to get up any more." Checked out. Done. It would be how Neil would deal with many things in the coming days and weeks. My heart broke for him.

I watched him for a long time. I wondered how he could possibly process that information. How completely unreal the whole thing must seem in his brain-injured, time-warped, drugged-out state. One minute you're walking down the street holding hands with your girlfriend. The next you're being told that while you were asleep, she passed away.

Despite our diligent preparation and all our "family rules" about how and when and where to tell Neil about Trista, Neil remembers the scene very differently—like those movies where the same story is told differently from each character's point of view. In his world, the information came quickly and cleanly. Like a guillotine.

"She died."

In mine there was forethought, a plan. A strategy worked out carefully over days, in consultation with others. Words well chosen and delivered in the warm embrace of family. I used to argue with Neil about it, tell him that's not how it was. I wouldn't have dropped those words like a hatchet on a chopping block. "She died." For him to remember it that way made me feel callous and cruel.

I once lamented to Neil that if only I hadn't said to him that night "Why don't you walk Trista home?" that maybe they would both be alive now. But he told me that if he hadn't walked her home, she would still be dead, and he would feel unbearably guilty for not being there. Maybe that helps him bear his wounds sometimes. By seeing them as penance. As proof that he was there. As the least he could do to protect her.

So maybe remembering my words the way he does is part of his healing. Maybe he has to remember them that way. Maybe he needs to feel the cruelty of the situation full on, not softened by a mother's touch. Maybe he has to feel it like a cutter has to feel a knife against her skin. Because pain makes things real. Whatever the reason, his memory is what it is. I have finally come to realize that it has nothing to do with me. It is his reality and part of his healing and his journey back. And I have to honor it.

16

A Hasty Getaway

OVER THE NEXT TWO DAYS, Neil became more alert. He still slept a lot, but he had more spontaneous words, more facial expression, and more eye contact. He was deemed well enough to be transferred from the trauma ICU to what they called the step-down unit. Here we had a private room with a view of the city streets. It was quieter here, away from the constant lights, the relentless noise of beeping monitors and alarms, and the ever-present eyes of the ICU nurses.

But although Neil's mind was clearing, the horrific reality he faced through that lifting haze haunted and depressed him. He seemed to give up. He spent his time in bed with a blanket pulled up over his head. I never heard a sob or saw a tear, but he always emerged from those covers looking weak and spent. He refused to eat. He declined physical therapy.

"You'll never walk right if you don't exercise your leg, Neil," the orthopedic surgeon told him.

"I don't care if I ever walk again," he spat back.

I asked for a psych consult—someone to evaluate his emotional stability, help him deal with his terrible loss. I told Neil someone would be stopping by to talk to him.

"Fine," he snarled. He aimed his one-word answers at us, hurling them like missiles in response to anything we said to him. Then, the blanket over the head.

We continued our "never leave him alone" policy. At first it was to protect him from the news of Trista's death. Now it was to protect him from himself.

"Think of it as a suicide watch, Dan," I told my oldest son, the words catching in my mouth. I didn't really think Neil would do that. Then again he'd never lost a girlfriend before.

We waited all day for the psychiatrist's visit, or at least a resident. It was getting late. I finally went out to the nurses' station to ask when the psych team was coming.

"Oh, they're not," the nurse informed me, a little too cheerily.

"Why not?" I asked, horrified that, number one, they weren't coming, and that, number two, I wasn't told.

"The team won't come unless a patient is actively suicidal," the nurse said, her voice now devoid of cheeriness.

"And how exactly are they supposed to make that determination without *actually seeing THE PATIENT?*" I asked. When the nurse took a step back, I realized just how loudly I'd raised my voice, but I was furious. I knew I'd better get a grip or someone would be calling Security on me.

I walked back to Neil's room and leaned against the wall outside the door, my heart pounding, my eyes stinging with pent-up tears. I tried to gather my thoughts and rein in my emotions. I felt that the hospital, my medical community, was failing us. First there was the social worker who was "here and not here," unwilling to stay a few minutes beyond her scheduled shift to see one of her families through. And now no one was coming to evaluate my child's mental health even though to me he was clearly at least passively suicidal. How could a world-class trauma center not recognize the emotional trauma that goes along with the broken bones and bleeding brains?

I walked back to the nurses' station and said in my calmest, quietest voice, "I want my son transferred back to Anna Jaques Hospital."

"I'll call the residents," she responded, her hand already on the phone before I'd even turned away from the desk to return to Neil. Here at Brigham and Women's Hospital, Neil's care had been excellent, the staff attentive and diligent. But we knew that there were so many sicker, more critical patients here. We could see it in the halls where staff raced to silence alarms and check beeping monitors. We knew it from our time in the waiting room, listening to other families rally then grieve. We heard it in the staff's upbeat assessment of our child. "He's gonna be just fine." Here a traumatic brain injury in which the patient speaks and stands was no big deal. Back home at Anna Jaques, Neil would be a very big deal. There he would be known. The son of a businessman in the community. A member of the synagogue. A classmate of the sons and daughters of the doctors and nurses caring for him. If the acute phase of Neil's injuries was behind him—he wasn't getting surgery on his brain; he'd had the first operation on his leg; if all he needed was rehab—I wanted to take him back to his hometown where family and friends could more easily visit and support him.

Back in his room, Neil slept. I told Saul about my encounter with the nurse and the missing-in-action psych residents. Saul sighed and shook his head.

"We should go back to Newburyport," he said, independently coming to the same conclusion I had. It made me feel better about my volatile encounter and my spontaneous demand for a retro-transport.

Neil had a few visitors that afternoon. Suzanne Bryan, his drama coach, was there. We had snuck her in after visiting hours the night before as "Aunt Suzanne," but now she was here legitimately, along with a few of Neil's friends. Brendan brought him comic books. Neil smiled at the pile, each edition carefully wrapped in a clear plastic sleeve. But Neil couldn't stay awake for long. So we took the conversation out into the hall.

"Thanks, Brendan," I told him. "You get the prize. That was Neil's first smile since the accident."

Later, Neil's friends Travis and Greg brought a movie and a VCR. The movie played. Neil slept.

"I'm sorry I'm so tired." He apologized each time he woke. "I'm sorry I'm in so much pain." The boys finally went home.

By the next morning we still did not know the status of our requested transfer back to our hometown. We asked the nurse to check on things for us.

Soon an alarmingly young-looking resident came in to round on Neil.

"He's all set to go," he proclaimed.

"What do you mean?" I asked

"He's discharged," the resident explained, still smiling, as if this were good news. But it wasn't good news to us. Neil wasn't ready to leave the hospital. He was weak. He had lost weight. Having refused physical therapy for the past two days, he had not even stood on his own, let alone walked or done stairs. Dan had even been carrying him to the bathroom. Then there was the issue of his fragile mental health.

"But he's not ready," I stammered.

"Oh, he'll do fine," the resident smiled, his teeth astonishingly white. His optimistic pronouncement reminded me of Chuck/Mitch's one-minute ER assessment. We asked to speak with the head of the ICU, the trauma surgeon who had been so concerned about a basilar skull fracture that first night in intensive care. But the attendings had switched rotations, and the new one seemed in agreement with his resident. He showed us stable head CTs and x-rays of Neil's newly aligned leg bones as evidence of his readiness.

"I'll get your paperwork ready."

"What about physical therapy at home?" I asked hopefully.

"Oh, kids bounce back so quickly. I don't think he'll need that."

And he was out the door. We felt defeated. We looked over at our thin, pale, sleeping son. He did not look very bouncy to us. Saul looked at his watch.

"Trista's funeral is at 12:30," he commented. "I'd like to try to make it." I nodded.

Neil suddenly sat up in bed.

"I want to go to Trista's funeral too," he announced. The idea was preposterous. He couldn't stay awake for more than an hour. He was still on IV fluids. Besides drinking a few smoothies, he really hadn't eaten anything. He was on IV Dilantin for seizure prevention and a patient-controlled analgesia pump for the pain. He had no experience with crutches.

"No one expects you there, Neil," Saul said, trying to discourage him from this impossible plan. "They know you're still in the hospital."

"But they said I can go. So what do I have to do to get out of here?"

He looked determined. I had to admit that just having that goal—to leave the hospital to attend his girlfriend's funeral—seemed to pump Neil up just a little. Put a little color in his face. Add a strength to his frame that wasn't there before.

Now Neil was on the going-home bandwagon too, along with the resident and attending. Saul and I were quickly losing this battle. "Well, Neil, you'd need to take your medicines in pill form and be able to walk on crutches," I offered.

"And you'd need to eat a little something as well," his father added.

Neil thought about that for a moment.

"Then get me a sandwich, bring me my pills, and get that lady with the crutches back here," he ordered. He tried to sit up at the edge of the bed, but the effort made sweat stand out on his forehead. His face was pale and gaunt. He closed his eyes and lay back down.

"Can you draw the shades please?" he asked in a whisper. But they were already drawn. I closed the door to squelch what little light was leaking in from the hallway.

Neil slept briefly. Then the physical therapist came. She was a tiny muscular blond woman with short hair. Her nametag read SHARI. Neil sat up. Standing next to Neil, she came up to his shoulders.

"I'm dizzy. I can't do this," he complained, lying back down on the bed.

"No problem," Shari responded cheerily. "I'll come back tomorrow."

Neil threw back the covers and winced.

"No," he snapped. "I'll do it."

The physical therapist showed Dan how to put the air cast on Neil's leg. Together they helped him stand, balancing a crutch under each arm. Neil made short jerky steps around the room. His long curls stuck to the sweat on his face. He blew them away. He seemed out of breath. After the brief session he collapsed onto the bed. Neil cried out when Dan swung his leg carefully up onto a pillow.

"Bring me a pain pill," he croaked.

"I'll be back tomorrow and we'll do stairs, Neil," Shari promised.

"No, now," Neil argued, eyes closed. The therapist looked at us, panicked, and shook her head.

"Neil, you rest," I suggested, watching Shari's face for cues. "Maybe Shari will come back in a little while."

"He wants to go home," I mouthed. She looked at her watch.

"Give me an hour," she agreed.

"Thanks," I said.

Neil's meal tray came. He picked at the offerings, forcing his mouth to chew, his throat to swallow. Dan helped him into the shower, his first since the accident. There he ripped his IV out, not wanting to take any chances that he wouldn't be allowed to leave the hospital.

With tremendous reservations, but with the endorsement of the Brigham and Women's Hospital team, we packed him up. Untouched fruit baskets, unread books, unwatched movies and unworn clothes; cards, flowers, cookie-grams all got loaded into Saul's car. We had planned for the two-week stay the doctors had forecast. Now we were gearing up for the abridged six-day version Neil was demanding.

We took two cars home—Saul's loaded up with hospital leftovers, mine loaded with Neil. I put the passenger seat down as far as it would go, wrapped his leg in my coat to act as a shock absorber, and had Dan climb into the backseat. Neil still winced and sucked in air through his teeth every time we went over a bump. A few blocks from the hospital, Neil announced, "I'd like to eat berries." I pulled the car into the Star Market parking lot on Brookline Avenue. Dan ran in to make the purchase. But by the time he came back out, Neil was asleep. I put the car in gear and drove as gingerly as I could.

I cried all the way home. I couldn't believe this was happening to us. Until now I hadn't allowed myself to think much about the drunk driver. I needed all my energy focused on helping Neil get well. But as I drove home down Interstate 95, my wounded son next to me crying out with every bump in the road, I was filled with anger. This was all so unfair. Neil and Trista were doing everything right. Studying together on a Tuesday night. Walking home before curfew. Wearing bright-orange clothing. Walking on the correct side of the street. Neil could have driven Trista home. He had a license. But he was a junior operator, not allowed to take passengers. He was following the rules. The drunk driver had not.

As we got closer to home, Neil started to stir next to me. In a half-awake state, he instinctively placed both his hands on either side of his coat-splinted leg, shifting position carefully but still wincing with the effort. He then settled back into a fitful sleep, his brow furrowed and sweaty.

He had taken a Percocet shortly before we were discharged, but that had been almost three hours ago. He would be due for his next pain med right about the time we'd be pulling into the driveway.

With one hand on the wheel, I fished Neil's prescriptions out of my purse. Then I dug out my cell phone and tossed it to Dan in the back seat, careful to keep my eyes on the road.

"Call the drug store at Port Plaza, Dan. Get the pharmacist on the line."

Dan sprang into action, getting the phone number from information, then winding his way through the Walgreen's phone tree, and finally handing me the phone.

"Hi, Mark. It's Carolyn Bornstein."

"Sorry, no. This is Tina. How can I help you?" a high-pitched Asian voice offered. Crap.

"Uh, this is Dr. Bornstein," I began.

"Oh, yes, Doctor," her voice picked up and I pictured her sitting up, pen in hand, ready to take dictation. Clearly, she didn't recognize our name.

"Well, I'm on my way home with Neil," I started. The line was silent. No recognition on the other end. "And I've got a Percocet prescription here."

"Oh, Doctor, you can't call in a narcotic," Tina stated, flustered.

"I know. I know. I'm not calling it in really. You see it's not my prescription. It's from Boston. I just thought you could get it ready." I was stumbling. I suddenly felt like a criminal, or at least a wayward doc trying to call in a favor. But really I just wanted Neil not to be in pain. I wanted him not to have to wait. I looked over at him. He was the color of sand.

The line momentarily cut out.

"Hey, Carolyn, Mark here. What's up?"

Relieved, I explained the situation, but before I could even finish my request, Mark responded, "I'll have it ready."

As we pulled up in front of the house, Saul was chipping away at the sidewalk with an ice chopper and spreading rock salt on the stairs. Unlike the stubborn January snow, my heart melted for my husband, desperately trying to make his son's way safe.

It was 12:15. Trista's funeral was scheduled to begin in 15 minutes. As I saw it, we had three options. One would be to drive to the funeral home early, giving Neil a chance to settle in. Or we could bring Neil into the house, wait the hour until he was due for the Percocet, and get to the funeral late. The third option seemed the most obvious to me. Neil would skip the event altogether. I roused him.

"Neil? We're home. The funeral is in fifteen minutes. What do you want to do?"

Neil grimaced, keeping his eyes closed.

"Get me into bed."

I sighed with relief.

Dan carried Neil down the hill in front of our house, down the frozen steps, and in the front door. The house was ice cold. We hadn't been home in a week. I pulled out the convertible couch and threw on some sheets and pillows while Dan held his brother patiently in his arms. We laid him carefully on the pullout, lifted his leg onto pillows, and piled blankets on top of him. His lips were blue. He shook violently.

I lit a fire in the wood stove then brought Neil a Percocet and a drink. It wasn't quite four hours, but he was in pain. I called the Brigham, not knowing what to do. I spoke with the attending who had discharged us. He assured us that, this once, it would be okay. Someone called on the phone. I cut them off. I was scared. What had I done? I should have insisted on a longer stay, or at least that transfer. The agonizingly long stretches of time in the ICU hadn't prepared me for this leap to action.

Saul came in from clearing the walk, threw on a jacket and tie. Trista's funeral was in five minutes. The three of us looked at one another, then at Neil. He was asleep under a pile of blankets, thin and weak. He had missed Trista's wake, and now it looked like he was going to miss her funeral too. He would rouse from this nightmare and she would be gone: dead and buried. Saul shrugged his shoulders, blew me a silent kiss, and closed the door quietly behind him.

17

Like Dogs

DETAILS ABOUT THE EVENTS that led to the drunk driver plow-ing into our kids came out gradually over the days and weeks following the crash. The drinking began at the home of a teen-aged boy whose parents were at work. He invited a bunch of his friends, and the drunk driver arrived with a bottle of red wine. At some point the teenaged host took a fake ID and bought a thirty-pack of beer at a liquor store just over the New Hampshire border. They played a drinking game called beer pong. When the teen host received a call from his mother saying she would soon be home, the boys all piled out of the house.

They loaded the empties into the drunk driver's SUV. It was apparent to everyone that he was way too intoxicated to get behind the wheel. One (or some) of the boys tried to take his keys away from him but were unsuccessful. He drove off into the night and ultimately into our children.

My mind fills in the details of the accident I did not wit-ness. I hear the shrill shriek of screeching brakes and the sharp shattering of broken glass. In terrifying dreams my mind con-jures up images of things I did not see and cannot know. I see our children, blinded by headlights that lurch unannounced from a pitch-black night. I hear the horrified screams of shocked witnesses, seeing it happen before their eyes, powerless to stop it.

But as time has gone by, I have learned the actual details from newspaper accounts and police reports. From first responders and passersby. From people who cannot get those nightmare images out of their heads. I want to suck those scenes right out of their brains and plant them inside mine then replay them again and again, making them my own.

From the crash reconstruction team, I have learned that there were no screeching brakes that night. There were no brakes at all. The drunk driver plowed into our children headlong, too drunk to notice them, too cowardly to stop.

There was no shattering windshield either. Just a crack in the glass. A single crack with hairs wedged into it, like a weed sprouting from a line in the sidewalk. This I learned from the police detective who came to my home. The one who asked me to pluck twenty-five hairs from my son's head so that they could extract his DNA and match it to the hairs at the scene. The ones sprouting from the lone crack.

And Trista and Neil were never blinded by headlights. They were hit from behind. They never saw it coming. It *was* pitch black that night. On Ferry Road where they were hit, there indeed are long stretches of unlit territory. Long sections with no sidewalk and nowhere to walk but the road itself. But they were run down under a street light by a drunk driver driving on the wrong side of the road. It was there that investigators found her watch, her book bag, his hat. ("Hats are never found more than twenty feet from the point of impact.") I learned all this from the police officers, waiting to testify before the grand jury, convened to indict the drunk driver.

And there were no horrified screams of shocked onlookers either. There were no witnesses to the crash at all. Only those who came later. There was Dick Sullivan, a retired firefighter who swerved to avoid being hit by a car out of control. Who radioed headquarters for backup. Who followed the driver, watched him flip his SUV, and then flee into the woods on foot. There was Wynn Damon, a local radio personality, whose driveway the drunkard was caught in, urinating on Wynn's wife's car. There was Steve Cutter, the fire chief, whose kids played soccer with Neil. Who heard the call from home. Who responded to Dick's report of an erratic driver. Who found two crash victims instead.

"Run over like dogs." That is how one officer described it to a newspaper reporter that night. An honest response from a weary rescuer, overwhelmed by what he saw. I can just see him shaking his head and sighing, "like dogs."

That printed comment turned out to be controversial. A woman who worked as a cashier at the local supermarket wrote a letter to the editor admonishing the officer for his word choice. She felt he maligned the drunk driver and showed little respect for us, the parents of the victims.

But we sympathized with the sergeant. In fact, we felt he was being too kind with his words. Who would run down a pair of dogs, let alone kids, then leave them for dead? But that is exactly what happened to Trista and Neil.

And this is what galls us most. What we cannot fathom, even now. This is what Neil cannot wrap his injured brain around.

"How could he just leave us, Mom?"

Neil asks me this question again and again, over and over.

"Why didn't he call 911?"

Trista's father, Dave, asks himself an even more pointed question: "Would my daughter be alive if he had?"

And I will never have an answer for them. Everyone had cell phones by then. And there were plenty of doors to knock on. Why, indeed. But he just left them there. To die. To freeze to death. Or get run over again by cop cars hurrying to apprehend an erratic driver, unaware that the drunkard had already begun leaving victims in his wake.

So now my dreams have detail. I have quilted together a new reality. No screeching brakes. No shattering glass. No screaming witnesses. Just a cold, clear night. A halo of light from a towering street lamp. A soft dull thud. A watch. A book bag. A hat. Two young lovers, hand in hand, unaware that their future ends now.

18

Drunk Driving

As DETAILS OF THE CRASH CAME OUT, so did the discussions about underage drinking and drunk driving: in the local newspaper and the *Boston Globe*, on talk radio, in conversations among friends at parties and grocery stores. If I had thought about it, I would have expected those discussions. What I didn't expect were the families who seemed okay with underage drinking. Who felt they were protecting their children by confiscating their keys and giving them a "safe place" to drink. Their comments filled the op-ed pages, even as the story of the crash and all its devastation was still fresh in everyone's mind.

But the dangers of underage drinking go beyond drinking and driving. I know this not just as a parent or even as a pediatrician; I know this as a citizen of my own community, one who reads the paper and knows the stories: A little girl in a nearby town wandered away from a drinking party and drowned in a shallow stream. A boy at another local drinking party cut his hand on a window and bled to death, discovered the next morning on the back stoop. Confiscating car keys may prevent drunk driving, but it doesn't prevent drunkenness, and bad things happen to drunken children, children of sleeping or inattentive parents. The misguided notion that if parents take away the car keys and let their children drink under their roof they will somehow keep them safe to me just ignores history.

Parents who allow their children to drink in their homes open themselves up to enormous risk. Many states, including Massachusetts, have social host laws that hold parents responsible for the actions of partygoers who drink alcohol in their homes, even if they were not present when the drinking took place and didn't provide the alcohol. A couple of years after the accident, a friend of mine hosted a party for her son's graduation from high school, and she served alcohol. Saul and I were incredulous. Not just because they had so much to lose but also because we had already lost so much. But there was no talking to her; her mind was made up. She just seemed to ignore all the bad possible outcomes.

But to me it's more than just the lawsuits. Assuming children can't have a good time without alcohol sets the bar of expectation pretty low for our young people.

Neil came to the same conclusion reading the array of editorials and responses.

"It's like they think we have to be drunk to have fun."

But Neil and his friends could have fun without alcohol. Neil was a theater kid in high school. Theater kids know how to party. They had bonfires at their drama teacher's house. They held coffeehouses between the performances and the judging at the Massachusetts Drama Guild Competition, a contest among over 120 high schools in the Commonwealth in which each theater team had to set up a stage, perform their play, and then strike the set—all in less than fifty minutes. All these events were alcohol-free.

They weren't angels. The police were called one night when Alex Wallace led a particularly rousing rendition of "She Bangs" while dancing on top of one of the tables at the local Wendy's to the thunderous applause of his fellow theater kids. Whom did they call from police custody? Their theater teacher, Suzanne Bryan, who came to get them with a stern look for the kids and a solemn plea to the police officer.

"Some of them are troubled kids, officer. Just let me take them home without calling their parents."

The officer acquiesced to Suzanne's requests.

"Are you gonna call our parents?" the kids nervously asked their teacher after they were safely in her custody.

Suzanne maintained her stern expression but shook her head no.

"You're not?"

"Uh-uh."

She paused, for dramatic effect no doubt, before pumping her fist in the air and shouting "because you're theater kids!"

The crowd erupted in cheers. No confiscation of car keys needed. No fake ID. No record. Just plain fun.

In my everyday life as a pediatrician, I often have the opportunity to talk to kids about underage drinking and drunk driving. While I'm generally reluctant to share events from my personal life with my patients, I do sometimes when I feel I'm not getting through to my kids—when my usual spiel on drugs and alcohol are making my young patients' eyes glaze over. Sometimes their parents are in the room with us, and I'll often catch a glimpse of

Mom out of the corner of my eye, nodding gratefully. I'm a new adult ally in the war on drugs. Sometimes it's just the kid and me in the room together, locked in a kind of health-care *Smack-Down:* them with their in-your-face-what-do-*you*-know swagger, me with my more quiet "Let me tell you how it is" stance. That's when I'll sometimes play the crash card.

After all, what's more effective? Telling them that 11,773 people died in 2008 in drunk driving accidents or recounting being asked to pluck twenty-five hairs from Neil's head so the crash scene investigator could match them to the ones sprouting from the drunk driver's cracked windshield? What if one of my teens tells me she doesn't drive drunk, just buzzed? Do I reach her with a discussion of blood alcohol levels and the minimum legal drinking age? Or do I tell her a story about watching my seventeen-year-old son say the mourner's prayer for his dead girlfriend in our synagogue?

It's not that I've become a doctor without borders. I believe in the usual boundaries between physicians and their patients. I don't parade the gory details of my life out for every family in my practice. In fact, I don't talk about the crash much at all. But when I do I'm simply trying to get my point across. A pediatrician I know keeps his daughter's crumpled bicycle helmet displayed prominently on his desk as a reminder of her survival. He pulls it out to show his patients whenever one of them claims not to believe in its use. I don't have a crumpled bike helmet. All I have are words. Are they effective? Who knows? I'm not going for shock value. I'm just trying to connect with my patients and make a difference in their world. Using my own family's narrative as street cred. Linking choices to consequences. Hoping that my words get through.

19

Home

I TRIED NOT TO PAY TOO MUCH ATTENTION to all the media in those early days. There was so much to do to help Neil recover. His first days home were terrifying. His head still ached from the slightest ray of light or shred of sound. We unscrewed light-bulbs and drew curtains. We tiptoed around the house. Our dog, Lucky, had been staying with Saul's brother, Louis, while Neil was in the hospital. We thought seeing her might do him some good, so we called Louis and asked him to bring her over. Then we worried that maybe this was not such a good idea. Perhaps her barking would be more than Neil could tolerate. It was even worse than that. Louis opened the door and Lucky padded over to where Neil lay, waiting to be petted.

"Go away, Lucky," Neil told her, a washcloth covering his eyes. "You breathe too loud."

Neil slept most of the time. He couldn't seem to keep him-self awake for more than an hour at a time.

Ever since we first told Neil of Trista's death, he would wake up from every dozing-off with the same question.

"Mom, have I been dreaming?"

Every time I'd have to tell him the same thing: "No, Neil. I'm sorry. I wish I could tell you it was all a dream. But it's not."

I'd have to wait for that news to settle in. Every time. Like a recurring nightmare. I felt like one of those Marines charged with telling a family that their soldier-son had died, only instead of delivering the body blow once, I was caught in a *Groundhog Day*-type scenario, having to tell Neil over and over again that Trista was no longer with us.

I arranged for a mental health worker to come to the house to provide that psychological evaluation that the Brigham had not. Bob had come recommended by a couple of friends, themselves therapists. I knew Neil couldn't participate very much in the process at first. He slept much and talked little. But that was precisely what scared me. I understood that a lot of his fatigue was physical, from the brain injury itself. But I worried that I might be letting him slip into a deep depression. I also knew that Neil was by nature a young man of few words. But was his silence now just part of that quiet personality, or was it something more? Part of the injury or a sign of an impending breakdown? I needed help here. I was out of my league. I needed another pair of eyes watching Neil; another set of ears listening for signs of worsening despair. Our family had never been through anything this traumatic before. I didn't know what to say to Neil. I needed help finding the right words.

The first time Bob came over, Neil was not up for a full therapy session. Bob knelt next to Neil's makeshift bed in the darkened living room for a short while. He spent most of the session with Saul and me in the kitchen, describing his experience, telling us what approach he would take with Neil, suggesting ways we might support our son.

Even in my own field—medicine, pediatrics—I felt at sea. I made charts for everything. I kept track of his daily Dilantin, afraid that if I forgot a dose, he'd have a seizure on me. I recorded his Percocet too, worried I would overdose him. It was overwhelming. I was terrified. I didn't know what parents with no medical or nursing background did in these situations. My own degrees were doing nothing to help me keep my own head above water.

Neil had changed physically in his short hospital stay. He had always been a thin young man, but a week in the ICU with near nothing to eat had reduced him to a disturbing package of skin and bones. I made him milk shakes with ice cream, Carnation Instant Breakfast, and raw eggs. I calculated the calories of each and entered them in a notebook. I cooked all his fattening favorites: matzo balls made with chicken fat, fettuccine Alfredo. I bought the cheap, fatty variety of hamburger for his American chop suey. I kept track of his "*I*s and *O*s," intake and output, as best I could. I measured every cc that went into him. I listened outside the bathroom door when he peed, making checkmarks in the output column. I worried he would get dehydrated.

I called the visiting nurses and arranged for a physical therapist to come to the house. Pat was a godsend. She taught us how to do daily exercises to stretch Neil's leg. His muscles had atrophied significantly—even Neil noticed it. She brought him a walker. She expertly looped a strap around his waist to steady him. Pat taught him to take stairs one at a time.

Friends called, both Neil's and ours. They wanted to pay us visits. They had gifts they wanted to bring. We appreciated their checking in and good wishes, but none of us were up to visitors just then, Neil physically, Saul and I emotionally. There was a real "circling of the wagons" feeling about our immediate post-hospital life. Neil needed the curtains drawn to protect his eyes from the light. We wanted them drawn as a symbolic cocoon— shielding us from a world we didn't feel ready to receive.

Those first days home, I pulled a mattress down from the attic and slept on the floor next to my boy. I listened for his breathing to grow even and deep before letting my own lids close. Even then I didn't sleep well, rousing at each cough or turn. It reminded me of my first restless nights as a new mother when my children were newborns. I listened intently to their breath in the dark, wondering if I would be able to detect something wrong.

That first week Neil did get stronger. He put on some weight. He was able to stay awake for longer periods, though he still tired easily. Pat lent us a shower chair and taught Neil how to transfer himself in and out of the tub. His first foray into the bathroom alone led to a major water leak when Neil left the shower curtain outside the tub. But Neil learned his lessons well. He gained strength and independence. At first I held onto the waistband of his pants to support him as he teetered around with his walker or crutches. Later I tried to resist the urge to spot him. Neil swatted my hands away, but I always went flying into the room whenever I heard the walker clang against the wall or over a doorjamb. Invariably he was okay, balancing himself on his crutches, giving me his stern "I'm fine, Mom" look.

By the end of his first week home, Neil insisted that I get rid of the mattress on the floor and return to my own bed upstairs. So we bought him a bell to ring if he needed something and a baby monitor so we could listen to his movements at night. He never rang his bell. And though we kept our ears glued to the tiny bedside monitor, no sounds ever alarmed us. By this time Saul had returned to work. He owned his own business. No one was taking over for him. Without him no orders were placed, and deliveries were piling up. With me it was different. There were more than seventy health care providers at the clinic where I worked. They could easily take over my patient panel. I spoke with the medical director and told him I'd be staying home taking care of Neil until further notice. Dan finally flew back to Mexico to finish his Spanish-language course. His brother was home and healing. He could sense his work here was done.

By our second week home, I was feeling better. Physical and mental health therapies were in place. Neil and I had our routine. I felt more confident and ready to let friends back into our changed world. Ready to open up the circled wagons just a bit.

Neil's friends from school came in bunches. They brought stuffed animals, stickers, comic books, and Heroclix, a kind of action figure that the mother of one of Neil's friends called their "stupid little men." Neil and his friends could play with them for hours. They sent journals with quilled pens, giant get-well cookies from Mrs. Fields called "cakies," packs of Old Maid cards, bags of movies. Our friends sent flowers and fruit baskets and pots of homemade soup. A friend of mine from work stopped by frequently with what she called "Lawrence food drops," fare from the ethnic neighborhood of the health center where we worked: tabouleh and stuffed grape leaves from George's Lebanese bakery, seaweed salad from the Asian Market. The owner of the artisan bakery in town made us four huge loaves of challah, big as breadboxes, with shiny brown crusts. They were sweet and eggy inside, the best I'd ever eaten.

"None of the get well cards I looked at seemed quite right," he told us sweetly.

My friends from town gave me lotions and bath soaps, passes to the gym, and invitations to the movies. They brought Neil word puzzles and gift certificates for video games they didn't understand. A friend's mother who lived in New York crocheted him a small afghan to throw over his shoulders or lap. Neil's dentist sent a huge floral arrangement signed by the entire office staff. A quilt from the Linus Project ladies arrived in the mail.

We all got tons of cards, letters, phone calls, and e-mails from people with warm thoughts and prayers and well wishes. Some were from people we didn't even know, people who were just moved by the whole tragedy and compelled to reach out. To touch Neil or us in some way.

One day Neil's theater friends dropped by after school. They gathered around his makeshift bed in the middle of the living room, acting out scenes from the musical they were doing at the high school.

"This is how Grant sounds when he sings," one would say and launch into an operatic falsetto. The crowd went wild.

"This is what Seamus looks like when he dances," another aped, flailing his arms and legs in exaggerated moves. Neil was grinning broadly. I ached seeing that beautiful smile again.

The doorbell rang. It was Neil's therapist, Bob. The theater kids parted to make room for him, starting to gather up their things.

"I guess we'll see you later, Neil."

Neil's disappointment was obvious—etched onto his face like a Greek tragedy mask. A moment ago he had been a part of the troupe, or at least part of the audience. Now he was different, alone, in need of treatment. It took Bob no time to decide what to do. He checked his watch then looked at Neil and me.

"No, you guys stay," he told them. "How about I come back after supper?"

Neil smiled. His friends set down their books and settled back in. I winked a thank-you, my heart melting with gratitude.

20

Please, Please, Please

I SUBSCRIBE TO the Anne Lamott school of prayer. She once wrote that, for her, there are only two kinds of prayers. The first one goes *please, please, please.* The second one goes *thank you, thank you, thank you.* During the early hours following the accident, I lived the *please, please, please,* beginning with running to the accident scene. *Please, please, please.* One foot in front of the other. Please let it not be him. Please not them. Deep down, I must have known that it was.

I prayed for so many things then. *Let it not be them* (denied). *Let Neil be alive* (granted). *Let Trista make it* (denied).

My God is not a father in heaven. He is not a presiding entity who watches over us. He may not even be a He. My God is more loving presence than omnipotent ruler. When I pray, it is more like hoping than asking. I am more likely to pray in a car than in a synagogue. For me prayer is part review: Okay, this is where my life is at. The other part of prayer is hope: Okay, this is where I want to be. *Please, please, please.*

Events such as accidents stop us dead in our tracks. They take whatever we were doing at that instant and make it suddenly trivial. In that one moment of the accident, every other thought melts away like sand castles on a beach, leaving just this one thing center stage. One minute I am working on my novel, happily typing away at the computer. The next, I am running through the cold praying *please, please, please.*

While I am very good at the *please, please, please,* in the days following the crash I always seemed to be a little late on the *thank you, thank you, thank you.* I don't know why that is. Baseball players seem to remember to thank God the moment their feet touch home plate. They put their hands together, or make the sign of the cross, or give God a big thumbs-up on national television. Look at Tim Tebow, so grateful to God for touchdowns that he sinks to one knee in the end zone, making the sign of the cross. I read a story in the *Boston Globe* once about a lottery winner who brought bouquets of flowers to three local churches to thank God for his kindness. Me? It can be days after Neil has made it through another surgery or received encouraging test results that I remember to say, oh, yeah, *thank you, thank you, thank you.*

It's not that I'm not thankful. I am. Maybe I worry about using up my quota of requests. Maybe there will be something bigger and more important to pray for down the road in Neil's recovery.

Maybe it's because I'm busy. With each new piece of information, each new event to be grateful for, I have to move on to the next task that needs to be completed. He made it through surgery? Great. Now there's pain to manage and physical therapy to arrange. The CAT scan shows the bleeding has stopped? Hallelujah! But there are still antiseizure drugs to titrate and mental health appointments to set up. One foot in front of the other. *Please, please, please.* Always something more to pray for.

In asking for things, in praying the *please, please, please,* I feel it in my gut. The anxiety of not knowing the outcome of an operation or a scan somehow makes the asking palpable. Praying for things feels visceral. I cannot know the future, but I strain to see it anyway. Gratitude comes more gradually to me, like a slow unwinding of the knot in my stomach. I can breathe again, releasing my angst like pent-up air.

I have probably sat cross-legged meditating more times than I have set foot in a church or synagogue. I slow my breath and clear my mind. I picture air flowing into me through the top of my skull, a point called One Hundred Meeting Places in acupuncture. It is a center of creativity and flow. I visualize good things streaming into me through that spot. As I exhale, I try to let go of my worries, releasing stress and strain. Maybe that's why I forget to say *thank you, thank you, thank you.* If gratitude feels like a cleansing breath, maybe I cleanse away any thought or reminder in my head of thanking a higher power.

But maybe it's more than that. Maybe I'm just not sure enough that there is a higher power to thank. They say there are no atheists in foxholes. Maybe Neil's bedside is my foxhole and I'm praying like there's no tomorrow during each operation or scan. But as each danger passes, as Neil survives the crash, comes through surgery, learns to walk, I come out of my foxhole, my doubts reemerging with me.

I use a mantra when I meditate. I was encouraged by a yoga practitioner years ago to choose a phrase that captures my belief system. It took me a very long time to come up with the mantra, mainly because I'm so squishy about what my belief system actually is. I was raised a Catholic. I loved the rituals: the smell of the smoking incense rising from the thurible our priest used to bless us congregants each Easter. I fingered rosaries and lit Advent candles. I walked the Stations of the Cross.

Later I converted to Judaism. I liked the liberal politics of my reform temple. There were also new rituals to learn and embrace. I could light candles on Friday nights, inhale spices on Saturday evenings. There were prayers for waking up and prayers for going to sleep. Prayers before eating fruit, breaking bread, or drinking wine. But how do you capture all that in a phrase: the religion that raised me and the one that called me? And the incense, the candles, the Hebrew, the prayers: Wasn't that just ceremony anyway? Catholicism and Judaism were my religions, but were they a belief system?

My mantra came to me one day in synagogue. It was right after the part of the service where we explicitly acknowledge our duty to teach our children our faith, to pass on the torch of religious tradition.

"These words I command you this day you shall take to heart. You shall teach them diligently to your children."

And there it was. My mantra: *L'dor Va'dor*. From generation to generation. It captured my belief system perfectly. Family. I believe in family. I believe in us: in me, my husband, my sons. We are there for one another. My husband and I have taken turns as breadwinner and homemaker over the years. Saul watched our children when I started medical school, laid off from his restaurant supply sales job. He later started his own business, selling plates and flatware out of our basement, boxes of the stuff piled under our Ping-Pong table. We have cared for each of our parents as they aged and passed on. Dan flew home to be with Neil, literally sleeping beside him in the ICU. That's what I believe in.

Maybe I take too much credit for things in my life. Maybe I owe more to higher powers than I know. Either way, I'll probably continue praying in this same random and haphazard way. To a God who may or may not be out there. Grateful when my prayers are answered but not looking for reasons why when they are not.

21

Reentry

ALMOST A MONTH AFTER THE ACCIDENT, Neil asked when he could go back to school. He had not yet had his follow-up appointments in Boston. He had one scheduled with the neurosurgeon who had seen him in the hospital and the orthopedist who had repaired his broken leg. Those were still a couple of weeks away. I assumed we would get their okay for Neil's return at those visits. But Neil was definitely improving day by day. He still had headaches, and his memory was not sharp. It was a struggle for him to read and recall. But he was able to remain awake most days. He could do crossword puzzles for short periods of time. He managed stairs with one crutch and had moved back into his second-floor bedroom. I didn't see any reason Neil shouldn't be allowed to try at least a part-time return to school. The semester had started without him, his last before the start of college. There would be a lot of catching up to do.

I called the school and spoke with the principal and the dean of Student Life. They agreed that Neil could return with a note from a doctor. I called his orthopedic surgeon in Boston, who faxed me the letter that same day. The school officials picked a start date later that week and scheduled a meeting to ease Neil back into his day. A lot had happened while he'd been gone, and the faculty wanted the chance to prepare him. I appreciated their efforts.

Reentry. That's what they called the meeting that launched the process of Neil returning to school. The name reminded me of those splashdowns in the early space program where a Gemini capsule would come hurtling down to Earth and plunge into the Indian Ocean. There it would bob helplessly until a helicopter hooked it with steel cables, hoisting it out of the water and dropping it onto the deck of a fighter ship to lie like a defeated flounder.

Reentry. Maybe the word was actually appropriate.

Neil and I got up early to get ready for the meeting, after which Neil was to attend a couple of classes. Then I would pick him up, an abbreviated day for him. The 10:00 a.m. time was chosen purposely so that the rest of the students would be settled into their day, the halls relatively clear and safe for travel for a boy and his walker.

Neil and I hadn't set an alarm clock in a month. He showered listening to the same song he always did, a song by They Might Be Giants, Trista's favorite band. One line talked about a bag of groceries expiring on the supermarket shelf. It always reminded me of Trista, certainly taken before her time. I wondered if Neil thought that too. I wondered if that was why he listened to that song, over and over, every morning. For weeks now Neil had been hobbling around the house in nothing but sweats and T-shirts. Now he balanced his crutches under his arms and fumbled with buttons and zippers.

It was still January, but the cold snap we were in the night Neil was hit and during our hospital stay had passed. Soggy puddles of snow replaced the treacherous chunks of ice on our walkway. Neil hadn't been out of the house since we'd carried him down these stairs over three weeks ago. He didn't even look up to take in the day. He just carefully surveyed the outside stairs. No handrail. He tucked both crutches under one arm like he'd been taught in PT and used my shoulder as the railing.

He negotiated the stairs and threw his crutches into the backseat. I followed with his collapsible walker; I thought the walker would be more stable for him. He climbed into the front seat, book bag on his lap. I hadn't driven Neil to school since he was little. Looking at him now I remembered the young middle school boy with the science project, a carefully constructed replica of a fourteenth-century lute made out of cereal boxes, rulers, and rubber bands, all balanced precariously in his lap. A proud smile lit up his face. How much had happened to him since those grammar school days; how much innocence had been lost.

The meeting took place in a conference room outside the principal's office. Seated around a long oval table were the principal, the dean of Student Life, the school nurse, a guidance counselor, and all of Neil's teachers. Some stood up and hugged Neil awkwardly. I understood that professional gray zone: They're the teachers; he's the student. But his loss was monumental, and they had lost someone too—and that had to be acknowledged in some way. Introductions were made, though I already knew most of the people in the room.

The first order of the day was to prepare Neil for some of what he would be seeing in the school's corridors: tributes to Trista, bulletin boards with photos and letters, a giant red heart painted in the snow in the school's courtyard. The principal put a sack of letters on the table that his fellow students had written him. Neil just stared at it; I swept it onto my lap. Neil sat, stone-faced, his eyes getting that glazed-over look of not wanting to hear this information; his jaw clenched as if resisting the urge to tell us so. I wanted to reach under the table and squeeze his hand, but he was too far away, so I just closed my eyes and mentally hugged my son.

The next agenda item was academic. The team had decided that Neil's grades for the semester would stand as they were at the time of the accident. He would be "medically exempt" from midterm exams. His calculus and physics teachers suggested he take the AP exams at some point, but no one was rushing him. None of us knew at this point how Neil's brain injury would affect his abilities. Neil, who had gotten a perfect eight hundred on his math SATs, would now need extra help, modifications, and accommodations to finish the school year.

Then the reentry team offered him physical help: a wheelchair, a "book buddy" to carry his backpack. Neil politely declined. He seemed anxious to be on his way, away from these adults and back with his peers.

The meeting, one that so many had prepared for, ended. It had taken all of about fifteen minutes. Still, I was grateful for the support, glad to know that all these caring grown-ups would be watching out for my son.

Neil swung his book bag over one shoulder and steadied himself against the walker I had insisted he use. He pushed it in front of him step by step, but found it slow.

"Can you go out to the car and get my crutches, Mom?" he asked me. I was reluctant, picturing hoards of teenagers jostling into him as the bell rang, even though I had just been assured that Neil would get a ten-minute head start in between classes to avoid just that. But I agreed. I went out to the car, dumped the sack of mail into the front seat, and grabbed his crutches from the back. I went back into the school and handed him the crutches. He pushed the walker toward me. Then he was gone, hobbling down the hall. It felt like it had dropping him off at kindergarten and watching him head off alone for the first time.

Maybe Neil didn't feel he'd needed a reentry meeting, but I had. I needed something. I didn't want to go home. After a month of spending every day together from beginning to end, I was not ready to just leave Neil. I wanted to be near my son, or at least just stay in the same building as he was. I stopped into the guidance office and talked with his counselor. I went to the theater and helped Suzanne, the drama teacher, pin stars onto a silk flag for an upcoming student production. I didn't want to go home to that empty house.

22

The Journal

I'VE JOURNALED ALL MY LIFE. As a little girl I called it a diary. I got one every year for Christmas: soft pink ledgers with tiny locks and thin metal keys. In them I detailed my middle school years: fishnet stockings and Girl Scout meetings. I poured my heart onto their pages in high school: my first kiss with Donny Gagne, tears spilled over Jim Croce's death.

Later in life I chronicled more salient events: my potluck hippie wedding, the birth of my children, my graduation from medical school. I wrote in spiral-bound notebooks. They sit stacked by the dozens on shelves in my bedroom closet. If my husband and I want to remember the meal we had on our anniversary in 1989, I can simply open the appropriate book and voila! Details!

"I had the grilled halibut with the chimichurri sauce. You had the peppercorn pâté. Remember?"

After the accident, all that changed. The ink dried up. I didn't write a word. Even the night Neil was admitted to the Brigham, when I gave Saul a list of things we might need in the hospital— a change of clothes, my knitting to pass the time—my journal was not on the list. It's as if I knew my energy was needed in the here and now, not reflecting, not writing.

Three CAT scans, an operation on his leg, low blood pressure, antiseizure medications. We went through it all. But my pen was silent. In the ICU, on the step-down unit, at home with physical and mental therapy, the page remained blank.

At first it just didn't occur to me to write. This was life, not art. My boy needed me. I listened to the doctors describe his injuries. I prayed for his recovery. I sat in the waiting room through his leg operation, too worried to pick up a pen. But as the days stretched out through long hours of physical therapy, as we moved from the ICU to the step-down unit, I knew it was more than fear or worry that paralyzed me. More than sheer writer's block. I knew I would write eventually, maybe even soon. But I needed some distance first. I felt too raw at that moment. Too *in* the moment.

The British novelist Graham Greene once called the necessary distance an author must have from his or her material "a sliver of ice in the heart of the writer." Right now I did not have that ice. My heart was still warm with worry for my boy.

Notebooks still lay all around my house. There was one for my essays, one for my health column for parents published in the local newspaper. There was one for fiction and one for my novel-in-progress. Then there was the one where I kept track of where each piece was submitted, when they were accepted, and when they would be published. Now all these notebooks seemed to be calling out to me, beckoning me back. I once went so far as to open up my journal to the last thing I wrote before the accident. But it was like watching a train approaching a woman on the tracks and having no way to warn her: blithely breezy words, then nothing.

I slammed it shut.

Partly my inability to write was due to the sheer amount of work it took to care for Neil each day, and a lack of energy to do anything else. Partly I wasn't yet sure how to write about the ways my son's life had so drastically changed. So I ignored my notebooks and focused on the tasks at hand: setting up equipment, arranging appointments.

After Neil's reentry meeting, I eventually went home. I paced. I puttered. I didn't know what to do with myself. I didn't want to be alone. I threw in a load of clothes. I ran the dishwasher. I sat at my dining room table looking out the window at the oak trees sloughing their leaves onto my yard. I drank black coffee, which probably didn't help my profound angst. I knew somehow I needed to gain control of my world again. I grabbed a notebook and pen and began to write.

The words came quickly. The phone call. The crash. The cries of pain. The weeks of hard work. Physical therapy. Antiepileptics. I got it all down. My hand cramped. I soaked the pages with my tears. I lost all track of time. I wrote right up to that very morning. His first day back at school. The meeting. The walker. My fears and anxiety.

At last I was done. I pushed the pen and notebook away in exhaustion. My breath was coming hard. I felt as though I'd run a marathon. I was spent. I looked at the clock, amazed to find that over three hours had gone by. But I was back, doing what I do: capturing my world in words on a page. Trying to make sense of something senseless. Pulling one word after another from some deep space in my heart. Writing was becoming less about documenting and more about understanding.

One day about a month after Neil had started back to school part-time, I came home from running some errand to find him sitting at the dining room table, my journal opened in front of him. My heart skipped a beat. What had I written there? I racked my brain: Neil pulling off his johnny. Neil lashing out at the hospital staff. Neil needing to be restrained.

But before I could decide whether to ask him to stop reading my private entries or let him continue, he looked up at me, his face blank as a plate.

"I'm sorry I yelled at you in the hospital, Mom."

My heart cracked. He didn't know he had. He didn't know anything. He was almost totally amnesic for his entire stay in the ICU, remembering only brief images, a few spoken words. I squeezed his shoulders and pressed my lips to the top of his head.

"It's okay, Neil. Read what you want. I'll be here if you have any questions."

I knew at that moment that he needed to recover information about those lost days. My journal was filling in the memory gaps for him. He was learning things from my writing that I could not bring myself to express out loud: the breadth and depth of my love for him, my deep sorrow at not being able to take away his pain, my guilt for being the mother of the one who survived this terrible accident, my guilt at feeling guilty. I hovered as Neil read: pretending to dust, rearranging piles of books, all the while keeping a wary eye on my son. Finally he closed the back cover of the notebook and looked up at me.

"I just like the song," he finally said.

Here he was reassuring me that his song choice was just that. No need to read anything into it. Here we were, reassuring each other that it was okay.

23

Vulnerability

Just as I was sending my boy back out into the world, it had suddenly become a very dangerous place. I went from controlling his day, his calorie count, and his medication to watching him hobble down the school hallway with his walker to his refusing all help from me.

The accident happened in January 2003. Terrorists had flown their planes into the World Trade Towers two autumns before, and now the president was beating the drums of war. Our days were branded with a colorful hierarchy of alertness, orange one day, red the next. News reports advised us to cover our windows with plastic and duct tape just in case of an anthrax attack.

To me life now felt fragile and unpredictable in a way it never was before. Not long ago war was far away and terrorists hurt other people and I knew where my children were. Now I was waiting for the other shoe to drop. My son had left home one night and come back a week later a different person. One with blood on his brain and metal in his leg. Minus a girlfriend and with an extra ache in his heart. When my children were little I remember feeling too lucky. I spent a lot of my time counting my blessings and wondering when it was all going to be taken away from me. We all try to protect our children as best we can. We vaccinate them. We watch them sleep. We buy them safe toys and warn them about strangers. But I had failed. I had sent my younger son out of the house and into the path of a killer. I had undone all those years of protection with one sentence.

"Why don't you walk her home, Neil?"

Almost losing one of my children makes him seem even more susceptible to danger. I worry about Neil in a way I don't Dan. With Dan I don't lose sleep over each rejection or disappointment. With Neil I want to smooth his way. I analyze the timber of his voice on the phone, mining the conversation for evidence of depression or angst. I wonder if it will be this way forever. If I will always feel the need to be his spotter. Cushioning each blow, softening the falls. Or if I can someday let go of him. And watch him stand. And walk tall. Maybe even fly.

24

School Days

NEIL CAME HOME from his first day of school exhausted. He collapsed onto the couch and slept until I woke him for dinner. He woke up with a headache. I gave him some Tylenol. At the supper table we fished for details about his first day. Neil could be a typical monosyllabic teenager at times, and our conversations sometimes felt more like interrogations than discourse. We learned that his two classes were physics and calculus, his two advanced placement courses. He had missed out on several weeks of work and had come home with stacks of makeup assignments.

"Do you think you can catch up?" I asked him.

"We'll see," he said into his pork chops, not lifting his head. He disappeared into his room after supper.

Neil woke up the morning after his first day sore. He showed me chafing bruises under each armpit where his crutches had rubbed his skin raw.

"Try to keep your weight in your hands, not your under-arms," I advised him. I padded the crutches with gauze and tape and drove him to his second day. I dropped him off at the side door where he could take the elevator and avoid the school's slick granite stairs. I sat in the car waiting several minutes until I thought Neil would be safely ensconced in his class. Then I entered the school too and went to find Neil's guidance counselor. I had met with Mrs. Bombard many times during Neil's junior and senior years. She had been invaluable at helping Neil put together a list of colleges to apply to. His top choice was Skidmore College in Saratoga Springs, New York. He had fallen in love with its bucolic campus the previous year on our college road trip. He had applied early decision but hadn't gotten in. Mrs. Bombard was fairly confident that if he could just bring up his physics grade, he could get in through the regular admissions process. Now that was all in question. Now I just wanted Neil to finish high school.

What I didn't know at the time, though maybe I should have, was that I could have applied for a 504 plan for Neil. Part of the Americans with Disabilities Act, it requires school systems to put in place accommodations for students with disabilities so they can participate fully in the school's curriculum. I hadn't known such a thing existed. I only learned about it years later at a Brain Injury Association conference. I knew I could have applied for disability for him, but I didn't really think of him as disabled. I also didn't want to saddle him with a label or stigmatize him among his peers. I also knew I could have applied for special education services that would have qualified him for an IEP, or Individualized Education Plan. But I feared that going from making the honor roll to needing special education services would wound Neil's ego or mark him like Nathaniel Hawthorne's Hester Prynne. Maybe a 504 plan wouldn't have looked so very different from the accommodations his school was already making for him—a shorter class day, exemption from midterm exams—but as a doctor and his mother, when I learned of the possibility of a 504 plan, I felt that I had let my son down.

I went to see Mrs. Bombard with the hopes that she could reassure me about Neil's abilities. That he would finish the year successfully, maybe even go on to college. But the guidance counselor was too caught up in her own uneasiness.

She offered me a chair at her desk. She asked about Neil. But she was obviously distracted.

"They keep sending me students to counsel over Trista's death and Neil's accident," she told me, clearly still shaken. "I don't even know how to deal with it myself. What am I supposed to say to them?"

I knew I wasn't going to get the reassurance I needed. At least not today. I shook her hand.

"No one knows what to say," I told her honestly. "I'm sure the students just want someone to talk to."

Neil gradually caught up with his classmates in every course except one. He dropped AP physics at his teacher's suggestion and replaced it with the regular level physics class. With that move he was able to bring up his grade in the one class his guidance counselor thought had doomed his early-decision chances at Skidmore.

I continued driving Neil to school every morning and picking him up every afternoon. I never asked him if he wanted to go back to taking the bus. He had ridden the bus with Trista every day since September. I thought riding the bus alone would have been too painful, her seat next to him now empty. Also, to catch the bus he would have had to traverse the same path he'd walked the night they were hit by the drunk driver. I didn't think he'd be anxious to retrace those fateful steps any time soon.

After just a few weeks of adjusting to this truncated schedule, Neil was able to ramp up to a full day. He traded in his crutches for a hand-carved walking stick he picked out himself at a camping store. At this point he could bear weight easily on his injured leg, using the stick more for security and balance than actual support. Once I was sure Neil was able to tolerate the full day, I too went back to work. But I kept my hours part-time, arriving later and leaving earlier than I used to so that I could continue transporting my son.

I liked driving him. I felt like I was contributing to his safety and his recovery. It also gave us some enforced alone time together. Sometimes we drove in silence. But sometimes he shared his struggles with me. He told me things were often awkward at school.

"Everybody stops talking whenever I walk into a room, Mom. When is that going to end?"

I didn't have an answer for him. This was a huge tragedy for the whole community. A teenage life had been lost. Another teenager would make his way through the courts—and the headlines—for many months to come. And Neil was the face of that tragedy: a living reminder of how this community had changed and all it had been through.

Neil tried to move on. He dated briefly in high school. He felt his friends were judging him for moving too quickly. The relationship eventually ended. He dated again in college, but he told me the girl acted a little too much like Trista, and so he broke things off.

If Neil reminded Newburyport of all it had been through, Newburyport reminded Neil of everything he'd lost. He ached to leave town, to move on. I suppose most teenagers feel the same way, anxious for the next phase of their lives to begin. But for Neil the future couldn't come fast enough, because the past carried so much pain.

25

Court

THE COURT APPEARANCES BEGAN immediately after the accident. The drunk driver was arrested the night of the crash and charged with reckless driving, two counts of driving while under the influence, being a minor in possession of alcohol and marijuana, and two counts of leaving the scene of an accident resulting in personal injury. He was arraigned the next day, the day of Neil's surgery, the day of Trista's death. It was the only court appearance where our families were unrepresented. It was the one time he would not have to look us in the eye. Either Saul or I and both Mary and David Zinck made it to all the other hearings, arraignments, sentencings, and changes of plea.

The wheels of justice turned slowly, and we did not always like the path it took. Two weeks after Trista died, the drunk driver incurred additional charges: motor vehicle homicide and leaving the scene of an accident resulting in death. He posted bail and was free that same afternoon. More than a year later, he finally changed his plea to guilty and was sentenced to three and a half years in the House of Correction. That lenient punishment was a tough blow for us. We had done our best to argue for a lengthier jail term. We had read our carefully constructed victim impact statements detailing all the difficulties Neil was having—all the ways the drunk driver had changed his life—but to no avail.

The spring after the accident, another young man was charged with providing the alcohol to the drunk driver. He had purchased beer across state lines with a fake ID and provided an unsupervised home for his buddies to get drunk. He was nineteen at the time. He had graduated from Newburyport High School the previous year. To his credit, he pleaded guilty. He was sentenced to a year in jail. But in the week he was given to get his affairs in order before serving his time, he had a change of heart. He hired a new lawyer and changed his plea to not guilty, necessitating more court appearances, including one before the State Supreme Court, where his lawyer challenged the legality of the original charge. (He lost.) I can understand a mother's desire to keep her child out of jail, but the change of plea and the appeal of his conviction added to our feeling of being pushed and pulled by the judiciary.

The owners of the liquor store where the alcohol was illegally purchased faced their own charges. They lost a civil suit against them and were ordered to pay eight million dollars, the largest penalty in Massachusetts history. Neither Neil nor the Zincks have ever seen a dime.

Neil rarely went to any of these appearances. At first he was not well enough. Later he did not want to replay Trista's death or face her killer. He once told me he feared he would attack him. I always let Neil know of each hearing, inviting him to say his piece. I have to admit, I was always relieved when he declined. I couldn't protect him against everything, but I could shield him from this.

26

The Media

FROM THE BEGINNING, ours was a story that people couldn't get enough of. For weeks our story led the evening news, or if there was a really big breaking story, we might come in second. Reporters hounded us for comments. We'd find evidence of them everywhere. Our answering machine was filled with messages from them. When we opened the front door, their business cards came fluttering down to the doorjamb like confetti. We'd even catch camera crews in front of our house, using it as background for their stories on the six o'clock news. Journalists and camera crews covered almost every court appearance the drunk driver made. Whenever we left the courthouse, microphones were thrust in our faces. Journalists' pads and pens were ever ready to copy down our responses: us, the victims.

Saul and I shied away from the coverage. We are both private people by nature. We knew there was no way to keep our story out of the papers altogether, but we weren't eager to add our personal take on things.

We also wanted to protect Neil.

We weren't always successful. Saul and I always tried to get to the phone first when it rang. We turned down reporters' requests for comments from our son.

But we had to go out for milk once in a while.

One day while I was out on a quick grocery store run, my cell phone rang. It was Neil.

"They want to interview me," he said. My heart raced.

"Who's they?" I asked. I had already abandoned my grocery cart and was headed toward my car.

"I don't know. I think she works at ABC. I told them you'd be back in an hour."

I exhaled.

"That's good, Neil. Stay put. I'll be right there."

It's one thing for the media to stick microphones in our faces and shout questions, but Neil still suffered from headaches and memory loss. His response time was slow. It took a few minutes for him to process things. They'd eat him alive.

When I got to the house (less than a five-minute drive from the store), Rhondella Richardson, an on-air reporter from ABC, was teetering down our brick steps in high heels. Behind her, an unkempt cameraman shouldered a huge video recorder, his middle-aged paunch stretching out against his white T-shirt and over his jeans.

"What are you doing?" I yelled, half in and half out of my car.

Rhondella turned, her made-up, camera-ready face souring at the sight of me.

"My son just told you his parents weren't home," I shouted.

"We were going to ask his permission," she huffed.

"He's seventeen. He told you to wait an hour until I got home. That was five minutes ago. You had to know he was alone," I railed.

My heart was racing. I am not a confrontational person by nature, and here I was confronting a famous Boston reporter. Then I remembered one spring when a robin built a nest in the rhododendrons in front of our house. When the baby birds hatched, the mother robin began dive-bombing us as we came and went through the front door. I felt like that protective bird dive-bombing perceived danger.

I asked her to leave my property.

"They all won't be as nice as me," she warned, her face turning ugly as she clicked back up the brick steps. "At least I called first." Her response was charged and accusatory, as if she were the victim by not being granted access to my son.

I ran inside locking the front door behind me. I called Saul.

"Rhondella Richardson was at our front door, ready to interview Neil," I panted, still short of breath from my uncharacteristic rant.

"Calm down. Where are they now?" Saul's voice smoothed my ruffled feathers.

I parted the blinds and looked up at the road. Rhondella Richardson was speaking into her microphone gesturing toward our house as the camera rolled.

"They're still here. They're at the top of the stairs filming."

"Just let it go, Cal. They won't be back."

And they weren't. Despite the reporter's insistence that others "wouldn't be as nice" as she, the fact was everyone else was very professional, keeping their distance, respecting our privacy when asked. The media attention gradually died down, flaring up only occasionally over the years, when the drunk driver changed his plea or came up for parole. They also stopped calling us for comments. They knew a journalistic dead end when they saw one.

Mary and David were much more eager to give quotes to the media. A drunk driver had stolen their only daughter from them. They were deeply wronged, wounded, filled with rage at the injustice of it all, and anxious for the public to hear their story. They quickly became the media's go-to family, always ready with a reaction to any verdict or sentence. Their sound bites were raw, agonizing.

"There's no spot in hell hot enough for him," David said after one sentencing.

"He is a murderer and he's free. My daughter's in the ground," Mary lamented bluntly when the drunk driver was let out of jail.

We did allow one reporter to spend time with Neil. Meredith Goldstein of the *Boston Globe* contacted us about a year after the crash to do a feature article. At the time, the drunk driver was less than a week away from his sentencing. Neil, Saul, and I talked about it together and weighed the pros and cons. None of us liked interviews, but perhaps we could have some positive impact. Perhaps whatever Meredith wrote would be read by the judge and influence him to administer a lengthy sentence. We agreed to the interview. Maybe it helped that she was a member of the tribe.

We met at The Grog, a local watering hole, and together crowded into one of the creaky wooden booths in the back of the dim, noisy restaurant. We ordered Cokes all around and talked for hours. We liked Meredith, a young woman not so many years older than our son. She treated us all with respect and listened closely to our responses to her queries.

By the end of the evening it was clear that what she was really interested in was doing a story on Neil—on how he was progressing after his loss. By now we felt comfortable enough with her to let her have an additional meeting with Neil, one-on-one and without us. They arranged to meet a few evenings later, again at The Grog. We kissed Neil good-bye then waited nervously for his return.

"How was it?" we asked when he came home several hours later.

"Kind of fun," he said. I wouldn't have predicted that would be the word he would use, but I was glad.

A photographer came to the house the next day, taking many photos of Neil in many poses. He helped pick one for the story.

What resulted was not the hard-driving judge-influencing piece we'd hoped for, but a thoughtful profile called "The Cadence of Grief." Meredith portrayed Neil as a sensitive, caring young man, doing his best to adjust to life without his first true love; trying hard to honor her memory by living his own life with quiet authenticity.

After so many bad experiences with reporters over that year—watching them get things wrong, having their microphones and cameras shoved in our faces, chasing them away from our home—here was a woman who seemed to focus on Neil as a person, not a story. She may not have completely restored our faith in the media, but Meredith showed us what one kind reporter was capable of.

27

Kaddish

ONE SATURDAY MORNING a couple of months after the accident, Neil decided he wanted to go to Sabbath services at our synagogue. In most synagogues kids disappear once their bar mitzvahs are over. While they are studying, they come religiously. They practice chanting the blessings before and after the haftarah and generally become familiar with the prayers and melodies of a Sabbath service. But once the bar mitzvah is over, they're gone. Sometimes when the last of the children has been bar mitzvahed, whole families disappear from temple life.

Not so with Neil. Neil loved everything about the shul. He enjoyed being called to the Torah. He liked that the rabbi knew his Hebrew name without having to ask him. He thrived in all the attention layered on him by the elders in the synagogue. But even he too eventually drifted away from the synagogue.

Until the accident.

Our shul is a conservative one. Much of the service is in Hebrew. We have a part-time rabbi who only comes to town every other week. The rest of the time we are on our own. Joe Goldman—a Holocaust survivor with a thick Eastern European accent, a big heart, and a smile for everyone—leads the services in the rabbi's absence. He once brought Neil home a hand-carved chess set from one of his many trips back to his native Poland to visit the Catholic family that hid him from the Nazis. He was also Neil's bar mitzvah tutor.

Services start at 9:00 a.m. in our shul, but they are a three-hour-plus affair, and the Torah service doesn't start until 10:00. So it was just before that when Neil and I entered the sanctuary. His hair was long, and he had a full beard and walked with his tall walking stick. As it happened, the Torah portion for that morning was from Exodus and involved Moses parting the Red Sea for the Israelites to pass out of Egypt into Canaan. Because Neil's Hebrew name was Moshe (Hebrew for Moses) and today he looked the part, there were many winks and nods directed his way as the parshe was read. Neil knew everyone in the room that day, and they knew him too. One by one, slowly, as the service moved on, each member of the congregation came over to Neil, embraced him warmly, and whispered into his ear.

Blessings, or berakhah, are part of the Saturday-morning service. There are blessings for those who are ill, for those who are called to the Torah, for mothers of newborns, for couples about to be married. If you can think of it, there's a blessing for it in our religion. They don't all get said at every service, just when appropriate. There is one particular berakhah said for someone who has recovered from a serious illness, has returned from a long journey, or has survived any type of danger. All three definitely applied to Neil. When the congregation recited the prayer in unison, we all cried tears of joy.

Then it came time to recite the Mourner's Kaddish, when everyone who has lost loved ones stands to remember them and pray for their souls. Neil leaned heavily on his walking stick, pulling himself to a standing position. He bowed his head so that only the top of his blue yarmulke was visible. His long heavy curls covered his face, but his quiet baritone was clear as he recited from memory the Mourner's Kaddish for Trista. He prayed. We cried.

After the service we all retired to the kitchen for a simple Kiddush meal of bagels and cream cheese, lox, pickled herring, gefilte fish, and, of course, schnapps. The men of the temple hoisted their glasses and sang an old up-tempo blessing in Hebrew that they all knew by heart. They tried to tempt Neil with a shot of the strong stuff. He declined.

Several of the men took Neil aside, their arms draped over his shoulders, heads bowed together in conversation. Mr. Goldman, especially, held Neil for a long time.

While the men of the congregation embraced Neil, the women in the shul embraced me. They were anxious for details of Neil's road to recovery, but they could see for themselves the most important thing: He was alive. He was here, happy to be back in the arms of his Jewish community. This time I remembered to say it: a silent *thank you, thank you, thank you.*

28

Hard Work

WHILE NEIL'S PHYSICAL THERAPY and mental health work began in our home just days after the accident, both continued for the rest of the school year and beyond. When Pat saw that Neil could manage stairs on his own, could transfer himself in and out of the tub alone, and had mastered his own leg-strengthening exercises, she discharged him from her care. But as I watched him walk, especially now that he was using his walking stick, I detected a subtle limp in his gait, a vague listing toward his right side. I sought the help of an outpatient physical therapist. I contacted the office affiliated with Anna Jaques Hospital. We met with Laurie one day after school for his initial evaluation. She worked in a large mirror-walled space where other therapists worked with other patients on beds and tables, bikes, and treadmills. It didn't take her long to assess Neil's stride.

"You have to relearn to walk," she told us. In favoring his injured left leg for so long Neil had basically developed an almost-permanent limp that would take the two of them months to correct.

So after school twice a week, Neil worked with Laurie, stretching and strengthening, working on balance and coordination. She had him ditch the walking stick, feeling it was contributing to his asymmetry. She gave him exercises to do on his own at home, which he did, when reminded.

Neil also worked hard to get his mental health back as well. It took him some time to see that he needed help, but he eventually did. He never quite clicked with his first therapist, Bob, so we looked elsewhere. Jan seemed more compatible with Neil's personality. I, of course, don't know all that went on in their weekly sessions, but he seemed to leave them in good spirits. I am proud of my son for working to process all that he'd been through. It would take more than a mother's love to help him find a way to live with his loss. He needed a professional to talk with, and I was glad he could see that and was willing to put the effort into his healing.

Saul and I also wondered if antidepressants might help his mood, so we found a nurse practitioner a couple of towns away who specialized in medication evaluation. She started Neil on a low dose of Lexapro. Neil was reluctant to take the medication at first, initially unconvinced that he needed it. He eventually agreed to give it a try. I couldn't really detect any change in Neil's outlook or personality. Neil's ways were always quiet, but he was friendly and made friends easily. But since the accident I found myself trying to analyze his moods, the sound of his voice, his eye contact, searching for signs of depression. Was this just typical teenage moroseness or something more ominous? Neil could also be a procrastinator. For me the trait now took on new meaning. Was it just his way, or was it a sign of impaired executive function? It would become a pattern of mine: observing my son and thinking, *Is this the injury, or is this just Neil?*

29

Present Perfect

On a cold February morning, I brought Neil to his follow-up visit with the orthopedist at Brigham and Women's Hospital. The doctor was taking out his metal staples that day. Neil wanted to be medicated for the procedure—he never liked the sight of blood. But having taken stitches and staples out of so many children over the years, I knew he could handle it and told him so.

Neil was less than convinced. When the doctor pulled back the gauze from the wound, revealing a colorful mix of rusty-orange Betadine and dark-maroon dried blood, Neil swooned, sweat beading up on his forehead. I held his hand and looked him straight in the eyes as the doctor worked.

"You're the most amazing person I know, Neil," I said. "A lot of other people would have just curled into a ball and checked out. But not you. You've kept going through everything."

Neil was grinning at the barrage of compliments, but he winced with each metallic snap of the staple remover as one after another was bent in half and slid out of his skin. But he never took his eyes off mine as I talked him through the pain.

"Physical therapy. Learning to walk again. Going back to school. You did it all, and I'm so proud of you."

The name of the game was distraction. When I was a resident, doing a lot of sewing of little children in the ER, I would often sing to them while I worked. A favorite song was "There Was an Old Lady Who Swallowed a Fly." Song, fairy tale, story, and joke all rolled into one, it kept the kids still and mesmerized while I sewed. If the cut was small, I'd be done suturing before I was done singing, but the kids were so into it, they'd make me finish the song before I discharged them. Neil might be too old for "There Was an Old Lady," but he wasn't too old to need distraction.

After the office visit we stopped for Cokes at the hospital's hospitality shop, referred as "the spit" by the hospital staff. I told Neil that I had recently put a sand dollar on the top of Trista's grave stone. It's a Jewish tradition when visiting a cemetery to place a rock on the headstone of the person you are visiting. There may be some deeper religious reason behind it, but to me it was just a way of showing that I was there. Although we were the only Jews visiting Trista's grave, others started following our tradition, and soon her tombstone was piled high with rocks.

"When do I get to clean these up?" her father, David, once asked me when we were visiting the grave together. He likened it to the top of his bureau collecting quarters, matchbooks, and odd paper receipts from emptied pockets at the end of the day. "I clean off my bureau from time to time, but what do I do with this?" he asked, gesturing to the rock pile on his daughter's grave. So I started bringing shells, I told Neil, just to change things up.

"Did Trista like the beach?" I asked as we sipped our Cokes. Neil thought about that for a few minutes, and then answered.

"I don't know. We haven't been."

He didn't say "We never went" or "She didn't go." Maybe that would sound too final. He said "We haven't been," like he could easily have tacked on a "yet" to the sentence. Like there was a possibility that they might still one day get to that beach.

I looked up the definition of the tense when I got home. Present perfect: It describes events in the indefinite past, while leaving room for the possibility of them happening again at some future date. Present perfect: the words themselves suggestive of freezing time, of keeping the present—that perfect present when Trista was alive and their futures were bright and together.

I was glad to be able to talk to Neil about her. Sometimes I felt like I couldn't. Sometimes it felt like an egg walk.

One day not long after Neil had been discharged from the hospital, he was sitting on the couch working on a crossword puzzle. It was a favorite activity of his, but it had been a long time since he had had the concentration or energy to attempt anything like that. I smiled over at him as I walked through the room, glad for this progress. But as I passed by him, I noticed the picture next to him on the end table. Why hadn't I seen it before? It was taken outside on our back deck, Neil and Trista framed in green trees. Trista smiling that half-smile that people with braces wear, even years after their braces come off. Neil in his "Dangerous Curves" T-shirt, a souvenir from the guitar exhibit Saul and I had taken him to at the Museum of Fine Art in Boston. His wiry hair and Jesus-like beard framed his own grinning face.

"Oh, Neil," I blurted out. "Does that bother you? Do you want me to put it away? Or do you like looking at it?" I felt like I was blathering.

Neil looked over at the picture as if noticing it for the first time. Then without a word, he lay down on the couch and pulled the afghan over his head.

I hurried out of the room so he wouldn't see me crying. I shoved a fist in my mouth so he wouldn't hear my sobs. I bit down hard on my own fingers to punish myself for acting so foolishly. How stupid I was. This was the first time Neil was awake and alert and engaged, and I had to go and mention the one thing he was trying to forget. I was so angry with myself. So ashamed.

But now, here in "the spit," he was talking about her. Not in the past. Sometimes in the present. And sometimes like this: in the present perfect. I was also glad he was in counseling. Someone needed to explore this with him. Someone with more background in grief work than I.

30

Our Education

I STARTED TAKING my first pre-med courses at Clark University in the 1980s. It was right down the street from where we were living practically rent-free in the rundown Main South area of Worcester, in an apartment owned by Saul's elderly grandfather. Before we moved in, the apartment was uninhabited and uninhabitable. We replaced broken appliances, hung new wallpaper, and painted window casings and ceilings, turning the five rooms into a cozy home.

I was pregnant with Dan when I started taking courses at Clark. Neil was two when I graduated. Saul's grandfather only lived to see Dan born. He was in his nineties but managed to climb up the two sets of stairs to see the new baby. He chucked him under the chin, calling him *Boychick* and asking over and over in his thick Russian accent, "How they make 'em so schveet?" (He also used to chuck my husband under his chin and call him "Beardy.")

I found a babysitter near the university who would take care of the children while I went to school. I'd walk one or both of them over in a cheap umbrella stroller then head off to class. One of the first courses I took was genetics. I was pregnant with

Dan at the time. I learned about the complex double helix, genotypes and phenotypes, and the laws of Mendellian inheritance. Adenosine, cytosine, guanine, thymine—how they shifted and paired, wound and unwound, determined features from height to hair color. One wrong turn in the chromosomal chain could mean the difference between a healthy baby and a fatal abnormality. With 247 million base pairs in its long strands of DNA, it was a wonder to me that any child was ever born whole.

It was a terrible time to be pregnant.

I took courses in biology and calculus, organic and inorganic chemistry. It was all fascinating, but it tested my brain power, stamina, and will. At twenty-eight, a commuter student, the mother of a two-year-old and pregnant with my second, I had little in common with my much younger peers. I was the only student in my physics class who hadn't taken the course in high school, and I struggled until an engineer friend of mine agreed to tutor me. Things finally clicked. I only made one real friend during those years. Even that friend was years younger than I.

"You know someone's really young when they're talking about Cheap Trick's old stuff," Saul once joked.

Even with a babysitter watching the kids during class time, my pre-med courses required hours of reading, studying, and cramming for midterm exams. I made time for my studies during naps and after bedtime and whenever Saul came home not too exhausted to take over the child care.

But sometimes the schoolwork just couldn't be done at home. During my anatomy course I had to memorize every muscle, bone, tendon, and ligament of my preserved, dissected cat. There was no possible way to do that from home, and paying a babysitter for the extra time just wasn't in the family budget. So I loaded Dan into a pack on my back and walked the six blocks to my anatomy lab. I told myself he wouldn't recognize the animal I was working on, gut filleted open, stinking of form-aldehyde. But when I slid my oblong white box from its spot in the refrigerator and lifted off its plastic lid, Dan pushed up on the metal frame of his back pack, peered over my shoulder, and cried, "Kitty!"

I felt like the worst mother in the world.

Throughout my undergraduate years, I still worked a few hours a week on the pediatric ward at City Hospital. The doctors and residents there all knew I was taking pre-med courses and applying to medical school.

They were not supportive.

"Don't you like your family?" one cynical resident asked.

"Do you *want* to get divorced?" another jaded colleague wanted to know.

Others were even less tactful.

"Are you crazy?"

True, I'd seen divorce statistics for physicians quoted at around 30 percent. But it varied among specialties and depended on where one was in one's career when one married. And it wasn't as high as in other professions: massage therapists, for example. Or bartenders. Besides, Saul and I were doing all right. Weren't we?

There was only one pediatrician, Jerry Durbin, the chief of Pediatrics at City Hospital at the time, who was supportive of my decision. Dr. Durbin always asked how things were going when he saw me on the ward. He answered specific questions

I had about the cases we were seeing as well as general ones about life as a doctor. He always waxed enthusiastic about his specialty of pediatrics and his subspecialty, infectious disease. He wrote me a letter of recommendation when I applied to medical school. He would become my friend and mentor throughout my career. I call him to this day for advice on my own sticky cases.

Applying to med school was an arduous task. My advisor at Clark, Dr. Trachtenberg, spent hours with me researching suitable schools, preparing me for interviews, and writing me letters of support. I made long drives to interview at schools I couldn't afford to fly to, sometimes staying overnight in cheap hotels. I missed my family.

The University of Massachusetts Medical School was my number-one choice. Med school would be stressful enough with two young children. I needed a support system in place. I got into New York Medical College first. I was glad I would at least be going to med school, but I still wanted to stay closer to home. At first I was just wait-listed at UMass, so I started making mental plans to move to New York.

But the envelope finally came. I nervously waited until Saul came home before opening it. I figured if the news was good, I wanted him there to celebrate with me; if it wasn't, I'd need him to catch me when I fell.

I don't remember the words of the letter beyond "congratulations" and "we're pleased to inform you…" I don't remember our words to each other either. I only remember my husband's viselike embrace and a wave of relief at not having to uproot my family for what I thought would surely be the most stressful years of my life.

Neil was in the middle of the college application process when the crash occurred. He had applied to just five schools. His college essay was entitled "Go for My Knees." In it he recounted an incident that occurred during his high school's production of *Romeo and Juliet,* in which he played Tybalt. Neil had learned fight choreography from Shakespeare & Co. in that play. He would go on to win an award for his own fight choreography from the Massachusetts High School Drama Guild.

One night, in their recurring fight scene, Romeo jousted with Tybalt/Neil, jabbing his sword repeatedly at him. Usually Neil was able to judge his steps, knowing just when and where to turn, back up, or leap forward. But on this particular night, Neil misjudged the space around him and fell backward off the stage and onto the floor at the feet of a surprised front row. The audience gasped. Hal, playing Romeo, was unsure if Neil was badly hurt. Neil was momentarily dazed.

"Get up, Tybalt," Romeo finally called down to Neil.

"Tybalt, rise." The other student-actors followed Hal's lead, improvising.

Neil finally shook his head and grabbed his sword. He crept stealthily up the four stairs onto the stage, looking menacing, circling an uncertain Hal.

"Go for my knees," Neil whispered to Hal to cue him as to where to pick up the fight scene Neil had interrupted by flying from the stage. Their swords resumed clashing. The audience cheered, unaware that the fall was not part of the original script.

In the essay Neil wrote about his ability to take a negative and turn it into a positive. He used his fall as a metaphor for the obstacles life throws our way and his leap back onto the stage as a sign of his ability to adapt and make the most of the hand he was dealt. The essay persuaded. He got into Skidmore on his second try.

The acceptance came one day while Neil was still at school. The envelope was fat, so I figured the news had to be good. When Neil came home, I eagerly handed him the manila package, then waited, biting my tongue. He unfastened the bracket and peeled off the tape from the flap, pulling out a stack of paper. He read the cover letter. He was silent for so long I began to worry that he'd been rejected. Finally, he looked up.

"Why am I not happy?" he asked.

My heart crumpled. Why, indeed. When Neil had first sent out his applications, life was good. He and Trista had chosen to remain a couple even though Neil would be two hundred miles away at school. She had probably read his essay, remembered the stage fall, maybe offered her own take on the moral of the story. Now here he was, accepted but alone. I put my arm around him, but he ducked out from under my embrace.

"I'm going over to the Zincks," he told me, stuffing the contents back into the envelope.

"Don't you want to tell Dad first?" I asked.

"I promised Trista she'd be the first to know," he answered. Now I guess the least he could do was to tell her parents.

The door bumped shut behind him.

31

Sailing Away

IT WAS A WARM, SAD DAY when Saul and I drove Neil the 238 miles to his temporary new home in Saratoga Springs. The road trips Neil and I had taken the year before to look at potential colleges were fun-filled. We had chosen CDs that we both liked, not a difficult task since Neil is a fan of the Beatles, the Grateful Dead, and early-seventies rock. (With Dan it had been Nirvana and Green Day.) I can remember every song we listened to like a soundtrack of our journey. This day was different. We alternated between NPR news stories and silence. Although it was only August, as we drove farther north and west, the occasional tree sported an early burst of rusty-orange leaves.

We found Neil's dorm room (Johnson Hall) and took the elevator to his floor (the eighth). His roommate had gotten there first, claiming the bed nearest the inner wall and also the most convenient closet and desk. Neil had to squeeze past his room-mate's bed to reach his closet. His bed was pushed up against the window.

Neil hates heights.

The campus is surrounded by sugar maples, white spruce, and pines. The views from the dorm room were spectacular, the smoky blue outline of the distant Adirondacks undulating along the horizon in the rising heat.

I tried the window. To my dismay it opened. Saul and I looked at each other, the same worried thought in our heads: Eight floors is a long way down.

Neil had been in therapy since the accident. He remained on antidepressants. Now that he was in college, we would hook him up with the mental health services here, part of the Student Health department, located, as it turned out, on the first floor of this very building. He had never been actively suicidal or expressed any thoughts of harming himself. Nevertheless, the eighth floor worried us.

We helped Neil unpack. His roommate slid color-coordinated stackable storage bins under his bed. Neil pulled rumpled shirts out of a black garbage bag and stuffed them in his drawers. The roommate's mother plucked a brand-new green-flowered quilt from a zippered plastic case, its Bed Bath and Beyond stickers still in place. Neil threw a musty, pilled blue blanket on top of his bed over wrinkled sheets. He hadn't let me help him pack.

Dan had been the same way, wanting to pack for college himself, using trash bags and pillowcases instead of more conventional travel trunks.

"Trash bags conform better than suitcases," Dan said every time I offered to buy him luggage.

There were awkward introductions and some small talk between the new roommate and us. Neil cleared his throat a lot, shuffled his feet, and eventually turned his back to us, pretending to set up his computer. We could leave now, his body language was saying. He would be fine. We finally did, reluctantly, waving at our son as the elevator door closed.

The tears started almost immediately on the car ride home. Every song on the radio seemed to remind me of something else I would miss about Neil.

Neil was moving on. He had been looking forward to going to college. To getting out of Newburyport. To going somewhere where nobody knew him. To stop being that kid in the accident. The one with the dead girlfriend. .

He wanted to start fresh, his heart in the wind. I turned up the volume and cried.

32

Eight Floors Up

WHAT SHOULD HAVE BEEN the time of Neil's life, his college years, turned out to be one long struggle. Neil had always been very bright and done well in high school without much effort. Now the maximum effort on his part yielded mediocre grades. He took advantage of every type of assistance available to him: the campus writing center, tutors, tape-recorded lectures, note-taking service. But all his efforts only produced Bs and Cs.

It wasn't just academically that Neil struggled either. Life was difficult for him socially as well. He suffered from short-term memory loss. He would be introduced to people then not remember them. When he came into a group of students, he would hang back, unsure if he had already met them or not. He'd get phone calls from friends returning calls he didn't remember making. His self-assurance faltered.

"I just don't think I have the confidence for the classroom anymore," he told me at one point, his dream of being a teacher starting to sink away from him.

Watching Neil struggle through his freshman year, we decided to have him tested by a neuropsychologist at Brigham and Women's Hospital before his second year, to make sure there wasn't any other help we could get for him. The testing was a grueling four hours. Neil enjoyed some of the cognitive challenges but resisted the more personal questions, especially when it came to Trista. He gave the doctor monosyllabic answers while staring at her coldly. ("Well-defended" the psychologist called it.) Some of the testing I stayed for. For other parts I was asked to leave. Neil was over eighteen at this point, and sometimes it was frustratingly difficult to get doctors and nurses to give information to me, his mother.

The conclusions the neuropsychologist came to were nothing we didn't already know about our son. He suffered from memory loss. He was depressed. The psychologist was impressed with his intellect. He compensated for his losses in interesting and complex ways. She suggested all the things that were already in place for Neil: counseling, extra help at school.

We also brought Neil to the neurologist for a follow-up appointment. They did a CAT scan of his head that showed some cerebral atrophy or "post-traumatic volume loss." Since it had now been a year since the accident, the changes, they told us, were permanent.

The neurologist was very upbeat, noting all that Neil was accomplishing: walking without a limp, speech intact, going to college. And it *was* all good. But they didn't see what we saw. Neil had changed. His personality wasn't the same. It was subtle at times, but it was there. Neil's very fine, dry sense of humor was in little evidence these days. In many ways he reminded me of my mother after her stroke. She worked hard in rehab. She relearned how to walk and talk. But she was changed. She rarely was the one to start a conversation, though she could keep up her end of one already going on.

One night in late April of Neil's sophomore year at Skidmore, things came to a head. It was reading week, and students were preparing for final exams. We knew Neil was stressed. We had been talking with or e-mailing him almost daily. But that night we got a phone call from the mother of one of his high school friends. Her daughter was in college up in northern Vermont; she and Neil were in pretty close touch. But lately Neil had been sounding more strained to her, more desperate. It scared her. Finally she called her mom, who called us, our bedside phone waking us from sleep.

I called Neil right away. His voice sounded panicked.

"What am I supposed to do, Mom?" he kept asking. "Just what am I supposed to do?"

I thought about his bed jammed up against that eighth-floor window.

The stress of final exams, the difficulties with his memories, the social challenges—everything was closing in on him, weighing him down like stacked stones. It was late at night. I kept him on the phone for almost half an hour until he had calmed down. He had a counselor on campus whom he saw from time to time. He was going to hang up and call her. In the meantime I called Security to go check on him. I contacted the head of Mental Health Services on campus, who would also look in. He also gave me the name of a private therapist in town, feeling that perhaps Neil needed something more than his department had to offer at this point.

All this time Saul was following me around the living room as I paced the floor, phone in hand. I had used all of the professional know-how I could muster. I reached for my husband, feeling drained.

"What else can I do?" I asked, more rhetorically than anything else, feeling I had covered all my bases.

"What about Anna?" Saul offered.

Of course. I quickly called Anna Smulowitz, an adult friend of Neil's, his old drama coach who had recently become an ordained minister. The hour didn't matter to Anna. She was trained to help and was a good friend to us all. Anna listened to my ardent but abridged version of events. She promised to reach out. At that point I threw on some clothes, tossed a banana and a bottle of water in the car, kissed Saul good-bye, and began the four-hour-plus trip to New York.

The sky was just beginning to lighten, salmon-colored stripes appearing in the east, when I pulled into the parking lot of Johnson Hall. I rode the elevator up to the eighth floor and gently knocked on Neil's dorm door. He opened the door and scowled.

"What are you doing here?" he asked, seemingly ignoring the events of the previous night.

"I just wanted to see you with my own eyes, Neil."

"I'm fine," he muttered.

I peeked behind him into his room. His desk was lined with pill bottles: antidepressants and Advil.

I put an arm around Neil's shoulder. He ducked my hug but let me rub his shoulder and smooth his curls. His roommate was gone, spending the night with a girlfriend somewhere. I wondered if that was one reason Neil escalated so in his worries. I wondered if his roommate usually helped neutralize things for him. But I wouldn't have the answer to that today. Neil wasn't talking. He was mad that I had called Security to check on him. Angry that I had driven all that way to see him. He insisted he was fine and that I leave immediately.

I offered to take Neil home with me right then and there. I would bring him back for finals or he could not go back at all. Just stay home. It would be his choice. But Neil was not about to go anywhere. He wanted to finish the year with his friends. I admired his persistence even as I agonized over him. But he did look okay. I did feel better seeing him. I had accomplished what I came for, to see him with my own eyes. I gave him the name of the private therapist, and he promised to make an appointment.

I called Anna from my car in the parking lot. She told me that they had had a long, good conversation the night before. She would have called me, she said, but it ended so late she didn't want to wake me. I laughed and told her where I was.

"He'll ask for help if he needs it, Carolyn. I promise he will."

As desperate as Neil had sounded on the phone, as angry as he was this morning, I still felt comforted by Anna's words. She would not be that reassuring if she were worried about his safety.

This was such a precarious place to be as a parent. I felt better seeing Neil for myself, touching him with my own hands. But I couldn't fix him. I couldn't make everything better for him. I was relying on other people in his world to take care of him for me. His friends, a therapist, a roommate. I had done everything I knew how to do to keep him safe and supported. I just hoped it was enough. I just hoped he could draw his own support from somewhere within himself too.

33

Replay

NEIL CAME HOME FOR CHRISTMAS BREAK after his first semester at Skidmore complaining of knee pain. He'd been living on Advil at school and told me sometimes the knee even got swollen toward the end of the day. His orthopedist at the Brigham had told him that he generally liked to leave the hardware in his patients forever. But sometimes the metal continued to cause pain.

"That usually happens with skinny people," he said, adding, "If it still bothers you in a year, Neil, we'll take it out."

I made an appointment with the local orthopedic surgeon at Anna Jaques Hospital. He took x-rays of Neil's leg and agreed to do the surgery. It would be an outpatient procedure; Neil would be in and out the same day.

It was January 7, one year to the day since the crash. I didn't acknowledge the anniversary to Neil. If he didn't remember or realize the significance of the date, I didn't want to remind him. This is something I would struggle with on many anniversaries over the years. Trista's birthday. The anniversary of the day they started going out. (They had celebrated their six-week mark eating chocolate pudding out of wine glasses.) Did Neil think about her on those days after so many years had passed? If he was thinking about her, then was I a bad mother for not acknowledging his pain and loss? But if he wasn't thinking of her—if he was truly trying to move on—wouldn't I just be scratching at scabs that have just barely begun to heal?

I drove Neil to the hospital that morning. I stayed with him while the nurse got him ready. Seeing him in his flimsy johnny with his curls tucked under a paper OR cap stabbed my heart in déjà vu. The last time he was dressed like that he didn't know where he was or what had happened to him. Now he looked at me with clear eyes and a shy smile. I blew him a kiss as they wheeled him away.

The nurse showed me to the lobby to wait for my son.

"It shouldn't be too long," she assured me. "I'll come get you when he's out."

Neil had opted for general anesthesia, not wanting to be awake while they worked on his leg. I thought back to the last time he was under anesthesia. Then he was unconscious at the same time as Trista. Now he was out cold all alone.

I pulled my notebook out of my bag. Ironically, the drunk driver was due in court for sentencing in a few weeks, and I was working on my victim impact statement.

"As I write this letter, Your Honor, I am sitting in a hospital lobby waiting for word as to how Neil's surgery went. It is the second operation in a year. The second necessitated by the actions of the man standing before you today."

Tears stained the page and smeared the ink. It was all so unfair. Neil's first Christmas break from his first year of college, and where is he? Under the knife. Trying to relieve the chronic ache of a joint. It sounded like something an eighty-year-old man should be doing, not a college student in his prime. He should be off traveling. He should be skiing. He should be at parties. Not under anesthesia. Not in another hospital bed. Not again.

I put away my notebook and tried to read a book I'd brought. I could not focus on the words. Even the insipid stories in the *People* magazines in the lobby couldn't distract me from my angst.

Finally the surgeon came out to the lobby. Things had gone well. He recommended another six weeks of physical therapy. We'd get in as many sessions as we could before Neil went back to school.

"If he's still in pain in another year, we can do another operation. There are other things we can try," he offered.

I shook his hand and thanked him and tried not to think of Neil in pain for another year.

34

World Cup Circle

NEIL'S DREAM SINCE MIDDLE SCHOOL had been to be a teacher. Through those precarious years after the crash, I worried that the accident had derailed those dreams. But on a rainy May day, Neil took his place on stage at Skidmore College to receive his degree: a bachelor of arts with double majors in mathematics and classics. He wore his long black robe proudly, his sandaled feet poking out the bottom, the beanie part of his mortarboard pulled down awkwardly over his ears.

Saul's mother was with us, the proud Bubbe watching her third grandchild graduate from college. Neil showed us around campus. We toured the Tang Museum of Art. We saw his messy apartment. We walked on the brick with his name on it, part of the senior class gift to the school. He introduced us to his girlfriend, a woman he'd met on the set of the *Fiddler on the Roof* play they both acted in. The romance had barely gotten off the ground and didn't make it past graduation day. But it was a start.

We bundled all of Neil's possessions into our two cars: boxes of textbooks, notebooks from class, and every yellowed copy of the *Skidmore News* that had ever been printed during his college years. They sit in my basement to this day, my soft-hearted son unable to part with even one of them. Neil had had this sentimental streak ever since he was a kid. He always liked routine. He disliked change. When we moved from our apartment in Worcester to our home on the North Shore, I cut pieces of wallpaper from every room and put them, along with the metal number four from the front door, into a shoe box he could take with him to his new home.

Neil is his mother's son. I am every bit the sentimental pack rat that he is. Recently Saul and I were cleaning our cellar, preparing for a yard sale. I have clear plastic boxes stacked six feet high with every report card and certificate my sons ever received, every art project and Mother's Day card they ever made. Saul has no such streak of sentimentality. He handed me a box of clothes to toss. But in it I saw a pair of Trista's socks, white with red reindeer. Was I supposed to give that away? Throw it away? Inside the box were also T-shirts with Trista's face and her locally famous expression, "Life's too short to be sad" iron-on transferred to its front. Surely those were not yard sale items. I retrieved them from the pile and slipped them into another box.

Next Saul handed me the letter that informed Neil he'd been chosen as one of the recipients of the Trista Rose Zinck scholarship fund.

"Here, throw this away," he instructed.

"Okay," I lied, folding it into my pocket.

When Neil had left for college, he had made me promise not to go into a drawer in his bedside table. He told me there were writings in there he would rather I not see. I respected his wishes. I dusted around it. Now the table was going to the curbside, up for sale. I took out the drawer with Neil's writings, tipped it over a shoebox, and closed my eyes.

After graduation many of Neil's college friends were leaving school with concrete plans: graduate school, paid internships, or real jobs in their chosen fields. Neil was leaving with the same hopes and dreams he started with.

He spent the summer job hunting. He worked with a head-hunter. He scoured the Sunday want ads. He utilized a website that specialized in finding teachers for private schools. He got callbacks. He went on interviews, always dressed the same: his one pair of pressed brown slacks, tan tasseled loafers, pressed white shirt. The accoutrements could vary. He had more than one tie, and he added a V-necked sweater, depending on the weather.

In the end his search came down to two schools: one in Vermont and one in New Hampshire. The New Hampshire school was a second-chance sort of a program for troubled kids. They really wanted Neil. They made him an offer and followed up with phone calls. But Neil was holding out for Vermont. The school catered to Olympic-level elite skiers. The day began and ended with ski practice. The vacation schedule was arranged to allow for national competitions. A large contingency of students spent several months skiing in Brazil. Neil kept putting off the school in New Hampshire, hoping the offer would come through from Vermont.

And it did. Finally. I was so happy for him, achieving his dream. And relieved too. There was a lot of breath-holding in our family at that time. Would Neil be able to find a job in his chosen field? The ecstatic answer? Yes! We once again helped our son pack up his belongings and move 175 miles away.

He shared faculty housing with a couple of roommates. He taught classes in pre-calculus and algebra II. He spent his evenings grading papers and planning lessons. He seemed happy enough.

Saul and I drove up to visit him in his new environs one beautiful fall day. As we drove farther north, the tips of the oaks and maples were starting to turn and "leaf-peeping" traffic became thicker.

Neil showed us his apartment, which took all of five minutes it was so small. He played a video for us that his friends from college had made for him. We walked around the campus with him.

"Hey, Mr. B," his students called to him. Neil smiled and waved back, clearly reveling in the warmth and respect he was being shown. My own peacock feathers spread out proudly as I strutted alongside him.

His classes went well. His students were highly motivated teenagers, used to success. He did get calls from parents, concerned that their son or daughter was being graded too severely, but he seemed to work it all out on his own.

And he was on his own. The headmaster was gone for weeks at a time, acting as an ambassador, promoting the school. Neil had no mentor. There were no faculty development programs. There was no set curriculum to inherit—no one ever observed him in the classroom or gave him any feedback on his teaching style.

Neil was also one of the only nonskiers on faculty. He tried to snowboard, outfitted by his students in their hand-me-down boards and helmets, goggles, and boots. But it didn't take.

I give him credit for trying. He and I are two peas in a pod—not big fans of heights or speed. When the kids were small and one of Saul's cousins owned a condo at a ski resort in Maine, Neil took lessons at the Ski-Wee program, making "pizza pies" with his skis and parallel skiing through a course of metal hoops, ringing the bell as he passed under each bridge. But at the end of the day, Neil thought the hot chocolate and coloring sessions were the best part of the program.

"C'mon, Neil, it'll be fun." I'd cajole Neil onto the lift even though my own heart was doing backflips in my chest at the prospect. He gave it a go, but he never really found his passion in skiing.

And he did the same here in Vermont. He tried. But in a place where skiing was the only game in town, being a novice at the sport didn't win you too many friends. The place itself was also very isolating. Groceries were a forty-minute drive away. The only people he knew were other teachers, all older than he. He did have a girlfriend for a time, but when that didn't work out, he spent more and more time by himself. He used to eat lunch with his students or "the ladies in the business office." They adored Neil and were constantly trying to fix him up, but toward spring he was eating alone.

I didn't realize how bad things had gotten until one day in April, when Neil called to say he was not being hired back for the fall.

"Too depressed" was the reason the headmaster gave for letting him go. He told Neil that he could either finish out the year, which ended the next month, or he could pack up and leave immediately. Neil chose the latter.

I'm embarrassed, as a doctor, to admit how little I knew back then about depression and traumatic brain injury. In college I thought Neil's depression was all about losing his girlfriend. In Vermont I thought it was the isolation. It took many years of reading and research, of going to conferences put on by the Brain Injury Association of Massachusetts, of observing my own son, to realize that his depression was organic, a result of his injury. I also learned that depression caused by a traumatic brain injury can be more recalcitrant, more difficult to treat than reactive depression or even a major depressive episode.

Over time Neil went to various therapists. He stayed on antidepressants for years. But his pattern—long months of stability followed (usually in the spring) by some kind of backslide—would repeat itself for a long time after the crash.

Never one to give up, Neil spent the summer looking for another teaching job. He landed one, this time in an inner-city public high school with no shortage of troubled and rebellious youth, a far cry from the elite skiers he was used to. He didn't last more than a few months. He was smoking marijuana pretty heavily over the summer ("self-medicating" my therapist friends called it), and although he had given up the stuff before he started work, his mandatory drug test came back positive and he was reluctantly let go.

"I'd love to keep you, Neil," the principal told him, "but my hands are tied."

He told Neil he could use him as a reference. He said his record would not reflect the reason for his being let go. I'm not sure that was true. I'm not sure those were his decisions to make. In any case, Neil hasn't taught in over two years now.

Saul and I worried that, unwittingly or not, he may have sabotaged his dreams of a teaching career. The economy also became bleak for teachers. Large-scale layoffs were common, and Neil was finding himself competing with teachers with many more years of experience.

His new strategy, implemented some years later, included a graduate program in math education. His dream was not dead, just on hold for now.

35

Med School

I WAS IN MY EARLY THIRTIES, married with children, when I got into medical school. I remember driving our Ford Tempo, maroon except for one mismatched black door, to my first day of class. It was a warm July morning in 1987. I drove with the windows all rolled down. I passed some railroad tracks where homeless men slept under heavy cardboard, their jackets balled up under their heads for pillows. I remember thinking how lucky I was. How blessed to be given this chance to be a doctor, to make a difference.

I had visited numerous day care centers trying to choose one that would be right for the boys. They were two and four at the time. This was their first time at full-time day care. I chose a YMCA center that was housed in the basement of a church near St. Vincent's Hospital. I assuaged my guilt by telling myself that I was setting an example for my sons by being a strong, intelligent, and capable woman. Maybe I was kidding myself.

I was one of only three women with children in my class. Karen, Pat, and I found one another right away and became fast friends over those four years. We sat in the same seats in Amphitheater A. It wasn't so much that we chose our seats; they chose us. With our wife-and-mother duties—fixing lunches, bringing the kids to school or day care—we wanted the seats right next to the side door, the ones we could spill into just seconds before the lecture was to begin, not to mention bolt out of if we got the call that one of the kids was throwing up.

The hardest part of being a mom and a medical student was finding time for everything. When I was studying I was feeling guilty that I wasn't spending time with my family. But when I took time from my studies to get down on the floor and play with my kids, I was convinced everyone else in my class was studying, and I was certain I was going to fail.

Luckily one of my boys' favorite games at that time was "shipwrecked." The three of us would gather our favorite toys, books, and snacks and climb up on the top of Dan's bunk bed and pretend we were lost at sea. I got pretty good at killing two birds with one stone, memorizing the Krebs cycle while pretending to fish.

One of the things that got me through those four years was a women's group that was started by two psychiatry residents. Maybe it fulfilled some course requirement for them; maybe they did it just to pay it forward. In any case I benefited enormously from those sessions. I saw that I was not the only one who struggled to balance home and academic commitments. I heard about other women's fears and goals, not so different from my own.

One of my fellow students, a second-generation Indian woman, always managed to put things in perspective for us.

When we would be commiserating about our struggles with work-life balance or our angst over this test result or that rotation, she would say, "These are the worries of the privileged," reminding us that women in some countries worried about their very survival. Reminding us of our blessings.

The most difficult course for all of us in medical school was gross anatomy. It wasn't just physically and academically challenging but emotionally hard as well. We were assigned our cadavers on the first day of medical school. We were nervous. Most of us had never been this close to death before. Few of us, I'm sure, had ever touched a dead body. We walked slowly into the cool tiled room, those of us near the back trying to peer over the heads of our classmates, the sharp smell of formaldehyde hitting our nostrils hard. Twenty-five stainless-steel tables were arranged around the room. On each lay a body, wrapped head to toe in plastic and bagged in a zippered white shroud.

Four of us were assigned to each cadaver. The only piece of information we were given about our cadavers was the cause of death. The instructors were respectful, even reverent in the care of the corpses. They were also mindful of the impact the experience would have on us, the students who would spend an entire year, scalpel in hand, carving every inch of these bodies, knowing them inside and out, more intimately than anyone ever had. The most human parts of them, their hands, their faces, were the last to be studied, kept wrapped in white gauze until after the chest, back, neck, arms, and legs were all thoroughly dissected.

Our cadaver was a gray-haired heavy-set elderly woman. She had a sweet, pudgy face. You could just picture her with a plate full of freshly baked chocolate-chip cookies for the grandchildren she surely had. We treated her gently; mindful of the ultimate gift she was giving us every day. The experience of dissecting a human body is one that few people share. It bonded us together in knowledge, in respect, as doctors.

In the spring we held a memorial service to honor all the people who had donated their bodies and contributed immeasurably to our education, both as doctors and as human beings. We learned our anatomy lessons of course. But we also learned to face death. We held death in our hands. We learned about sacrifice. The families of some of the living donors, as they are called, came to the ceremony, anxious to see for themselves, I'm sure, that their loved ones were treated with dignity. We were not introduced. The donors remained anonymous to us.

Each student contributed in some way. Some students made art projects, paintings, drawings, or sculptures. Some sang movingly. One woman played the harp. I remember sobbing as I watched my fellow classmate Ray Colon perform a beautiful ballet of thanks. His lithe body arced and drifted across the stage, his expression strained with emotion.

That night, as I read my children a bedtime story and tucked them into their beds with a kiss, I thought about my cadaver; her wisps of gray curls, her friendly face, her pudgy hands. I felt her watchful presence, another blessing in my life.

My first two years of medical school were all academic: lectures, workshops, and labs. Third and fourth years were our clinical years, with clerkships in medicine, surgery, pediatrics, obstetrics, and psychiatry. We took call every third or fourth night, depending on the rotation. We could choose to do some of our electives at different hospitals. I did a pediatric intensive care elective at Mass General, a cardiology and hematology-oncology rotation at Children's in Boston.

The time away from my family stung. One night in the pediatric intensive care unit at Mass General, I got a call from Saul. Dan had cut himself on some metal on the ladder of the swimming pool at the Jewish Community Center. Saul had taken him for stitches. Saul told Dan that they were just going to the hospital to have "one of Mom's friends" take a look at his cut. Dan was fine until they pulled into the parking lot. Saul decided to warn his son about his impending sutures. On hearing that, Dan wound his arms around the seat belts in the car, refusing to let Saul pull him out. He needed "one of Mom's friends" just to extract him from the front seat. The next day, knowing all about this scene in the parking lot, I nevertheless commended Dan.

"That must have really hurt Dan. You must have been so scared."

Dan rolled his eyes, scoffing at the thought.

"Don't make me laugh," he said, as if he'd been the bravest patient in the ER. I smiled at his bravado but was secretly guilty that I had been away when his accident occurred.

Neil had his share of trips to the emergency room during my time at UMass too. One day we were kneeling in the garden planting green beans. When Neil stood up, blood dripped from his knee. I searched briefly in the dirt for the broken glass that surely must have been there, but I didn't come up with anything. I washed and wrapped his knee then told him I'd need to take him in to "my hospital" for stitches. At the mention of the word, all color drained from his face and he staggered visibly.

At the hospital, the triage nurse took our information, typing down our answers to her questions.

"How did this happen?" she asked.

"I don't know," I stammered. "We were out in the garden. When he stood up he was bleeding."

Son cut knee. Mother has no idea how it happened, she typed.

"That's not exactly what I said," I pointed out, making her change the wording before anyone called DCF on me.

One of my fellow residents stitched Neil up expertly. His only advice was that he find another story for his scar.

"Tell him a tiger got you, Neil," he told us. I was grateful for his humor and his skill.

Neil would remain my "woozy one." The one to get queasy at the sight of blood. The one to catch every virus in his school and be hit hardest. Dan was stocky as a boy and much hardier than his brother. A cold that landed Neil in bed for days with a fever and chills barely roused a sniffle in Dan. Neil had strep throat four times as a boy while the rest of the household escaped unscathed.

Each time one of the children became ill (usually Neil), Saul and I had to figure out who was staying home as the caretaking parent. One day Neil was home ill and Saul was the one to stay home with him.

"I'm sorry, Neil," I told him before leaving for my shift. "I can't miss a day from this rotation. There are lots of sick children in the hospital who need me. Besides, you've got Dad."

Neil didn't miss a beat, laying the guilt on pretty thick.

"So not only are you not staying home with me," he said accusingly, "but you probably brought the germs home that got me sick in the first place."

We couldn't have predicted then that such a vulnerable child would grow up to be such a resilient young man. The brain injury, the broken leg: They took their toll, but they never broke Neil's spirit. He just did what he had to do, one foot in front of the other.

36

Residency

THE KIDS WERE SIX AND EIGHT when I began my residency, nine and eleven when I finished. They went from "Oh, Mom. You're on call again?" (Translation: You bad mother. You've already left us twice this week.) to "Oh, Mom. You're on call again?" (Translation: Poor Mom isn't going to get any sleep tonight either.)

On most rotations we were on call every third night. Surgery rotations could be worse. There's a well-known saying among surgeons: "What's the worst part of being on call every other night? Missing half the cases." On our post-call days we rounded on our patients and wrote orders before signing out to our colleagues. Our goal was to finish work by twelve o'clock, attend noon conference, then go home, hoping to catch some sleep before arriving early the next day to pre-round on our patients. Sometimes we didn't leave until three.

Nowadays the Accreditation Council for Graduate Medical Education regulates resident work hours, the idea being that sleep-deprived doctors make mistakes. I agree with the sentiment, but I wouldn't trade my long hours of patient care for anything. I only learned about the stages of a woman's labor and delivery by seeing them, hour by hour. Serial abdominal exams helped me divine the diagnosis of appendicitis when the initial history and physical exam were equivocal. Today many residents sign out after morning rounds, required by their programs to be out the door by 8:00 a.m. But I wanted to write the orders on my own patients, because no one knew them better than I. I wanted to go to morning rounds and present my own patients to the chief, hear his feedback. I learned from my mistakes, but only because I knew I had made them.

There are trade-offs that come with shorter working hours, not only in resident learning but also in patient care. The shorter residents' hours become, the more sign-outs are required to pass on patient information from one team to the next. As careful as we are to communicate to our colleagues what needs to be done, we've all played the game of telephone. Invariably at times messages aren't heard or information is misinterpreted.

Maybe the ultimate answer is a longer residency program. There seems to be an infinite amount of information to learn but a finite amount of time to learn it in.

Saul brought the kids to see me when I was on call whenever both of our schedules allowed. We'd have supper together in the cafeteria or out on the patio under umbrellaed picnic tables. After dinner the boys had fun rolling down the grassy hill between the edge of the cafeteria lawn and the ambulance bays of the ER. If they were really lucky, they'd get to watch a Med-Flight helicopter land or take off. The boys would stand shoulder to shoulder, heads turned up to the sky, sometimes shading their eyes from the setting sun. The copter's rotors whipped their in-need-of-a-haircut curls while Saul and I looked on and smiled. This is as close as we would ever come to being "helicopter parents."

Sometimes on a quiet night they'd come up to the floor with me. We'd watch a video in the call room, or sometimes my kids would play with some like-aged patients in the playroom.

Those were the good times.

⁓

Both my parents were admitted to my hospital during my residency.

My father went first. He had not been feeling well for a couple of weeks. His stomach was bloated. The whites of his eyes had begun to muddy. He had gone to his family doctor, who was running some tests. My sister and I went to pick him up and take him to the doctor's office to get his results. He was weak and tired. Our father, who prided himself on never being sick a day in his life, had aged years since the last time I'd seen him just a few weeks before. He leaned heavily on my mother on his way to the car. When we got to the doctor's, I went inside to get a wheelchair, afraid he'd never make it across the parking lot.

The news wasn't good. My father had cancer. At the sound of the word, his shoulders slumped and he exhaled heavily. It sounded like the life was being let out of him right before our eyes, as deflated as a child's spent balloon.

The doctor outlined his plan. He was hospitalizing my father right then and there. He would hydrate him over the weekend, beef up his nutrition. On Monday they would run more tests to find out where the cancer had started and how far it had spread and formulate a plan for treating it.

My father had stopped listening. He had stopped hearing anything after "the C word," as his generation called it.

I registered my father in the emergency room at UMass. He was placed in a johnny by nurses I knew, examined by residents in my program, his care supervised by an attending who had supervised me.

I held his tanned hand in mine.

"It'll be okay, Dad," I said, words with no faith behind them.

He stared back at me not saying anything, his face blank. I couldn't blame him for not believing me. I didn't believe myself. His eyes were vacant. As his eyelids closed, I looked up at his monitor. The neat green blips of his normal rhythm had turned into an erratic lightning strike across the screen.

"Dad!" I screamed, shaking his shoulders.

"Dad!"

I ripped the call bell from the wall. But the team was already pushing their way through the curtain and into his cubicle, alerted to the dangerous rhythm by the telemetry unit at the nurses' station. The drawers of the red crash cart were flying open before it had even come to a stop.

"Dad." My voice caught in my throat like a chicken bone.

One of my fellow residents appeared out of nowhere, her gentle hands on my shoulders, leading me, my sister, and mom into the family room. There we waited, huddled and afraid, until they came to tell us what was going on.

The "they" turned out to be Cynthia Adams, one of the more aggressive attendings in the ER. In the pediatric department we used to joke that she wouldn't know a well child if she tripped over one. She was a large woman, always in scrubs, and walked with a manly swagger. Now she was standing over us, hands on hips.

"Well, he's stable," she told us. We let out a collective sigh of relief.

"Yup, we tubed him and thumped him," she went on.

Now it was my turn to tune out. By "tubed him" the doctor meant that my father had stopped breathing and that the code team had had to insert a tube into his throat and hook it up to a ventilator to breathe for him. By "thumped him" she meant that someone had either literally delivered a decisive fist to his chest to get him out of that dangerous rhythm or, more likely, shocked his heart using electrical defibrillator paddles. Somewhere in the back of my mind I was appalled that Dr. Adams would use this ER cowboy lingo to describe what had happened to my father, but at the time I was sick with worry and fear and anxious to get back to his side.

By now his bedside was crammed with machines and monitors. IV fluid and meds dripped into his skinny arms. A glowing red clip on his finger monitored his oxygen levels. His breathing tube was taped to his slack-jawed face; the ventilator's bellows whooshing, regular as a metronome. The lightning strike rhythm had evened itself out into orderly green blips again.

I explained what was going on to my family. But as I spoke, his heart went into V-fib again. Again we were herded out of the room while they worked on him. Now an ICU attending was involved, telling us he needed a pericardial window. His heart was filling up with blood and needed to be drained.

My brother arrived. We conferred. Our dad would definitely not want this. Here was our father, healthy as a horse his entire life, now hooked up to medications and machines. Facing a diagnosis that felt like a death sentence to him and a treatment he may in fact have refused.

But I was out of my league here. I was a pediatric resident, not an intensivist or an oncologist or a cardiologist. I wasn't even an attending. I called the only person I thought could help us—someone who knew my dad and also took care of many sick and elderly patients in the office and on the floor: my father's family doctor.

I explained the situation.

"He keeps going into V-fib. They keep coding him. Now they're talking about a pericardial window."

I wanted to know what to do. I wanted some numbers. I wanted statistics. What were my father's chances of survival? I knew I was asking his doctor a lot. At this point, he didn't even know what kind of cancer my father had. But he knew *him*. He knew the man. He had cared for him for over forty years.

"If he has a pericardial effusion, it's probably metastatic," he began, waiting for that news to sink in.

"And?"

"Well, Carolyn, I can tell you this much." He spoke slowly, as if choosing his words very carefully. "No one in that situation—metastatic effusion around the heart, going into runs of V-fib—has ever left the hospital."

I don't know where he got that statistic. He didn't quote a study. Maybe he was just relaying his own experience. But he knew what I was asking, and I think he was telling me what I needed to know.

I conferred with my family, and we all agreed. My dad wouldn't want what was happening to him to continue unless he could be assured of some good quality years ahead, and his doctor was telling me that wasn't going to happen.

We signed the DNR papers. Do Not Resuscitate. We got him settled into a bed in the ICU. He was kept comfortable on morphine.

"Is he on the dope?" my mother asked when he didn't respond to her voice.

"Yeah, Mom, he is, but he can still hear you."

I honestly didn't know if that was true, but I knew we always said that to families in the ICU, and it seemed to give everybody comfort to be able to still talk to their loved one. And we talked to my father now.

"I love you, Dad," I said. My brother and sister followed suit.

But the next time his heart rhythm turned into V-fib, the next time lightning struck, instead of coming in with a crash cart, the nurse just came in. She turned the monitors off. We held Dad's hands and laid our heads on his chest and waited for his quivering heart to lay quiet in its cage.

My mother's end was not so quick. Her first stroke happened on my surgery rotation. I was scrubbed in on a routine appendectomy, excited because with these relatively minor routine surgeries, we sometimes got to do more than hold retractors and sew up the wound. Sometimes we got to cut.

When we were in surgery, we left our beepers with the nurse at the front desk, who answered the pages and relayed messages. She usually just called in by phone or over the intercom system. So when she appeared at the door in person and called me by name, I knew something was wrong.

I didn't get much information initially. Just that my mother was down in the ER. I took the stairs two at a time, found my mother's name on the board outside Triage, and stepped into her cubicle. She was alone in the room, in a johnny and on a stretcher with the side rails pulled up, but otherwise looking fine. No monitors. No IVs. Her color looked good. I smiled in relief.

"Hi, Mom."

She turned her head toward me, but just stared. It occurred to me that she might not see me.

"Mom?" I repeated, walking toward her. She seemed to not know who I was. She opened her mouth to speak, but no words came out. My heart plummeted in free fall, crash-landing in the pit of my stomach as I realized what I was watching: my mother's stroke in evolution.

There was nothing for me to do. There wasn't the same urgency to her situation as there had been to my father's. My mother had had rheumatic fever as a child, which left her heart with leaky valves. Her rhythm was chronic atrial fibrillation or A-fib. Though not as lethal as the kind of fibrillation my father had suffered, it did put her at risk for blood clots, which could travel to the brain in the form of a stroke. She was on a blood-thinning medicine to make clotting less likely, but that put her at risk for a different kind of stroke—a hemorrhagic stroke in which the brain, instead of having its blood supply cut off by a clot, is actually flooded with blood with nowhere to go. She was between the proverbial rock and a hard place. We wouldn't know which kind of stroke she'd had or what her treatment would be until more testing was done.

Meanwhile she was admitted to a medical-surgical floor. I rode up in the elevator with her, holding her hand. I helped the nurses transfer her from stretcher to bed. A neurology resident came by to examine her. He tested her gag reflex, determined it was absent, and ordered a feeding tube. I refused. I spooned tiny amounts of ice chips into her mouth instead. She didn't choke once. They also ordered a Foley catheter to be placed in her bladder so that she would not be incontinent and suffer skin breakdown. Again I sent the nurse away, turning my mother every two hours and putting her on the bedpan myself. My friend and fellow resident Mike Zackin took my shift that night so I could spend it next to my mom on a foldout recliner, fending off nurses with tubes.

My mother recovered well from that stroke but suffered several more over the years. The last one was devastating, leaving her lingering in a not-quite-vegetative state for weeks. She underwent CAT scan after CAT scan, baffling the doctors, who saw no lesion on her scans that accounted for the state she was in. She was intubated but breathing on her own much of the time. But every time the doctors tried to extubate her, to let her breathe on her own, she failed.

My siblings and I watched our mother endure one invasive procedure after another. But with the doctors not being able to see any reason for her state, we all held out hope that she might turn around, open her eyes, speak.

It never happened. Weeks passed. We went from constant bedside vigilance to gradually returning to work, visiting her in the evenings like other visitors: like she'd just had her appendix out.

The staff began to talk about nursing homes, long-term care facilities. My brother and sister were the first ones to broach the subject of taking her off life support.

"Mom wouldn't want this," they told me.

I was the holdout. As much as I championed patients' right to die, as much as I believed in families deciding the fates of their loved ones, this was one decision I felt incapable of making.

I eventually succumbed. So did my mother. We siblings made a plan. We would all be with her. We would not leave her alone. We called our children. Everyone came. The nurses removed my mother's breathing tube, gave her a little morphine, then left us alone as a family. The grandchildren were taking it pretty hard, crying in turns. My mother continued breathing. She got congested from time to time. When she coughed or grimaced, the nurses gently cleared her airway and gave her more morphine. The day passed. We took turns going to the cafeteria for lunch, then dinner. We chatted with one another, catching up on family news. Nursing shifts changed: seven to three, then three to eleven, and finally eleven to seven. Around midnight it became clear my mother wasn't going anywhere. Our plan to all be at her side when she died now morphed into one in which one of us would stay with her at all times. She would never be alone.

"I'll take the first shift," I volunteered.

We all began saying our good-byes to one another, slipping into our coats, moving out into the hall.

Suddenly the steady rhythmic beeping of my mother's cardiac monitor slowed. We all turned in unison to watch her heart rate drop. Sixty . . . fifty . . . thirty. We rushed back to her side, held her hands, looked at each other in wonder. It was as if she were aware all along. As if she had just been sleeping, or even playing possum, happily listening to the chatter of her brood, happy to be in the middle of it. It was as if faced with the prospect of dying with us all around her versus carrying on longer with just me, she had chosen the former.

~

With both my parents, we were there. That is one thing I feel good about. Family supporting family. Being there when it matters. It is the same with Neil now. Dan flying back from Mexico to be with him. Me taking work leave to take care of him. Never any question of where our priorities lie. Never any question of where we belong.

37

"& Sons"

WHILE NEIL ALWAYS WANTED to be a teacher, Dan always wanted to be a comedian. He made that decision in the sixth grade and never looked back. We tried to be supportive. We took him to comedy clubs all over the Boston area starting when he was about twelve. Sometimes we'd be embarrassed at the foul language and the raunchiness of the routines. Often, in midsentence, the comedian would notice there was a kid in the crowd. The jokes invariably ensued.

"Hey, who's carding at the door?"

"Hey, kid. Your parents know you're here?"

We'd sheepishly raise our hands. A few more gags would follow, but once they got over the initial shock of Dan, the show eventually went on.

When Dan was in high school, he signed up for Talent Night. So did Neil. But while Neil performed a more traditional musical number, Dan wrote jokes. He rehearsed in his room. Nobody from the school ever previewed his work. Maybe we should have been suspicious when he wouldn't allow us to go to opening night, but I figured he was just self-conscious, that having his parents in the audience would make him nervous. If Neil knew what Dan had written in his routines, he didn't let on.

He came home late the night of the performance. He made a grand entrance, flinging the door open wide, launching his arms straight up into the air, throwing his head back and announcing in a booming voice, "I was made for the stage!" I had never seen him so happy.

He didn't tell us much about his actual act, but he had clearly enjoyed himself. We were so proud of him. Dan at that stage was pretty awkward. He was still the new kid in town, having only moved here a few years before. A bit overweight, unlike gregarious Neil he didn't make friends that easily. When we would take the boys to the beach for the day when they were small, Neil would come back to our blanket telling us the name of each child he'd befriended that day. Dan was more or less oblivious to them. This success on stage was great for his self-esteem.

Until we got the call from the principal's office the next day.

There had been complaints about some of Dan's material. This was not long after the Columbine school shootings, and Dan had performed in a long black trench coat. One of his jokes involved guns.

Saul and I went together to the high school the next morning. The principal stuck a tape of the show into the VCR in his office.

"See for yourself," he told us, pressing PLAY and leaving the room.

We were amazed. Dan was fantastic. He strutted back and forth across the stage, voice strong, material memorized, the audience eating out of his hand. The kids went wild, laughing uproariously, clapping like thunder. Sure there was the occasional scatological reference we could have done without. The joke the principal had complained about involved airport security and body searches. But Dan was just doing what comedians do: writing routines from their life experiences. We had just gone on a family vacation to Florida to Saul's brother Louis's graduation from acupuncture school. The trip had involved x-ray scanners and metal detectors. The worst part of his performance, as far as we were concerned, was an inappropriate dumb-blond joke. We would speak to him about that one later.

Dan even handled a heckler with aplomb.

"Soooo, this guy wants me to stop! Do *you* want me to stop?!!" Dan yelled to his fans.

"NO!!!" the crowd roared back at him.

When the principal returned, we had to admit to him: We thought our son was great. We would speak to him about some of the jokes. Luckily he left it at that. No suspension. No punishment at all.

When Dan and I were touring potential colleges during his senior year of high school, the presidents who came out to greet the applicants always wanted to talk to Dan. He stood out from the crowd.

"What does everyone want to be?" the presidents would ask.

"Doctor. Lawyer. Lawyer. Doctor."

"Comedian."

"Really?" they'd say and sit down next to Dan, fascinated.

He majored in English, figuring that would be his best bet for learning to write comedy routines. Every class he took, every piece he turned in, he aimed to amuse.

The faculty recognized Dan's talent as a writer and tried to get him to see it too.

"Dan, I don't want another comedic piece from you," one of his professors finally told him. "The next piece you turn in has to be serious or I won't accept it."

Then the accident happened. Dan wrote a piece of creative nonfiction about the night he learned of Neil's accident. Called *A Quiet Night in Mexico*, it got published in an anthology. Another short story got published in the online literary journal *VerbSap .com*. People were starting to take him seriously as a writer, and so he started to see himself as one too.

Dan has shared many of his stories with me over the years. His themes are often dark but emotionally evocative. He has moved me to tears with his words. I believed in him as a comedian, but I adored him as a writer.

But ever the pragmatist, Dan ultimately turned his minor in business into a double major. "In case the writing thing doesn't work out," he said.

Dan walked for his graduation from Goucher College but didn't actually receive his diploma until the following semester. To qualify for a full degree in business, he needed to complete an internship. He went to work for Saul and turned in a project analyzing the failure of a seasonal kitchen shop we had tried to open in a New Hampshire mall.

When he got his degree, he astonished us all by announcing, "I want to take over the family business."

So Dan was on board, his father's apprentice. When Saul opened a second location in Portland, Maine, it became "Dan's store." He fell for the business hook, line, and sinker. He has a big personality, perfect for sales. He's an adept conversationalist and a natural schmoozer. He spent every summer in college working for Bridges Brothers moving company, a real handy skill in the restaurant world. And he was smart, which helps too. There is so much to know.

After Neil's second teaching job ended, he too joined the family business, first working with Saul in Portsmouth learning the ropes. He made a spreadsheet of the store's entire inventory in preparation for a new equipment-tracking computer system. He eventually moved in with his brother to help him run the Portland store. They have a nice division of labor. Dan is definitely the boss. He makes sales calls and does the negotiating with customers. Neil is in charge of inventory. Dan doesn't know where anything is or when to order new supplies without asking Neil.

But while restaurant supply may have been in Dan's blood, for Neil the family business was always temporary. Neil's plan remains to teach, though the strategy has changed—he's started a graduate program in math education.

38

Get Over It

OUR LOCAL PAPER COVERED the accident from the beginning. So did the *Boston Globe*. At first there were updates on the conditions of Trista and Neil. Then came Trista's obituary and biopic-type stories about Neil and how the two of them had met.

As the drunk driver and the teen who supplied him with alcohol were arrested and their cases moved through the courts, those stories too made the paper.

We followed these articles only sporadically from the hospital, logging onto the computer in the ICU's waiting room whenever the nurses sent us away from Neil's side. We sometimes read the comments readers posted, one friend or neighbor after another expressing sympathy for our two families and dismay or anger or disgust at the drunk driver.

But as time went on, when he was sentenced to two and a half years in the County House of Correction for motor vehicle homicide with one additional year for leaving the scene, and especially when he got five to seven years in state prison for violating his probation, there began to percolate up through the comments a tiny groundswell of support for his case. There was a small but distinct group of responders who thought he was being punished for "having a beer."

The original sentencing judge had made it quite clear that abstaining from alcohol for five years was one of the terms of the drunk driver's probation. The drunk driver also knew that the entire fifteen-year state prison sentence was still hanging over his head if he violated any one of those conditions set down by the judge. Yet he chose not only to drink, not only to drink publicly at a 99 Restaurant where a friend of Trista was his server, but to even order a "blockbuster"—a full twenty-four ounces of Sam Adams beer. To me he was flaunting it.

To the judge his decision "made a mockery of the harm done." He believed the drunk driver showed not just a lack of remorse for Trista's death and Neil's injuries but that "he just doesn't get it." In court the judge said that if the drunk driver had understood his role and felt true remorse, "alcohol would never touch his lips."

But somehow these commenters viewed our role in the sentencing, which was just showing up in court and reading our victim impact statements, as "seeking revenge." We still just viewed it as seeking justice. Many of the responders wrote that the Zincks and the Bornsteins should just move on with our lives. Get over it. As if our diligence in speaking out in court, in making sure each judge knew just what we had lost, was somehow an obsession that would be better off let go.

I have seen this mind-set in other situations as well—this lack of sensitivity when a person has not directly experienced a victim's particular trauma. I remember reading a report of a Catholic Youth rally in Austria that was being protested by child sexual abuse victims. The report quoted a church official as saying the protesters should not "wait crankily" for an apology. Such dismissiveness minimizes victims' suffering.

This idea that victims can easily move on and that any discussion of their pain marks a stubborn willfulness to stay mired in the past is false. This idea of closure is fraudulent. The word itself feels made up, its attainability impossible and unrealistic.

I would love to move on. I would love to let go. But moving on is easier said than done. Neil had two operations a year apart to repair his broken leg bones. He spent his first Christmas break from college recovering from his second surgery and working through physical therapy He has no memory of the accident or his days in the ICU. He struggled with memory loss, depression, anxiety, and posttraumatic stress disorder, or PTSD. He was in therapy and on antidepressants for years. It's hard to move on from that.

Unfortunately, it wasn't hard for some of Neil's friends to move on from him. His personality has changed. He will be the first to tell you he isn't the same person he was before the crash. Some friends who initially stood by him ultimately didn't know how to deal with this "new Neil." Some of course remained. Neil took Trista's best friend, Jess, to the senior prom. She, Max, Jeff, Ari, Greg, all keep in touch with Neil to this day and are a great support.

And he's needed it. When he struggled with academics, we arranged for neuropsychological testing, which revealed deficiencies in attention to visual detail, verbal reasoning, and rapid sequencing. He showed inattention and encoding problems when there were competing distractions around him. He had difficulties with executive function, frontal lobe skills of organization and interpretation, lobes that were contused in the crash. We would love to let go of all of that.

We don't obsess about the accident. We are not negatively focused. We celebrate with Neil each accomplishment: graduation from high school and college, first job, getting into graduate school. But each new accomplishment brings some new challenge as well. When Neil called to tell us he had gotten into grad school, he didn't want to talk about it.

"Don't congratulate me on it. I'm really, really nervous."

Let it go? Move on? I wish someone could tell me how.

39

Fate

"Things happen for a reason."

It's a line a lot of people use to try to comfort someone who is going through a tough period. It's a line I've heard many times as people try to help me to deal with Neil's losses. Folks mean well. They take comfort in believing that events are part of a larger, more complex or holier plan. God's plan.

But I am not a fatalist. I do not believe things happen for a reason. I just can't. Because what possible reason could exist for a kid to be driving so drunk on a Tuesday night that he kills one person and maims another and just keeps on going? I believe in the beautiful randomness of this world. I believe in finding our own meanings along the way. I am not the kind of person who takes things for granted. I did not need this accident to show me how precious my child is. I did not need to have him almost taken from me to appreciate his sweetness and intelligence and wit.

But people who believe in this concept of fate, of unalterable predestiny, believe in it strongly. The whole concept became a tense discussion point one night in my writing group. After reading this very chapter, Lisa, a member of the group, told me a story about a friend of hers who had lost her job as a nurse at Anna Jaques Hospital.

"Things happen for a reason," Lisa told her. Cold comfort in the unemployment line, I thought.

But a year later her friend found another nursing job at a distant hospital with a lengthy commute. One day at work she didn't feel so well. If she were at Anna Jaques, in the town where she lived, she would have simply gone home sick. But working so far from home, she did the next best thing; she ran an EKG on herself. When she handed it to one of the staff physicians to read, he packed her into an ambulance immediately and sent her to Boston. She was having a heart attack.

"If I was at my old job, I would have just gone home and lain down. I would've died," she told Lisa.

To Lisa this was proof positive of her fatalistic view of the world.

"See, Carolyn? It may be hard for you to hear right now, but things really do happen for a reason. You may not even know what the reason is, but someday you'll see it, just like my friend."

I shook my head. To me the events in Lisa's story were just random occurrences. Lisa was attaching her own significance to them.

"I just can't believe that, Lisa. I just can't."

Lisa sat up a little straighter and gave her shoulders a little "believe what you want" shrug. We went back to our work. Lisa and I have been writing together for fourteen years. This was the tensest exchange we've ever had.

I give a talk as part of the ambassador program of the Brain Injury Association of Massachusetts. The program is designed to increase awareness of the devastating effects of brain injury as well as the BIA's many prevention programs. Having speakers who are personally familiar with brain injury puts a human face on a very large statistic. Toward the end of my speech, I speak about this concept of fate and of my not believing things happen for a reason. I talk about taking the hand we are dealt and creating our own meaning.

"That's what I'm trying to do here today," I told one recent audience. "Taking the nasty hand my family was dealt and doing something positive with it."

The speech is always well received. But on this particular day, as I left the building, an older gentleman chased me out into the parking lot. He put one hand on my shoulder and leaned the other hand against the door of my car, blocking my entrance.

"Look, I know you don't think things happen for a reason," he told me, a weighty look in his eye. "But I gotta tell ya. They do."

With that he gave a little nod and strode off.

***

Maybe I should give it a try. Look for reasons this whole thing happened. Why Trista died. Why Neil didn't. To the accident reconstruction team, the answer was simple. Trista was short. She went under the car. Neil is tall. He was thrown over it. There might not be any more to it than that. I don't know.

But maybe we're saying the same thing, the fatalists and I. Lisa says things are presented to us when they need to be. Events change us, or we change to adapt to them. I have learned things about myself and my family because of it. We may be stronger and closer as a result. But I am fundamentally the same person I was before the crash, just one with a different life experience. All that makes me a humanist, not a believer in fate.

40

The Offender

FOR ALL MY FAMILY HAS BEEN THROUGH, I still cannot say that I hate the drunk driver.

I don't wish him harm. I don't spend my every waking moment fantasizing about his demise. I feel sorry for him. Not in the same way you feel sorry for an orphan, say, or a lost puppy, but sorry in a pathetic kind of way. Sorry that no one cared. No one in the juvenile justice system cared enough about this kid to permanently take away his license after the first time he ran somebody down. No one in his family cared enough to get him the help he needed for his drinking problem. Maybe no one even noticed that he had one. I feel sorry in a regretful kind of way; that maybe if someone had cared enough to intervene, he wouldn't have been drinking that night—or at the very least not on the road.

From the beginning the drunk driver took no responsibility for his actions. He tried to claim he wasn't driving, even though an off-duty firefighter had witnessed the rollover of his SUV. He even tried to pretend he was noble, telling the arresting officer, "I won't rat out my friends."

For Trista's family, the hate started early.

I didn't have room for the hatred that first night. I didn't have time for it. I needed to put all my energy into helping my boy get better. He had a total of three CAT scans to monitor his bleeding brain. His acute confusion and agitation gradually gave way to chronic memory loss, personality changes, and depression. He had two operations on a leg that wouldn't heal. He was on painkillers, antiseizure medications, and antidepressants. I was a little busy.

But if in the beginning I had no time for the hatred, in the end I just didn't feel it. Later I did my part to get the drunk driver convicted. I took time off from work to make his every court appearance. I argued for a lengthy sentence. And when he didn't get one, I showed up at every parole hearing to plead for his continued incarceration. I felt I owed that much to Neil and Trista. But do I owe it to them to hate? Do I have to carry that hatred around inside of me? Do I have to wear it like a badge? I hope not, because I can't. I cannot pin all my hopes on justice. I cannot let my healing depend on getting this guy the sentence he deserves. I tried my best, I showed up, but I cannot let his sentence define my peace.

I've heard a definition of revenge that goes something like this: It's like taking poison then waiting for the other person to die. Trista's parents' hatred was poisonous. Understandable, but chilling in its matter-of-factness. Mary talked frequently in those early days after the accident about running the drunk driver over with her car if she ever met him on the street after he got out of jail. She added that before she hits him, she will knock back the nip she keeps in her glove compartment just for the occasion, because "obviously if you're a drunk driver, you can get away with murder." I suspect she was only half kidding.

Trista's father, David, once told the judges at one of the drunk driver's parole hearings that justice will only be served when they cut his body down from a pipe after he hangs himself in his jail cell. He broke down as he said it. Mary comforted him. "Don't say that, David, don't say it," she soothed. They really did seem to want this young man dead. Would I if he had killed my son? Should I because he changed Neil's life forever? It's been some time since the accident. Perhaps the Zincks' position has softened.

The drunk driver has never shown any remorse. Remorse first requires that one understand the pain and damage one has caused. The drunk driver has never made this first step. In his small mind and with his concrete thinking, he seems to believe that he cannot be held accountable for events he cannot remember. He did not make parole at any of his three attempts. He was inarticulate, shallow, and unintelligent. When asked by the judge why he should be let out of jail early, he replied, "So I can get on with my life," like killing someone was just a minor inconvenience to be waited out or stepped over. He took an alcohol recovery course in jail to chip some time off his sentence, but he seemed to miss the whole point of the program. Asked if he had a problem with alcohol, he answered, "I guess I don't have a problem in here because I can't drink in here." It sounded like a bad Lenny Bruce joke. But it didn't fill me with anger. It didn't fill me with anything at all. It left me empty. Astonished at this monstrous lack of humanity. Completely mystified as to how someone could take a person's life and not realize its impact, not feel shame or sorrow or regret.

The drunk driver had mown down people before. Several years earlier he had run a red light and hit a woman on a bicycle in a pedestrian crosswalk. Her injuries were serious, and she, like Neil, required multiple operations to heal. At one of his parole hearings, the drunk driver seemed to forget about this incident. (He also seemed to forget that the parole board had access to his complete record.) When they reminded him of this earlier infraction, the drunk driver responded, "Oh yeah. But thank God she's okay." One of the members of the board was not impressed.

"So by 'okay' you mean not dead."

At trial he was asked over and over by the lawyer what he remembered of that night. Apparently the answer was nothing.

"Do you remember getting into a car with thirty empty beer cans in it?"

"Nope."

"Do you remember striking Mr. Bornstein and Ms. Zinck?"

"Nope."

"Do you remember rolling your SUV?"

"Nope."

"Do you remember running away from the police then being caught?"

"Nope. Nope. Nope."

Each time he answered in the negative, he gave his head a definitive shake, as if trying to leave no doubt in the jury's mind that he should be found not guilty by reason of amnesia.

The drunk driver faced a variety of charges, each with its own potential sentence. The manslaughter he was charged with carried a maximum twenty-year sentence. Vehicular homicide, ten. Leaving the scene of an accident, operating under the influence, and possession of a class D substance together brought his potential sentence to forty years in state prison. He received a three-and-a-half-year sentence in the Essex County House of Correction. He was out in thirty-three months.

I believe in redemption. I really do. I have to. I've parented two teenaged boys. I am a pediatrician with a large adolescent practice. I know kids make mistakes. I believe in second chances. But this drunk driver had his second chance; he blew it. That doesn't mean I hate him. When I argued before the judges for a lengthy sentence, I wasn't seeking revenge. I was looking for justice.

<hr />

There are only two ways I can travel to and from work. On one route I pass the cemetery where Trista is buried. Her grave marker is a large granite heart with a photograph of her and her family at Disney World embedded in it. Soggy teddy bears, deflated balloons, and dead bouquets clutter the space around it. Trista's famous quote is engraved along the bottom of the tombstone: LIFE'S TOO SHORT TO BE SAD. The other route I can choose takes me past the scene of the accident itself. A makeshift shrine with photographs of Trista, ribbons, and candles marks the spot. They are daily reminders of our loss and what Neil has overcome. I don't dwell on the past. It dwells on me. Driving by these two scenes evokes many emotions in me; but hatred isn't one of them. I do feel the injustice of the drunk driver breathing air that Trista cannot. But I don't feel it as hatred. I feel it as pity and hopelessness and amazement that there is a human being on this earth who so completely doesn't get it.

41

The Three White Envelopes

BECAUSE WE WERE VICTIMS in a criminal case, the district attorney's office assigned us a victim/witness advocate. We have had seven or eight different ones over the years, changing as they retire or move on to other jobs. We were also assigned a new advocate each time the drunk driver changed correction facilities.

I have always appreciated the advocates. They accompanied us to every hearing, trial, and sentencing. The court can be a very intimidating place. While waiting for our case to be called, we have been witnesses to all manner of tragedy. We unwittingly were at the trial of an elderly man accused of poisoning a toddler at a barbecue at his home. We witnessed part of the trial of a doctor who allegedly walked into his wife's hospital room and shot her dead along with her lover. Prisoners in orange jumpsuits, their wrists manacled, shuffled within inches of us, their shackles clanging with each step. Although our advocates couldn't really do anything about who was in court with us, I was grateful for their experienced presence.

They weren't just hand-holders though. They explained the system to us as we went along: the role of the grand jury in the indictment of the drunk driver; the array of possible charges that could be brought against him and the advantages and limitations of each; the range of sentences possible. The learning curve was very steep, and the district attorney did not always have the time to explain all the details to us himself. There was also an endless number of Latin terms to puzzle through. The *voir dire*: a fancy phrase for jury selection. The *colloquy*: the process by which the judge ensures that the person charged understands the rights he is giving up if he changes his plea to guilty. *Ex parte*: the sidebars in which the lawyers conferred with the judge, hands over microphone to mask their words. It was a bewildering new world to be mastered quickly. The advocates helped us cram.

They tried not to let anything surprise us. They didn't want us reading about developments in the case with the rest of the region in the *Boston Globe*. They called us on the phone whenever the drunk driver's lawyer made any motions. Whether he asked for a parole hearing or requested to be moved to a different corrective facility, the advocates made sure we knew first.

They are always happy to answer any questions we have about the drunk driver. From their answers we learned what classes he took in jail, what infractions he committed while there, and who came to visit him. Sometimes it felt voyeuristic. But I guess he surrendered certain rights when he took a life, left the scene, violated his probation.

Now, eight years after the crash, our contacts with the victim/witness advocates are few and far between. Often it seems that just when our lives are getting back on track and back to normal, the envelopes appear. Always three: one for Saul, one for me, one for Neil (even though he hasn't lived at this address for years). All with the same telltale blue coat of arms of the Commonwealth of

Massachusetts in the upper left-hand corner. All with Victim Service Unit typed in the return address. My heart always drops when I see them. Those three white envelopes, all the same. I worry that he's been let out of jail—proclaimed free and innocent. Or out on some technicality.

The most recent letter informed us that inmate W92140 had been approved for transfer from minimum security to a prerelease program in Boston. My heart skipped a beat. Were they letting him go? I called and spoke with my latest advocate. I have never met him. We had never spoken before. But he knew all the facts of the case and assured me that the earliest the drunk driver would be released was more than a year away; that he could still serve his entire sentence until 2014.

We will know when his parole hearing comes. The advocates will make sure of that. We've done this before many times. We'll argue for continued incarceration in front of the parole board. We'll write our victim impact statements and read them to the board. I have a drawer full of them now, including the one I wrote from Neil's hospital room at Anna Jaques.

After all these years I am quite used to this roller coaster of a judicial ride. But the predictable is still painful. The prosaic still smarts. Try as I might not to allow the drunk driver to rule my emotions, the sight of those three white envelopes showing up in my mailbox, all the same, brings me to my knees every time.

42

Of Grief and Gratitude

"THE ROAD TO RECOVERY after a traumatic brain injury is not linear." Those words were spoken by Marilyn Lash, a publisher of books on brain injury, at a conference put on by the Brain Injury Association of Massachusetts a few years ago. Truer words were never spoken.

When I first learned of the accident …

"Where are the kids?"

"They should have gotten to your house by now."

"Two kids were hit on Ferry Road,"

… I was stunned into disbelief. I ran all the way to the crash scene, praying that Mary was wrong. That it wasn't our kids. That Neil was all right.

And he was all right. Or so I thought. In the span of one breath I went from gratitude to grief. Breathe in. He's alive. Breathe out. He's confused. Breathe in. Thank God. Breathe out. Oh no. Breathe in. "He's gonna be just fine." Breathe out. But will he still be Neil?

As glad as I was that Neil had survived the crash, I was still, even that very first night, worried about his future. His personality. His IQ. As grateful as I was, I still grieved for his losses. And with good reason. Those are the very aspects of his life that are affected to this day.

But with that grief came guilt. For even as I stood over my shivering son in the emergency room at Brigham and Women's Hospital, wishing I could warm him with my coat, my body, I thought of Mary—of how she would love to feel Trista cold and shivering instead of just plain cold.

And later, when Neil was screaming at me, I thought of Mary. Of how she'd give anything to hear Trista's voice again. Even if she were yelling; even if she were angry or confused.

The road is not linear, indeed.

It can take a very long time to realize all the effects of a traumatic brain injury. It can be a very long time before you realize that your son, who looks so perfectly fine on the outside, isn't really so perfectly fine.

It was easy to feel gratitude when Neil opened his eyes and said, "Hi, Mom." It was harder to feel grateful five years later when he's still seeing a therapist and taking Lexapro and smoking cigarettes.

For years I felt like I was standing in the shadow of the other mother: the one whose child was killed in the same accident that injured mine. To even use the word *grief* when talking about Neil's losses felt fraudulent, like I was hijacking the very word from someone who knew true loss. Whose loss was terminal.

But as time has passed—as Neil has continued with his memory loss, learning disabilities, and personality changes—I have owned my grief. Spread out in it and made myself at home. Year after year I attend the Brain Injury Association's conferences. I am comfortable there. I feel like people understand me there. We get one another in this disenfranchised grief. I always learn something new at the conference. Every year I feel like I understand Neil and his injury a little bit more.

For years after the accident, Mary and I went to court, over and over. We stood side by side before judge after judge, telling our respective stories, chronicling our individual loss. Our parallel if uneven tragedies were held up for display over and over. I stated my disclaimer up front. I haven't suffered like she has. The whole time I was writing my impact statement, I was making comparisons. Myself to Mary. Neil to Trista. Every time, my own losses came up short.

Sometimes Mary and David spoke ahead of me. Occasionally I went first. Sometimes they read from prepared statements, but often they just spoke from the heart. They told of memories: shopping trips and Girl Scout camps, school plays and holding hands—all the things they would miss about their daughter.

"What yardstick do we use to measure that?" they asked.

But I need a yardstick too. It may be different from Mary's. With tinier notches perhaps. Or at least spaced more widely apart. But I have things to measure, too. Neil's pain from fractures and blood. From stitches and metal and scars. His slow progress through physical therapy. His struggles with memory loss, depression, anxiety, and learning difficulties. His pain from the loss of his girlfriend and having his whole world shattered in an instant. Neil wonders too what is a result of the accident and what is just his personality. But he's coming to grips with the fact that it doesn't really matter. It's just who he is now.

I believe now that grief has many faces. There is no one right way to behave in the face of it. No correct approach. There is no one set of circumstances that warrants it as a reaction and no specific set of behaviors that qualifies as appropriate in response to it. It just is. Mary's rawness. My reserve. Her guts and grit. My reticence and guilt. I have come to understand that the whole gamut of human emotion is legitimate when it comes to coping with loss. Even how we define our loss is personal and valid, different as it may be for each of us. I'm not sure where I stand in this hierarchy of grief. I may not be on the top rung, but I'm not on the bottom either. I just know that I belong on the ladder.

For years I bounced around between grief and gratitude and guilt. But over time, all three of these "Gs" have given way to another "G" on this very nonlinear road, and that is grace. We've had our struggles as a family, but we're here. We are survivors. Neil may not be the same person he was before the accident, but who really is the same person he or she was at seventeen? Neil has his limitations, but don't we all? I don't want to focus on what Neil might have accomplished without his brain injury. Instead I want to celebrate everything he has accomplished with it. Despite it. That is grace.

I also choose not to make my life all about the drunk driver's punishment. I had to show up. I had to voice my opinion to the judge about what I thought that punishment should be. But I can't make my peace depend on justice. I can't make my happiness be about that. Again, there is grace.

I don't believe in fate. I believe we deal with the hand we are given. We make our own meaning. We find our own grace. Grace as a kind of acceptance. Grace as thankfulness. Grace as new meaning for a changed life.

Afterword

THE ACCIDENT HAS BECOME a defining part of our family's narrative. Tragedies can break families. Ours is not broken. I am proud of the way we came together. I am proud that Dan's immediate reaction to the news of the crash was "get me home." There was no question that I would take time off from my job at the community health center. The vastness of staff led to many frustrations with my job there, but it also meant that there were many hands to take over caring for my patients while I cared for Neil. Saul's role, after those precarious first days in the ICU, went back to being chief provider for us. Our rock.

As a doctor I am ashamed of how much I didn't know about brain injury. I didn't know fundamental things, like that traumatic brain injury can cause an organic type of depression. I'm embarrassed to say that it was Neil's lawyer who told me this. We were preparing for trial.

"We have to be sure the jury understands that Neil's depression was caused by his brain injury, not by losing Trista."

I was a bit taken aback. It was the first time I had considered this. His lawyer was top-notch. I trusted her completely. But surely Neil *was* grieving for Trista. Was she asking me to lie on the witness stand?

After that day in court, I went home and did some research. I learned how wrong I was in thinking Neil was simply mourning for his lost love. Of course his lawyer wasn't asking me to lie. Neil's depression *was* organic. All the areas of the brain that regulate emotional stability were areas that were injured in the crash: frontal lobes, right temporal horn, the amygdala. Contusions, hemorrhages, fractures, volume loss. All in the right places to disturb the ability to modulate feelings. To be happy. What a fool I was.

But I wasn't the only doctor in the field naïve to the long-term subtle deficits people with traumatic brain injury suffer. When Chuck/Mitch told us, "He's gonna be just fine," he believed it. He is an intensivist, geared toward the acute. In his world a patient who knows who he is, can blink on command, and can accurately identify how many fingers are being held up in front of his face is worlds better than the lot he sees every day. Neil didn't need a stint in a rehab facility. But he did need physical therapy, mental health support, antidepressants, and modified educational plans, none of which were provided for or even suggested at discharge, all of which I subsequently arranged myself. I was not the only one ignorant of what the future could hold for a brain-injured boy.

I've tried to compensate for these deficiencies in my knowledge of brain injury by obsessively reading all that I can on the subject. I subscribe to a cite-tracking news-alert system, receiving almost daily articles about all aspects of head trauma and brain injury:

"Efficacy and Safety of Dopamine Agonists in Traumatic Brain Injury."

"Time and Dose Dependent Neuroprotective Effects of Sex Steroid Hormones on Inflammatory Cytokines after Traumatic Brain Injury."

"Is Traumatic Brain Injury a Risk Factor for Schizophrenia?"

I get them all, trying to become something of an expert in a field I knew so little about until it struck at home.

I've since written articles on various aspects of brain injury for local publications as well as national pediatric newsletters. I edit a column in *Heads Up*, the Brain Injury Association of Massachusetts' quarterly newsletter. I've blogged about the new concussion guidelines for young athletes.

I use every available avenue I have to get out the word about traumatic brain injury. It's the signature wound for our soldiers coming back from Iraq and Afghanistan. The frequency and severity of head trauma in professional sports has prompted new rules for them as well. The nation watches with amazement and respect as Gabby Giffords recovers from her traumatic brain injury. We can only guess what she and her family are going through. I am kindred spirits with all the soldiers and athletes and victims and families who have been through the TBI experience. I am at once their comrade and their advocate.

I also address audiences about the subtle and not-so-subtle effects of brain injury. I am in the Ambassador Program, a speakers' bureau for the Brain Injury Association of Massachusetts. The program aspires to put a human face on a grim statistic: One and a half million people in the United States suffer from brain injury each year. That's 2 percent of the population. That's a brain injury every twenty-three seconds. There are five million children and adults living with long-term disabilities as a result. I speak to Rotary Clubs, Kiwanis Clubs, and Lions Clubs. I've spoken to college students and high school classes. I've spoken during Alcohol Awareness week and given pre-prom talks. I was the keynote speaker last fall for the Pediatric Brain Injury Conference put on by the Brain Injury Association of Massachusetts (BIA-MA). In just one week, at the end of this month, I will have attended two brain injury conferences, one sponsored by BIA-MA and one at Boston University. I will have lectured at the Trauma Care Symposium at the Lahey Clinic in Boston and spoken to 150 high school students, members of the Students against Destructive Decisions (SADD) chapter in North Attleboro. This has become not just part of my day and part of my work but also part of who I am. In the book world it's called platform. In my world it's my passion.

In the years since the accident, my creative writing has also evolved. The short stories I wrote always had medical themes. That's my world. "Write what you know," as they say. But the subjects and motifs have narrowed into sharp focus for me now. My roles as mother, physician, and writer have merged into a life of purpose, passion, and prose. To riff on a phrase of Descartes: I write, therefore I am.

I will always be a mother: checking in with my sons, helping them move and move on, cheering their successes, shouldering their disappointments. I will continue to work: the doctoring, the taking care of babies, working with families, learning about head injury, lecturing on what I've gleaned. And, of course, I will write about it all, putting pen to paper as I try to explore this world and my place in it.

It has been almost ten years since the crash. Neil has been through a lot. We all have. Although we haven't come through the ordeal unscathed, we have come through. And we've done it together, as a family.

Five years after the accident, Neil came home from a trip to Israel with a present for me: a necklace engraved with the Hebrew words *L'dor Va'dor*, which means "from generation to generation." The words were straight out of our Jewish prayer book and are spoken every Sabbath. Neil knew those words well from his many hours in synagogue.

"Thank you, Neil. It's beautiful."

Neil beamed, clearly pleased that I liked his gift so well.

"I read your essay on the computer," he told me.

Say what? I was a bit taken aback. I thought Neil had chosen these words to engrave based on the Jewish prayer. I had no idea he'd read my essay. I'd never exactly invited Neil to read my work. Then again, I hadn't discouraged him either. They were right there on the computer. Saved documents in Microsoft Word. No password required. As personal essays go, the piece Neil had read wasn't particularly personal. But it also wasn't something I would normally share with my son. Once again I realized that my son had learned something about me that he wouldn't have gotten otherwise.

People ask me all the time, "Does Neil know you're writing a book?" "Has he read it?" and "What does he think?" The answer is he does know and he has read it. We have supported each other through its writing, submission, publication. He is proud of me, as I am of him.

The truth is Neil wants to get the word out about brain injuries too. The truth is he understands what it's like to have problems no one else can see.

In college Neil had wanted to play soccer. We were told by his neurosurgeon at the time that he should wait at least a year before engaging in contact sports. I was so disappointed for him. Later that year I was attending a Grand Rounds lecture on traumatic brain injury held at Lawrence General Hospital. The speaker was William Meehan, director of the Sports Concussion Clinic at Children's Hospital Boston. After the lecture I spoke with him, describing Neil's injuries: subarachnoid hemorrhage, subdural bleeds, frontal lobe contusions, fractured skull. I asked him what he thought about Neil playing soccer in college. He advised against it—not that semester, not that year, not ever. His lecture had been about sports concussions, but his advice applied to any brain injury.

"The brain doesn't know how it was injured, Carolyn," he told me.

As it turned out, Neil never tried out for the soccer team. While we were worried about his head, he was worried about his leg. He was afraid he would rebreak it if he played soccer. He even worried about playing hacky sack.

The summer after his first year of college, a year and a half after the accident, he rented a beach house with some friends. One day he called me from his cell phone, all excited.

"Mom, I jumped!"

I thought I had misheard him at first.

"You what?"

"I jumped!"

207

He explained that he and his friends were leapfrogging from rock to rock at the seashore and he suddenly realized that, without thinking, he too was jumping. Not only that, but his leg didn't hurt to do it. It was holding him up and not rebreaking. This was such a major milestone for Neil.

For most kids his age, this was a time characteristically marked by a feeling of immortality. I work every day with teenagers who are immune to my messages about seat belts and condoms and designated drivers. This is the mind-set of the teenager and young adult: Other people get into accidents, fall, get hurt. This cannot happen to me. In their minds they will live forever. But here was my son who came so close to losing his life that he's afraid of having a seizure, he's afraid to *jump*, for God's sake. He felt none of the invincibility that usually defines this stage in life.

Neil also wanted to help other people avoid what he had suffered, but he did it on his own terms. He didn't join the SADD group at his high school, newly formed after his accident. He didn't want to drop the first puck at a hockey game raising funds for a scholarship in Trista's name. The Newburyport Police would all be there. Neil was certainly not ready to face the detective from the accident reconstruction team who wanted twenty-five hairs from his head.

He did help put together a video on underage drinking and drunk driving with his friend and mentor, Anna Smulowitz, to be used in the high schools and by local police to discourage those practices. He showed up in court infrequently but as much as he could, seeking just sentencing for the drunk driver from the judge. Even when he wasn't physically there, he wrote his own victim impact statements for the judge. And he still wants to learn about other people with brain injuries.

One night Neil was visiting us and we all were watching a biopic on Mohammed Ali. At a commercial during the show, Neil said, "I hope Scal retires." He was referring to Brian Scalabrine, the Boston Celtics forward who, that year, was sitting on the bench after suffering three concussions in one season. Neil understood the risk he would be taking if he returned to play: the risk that another concussion might be life-threatening. He was afraid for this player. He didn't want him to take that risk. He can relate to people with traumatic brain injuries.

Neil has a friend named Emily whom he has known since the third grade. She was diagnosed with a brain tumor when she was a little girl. She was told at her local hospital that her tumor was inoperable, but her parents took her to Mount Sinai Hospital in New York, where they treated her despite all the risks. She survived. She is legally blind and walks with a limp and suffers crippling headaches at times, but she is Neil's age and is alive.

Neil and Emily had lost touch with each other for a number of years until, a few years back, Neil heard Emily being interviewed on WBUR about her amazing story of survival. She was a freshman at Harvard University, majoring in mathematics. Neil called her up right away.

"I heard you on the radio," he told her.

"I read all about you in the newspapers last year," she said.

Since that telephone reunion, they have become good friends again. They share a love of music. Neil plays piano and guitar. Emily's father is a professional musician. Emily sometimes played on stage with her parents, a popular local band called The Crocketts. Neil and Emily both love higher education and mathematics. When Neil fell in love with the book *Flatland*, a novel of mathematical fiction, he described it enthusiastically to Emily, who, of course, could not see to read it. Not finding it on books on tape, Neil spent an entire summer recording himself reading the book. He recently gave the CD he'd recorded to his friend.

They also share their experience of brain injury. Emily has suffered longer and harder than Neil, but Neil understands her in a way few others can.

Though he isn't the same person he was before the crash, the "new Neil" is well on his way. He is enrolled in a PhD program in mathematics education and hopes the advanced degree will help him land a job teaching at another private high school or maybe even college. He has all kinds of hopes and dreams for his life and talents to offer. He is looking forward to tutoring during graduate school. He wants to be a teaching assistant. He would like to be active coaching high school athletes or helping out with theater productions.

I've thought a lot about how to end this book. How do I end a book about one of the dearest people in the world to me? How do I end what has at times taken every ounce of my strength to simply show up at the page? The writer Red Smith once said, "Writing is easy. All you do is sit down at the typewriter and open up a vein." Obviously Red was writing in another era: an era of Royals and Remingtons and Underwoods. But the sentiment is timeless. Writing and bleeding have at times felt very much the same to me.

But Neil's story, in many ways, is just beginning. His future, though informed by a very arduous and obstacle-filled past, is brightening. It is a new start for us all.

Book Group Discussion Points

- Guilt is a major theme in *Crash*. Under what circumstances does guilt emerge in the author? Is the guilt justified?
- In "The Offender" what is the importance of the distinction between anger and hatred? Why is one acceptable and the other not?
- In the prologue the crash is identified as a dividing line, separating the before and after. What other dividing lines emerge as the story moves on?
- In "Please, Please, Please" the author makes a distinction between faith and fatalism. What is the difference between these two concepts, and why is that difference important?
- Grief is another overarching motif in the book. Is grief the same thing as bereavement? Or is grief in the eye of the beholder, so to speak? Is there any grief that is not valid?
- In "POV" Neil's learning of Trista's death is seen from two different points of view: mother and son. How does our point of view color our perception of events? Consider age, timing, event, and circumstances.

- How does the way each parent learned of the events shape his or her ultimate interpretation of outcomes?
- How is Dr. Roy-Bornstein supported by and failed by her medical community?
- The family struggles with its interactions with the media. What role do modern media play in private tragedy?
- What role does the author's medical background play in how she reacts to her son's accident?
- Define grace. What role does grace play in the family's healing?

Acknowledgments

I HAVE TO THANK the members of my writing group—Lisa Mahoney, Shelley Carpenter, and Margaret Flaherty—for their tireless willingness to read essay after essay, chapter after chapter, and rewrite after rewrite, offering feedback on everything from the placement of a comma to the impact of a word. Ladies, this was truly a group effort.

To my husband, Saul, and my son Dan: Thank you for being my shared memory in this journey and my eye to the details that escaped me in my fear and angst.

To my agent, Daniel Bial, and my editor, Mary Norris, this book would not have been possible without your confidence, dedication, and work on my behalf. Thanks for believing in me.

To Shannon Berning, I am grateful to you for seeing the book that was trying to emerge from the one I was originally writing.

To Mary Zinck, the "other mother" in this story. We've been in this together from the beginning. I have learned much from your brave, no-holds-barred attitude.

Most of all, to Neil: You are the hero of this book and of my life. Your ability to grow, to learn, to adapt, and to teach has been an inspiration to me. I am not a good enough writer to put into words my love for you. Just know that it is there, constant, certain, everlasting.

About the Author

DR. CAROLYN ROY-BORNSTEIN is an award-winning writer who is also a practicing pediatrician. She writes a monthly health column, "Pediatric Points," in the national newsletter *Pediatrics for Parents*. She is also an ambassador with the Brain Injury Association of Massachusetts (BIA-MA), giving speeches to civic groups, schools, and businesses. She lives in Massachusetts.

Copyright © 2010 by Carmine Gallo. All rights reserved. Printed in the United States of America. Except as permitted under the United States Copyright Act of 1976, no part of this publication may be reproduced or distributed in any form or by any means, or stored in a database or retrieval system, without the prior written permission of the publisher.

24 25   LCR   21 20 19

ISBN   978-0-07-163608-7
MHID   0-07-163608-0

e-ISBN   978-0-07-163675-9
e-MHID   0-07-163675-7

The Presentation Secrets of Steve Jobs is in no way authorized, prepared, approved, or endorsed by Steve Jobs and is not affiliated with or endorsed by any of his past or present organizations.

Library of Congress Cataloging-in-Publication Data

Gallo, Carmine.
      The presentation secrets of Steve Jobs : how to be insanely great in front of any
      audience / Carmine Gallo.
            p.   cm
      Includes bibliographical references.
      ISBN 978-0-07-163608-7 (alk. paper)
      1. Business presentations.   2. Business communication.   3. Jobs, Steven,
      1955–   I. Title.

      HF5718.22.G35 2010
      658.4'52—dc22   2009008623

Interior design by Think Design LLC

McGraw-Hill books are available at special quantity discounts to use as premiums and sales promotions, or for use in corporate training programs. To contact a representative please e-mail us at bulksales@mcgraw-hill.com.

This book is printed on acid-free paper.

The Presentation
Secrets of
Steve Jobs

How to Be
Insanely Great
in Front of Any Audience

Carmine Gallo
Columnist, Businessweek.com

New York   Chicago   San Francisco   Lisbon   London   Madrid   Mexico City
Milan   New Delhi   San Juan   Seoul   Singapore   Sydney   Toronto

To my father, Franco, an insanely great man

who has lived an extraordinary life

CONTENTS

ACKNOWLEDGMENTS

This book is a collaborative effort. The content took shape with the help of family, colleagues, and the amazing staff at McGraw-Hill. Big thanks to my editor, John Aherne, for his enthusiasm and counsel, and to Kenya Henderson, for making it all happen! McGraw-Hill design, marketing, and public relations staff are among the best in the book publishing industry. I'm honored they share my excitement about the subject.

My wife, Vanessa, manages our business at Gallo Communications Group. She worked tirelessly to prepare the manuscript. How she found the time between juggling our business and caring for our two children is beyond the scope of "mere mortals."

Many thanks to my editor at BusinessWeek.com, Nick Leiber, who always seems to find a way to improve my columns. As always, thank you, Ed Knappman, my encouraging agent at New England Publishing Associates. Ed's knowledge and insight are second to none.

I owe thanks to my parents, Franco and Giuseppina, for their unwavering support. Thank you, Tino, Donna, Francesco, Nick, Patty, Ken, and many other close friends and family members who understood why I couldn't be around or why I had to skip golf on weekends. Back to the course!

My girls, Josephine and Lela. You are Daddy's inspiration. All your patience during Daddy's absence will be rewarded with an insanely great visit to Chuck E. Cheese.

How to Be Insanely Great in Front of Any Audience

A person can have the greatest idea in the world— completely different and novel—but if that person can't convince enough other people, it doesn't matter.

—GREGORY BERNS

The concepts in this book will help you win over an audience in ways that you've never imagined. I've seen it happen. I've watched business professionals around the world adopt these techniques to win multi-million dollar accounts. I've met Apple Store employees who use the book to learn to pitch new products on the showroom floor. Thousands of readers in North America, Asia, Europe, and South America have reinvented their presentations with these techniques. If you read this book and study its examples, your presentations will never be the same. And that's the point. Your customers, employees, investors, and partners are bored to death with the same old lackluster style of presentation design and delivery. But a Steve Jobs presentation is unlike anything you've ever seen. It informs, educates, and entertains.

It illuminates and inspires. Best of all, because Steve Jobs does presentations "by the book," you can adopt his template to rock the house in your very next presentation!

Since *The Presentation Secrets of Steve Jobs* was first published, many individuals and businesses have used this book to change the way they tell their own stories. Those case studies alone can, well, fill an entire book. There's the story of a major medical device manufacturer whose marketing team has completely overhauled its presentations based on this book. There's the story of a global energy company whose leaders are using the book to change the way they pitch foreign governments. There's the story of the law firm managing partner who bought the book for every one of the firm's attorneys. There's the story of the CEO for a major European media conglomerate who read the book and admonished his sales staff, "no more bullet points!" There's the story of the sales team at a popular social networking site who used the book to pitch their company prior to launching a hugely successful IPO. There's also the story of the prominent technology analyst who called Steve Jobs's business rival and urged him to read the book. (The CEO wasn't pleased to get the tip so the analyst added the caveat, "I think every CEO should read it.") There are the stories of MBA students at Stanford, Berkeley, UCLA, and other universities who are learning ideas that are not taught in school. This book has touched professionals in every industry and in nearly every part of the world. It will touch you and transform the way you tell your brand story.

Why study Steve Jobs? The Apple cofounder is the most captivating communicator on the world stage. No one else comes close. A Jobs presentation unleashes a rush of dopamine into the brains of his audience. Some people go to great lengths to get this hit, even spending the night in freezing temperatures to ensure the best seat at one of his speeches. When they don't get that buzz, they go through withdrawal. How else do you explain the fact that some fans threatened to protest Jobs's absence from a conference he had keynoted for years? That's what happened when Apple announced that Jobs would not deliver his traditional keynote presentation at Macworld Expo in 2009. (Apple also announced that it would be the last year in which the company would participate in this annual trade show produced by Boston-based IDG World Expo.) Due to health-related reasons, Jobs has done fewer presentations than in the past but he still manages to make appearances for major announcements like he did for the iPad2 in March 2011 and for the unveiling of Apple's "cloud" strategy in June 2011. Even so, there are fewer and fewer Steve Jobs keynotes. As reporter Jon Fortt[1] wrote: "The sun is setting on the first generation of rebellious whiz kids who invented the PC, commercialized the Internet, and grew their companies into powerhouses."

A Steve Jobs keynote presentation is an extraordinary experience and, since there might be fewer opportunities to see a master at a craft he has honed for more than three decades, I wrote this book to capture the best of Jobs's presentations and to reveal, for the first time, the exact techniques he uses to inspire his audience. Best of all, you can learn his skills and adopt his techniques to blow away your audience, giving people a high they will crave again and again.

Watch a Macworld keynote—"Stevenotes," as they are known among the Mac faithful—and you will begin to reconsider everything about your current presentations: what you say, how you say it, and what your audience sees when you say it. I wrote a column about Steve Jobs and his presentation skills for BusinessWeek.com. It quickly became hugely popular around the world (Daniel Lyons, aka "Fake Steve Jobs," even featured it). It appealed to Mac and PC owners alike who wanted to improve the way they sell themselves and their ideas. A select few readers had seen Jobs in person, while others had watched video of Jobs online, but the vast majority of readers had never seen him give a keynote. What they learned was eye-opening and forced many of them to go back to the proverbial drawing board.

For educational purposes, use YouTube as a complement to the techniques revealed in the pages to follow. At this writing, there are more than 70,000 clips of Steve Jobs on YouTube, a far larger number than for most other high-profile CEOs. In this case, YouTube offers a rare opportunity to read about a particular individual, learn about specific techniques that make him successful, and see those techniques in action.

What you'll learn is that Jobs is a magnetic pitchman who sells his ideas with a flair that turns prospects into customers and customers into evangelists. He has charisma, defined by the German sociologist Max Weber as "a certain quality of an individual personality, by virtue of which he is set apart from ordinary people and treated as endowed with supernatural, superhuman, or at least specifically exceptional powers or qualities."² Jobs has become superhuman among his most loyal fans. But Weber got one thing wrong. Weber believed that charisma was not "accessible to the ordinary person." Once you learn *exactly* how Jobs crafts and delivers one of his famous presentations, you will realize that these exceptional powers are available to you as well. If you adopt just *some* of his techniques, yours will stand out from the legions of mediocre presentations delivered on any given day. Your competitors and colleagues will look like amateurs in comparison.

"Presentations have become the de facto business communication tool," writes presentation design guru Nancy Duarte in *Slide:ology*. "Companies are started, products are launched, climate systems are saved—possibly based on the quality of presentations. Likewise, ideas, endeavors, and even careers can be cut short due to ineffective communication. Out of the millions of presentations delivered each day, only a small percentage are delivered well."³

Duarte transformed Al Gore's 35 mm slides into the award-winning documentary *An Inconvenient Truth*. As with Al Gore, who sits on Apple's board, Steve Jobs uses presentations as a transformative experience. Both men are revolutionizing business communications and have something to teach us, but where Gore has *one* famous presentation repeated a thousand times, Jobs has been giving awe-inspiring presentations since the launch of the Macintosh in 1984. In fact, the Macintosh launch, which you will read about in the pages to follow, is still one of the most dramatic presentations in the history of

Why Not Me?

When I appeared on CNBC's "The Big Idea with Donny Deutsch," I was struck by the host's infectious energy. Deutsch offered his viewers this piece of advice: "When you see someone who has turned his passion into a profit, ask yourself, 'Why not me?' "[6] I urge you to do the same. When you read about Jobs in the pages to follow, ask yourself, "Why not me? Why can't I energize my listeners like Jobs?" The answer is, "You can." As you'll learn, Jobs is not a natural. He works at it. Although he always had a theatrical flair, his style has evolved and improved over the years. Jobs is relentlessly focused on improvement, laboring over every slide, every demo, and every detail of a presentation. Each presentation tells a story, and every slide reveals a scene. Jobs is a showman and, as with all great actors, he rehearses until he gets it right. "Be a yardstick of quality," Jobs once said. "Some people aren't used to an environment where excellence is expected."[7] There are no shortcuts to excellence. Presenting like Jobs will require planning and practice, but if you are committed to reaching the top, there is no better teacher than Apple's master showman. (See Figure 1.)

Performance in Three Acts

The Presentation Secrets of Steve Jobs is structured like one of Jobs's favorite presentation metaphors: a three-act play. In fact, a Steve Jobs presentation is very much like a dramatic play—a finely crafted and well-rehearsed performance that informs, entertains, and inspires. When Jobs introduced the video iPod on October 12, 2005, he chose the California Theatre in San Jose as his stage. It was an appropriate setting as Steve divided the product introductions into three acts, "like every classic story." In act 1, he introduced the new iMac G5 with built-in video camera. Act 2 kicked off the release of the fifth-generation iPod, which played video content for the first time. In act 3, he talked about iTunes 6, with the news that ABC would make television shows available for iTunes and the new video iPod. Jobs even introduced jazz legend Wynton Marsalis as an encore.

Figure 1 Apple's master showman turns presentations into theatrical experiences.

Photo by Justin Sullivan/Getty Images

In keeping with Jobs's metaphor of a presentation as a classic story, *The Presentation Secrets of Steve Jobs* is divided into three acts:

» **Act 1: Create the Story.** The seven chapters—or scenes—in this section will give you practical tools to craft an exciting story behind your brand. A strong story will give you the confidence and ability to win over your audience.

» **Act 2: Deliver the Experience.** In these six scenes, you will learn practical tips to turn your presentations into visually appealing and "must-have" experiences.

» **Act 3: Refine and Rehearse.** The remaining five scenes will tackle topics such as body language, verbal delivery, and making "scripted" presentations sound natural and conversational. Even your choice of wardrobe will be addressed. You will learn why mock turtlenecks, jeans, and running shoes are suitable for Jobs but could mean the end of your career.

Short intermissions divide the acts. These intermissions contain nuggets of great information culled from the latest findings in cognitive research and presentation design. These findings will help you take your presentations to an entirely new level.

What Are You Really Selling?

Jobs is "the master at taking something that might be considered boring—a hunk of electronic hardware—and enveloping it in a story that made it compellingly dramatic," writes Alan Deutschman in *The Second Coming of Steve Jobs*.[8] Only a handful of leaders whom I have had the pleasure of meeting have this skill, the ability to turn seemingly boring items into exciting brand stories. Cisco CEO John Chambers is one of them. Chambers does not sell routers and switches that make up the backbone of the Internet. What Chambers *does* sell is human connections that change the way we live, work, play, and learn.

The most inspiring communicators share this quality—the ability to create something meaningful out of esoteric or everyday products. Starbucks CEO Howard Schultz does not sell coffee. He sells a "third place" between work and home. Financial guru Suze Orman does not sell trusts and mutual funds. She sells the dream of financial freedom. In the same way, Jobs does not sell computers. He sells tools to unleash human potential. Throughout this book, ask yourself, "What am I really selling?" Remember, your widget doesn't inspire. Show me how your widget improves my life, and you've won me over. Do it in a way that entertains me, and you'll have created a true evangelist.

Along the way, you'll also discover that Steve Jobs is motivated by a messianic zeal to change the world, to put a "dent in the universe." In order for these techniques to work, you must cultivate a profound sense of mission. If you are passionate about your topic, you're 80 percent closer to developing the magnetism that Jobs has. From the age of twenty-one when Jobs cofounded Apple with his friend Steve Wozniak, Jobs fell in love with the vision of how personal computing would change society, education, and entertainment. His passion was contagious, infecting everyone in his presence. That passion comes across in every presentation.

We all have passions that drive us. The purpose of this book is to help you capture that passion and turn it into a story so mesmerizing that people will want to help you achieve your vision. You see, it's quite possible that your ideas or products vastly improve the lives of your customers—from computers, to automobiles, to financial services, to products that create a cleaner environment—but the greatest product in the world will be useless without a strong brand evangelist to promote it. If you cannot get people to care, your product will never stand a chance of success. Your audience will not care, they will not understand, nor will they be interested. People do not pay attention to boring things. Do not let your ideas die because you failed to present them in a way that sparked the imagination of your listeners. Use Jobs's techniques to reach the hearts and the minds of everyone you hope to influence.

As Jobs often says to kick off a presentation, "Now let's get started."

ACT I

Create the Story

C reating the story, the plot, is the first step to selling your ideas with power, persuasion, and charisma. Succeeding at this step separates mediocre communicators from extraordinary ones. Most people fail to think through their story. Effective communicators plan effectively, develop compelling messages and headlines, make it easy for their listeners to follow the narrative, and introduce a common enemy to build the drama. The seven chapters—or scenes—in Act 1 will help set the foundation for presentation success. Each scene will be followed by a short summary of specific and tangible lessons you can easily apply today. Let's review the scenes here:

» **SCENE 1: "Plan in Analog."** In this chapter, you will learn how truly great presenters such as Steve Jobs visualize, plan, and create ideas well before they open the presentation software.

» **SCENE 2: "Answer the One Question That Matters Most."** Your listeners are asking themselves one question and one question only: "Why should I care?" Disregard this question, and your audience will dismiss you.

» **SCENE 3: "Develop a Messianic Sense of Purpose."** Steve Jobs was worth more than $100 million by the time he was twenty-five, and it didn't matter to him. Understanding this one fact will help you unlock the secret behind Jobs's extraordinary charisma.

» **SCENE 4: "Create Twitter-Like Headlines."** The social networking site has changed the way we communicate. Developing headlines that fit into 140-character sentences will help you sell your ideas more persuasively.

» **SCENE 5: "Draw a Road Map."** Steve Jobs makes his argument easy to follow by adopting one of the most powerful principles of persuasion: the rule of three.

» **SCENE 6: "Introduce the Antagonist."** Every great Steve Jobs presentation introduces a common villain that the audience can turn against. Once he introduces an enemy, the stage is set for the next scene.

» **SCENE 7: "Reveal the Conquering Hero."** Every great Steve Jobs presentation introduces a hero the audience can rally around. The hero offers a better way of doing something, breaks from the status quo, and inspires people to embrace innovation.

Plan in Analog

**Marketing is really theater.
It's like staging a performance.**

—JOHN SCULLEY

Steve Jobs has built a reputation in the digital world of bits and bytes, but he creates stories in the very old-world tradition of pen and paper. His presentations are theatrical events intended to generate maximum publicity, buzz, and awe. They contain all of the elements of great plays or movies: conflict, resolution, villains, and heroes. And, in line with all great movie directors, Jobs storyboards the plot before picking up a "camera" (i.e., opening the presentation software). It's marketing theater unlike any other.

Jobs is closely involved in every detail of a presentation: writing descriptive taglines, creating slides, practicing demos, and making sure the lighting is just right. Jobs takes nothing for granted. He does what most top presentation designers recommend: he starts on paper. "There's just something about paper and pen and sketching out rough ideas in the 'analog world' in the early stages that seems to lead to more clarity and better, more creative results when we finally get down to representing our ideas digitally," writes Garr Reynolds in *Presentation Zen*.[1]

Design experts, including those who create presentations for Apple, recommend that presenters spend the majority of their time thinking, sketching, and scripting. Nancy Duarte is the genius behind Al Gore's *An Inconvenient Truth*. Duarte suggests that a presenter spend up to ninety hours to create an hour-long presentation that contains thirty slides. However, only one-third of that time should be dedicated to *building* the slides, says Duarte.[2] The first twenty-seven hours are dedicated to researching the topic, collecting input from experts, organizing ideas, collaborating with colleagues, and sketching the structure of the story.

Bullets Kill

Think about what happens when you open PowerPoint. A blank-format slide appears that contains space for words—a title and subtitle. This presents a problem. There are very few words in a Steve Jobs presentation. Now think about the first thing you see in the drop-down menu under Format: Bullets & Numbering. This leads to the second problem. There are no bullet points in a Steve Jobs presentation. The software itself forces you to create a template that represents the exact opposite of what you need to speak like Steve! In fact, as you will learn in later scenes, texts and bullets are the *least* effective way to deliver information intended to be recalled and acted upon. Save your bullet points for grocery lists.

Visually engaging presentations will inspire your audience. And yes, they require a bit of work, especially in the planning phase. As a communications coach, I work with CEOs and other top executives on their media, presentation, and public speaking skills. One of my clients, a start-up entrepreneur, had spent sixty straight days in Bentonville, Arkansas, to score an appointment with Wal-Mart. His technology intrigued company executives, who agreed to a beta test, a trial run. Wal-Mart asked him to present the information to a group of advertisers and top executives. I met with my client over a period of days at the offices of the Silicon Valley venture capital firm that invested in his company. For the first day, we did nothing but sketch the story. No computer and no PowerPoint—just pen and paper (whiteboard, in this case). Eventually we turned the sketches into slide ideas. We needed only five slides for a fifteen-minute presentation. Creating the slides did not take as much time as developing the story. Once we wrote the narrative, designing the slides was easy. Remember, it's the story, *not the slides*, that will capture the imagination of your audience.

The Napkin Test

A picture is the most powerful method for conveying an idea. Instead of booting up your computer, take out a napkin. Some of the most successful business ideas have been sketched on the back of a napkin. One could argue that the napkin has been more important to the world of business ideas than PowerPoint. I used to think that "napkin stories" were just that—stories, from the imagination of journalists. That is until I met Richard Tait, the founder of Cranium. I prepared him for an interview on CNBC. He told me that during a cross-country flight from New York to Seattle, he took out a small cocktail napkin and sketched the idea of a board game in which everyone had a chance to excel in at least one category, a game that would give everyone a chance to shine. Cranium became a worldwide sensation and was later purchased by Hasbro. The original concept was simple enough to write on a tiny airline napkin.

One of the most famous corporate napkin stories involves Southwest Airlines. A lawyer at the time, Herb Kelleher met with one of his clients, Rollin King, at the St. Anthony's Club, in San Antonio. King owned a small charter airline. He wanted to start a low-cost commuter airline that avoided the major hubs and instead served Dallas, Houston, and San Antonio. King sketched three circles, wrote the names of the cities inside, and connected the three—a strikingly simple vision. Kelleher understood immediately. Kelleher signed on as legal counsel (he later became CEO), and the two men founded Southwest Airlines in 1967. King and Kelleher would go on to reinvent airline travel in the United States and build a corporate culture that would earn Southwest's place among the most admired companies in the world. Never underestimate the power of a vision so simple that it can fit on a napkin!

The Story Takes Center Stage

In *Beyond Bullet Points*, Cliff Atkinson stresses, "The single most important thing you can do to dramatically improve your presentations is to have a story to tell *before* you work on your PowerPoint file."[3] Atkinson advocates a three-step storyboard approach to creating presentations:

Writing → Sketching → Producing

Only after writing—scripting—the scenes does he advocate thinking visually about how the slides will look. "To write a script, you need to momentarily set aside PowerPoint design issues like fonts, colors, backgrounds, and slide transitions. Although it might sound counterintuitive, when you write a script first, you actually expand your visual possibilities, because writing defines your purpose before you start designing. A script unlocks the undiscovered power of PowerPoint as a visual storytelling tool in ways that might surprise and delight you and your audiences."[4] With a completed script in hand, you'll be ready to sketch and "produce" the experience. The script, however, must come first.

Nine Elements of Great Presentations

Persuasive presentation scripts contain nine common elements. Think about incorporating each of these components before you open the presentation program, whether you work in PowerPoint, Keynote, or any other design software. Some of these concepts will be explored in more detail later, but for now keep them in mind as you develop your ideas.

HEADLINE

What is the one big idea you want to leave with your audience? It should be short (140 characters or less), memorable, and written in the subject-verb-object sequence. When Steve Jobs unveiled the iPhone, he exclaimed, "Today Apple reinvents the phone!"[5] That's a headline. Headlines grab the attention of your audience and give people a reason to listen. Read *USA Today* for ideas. Here are some examples from America's most popular daily newspaper:

> » "Apple's Skinny MacBook Is Fat with Features"
> » "Apple Unleashes Leopard Operating System"
> » "Apple Shrinks iPod"

PASSION STATEMENT

Aristotle, the father of public speaking, believed that successful speakers must have "pathos," or passion for their subject. Very few communicators express a sense of excitement about their topic. Steve Jobs exudes an almost giddy enthusiasm every time he presents. Former employees and even some journalists have claimed that they found his energy and enthusiasm completely mesmerizing. Spend a few minutes developing a passion statement by filling in the following sentence: "I'm excited about this product [company, initiative, feature, etc.] because it _____." Once you have identified the passion statement, don't be bashful—share it.

THREE KEY MESSAGES

Now that you have decided on your headline and passion statement, write out the three messages you want your audience to receive. They should be easily recalled without the necessity of looking at notes. Although Scene 5 is dedicated to this subject, for now keep in mind that your listeners can recall only three or four points in short-term memory. Each of the key messages will be followed by supporting points.

METAPHORS AND ANALOGIES

As you develop key messages and supporting points, decide on which rhetorical devices will make your narrative more engaging. According to Aristotle, metaphor is "the most important thing by far." A metaphor—a word or phrase that denotes one thing and is used to designate another for purposes of comparison—is a persuasive tool in the best marketing, advertising, and public relations campaigns. Jobs uses metaphors in conversations and presentations. In one famous interview, Jobs said, "What a computer is to me is the most remarkable tool that we have ever come up with. It's the equivalent of a bicycle for our minds."[6]

Sales professionals are fond of sports metaphors: "We're all playing for the same team"; "This isn't a scrimmage; it's for real"; or "We're batting a thousand; let's keep it up." While sports metaphors work fine, challenge yourself to break away from what your audience expects. I came across an interesting metaphor for a new antivirus suite of applications from Kaspersky. The company ran full-page ads (the one I saw was in *USA Today*) that showed a dejected medieval soldier in a full suit of armor walking away, with his back toward the reader. The headline read, "Don't be so sad. You were very good once upon a time." The metaphor compared today's Internet security technologies (Kaspersky's competitors) to slow, cumbersome medieval armor, which of course is no match for today's military technology. The company extended the metaphor to the website with an image of a suit of armor and the same tagline. The metaphor was consistent throughout the company's marketing material.

Analogies are close cousins of metaphors and also are very effective. An analogy is a comparison between two different things in order to highlight some area of similarity. Analogies help us understand concepts that might be foreign to us. "The microprocessor is the brain of your computer" is an analogy that works well for companies such as Intel. In many ways, the chip serves the same function in the computer as a brain serves in a human. The chip and the brain are two different things with like features. This particular analogy is so useful that it is widely picked up by the media. When you find a strong analogy that works, stick with it and make it consistent across your presentations, website, and marketing material. Jobs likes to have fun with analogies, especially if they can be applied to Microsoft. During an interview with the *Wall Street Journal*'s Walt Mossberg,

Jobs pointed out that many people say iTunes is their favorite application for Windows. "It's like giving a glass of ice water to someone in hell!"[7]

DEMONSTRATIONS

Jobs shares the spotlight with employees, partners, and products. Demos make up a large part of his presentations. When Jobs unveiled a new version of the OS X operating system, code-named Leopard, at Apple's Worldwide Developers Conference (commonly abbreviated WWDC, the annual conference is an Apple event to showcase new software and technologies) in June 2007, he said Leopard had three hundred new features. He chose ten to discuss and demonstrate, including Time Machine (automated backup), Boot Camp (runs Windows XP and Vista on Mac), and Stacks (file organization). Instead of simply listing the features on a slide and explaining them, he sat down and showed the audience how they worked. He also chose the features *he* wanted the press to highlight. Why leave it to the media to decide which of three hundred new features were the most compelling? He would tell them.

Does your product lend itself to a demonstration? If so, script it into the presentation. Your audience wants to see, touch, and experience your product or service. Bring it to life.

I worked with Goldman Sachs investors to prepare the CEO of a Silicon Valley semiconductor start-up that was about to go public. The company shrinks chips that create audio sound for mobile computers. As we were planning the investor presentation, the CEO pulled out a chip the size of a fingernail and said, "You wouldn't believe the sound that this generates. Listen to this." He turned up the volume on his laptop and played music that impressed those of us who were in the room. It was a no-brainer to use the same demonstration (with a more dramatic buildup) when the executive pitched the company to investors. The IPO went on to become a huge success. An investor who had underwritten the company later called me and said, "I don't know what you did, but the CEO was a hit." I didn't have the heart to say that I stole the idea from the Steve Jobs playbook.

PARTNERS

Jobs shares the stage with key partners as well as his products. In September 2005, Jobs announced that all of Madonna's albums would be available on iTunes. The pop star herself suddenly appeared via webcam and joked with Jobs that she had tried to hold out as long as possible but got tired of not being able to download her own songs. Whether it's an artist or an industry partner like the CEOs of Intel, Fox, or Sony, Jobs often shares the stage with people who contribute to Apple's success.

CUSTOMER EVIDENCE AND THIRD-PARTY ENDORSEMENTS

Offering "customer evidence" or testimonials is an important part of the selling cycle. Few customers want to be pioneers, especially when budgets are tight. Just as recruiters ask for references, your customers want to hear success stories. This is especially critical for small companies. Your sales and marketing collateral might look great in that glossy four-color brochure, but it will be met with a healthy degree of skepticism. The number one influencer is word of mouth. Successful product launches usually have several customers who were involved in the beta and who can vouch for the product. Incorporate customer evidence into your pitch. Including a quote is simple enough, but try going one step further by recording a short testimonial and embedding the video on your site and in your presentation. Even better, invite a customer to join you in person (or via webcam) at a presentation or an important sales meeting.

Do you have third-party reviews of your product? Always use third-party endorsements when available. Word of mouth is one of the most effective marketing tools available, and when your customers see an endorsement from a publication or an individual they respect, it will make them feel more comfortable about their purchasing decisions.

VIDEO CLIPS

Very few presenters incorporate video into their presentations. Jobs plays video clips very often. Sometimes he shows video of employees talking about how much they enjoyed working on a product. Jobs is also fond of showing Apple's most recent television ads. He does so in nearly every major new product announcement and has been doing so since the launch of the famous Macintosh 1984 Super Bowl ad. He's been known to enjoy some ads so much that he showed them twice. Near the end of his presentation at Apple's WWDC in June 2008, Jobs announced the new iPhone 3G, which connects to higher-speed data networks and costs less than the iPhone that was currently on the market. He showed a television ad with the tagline "It's finally here. The first phone to beat the iPhone." When the thirty-second spot ended, a beaming Jobs said, "Isn't that nice? Want to see it again? Let's roll that again. I love this ad."[8]

Including video clips in your presentation will help you stand out. You can show ads, employee testimonials, scenes of the product or of people using the product, and even customer endorsements. What could be more persuasive than hearing directly from a satisfied customer—if not in person, then through a short video clip embedded in your presentation? You can easily encode video into digital formats such as MPEG 1, Windows Media, or Quicktime files, all of which will work for most presentations. Keep in mind that the average viewed clip on YouTube is 2.5 minutes. Our attention spans are shrinking, and video, while providing a great way to keep the audience engaged, can be overused if left to run too long. Use video clips in your presentations, but avoid clips that run much longer than two to three minutes.

Video is a terrific tool for even the most nontechnical of presentations. I was helping the California Strawberry Commission prepare for a series of presentations set to take place on the East Coast. Commission members showed me a short video of strawberry growers expressing their love of the land and the fruit. The images of strawberry fields were gorgeous, and I suggested they create a digital file of the video clip and embed it in the presentation. In the presentation itself, they introduced the video by saying something like this: "We realize that you probably have never visited a California strawberry field, so we decided to bring the farmers to you." The video clip was the most memorable part of the presentation, and the East Coast editors loved it.

FLIP CHARTS, PROPS, AND SHOW-AND-TELL

There are three types of learners: visual (the majority of people fall into this category), auditory (listeners), and kinesthetic (people who like to feel and touch). Find ways to appeal to everyone. A presentation should comprise more than just slides. Use whiteboards, flip charts, or the high-tech flip chart—a tablet PC. Bring "props" such as physical products for people to see, use, and touch. In Scene 12, you'll learn much more about reaching the three types of learners.

Most communicators get so caught up in the slides: Which font should I use? Should I use bullets or dashes? Should I include a graph here? How about a picture there? These are the wrong questions to be asking in the planning stage. If you have a tangible product, find other ways outside of the slide deck to show it off. On October 14, 2008, Steve introduced a new line of MacBooks carved out of one piece of aluminum, a "unibody enclosure." After Jobs discussed the manufacturing process, Apple employees handed out examples of the new frame so audience members could see it and touch it for themselves.

Incorporating all of these elements in a presentation will help you tell a story worth listening to. Slides don't tell stories; you do. Slides complement the story. This book is software agnostic; it avoids a direct comparison between PowerPoint and Keynote because the software is not the main character in an effective presentation—the speaker is. Jobs himself started using Apple's Keynote software in 2002, so what are we to make of the extraordinary presentations Jobs gave dating back to 1984? The software is not the answer. The fact that Steve Jobs uses Keynote instead of PowerPoint does not mean your presentation will look more like his if you make the switch. You will, however, win over your audience by spending more time creating the plot than producing the slides.

Use a notepad or whiteboard to script your ideas. It will help you visualize the story and simplify its components. When Jobs

Aristotle's Outline for Persuasive Arguments

A Steve Jobs presentation follows Aristotle's classic five-point plan to create a persuasive argument:

1. Deliver a story or statement that arouses the audience's interest.
2. Pose a problem or question that has to be solved or answered.
3. Offer a solution to the problem you raised.
4. Describe specific benefits for adopting the course of action set forth in your solution.
5. State a call to action. For Steve, it's as simple as saying, "Now go out and buy one!"

returned to Apple in 1996, taking over for ousted Gil Amelio, he found a company with more than forty different products, which confused the customer. In a bold move, he radically simplified the product pipeline. In *Inside Steve's Brain*, Leander Kahney writes that Jobs called senior management into his office. "Jobs drew a very simple two-by-two grid on the whiteboard. Across the top he wrote 'Consumer' and 'Professional,' and down the side, 'Portable' and 'Desktop.'"[9] Under Jobs, Apple would offer just four computers—two notebooks and two desktops—aimed at consumer and professional users. This is one of many stories in which we learn that Jobs does his best thinking when he's thinking visually. Whether you plan best on a whiteboard, a yellow legal pad, or Post-it notes, spend time in analog before jumping to digital. Your ultimate presentation will be far more interesting, engaging, and relevant.

DIRECTOR'S NOTES

» Start planning before you open the presentation software. Sketch ideas on paper or whiteboards.

» Incorporate some, if not all, of the following nine elements to make your presentation come alive: headline, passion statement, three key messages, analogies, demonstrations, partner showcase, customer evidence, video clips, and props.

» Speaking like Jobs has little to do with the type of presentation software you use (PowerPoint, Keynote, etc.) and everything to do with how you craft and deliver the story.

Answer the One Question That Matters Most

You've got to start with the customer experience and work back toward the technology—not the other way around.

—STEVE JOBS, MAY 25, 1997, WORLDWIDE DEVELOPERS CONFERENCE

n May 1998, Apple launched a splashy new product aimed at shoring up its dwindling share of the computer market, which had sunk to under 4 percent. When Jobs unveiled the new translucent iMac, he described the reason for building the computer, the target market, and the benefit customers would see from buying the new system:

> Even though this is a full-blown Macintosh, we are targeting this for the number one use consumers tell us they want a computer for, which is to get on the Internet simply and fast. We're also targeting this for education. They want to buy these. It's perfect for most of the things they do in instruction . . . We went out and looked at all of the consumer products out there. We noticed some things about them pretty much universally. The first is they are very slow. They are all using last year's processor. Secondly, they all have pretty crummy displays on them . . . likely no networking on them . . . old-generation I/O devices, and what that means is they are

lower performance and harder to use . . . and these things are uuugly! So, let me tell you about iMac.[1]

After describing the weaknesses of current products in the preceding excerpt, Jobs drew a verbal road map for his audience, listing the features he would explain in more detail. (Learn more about drawing a road map in Scene 5.) The audience learned that the new iMac was fast ("it screams") and that it had a "gorgeous" fifteen-inch display, a large amount of built-in memory, and components that would make accessing a network easier for students and home users. In one of his typical surprise moments, Jobs then walked to the center of the stage and pulled the cover off the new computer.

Your audience wants to be informed, educated, and entertained: informed about your product, educated on how it works, and entertained while learning about it. Above all, people want to know the answer to one question: Why should I care? Let's take a closer look at that iMac excerpt. Jobs told the audience, "what that means is . . ." Jobs connects the dots for his listeners. Although he might leave the industry in the dark about future Apple releases, he never leaves his audience guessing when the product is finally introduced. Why should you care about Apple's new computer, MP3 player, phone, or gadget? Don't worry. Jobs will tell you.

The Rumors Are True

For years, Apple had a rivalry with Intel—even setting fire to an Intel bunny man in a 1996 TV spot. One decade later, Apple put its rivalry to rest and announced that Intel processors would power its new Macintosh systems, replacing IBM's PowerPC chips. On June 6, 2005, Jobs announced the switch at Apple's Worldwide Developers Conference in San Francisco.

Rumors of the switch had been floating around for months, and many observers expressed concern about the transition. Reporters for *eWeek* magazine found it difficult to believe Apple would swap the PowerPC for Intel, since the PowerPC had worked well for the brand. Developers were grumbling. Jobs had to convince the audience that the switch was the right thing to do. His presentation was enormously persuasive in changing people's opinions because, using plain and direct language, he answered the one question that mattered most: Why should Apple's customers and developers care?

> Yes, it's true. We are going to begin the transition from PowerPC to Intel processors. Now, why are we going to do this? Didn't we just get through going from OS 9 to OS X? Isn't the business great right now? Because we want to make the best computers for our customers looking forward. Now, I stood up here two years ago and promised you this [slide shows desktop computer with 3 GHz], and we haven't been able to deliver it to you. I think a lot of you would like a G5 in your PowerBook, and we haven't been able to deliver it. But these aren't even the most important reasons. As we look ahead, though we have some great products now, we can envision some amazing products we want to build for you, and we don't know how to build them with the future PowerPC road map. That's why we're going to do this.[2]

Jobs articulated the argument so convincingly that few people in the audience that day left without a high degree of confidence that the transition had been the right thing for Apple, its developers, and its customers.

Why Should I Care?

During the planning phase of your presentation, always remember that it's not about you. It's about them. The listeners in your audience are asking themselves one question—"Why should I care?" Answering that one question right out of the gate will grab people's attention and keep them engaged.

I was preparing a CEO for a major analyst presentation and asked how he planned to kick it off. He offered this dry, boring, and confusing introduction: "Our company is a premier developer of intelligent semiconductor intellectual property solutions that dramatically accelerate complex system-on-a-chip designs while

Channel Your Best Steve Jobs Impression

In the summer of 2006, Intel released a processor branded Core 2 Duo. The "duo" stood for dual-core, meaning there were two cores, or brains, on each microprocessor. That may not sound exciting, but if you answer the *one* question that matters—Why should I care?—it becomes very interesting.

Take two scenarios: In both scenarios, a customer walks into a computer store and asks the salesperson for information about notebook computers. The sales professional in the first scenario has not read this book and fails to answer the one question that matters. The salesperson in the second scenario is more likely to win the sale, by virtue of channeling his or her inner Steve Jobs and answering the one question on the mind of the customer: Why should I care?

Scenario One

CUSTOMER: Hi, I'm looking for a notebook computer that is light and fast and includes a DVD.

SALESPERSON: You should look for an Intel Core 2 Duo.

CUSTOMER: OK. I didn't know Intel makes computers.

SALESPERSON: They don't.

CUSTOMER: Can you tell me more?

SALESPERSON: An Intel dual-core processor has two performance engines that simultaneously process data at a faster rate.

CUSTOMER: Oh. Maybe I should look somewhere else.

Of course the customer in this scenario will look somewhere else. Although the salesperson was technically accurate, the customer had to work far too hard to figure out how the new system would make the person's life better. It took too much brainpower, and as you'll learn, the brain is a lazy piece of meat that tries to preserve energy. Make the brain work too hard, and you'll lose your audience. The customer had one question in mind and one question only. The salesperson failed to answer it and seemed indifferent, even arrogant. Let's try it again. This time, the salesperson will do a stellar Steve Jobs impression.

Scenario Two

> **SALESPERSON:** Hi, can I help you find something?
>
> **CUSTOMER:** Sure. I'm looking for a notebook computer. One that is light and fast and includes a DVD.
>
> **SALESPERSON:** You've come to the right place. We have a huge selection of small notebooks that are blazingly fast. Have you considered a system with an Intel Core 2 Duo?
>
> **CUSTOMER:** Not really. What's that?
>
> **SALESPERSON:** Think of the microprocessor as the brain of your computer. Now, with these Intel chips, you get two brains in one computer. *What that means to you* is that you can do a lot of fun and productive stuff at the same time. For example, you can download music while your computer is running a full virus scan in the background, and it won't slow down the system at all. Your productivity applications will load much faster, you can work on multiple documents at the same time, your DVDs will play much better, and you get much longer battery life on top of it! And that's not all: the displays are gorgeous.
>
> **CUSTOMER:** Great. Please show me those computers!

In this scenario, the salesperson spoke in plain English, used tangible examples to make the product relevant, and answered the only question that really mattered to the customer: Why should I care about the processor? Retailers who train their sales staffs to describe products in this way will stand out from the competition. Come to think of it, there is a retailer that does exactly that—Apple. Walk into most any Apple store, and you will be greeted by enthusiastic men and women who are eager to explain how Apple products will make your life better.

minimizing risk." I was dumbfounded and suggested he take a page from the Steve Jobs playbook, eliminating all of the buzzwords such as *intelligent* and *solutions* and simply answering one question: Why should your customers care about your product?

The CEO revised his introduction. He decided to walk onstage and ask everyone to take out his or her cell phone. He said, "Our company creates software that is used to build the chips inside many of the phones you're holding up. As those chips get smaller and cheaper, your phones will get smaller, last longer on a single charge, and play music and video, all thanks to our technology working behind the scenes."

Which introduction would be more effective in grabbing your attention? The second one, of course. It is free of jargon and, by answering the *one* question that matters, gives the audience a reason to listen.

Reporters are skilled at answering the one question for their readers. Pay attention to product descriptions in the *New York Times* or *USA Today*. Articles are written to be followed and understood. For example, on January 20, 2009, Cisco Systems announced that it planned a big push into the server market, a category dominated by IBM, HP, and Dell. The product would be a server with virtualization software. Now, virtualization is one of the most complicated concepts to explain. Wikipedia defines server virtualization as "a method of partitioning a physical server computer into multiple servers such that each has the appearance and capabilities of running on its own dedicated machine."[3] Got it? Didn't think so. The *New York Times'* Ashlee Vance took a different approach: "Virtualization products let companies run numerous business applications, rather than just one, on each physical server, allowing them to save electricity and get more out of their hardware purchases."[4]

The difference, of course, is that Vance answered the one question on the minds of his readers—What does "virtualization" mean to me? In this case, he identified his audience as investors, IT decision makers, and business leaders who would care about such things.

Your listeners are asking themselves, "Why should I care?" If your product will help your customers make money, tell them. If it helps them save money, tell them. If it makes it easier or more enjoyable for them to perform a particular task, tell them. Tell them early, often, and clearly. Jobs doesn't leave people guessing. Well before he explains the technology behind a new product or feature, he explains how it will improve the experience people have with their computers, music players, or gadgets.

Table 2.1 offers a review of some other examples of how Jobs sells the benefit behind a new product or feature.

TABLE 2.1 JOBS SELLING THE BENEFIT

DATE/PRODUCT	BENEFIT
January 7, 2003 Keynote presentation software	"Using Keynote is like having a professional graphics department to create your slides. This is the application to use when your presentation really counts."[5]
September 12, 2006 iPod nano	"The all-new iPod nano gives music fans more of what they love in their iPods—twice the storage capacity at the same price, an incredible twenty-four-hour battery life, and a gorgeous aluminum design in five brilliant colors."[6]
January 15, 2008 Time Capsule backup service for Macs running Leopard OS	"With Time Capsule, all your irreplaceable photos, movies, and documents are automatically protected and incredibly easy to retrieve if they are ever lost."[7]
June 9, 2008 iPhone 3G	"Just one year after launching the iPhone, we're launching the new iPhone 3G. It's twice as fast at half the price."[8]
September 9, 2008 Genius feature for iTunes	"Genius lets you automatically create playlists from songs in your music library that go great together, with just one click."[9]

Avoid Self-Indulgent, Buzzword-Filled Wastes of Time

Answer the one question in all of your marketing materials: website, presentation slides, and press releases. The people who should know better—public relations professionals—are often the worst violators of this rule. The majority of press releases are usually self-indulgent, buzzword-filled wastes of time. Few members of the press even read press releases, because the documents fail to answer the *one* question that matters most to a reporter—Why should my readers care? As a journalist, I've seen thousands of press releases and rarely, if ever, covered a story based on one. Most other journalists would concur. Far too many press releases focus on corporate changes (management appointments, new logos, new offices, etc.) that nobody cares about, and if people should happen to care, the information is far from clear. Read press releases issued on any given day, and you will go numb trying to figure out why anyone would care about the information.

For fun, I took a few samples from press releases issued within hours of one another. The date does not matter. The majority of all press releases violate the same fundamental principles of persuasion:

"_____ Industries announced today that it has signed an exclusive distribution agreement with _____ . Under terms of the agreement, _____ will be the exclusive national distributor of _____ 's diesel exhaust fluid." Now, seriously, who cares? I wish I could tell you how the new distribution agreement benefits anyone, even shareholders. I can't, because the rest of the press release never answers the question directly.

"_____ has been named 2008 Pizza Chain of the Year by *Pizza Marketplace*." The press release said this honor comes after the chain delivered consistent profits, six quarters of same-store sales increases, and a new management team. Now, if the chain offered its customers a special discount to celebrate this honor, it would be newsworthy, but the press release mentions nothing that distinguishes this pizza chain from the thousands of other pizza parlors. This type of release falls under the "look at us" category—announcements that are largely meaningless to anyone outside the executive suites.

"_____ has announced the addition of the 'Annual Report on China's Steel Market in 2008 and the Outlook for 2009' report to their offering." Really? I'm sure millions of people around the world were waiting for this new report! Just kidding. This is another example of a wasted opportunity. If this release had started with one new, eye-opening piece of information from the new report, I might have been slightly more interested. However, that would have meant putting the reader first, and, sadly, most PR pros who write press releases intended for journalists have never been trained as journalists themselves.

Here's another gem, courtesy of an electric company in Hawaii:

"_____ today announced that _____ has been named president and CEO, effective January 1, 2009. _____ replaces _____ , who stepped down as president and CEO in August of this year." We also learned that the new CEO has thirty-two years of experience in the utilities industry and has lived on the big island for twenty years. Isn't that wonderful? Doesn't it give you a warm feeling? Again, this press release represents a lost opportunity to connect with the company's investors and customers. If the release had started with one thing that the new CEO planned to do immediately to improve service, it would have been far more interesting and newsworthy.

For the most part, press releases fail miserably at generating interest because they don't answer the one question that matters most to the reader. Do not make the same mistake in your presentation, publicity, and marketing material.

Nobody has time to listen to a pitch or presentation that holds no benefit. If you pay close attention to Jobs, you will see that he doesn't "sell" products; he sells the dream of a better future. When Apple launched the iPhone in early 2007, CNBC reporter Jim Goldman asked Jobs, "Why is the iPhone so important to Apple?" Jobs avoided a discussion of shareholder value or market share; instead, he offered the vision of a better experience: "I think the iPhone may change the whole phone industry and give us something that is vastly more powerful in terms of making phone calls and keeping your contacts. We have the best iPod we've ever made fully integrated into it. And it has the Internet in your pocket with a real browser, real e-mail, and the best implementation of Google Maps on the planet. iPhone brings all this stuff in your pocket, and it's ten times easier to use."[10] Jobs explains the "why" before the "how."

Your audience doesn't care about your product. People care about themselves. According to former Apple employee and Mac evangelist Guy Kawasaki, "The essence of evangelism is to passionately show people how you can make history together. Evangelism has little to do with cash flow, the bottom line, or co-marketing. It is the purest and most passionate form of sales because you are selling a dream, not a tangible object."[11] Sell dreams, not products.

DIRECTOR'S NOTES

» Ask yourself, "Why should my listener care about this idea/information/product/service?" If there is only one thing that you want your listener to take away from the conversation, what would it be? Focus on selling the benefit behind the product.

» Make the *one thing* as clear as possible, repeating it at least twice in the conversation or presentation. Eliminate buzzwords and jargon to enhance the clarity of your message.

» Make sure the *one thing* is consistent across all of your marketing collateral, including press releases, website pages, and presentations.

Develop a Messianic Sense of Purpose

We're here to put a dent in the universe.

—STEVE JOBS

Ew York's luxury, Upper West Side apartment building, the San Remo, is located on Seventy-Fifth Street with commanding views of Central Park. Its most famous residents read like a who's who of contemporary culture: Tiger Woods, Demi Moore, Dustin Hoffman, Bono, and, at one time, a young man on a mission—Steve Jobs.

In 1983, Jobs was aggressively courting then PepsiCo president John Sculley. Apple desperately wanted to bring in someone with Sculley's marketing and managing experience, but despite Steve's charm, Sculley failed to budge. The position would require that Sculley relocate his family to the West Coast, and it paid less than he wanted. One sentence would change everything. One sentence that would transform Apple, shift the trajectory of Sculley's career, and begin Jobs's amazing path from whiz kid to failure to hero and, finally, to legend. In his book *Odyssey*, Sculley recounts the conversation that would lead to his decision to take the job. The conversation also provided one of the most famous quotes in the history of corporate America.

According to Sculley, "We were on the balcony's west side, facing the Hudson River, when he [Jobs] finally asked me directly: 'Are you going to come to Apple?' 'Steve,' I said, 'I really love what you're doing. I'm excited by it; how could anyone not be captivated? But it just doesn't make sense. Steve, I'd love to be an adviser to you, to help you in any way. But I don't think I can come to Apple.'"

Sculley said Jobs's head dropped; he paused and stared at the ground. Jobs then looked up and issued a challenge to Sculley that would "haunt" him. Jobs said, "Do you want to spend the rest of your life selling sugared water or do you want a chance to change the world?"[1] Sculley said it was as if someone delivered a stiff blow to his stomach.

The Reality Distortion Field

Sculley had witnessed what Apple's vice president Bud Tribble once described as Jobs's "reality distortion field": an ability to convince anyone of practically anything. Many people cannot resist this magnetic pull and are willing to follow Jobs to the promised land (or at least to the next cool iPod).

Few people can escape the Jobs charisma, a magnetism steeped in passion for his products. Observers have said that there is something about the way Jobs talks, the enthusiasm that he conveys, that grabs everyone in the room and doesn't let go. Even journalists who should have built up an immunity to such gravitational forces cannot escape the influence. Wired .com editor Leander Kahney interviewed Jobs biographer Alan Deutschman, who described a meeting with Jobs: "He uses your first name very often. He looks directly in your eyes with that laser-like stare. He has these movie-star eyes that are very hypnotic. But what really gets you is the way he talks—there's something about the rhythm of his speech and the incredible enthusiasm he conveys for whatever it is he's talking about that is just infectious."[2]

Do What You Love

Deutschman said the Steve Jobs "X" factor is "the way he talks." But what exactly is it about the way he talks that pulls you in? Jobs speaks with passion, enthusiasm, and energy. Jobs himself tells us where his passion comes from: "You've got to find what you love. Your work is going to fill a large part of your life, and the only way to be truly satisfied is to do what you believe is great work. And the only way to do great work is to love what you do. If you haven't found it yet, keep looking. Don't settle."[3]

We all have a unique purpose. Some people, such as Jobs, identify that purpose from an early age; others never do, because they are caught up in catching up with the Joneses. One sure way to lose sight of your purpose is to chase money for the sake of chasing money. Jobs is a billionaire and an extraordinary communicator precisely because he followed his heart, his passion. The money, he most certainly knew, would come.

FINDING YOUR CORE PURPOSE

What is your core purpose? Once you find it, express it enthusiastically. One of the most profound experiences of my journalism career happened during an interview with Chris Gardner. Actor Will Smith played Gardner in the movie *The Pursuit of Happyness*.

In That Craziness, We See Genius

> I think you always had to be a little different to buy an Apple computer. I think the people who do buy them are the creative spirits in this world. They are the people who are not out just to get a job done; they're out to change the world. We make tools for those kinds of people . . . We are going to serve the people who have been buying our products since the beginning. A lot of times, people think they're crazy. But in that craziness, we see genius. And those are the people we're making tools for.[4]
>
> —STEVE JOBS

In the eighties, the real-life Gardner pursued an unpaid internship to become a stockbroker. He was homeless at the time, spending nights in the bathroom of an Oakland, California, subway station. To make the situation even harder, Gardner took care of his two-year-old son. The two slept together on the bathroom floor. Every morning, Gardner would put on the one suit he had, drop his son off at a very questionable day care, and take his classes. Gardner finished top of his class, became a stockbroker, and earned many millions of dollars. For a *BusinessWeek* column, I asked him, "Mr. Gardner, how did you find the strength to keep going?" His answer was so profound that I remember it to this day: "Find something you love to do so much, you can't wait for the sun to rise to do it all over again."[5]

In *Built to Last: Successful Habits of Visionary Companies*, authors Jim Collins and Jerry Porras studied eighteen leading companies. Their conclusion: individuals are inspired by "core values and a sense of purpose beyond just making money."[6] From his earliest interviews, it becomes clear that Jobs was more motivated by creating great products than by calculating how much money he would make at building those products.

In a PBS documentary, *Triumph of the Nerds*, Jobs said, "I was worth over a million dollars when I was twenty-three, and over ten million dollars when I was twenty-four, and over a hundred million dollars when I was twenty-five, and it wasn't that important, because I never did it for the money."[7] *I never did it for the money.* This phrase holds the secret between becoming an extraordinary presenter and one mired in mediocrity for the rest of your life. Jobs once said that being "the richest man in the cemetery" didn't matter to him; rather, "going to bed at night saying we've done something wonderful, that's what matters to me."[8] Great presenters are passionate, because they follow their hearts. Their conversations become platforms to share that passion.

Malcolm Gladwell shares a fascinating observation in *Outliers*. He argues that most of the leaders who are responsible for the personal computing revolution were born in 1955. That's the magic year, he says. According to Gladwell, the chronology makes sense because the first "minicomputer," the Altair, was introduced in 1975, marking one of the most important developments in the history of personal computers. He states: "If you were more than a few years out of college in 1975, then you belonged to the old paradigm. You had just bought a house. You're married. A baby is on the way. You're in no position to give up a good job and pension for some pie-in-the-sky $397 computer kit."[9] Likewise, if you were too young, you would not be mature enough to participate in the revolution.

Gladwell speculates that the ideal age of tech industry titans was around twenty or twenty-one, those born in 1954 or 1955. Steve Jobs was born on February 24, 1955. He was born at the right time and in the right neighborhood to take advantage of the moment. Gladwell points out that Jobs is one of an amazing number of technology leaders born in 1954 and 1955 (including Bill Gates, Paul Allen, Steve Ballmer, Eric Schmidt, Scott McNealy, and others). Gladwell's conclusion is that these men became successful precisely because computers were not big moneymakers at the time. They were cool, and these men loved to tinker. The message, claims Gladwell, is: to achieve success, do what you find interesting. Do what you love, and follow your core purpose. As Jobs has said, your heart knows where it wants to be.

THE LUCKIEST GUYS ON THE PLANET

On May 30, 2007, Steve Jobs and Bill Gates shared the stage in a rare joint appearance at the technology conference D: All Things

Lust for It

In a *New York Times* article after the launch of the MacBook Air, John Markoff wrote about witnessing Steve's enthusiasm in person. Markoff spent thirty minutes with Jobs after the conference and noted that Jobs's passion for personal computing came across even more so than it did when he was performing onstage. Jobs excitedly told Markoff, "I'm going to be the first one in line to buy one of these. I've been lusting after this."[10]

Digital. *Wall Street Journal* columnists Walt Mossberg and Kara Swisher covered a variety of topics with the two tech titans. In response to a question about Bill Gates's "second act" as a philanthropist, Jobs credited Gates for making the world a better place because Gates's goal wasn't to be the richest guy in the cemetery.

> You know, I'm sure Bill was like me in this way. I mean, I grew up fairly middle-class, lower middle-class, and I never really cared much about money. And Apple was so successful early on in life that I was very lucky that I didn't have to care about money then. And so I've been able to focus on work and then later on, my family. And I sort of look at us as two of the luckiest guys on the planet because we found what we loved to do, we were at the right place at the right time, and we've gotten to go to work every day with superbright people for thirty years and do what we love doing. And so it's hard to be happier than that. And so I don't think about legacy much. I just think about being able to get up every day and go in and hang around these great people and hopefully create something that other people will love as much as we do. And if we can do that, that's great.[11]

Nowhere in that quote do you hear Jobs speak of wealth, stock options, or private planes. Those things are nice, but they don't motivate Jobs. His drive comes from doing what he loves—designing great products that people enjoy.

Rally People to a Better Future

Donald Trump once remarked, "If you don't have passion, you have no energy, and if you don't have energy, you have nothing." It all starts with passion. Passion stirs the emotions of your listeners when you use it to paint a picture of a more meaningful world, a world that your customers or employees can play a part in creating.

Marcus Buckingham interviewed thousands of employees who excelled at their jobs during his seventeen years at the

Oprah Shares Jobs's Secret to Success

> *Follow your passion. Do what you love, and the money will follow. Most people don't believe it, but it's true.*[12]
>
> —OPRAH WINFREY

Gallup organization. After interviewing thousands of peak performers, he arrived at what he considers the single best definition of leadership: "Great leaders rally people to a better future," he writes in *The One Thing You Need to Know*.[13]

According to Buckingham, a leader carries a vivid image in his or her head of what a future could be. "Leaders are fascinated by the future. You are a leader if, and only if, you are restless for change, impatient for progress, and deeply dissatisfied with the status quo." He explains, "As a leader, you are never satisfied with the present, because in your head you can see a better future, and the friction between 'what is' and 'what could be' burns you, stirs you up, propels you forward. This is leadership."[14] Jobs's vision must have certainly burned him, stirred him, and propelled him forward. Jobs once told John Sculley he dreamed that every person in the world would own an Apple computer. But Jobs did not stop there. He shared that dream with all who would listen.

True evangelists are driven by a messianic zeal to create new experiences. "It was characteristic of Steve to speak in both vivid and sweeping language," writes Sculley. " 'What we want to do,' he [Steve Jobs] explained, 'is to change the way people use computers in the world. We've got some incredible ideas that will revolutionize the way people use computers. Apple is going to be the most important computer company in the world, far more important than IBM.' "[15] Jobs was never motivated to build computers. Instead, he had a burning desire to create tools to unleash human potential. Once you understand the difference, you'll understand what sparked his famous reality distortion field.

An Incredible Journey

Apple was this incredible journey. I mean, we did some amazing things there. The thing that bound us together at Apple was the ability to make things that were going to change the world. That was very important. We were all pretty young. The average age in the company was mid to late twenties. Hardly anybody had families at the beginning, and we all worked like maniacs, and the greatest joy was that we felt we were fashioning collective works of art much like twentieth-century physics. Something important that would last, that people contributed to and then could give to more people; the amplification factor was very large.[16]

—STEVE JOBS

What Computers and Coffee Have in Common

Lee Clow, chairman of TBWA/Chiat/Day, the agency behind some of Apple's most notable ad campaigns, once said of Jobs, "From the time he was a kid, Steve thought his products could change the world."[17] That's the key to understanding Jobs. His charisma is a result of a grand but strikingly simple vision—to make the world a better place.

Jobs convinced his programmers that they were changing the world together, making a moral choice against Microsoft and making people's lives better. For example, Jobs gave an interview to *Rolling Stone* in 2003 in which he talked about the iPod. The MP3 player was not simply a music gadget, but much more. According to Jobs, "Music is really being reinvented in this digital age, and that is bringing it back into people's lives. It's a wonderful thing. And in our own small way, that's how we're going to make the world a better place."[18] Where some people see an iPod as a music player, Jobs sees a world in which people can easily access their favorite songs and carry the music along with them wherever they go, enriching their lives.

Jobs reminds me of another business leader whom I had the pleasure of meeting, Starbucks CEO Howard Schultz. Prior to our interview, I read his book, *Pour Your Heart into It*. Schultz is passionate about what he does; in fact, the word *passion* appears on nearly every page. But it soon became clear that he is not as passionate about coffee as he is about the people, the baristas who make the Starbucks experience what it is. You see, Schultz's core vision was not to make a great cup of coffee. It was much bigger. Schultz would create an experience; a third place between work and home where people would feel comfortable gathering. He would build a company that treats people with dignity and respect. Those happy employees would, in turn, provide a level of customer service that would be seen as a gold standard in the industry. When I reviewed the transcripts from my time with Schultz, I was struck by the fact that the word *coffee* rarely appeared. Schultz's vision had little to do with coffee and everything to do with the experience Starbucks offers.

"Some managers are uncomfortable with expressing emotion about their dreams, but it's the passion and emotion that will attract and motivate others," write Collins and Porras.[19] Communicators such as Steve Jobs and Howard Schultz are passionate about how their products improve the lives of their customers. They're not afraid to express it. Coffee, computers, iPods—it doesn't matter. What matters is that they are motivated by a vision to change the world, to "leave a dent in the universe."

This book is filled with techniques to help you sell your ideas more successfully, but no technique can make up for a lack of passion for your service, product, company, or cause. The secret is to identify what it is you're truly passionate about. More often than not, it's not "the widget," but how the widget will improve the lives of your customers. Here is an excerpt from an interview Jobs gave *Wired* magazine in 1996: "Design is a funny word. Some people think design means how it looks. But of course, if you dig deeper, it's really how it works. The design of the Mac wasn't what it looked like, although that was part of it. Primarily, it was how it worked. To design something really well, you have to get it. You have to really grok what it's all about. It takes a

The Charismatic Leader

> *When I wasn't sure what the word charisma meant, I met Steve Jobs and then I knew.*[20]
>
> —FORMER APPLE CHIEF SCIENTIST LARRY TESLER

passionate commitment to really thoroughly understand something, chew it up, not just quickly swallow it. Most people don't take the time to do that."[21] Yes, *grok* is the word Jobs used. Just as Howard Schultz isn't passionate about the product itself, coffee, Jobs isn't passionate about hardware. He's passionate about how design enables something to work more beautifully.

Think Different

Los Angeles ad agency TBWA/Chiat/Day created an Apple television and print advertising campaign that turned into one of the most famous campaigns in corporate history. "Think Different" debuted on September 28, 1997, and became an instant classic. As black-and-white images of famous iconoclasts filled the screen (Albert Einstein, Martin Luther King, Richard Branson, John Lennon, Amelia Earhart, Muhammad Ali, Lucille Ball, Bob Dylan, and others), actor Richard Dreyfuss voiced the narration:

> Here's to the crazy ones. The misfits. The rebels. The troublemakers. The round pegs in the square hole. The ones who see things differently. They're not fond of rules. And they have no respect for the status quo. You can quote them, disagree with them, glorify or vilify them. About the only thing you can't do is ignore them. Because they change things. They push the human race forward. And while some may see them as the crazy ones, we see genius. Because the people who are crazy enough to think they can change the world are the ones who do.[22]

The campaign won a ton of awards, became a cult favorite, and lasted five years, which is an eternity in the life cycle of ad campaigns. The campaign reinvigorated the public's appetite for all things Apple, including an interest in one of the most influential iconoclasts in the computer world, Steve Jobs himself.

In *The Second Coming of Steve Jobs*, Alan Deutschman, who, as mentioned earlier, was pulled into Jobs's reality distortion field, describes a meeting between Jobs and *Newsweek*'s Katie Hafner, the first outsider to see the new "Think Different" ads. According to Deutschman, Hafner arrived at Apple's headquarters on a Friday morning and waited a long time for Jobs to show up. "Finally he emerged. His chin was covered by stubble. He was exhausted from having stayed up all night editing footage for the 'Think Different' television spot. The creative directors at Chiat/Day would send him video clips over a satellite connection, and he would say yes or no. Now the montage was finally complete. Steve sat with Katie and they watched the commercial. Steve was crying. 'That's what I love about him,' Katie recalls. 'It wasn't trumped up. Steve was genuinely moved by that stupid ad.' "[23]

Those ads touched Jobs deeply because they reflected everything that pushed Jobs to innovate, excel, and succeed. He saw himself in the faces of those famous people who advanced the human race and changed the world.

As a journalist, I learned that everyone has a story to tell. I realize we are not all creating computers that will change the way people live, work, play, and learn. Notwithstanding, the fact is that most of us are selling a product or working on a project that has some benefit to the lives of our customers. Whether you work in agriculture, automobiles, technology, finance, or any number of other industries, you have a magnificent story to tell. Dig deep to identify that which you are most passionate about. 'Once you do, share that enthusiasm with your listeners. People want to be moved and inspired, and they want to believe in something. Make them believe in you.

"There's an old Wayne Gretzky quote that I love," Steve Jobs once said: " 'I skate to where the puck is going to be, not where it has been.' We've always tried to do that at Apple. Since the very, very beginning. And we always will."[24]

DIRECTOR'S NOTES

» Dig deep to identify your true passion. Ask yourself, "What am I really selling?" Here's a hint: it's not the widget, but what the widget can do to improve the lives of your customers. What you're selling is the dream of a better life. Once you identify your true passion, share it with gusto.

» Develop a personal "passion statement." In one sentence, tell your prospects why you are genuinely excited about working with them. Your passion statement will be remembered long after your company's mission statement is forgotten.

» If you want to be an inspiring speaker but you are not doing what you love, consider a change. After interviewing thousands of successful leaders, I can tell you that, while it's possible to be financially successful in a job you hate, you will never be considered an inspiring communicator. Passion—a messianic zeal to make the world a better place—makes all the difference.

Create Twitter-Like Headlines

Today Apple reinvents the phone!

—STEVE JOBS, MACWORLD 2007

"Welcome to Macworld 2008. There is something clearly in the air today."[1] With that opening line, Steve Jobs set the theme for what would ultimately be the big announcement of his keynote presentation—the introduction of an ultrathin notebook computer. No other portable computer could compare to this three-pound, 0.16-inch-thin "dreambook," as some observers called it. Steve Jobs knew that everyone would be searching for just the right words to describe it, so he did it for them: "MacBook Air. The world's thinnest notebook."

The MacBook Air is Apple's ultrathin notebook computer. The best way to describe it is as, well, the world's thinnest notebook. Search for "world's thinnest notebook" on Google, and the search engine will return about thirty thousand citations, most of which were written after the announcement. Jobs takes the guesswork out of a new product by creating a one-line description or headline that best reflects the product. The headlines work so well that the media will often run with them word for word. You see, reporters (and your audience) are looking for a category in which to place your product and a way of describing the product in one sentence. Take the work out of it and write the headline yourself.

140 Characters or Less

Jobs creates headlines that are specific, are memorable, and, best of all, can fit in a Twitter post. Twitter is a fast-growing social networking site that could best be described as your life between e-mail and blogs. Millions of users "tweet" about the daily happenings in their lives and can choose to follow the happenings of others. Twitter is changing the nature of business communication in a fundamental way—it forces people to write concisely. The maximum post—or tweet—is 140 characters. Characters include letters, spaces, and punctuation. For example, Jobs's description of the MacBook Air takes thirty characters, including the period: "The world's thinnest notebook."

Jobs has a one-line description for nearly every product, and it is carefully created in the planning stage well before the presentation, press releases, and marketing material are finished. Most important, the headline is consistent. On January 15, 2008, the day of the MacBook Air announcement, the headline was repeated in every channel of communication: presentations, website, interviews, advertisements, billboards, and posters.

In Table 4.1, you see how Apple and Jobs consistently delivered the vision behind MacBook Air.

Most presenters cannot describe their company, product, or service in one sentence. Understandably, it becomes nearly

Setting the Stage for the Marketing Blitz

The minute Jobs delivers a headline onstage, the Apple publicity and marketing teams kick into full gear. Posters are dropped down inside the Macworld Expo, billboards go up, the front page of the Apple website reveals the product and headline, and ads reflect the headline in newspapers and magazines, as well as on television and radio. Whether it's "1,000 songs in your pocket" or "The world's thinnest notebook," the headline is repeated consistently in all of Apple's marketing channels.

TABLE 4.1 JOBS'S CONSISTENT HEADLINES FOR MACBOOK AIR

HEADLINE	SOURCE
"What is MacBook Air? In a sentence, it's the world's thinnest notebook."[2]	Keynote presentation
"The world's thinnest notebook."[3]	Words on Jobs's slide
"This is the MacBook Air. It's the thinnest notebook in the world."[4]	Promoting the new notebook in a CNBC interview immediately after his keynote presentation
"We decided to build the world's thinnest notebook."[5]	A second reference to MacBook Air in the same CNBC interview
"MacBook Air. The world's thinnest notebook."	Tagline that accompanied the full-screen photograph of the new product on Apple's home page
"Apple Introduces MacBook Air—The World's Thinnest Notebook."[6]	Apple press release
"We've built the world's thinnest notebook."[7]	Steve Jobs quote in the Apple press release

impossible to create consistent messaging without a prepared headline developed early in the planning stage. The rest of the presentation should be built around it.

Today Apple Reinvents the Phone

On January 9, 2007, *PC World* ran an article that announced Apple would "Reinvent the Phone" with a new device that combined three products: a mobile phone, an iPod, and an Internet communicator. That product, of course, was the iPhone. The iPhone did, indeed, revolutionize the industry and was recognized by *Time* magazine as the invention of the year. (Just two years after its release, by the end of 2008, the iPhone had grabbed 13 percent of the smartphone market.) The editors at *PC*

World did not create the headline themselves. Apple provided it in its press release, and Steve Jobs reinforced it in his keynote presentation at Macworld. Apple's headline was specific, memorable, and consistent: "Apple Reinvents the Phone."

During the keynote presentation in which Jobs unveiled the iPhone, he used the phrase "reinvent the phone" five times. After walking the audience through the phone's features, he hammered it home once again: "I think when you have a chance to get your hands on it, you'll agree, we have reinvented the phone."[8]

Jobs does not wait for the media to create a headline. He writes it himself and repeats it several times in his presentation. Jobs delivers the headline before explaining the details of the product. He then describes the product, typically with a demo, and repeats the headline immediately upon ending the explanation.

For example, here is how Jobs introduced GarageBand for the first time: "Today we're announcing something so cool: a fifth app that will be part of the iLife family. Its name is GarageBand. What is GarageBand? GarageBand is a major new pro music tool. But it's for everyone."[9] Jobs's slide mirrored the headline. When he announced the headline for GarageBand, the slide on the screen read: "GarageBand. A major new pro music tool." Jobs followed the headline with a longer, one-sentence description of the product. "What it does is turn your Mac into a pro-quality musical instrument and complete recording studio," Jobs told the audience. This is typical Jobs method for introducing a product. He reveals the headline, expands on it, and hammers it home again and again.

The Excitement of the Internet, the Simplicity of Macintosh

The original iMac (the "i" stood for Internet) made getting on the Web easier than ever. The customer had to go through only two steps to connect to the Internet. ("There's no step three," actor Jeff Goldblum declared in one popular ad.) The introduction captured the imagination of the computer industry in 1998 and was one of the most influential computer announcements of the decade. According to Macworld.com, the iMac redeemed Steve Jobs, who had returned to Apple in 1997, and it saved Apple itself at a time when the media had pronounced the company all but dead. Jobs had to create excitement about a product that threw some common assumptions out the window—the iMac shipped with no floppy drive, a bold move at the time and a decision met with considerable skepticism.

"iMac combines the excitement of the Internet with the simplicity of Macintosh," Jobs said as he introduced the computer. The slide on the screen behind Jobs read simply: "iMac. The excitement of the Internet. The simplicity of Macintosh." Jobs then explained whom the computer was created to attract: consumers and students who wanted to get on the Internet "simply and fast."[10]

The headlines Steve Jobs creates work effectively because they are written from the perspective of the user. They answer the question, Why should I care? (See Scene 2.) Why should you care about the iMac? Because it lets you experience "the excitement of the Internet with the simplicity of Macintosh."

One Thousand Songs in Your Pocket

Apple is responsible for one of the greatest product headlines of all time. According to author Leander Kahney, Jobs himself settled on the description for the original iPod. On October 23, 2001, Jobs could have said, "Today we're introducing a new, ultraportable MP3 player with a 6.5-ounce design and a 5 GB hard drive, complete with Apple's legendary ease of use." Of course, Jobs did not say it quite that way. He simply said, "iPod. One thousand songs in your pocket."[11] No one could describe it better in more concise language. One thousand songs that could fit in your pocket. What else is there to say? One sentence tells the story and also answers the question, Why should I care?

Many reporters covering the event used the description in the headline to their articles. Matthew Fordahl's headline in the Associated Press on the day of the announcement read, "Apple's

New iPod Player Puts '1,000 Songs in Your Pocket.'"[12] Apple's headline was memorable because it meets three criteria: it is *concise* (twenty-seven characters), it is *specific* (one thousand songs), and it offers a *personal benefit* (*you* can carry the songs in your pocket).

Following are some other examples of Apple headlines that meet all three criteria. Although some of these are slightly longer than ten words, they can fit in a Twitter post:

» "The new iTunes store. All songs are DRM-free." (Changes to iTunes music store, January 2009)

» "The industry's greenest notebooks." (New MacBook family of computers, introduced in October 2008)

» "The world's most popular music player made even better." (Introduction of the fourth-generation iPod nano, September 2008)

» "iPhone 3G. Twice as fast at half the price." (Introduction of iPhone 3G, July 2008)

» "It gives Mac users more reasons to love their Mac and PC users more reasons to switch." (Introduction of iLife '08, announced July 2007)

» "Apple reinvents the phone." (Introduction of iPhone, January 2007)

» "The speed and screen of a professional desktop system in the world's best notebook design." (Introduction of the seventeen-inch MacBook Pro, April 2006)

» "The fastest browser on the Mac and many will feel it's the best browser ever created." (Unveiling of Safari, January 2003)

Keynote Beats PowerPoint in the Battle of the Headlines

Microsoft's PowerPoint has one big advantage over Apple's Keynote presentation software—it's everywhere. Microsoft commands 90 percent of the computing market, and among the 10 percent of computer users on a Macintosh, many still use

Headlines That Changed the World

When the "Google guys," Sergey Brin and Larry Page, walked into Sequoia Capital to seek funding for their new search-engine technology, they described their company in one sentence: "Google provides access to the world's information in one click." That's sixty-three characters, ten words. An early investor in Google told me that with those ten words, the investors immediately understood the implications of Google's technology. Since that day, entrepreneurs who walk into Sequoia Capital have been asked for their "one-liner," a headline that describes the product in a single sentence. As one investor told me, "If you cannot describe what you do in ten words or less, I'm not investing, I'm not buying, I'm not interested. Period." Following are some more examples of world-changing headlines that are ten words or less:

» "Cisco changes the way we live, work, play, and learn."—Cisco CEO John Chambers, who repeats this line in interviews and presentations

» "Starbucks creates a third place between work and home." —Starbucks CEO Howard Schultz, describing his idea to early investors

» "We see a PC on every desk, in every home."—Microsoft co-founder Bill Gates, expressing his vision to Steve Ballmer, who, shortly after joining the company, was second-guessing his decision. Ballmer, currently Microsoft's CEO, said Gates's vision convinced him to stick it out. With a personal net worth of $15 billion, Ballmer is glad he did.

PowerPoint software designed for Macs. While the actual numbers of presentations conducted on PowerPoint versus Keynote are not publicly available, it's safe to say that the number of Keynote presentations given daily is minuscule in comparison with PowerPoint. Although most presentation designers who are familiar with both formats prefer to work in the more elegant Keynote system, those same designers will tell you that the majority of their client work is done in PowerPoint.

As I mentioned in Scene 1, this book is software agnostic because all of the techniques apply equally to PowerPoint or Keynote. That said, Keynote is still the application that Steve Jobs prefers, and the Twitter-like headline he created to introduce the software was certainly an attention grabber. "This is another brand-new application that we are announcing here today, and it is called Keynote," Jobs told the audience at Macworld 2003. Then:

> Keynote is a presentation app for when your presentation really counts [slide reads: "When your presentation really counts"]. And Keynote was built for me [slide reads: "Built for me"]. I needed an application to build the kind of slide show that I wanted to show you at these Macworld keynotes: very graphics intensive. We built this for me; now I want to share it with you. We hired a low-paid beta tester to beta test this app for an entire year, and here he is [audience laughs as screen shows photo of Jobs]. Rather than a bunch of slides about slides, let me just show you [walks to stage right to demo the new software].[13]

Again, we see a remarkable consistency in all of Apple's marketing material surrounding the new product launch. The Apple press release for Keynote described it as "The application to use when your presentation really counts."[14] This headline can easily fit in a Twitter post and, without revealing the details, tells a story in one sentence. A customer who wanted more details could read the press release, watch Jobs's demonstration, or view the online demo on Apple's website. Still, the headline itself offered plenty of information. We learned that it was a new application specifically for presentations and made for those times when presentations can make or break your career. As a bonus, it was built for Jobs. For many people who give frequent presentations, that headline was enough to pique their interest and give the software a try.

Journalists learn to write headlines on the first day of J-school. Headlines are what persuade you to read particular stories in newspapers, magazines, or blogs. Headlines matter. As individuals become their own copywriters for blogs, presentations, Twitter posts, and marketing material, learning to write catchy, descriptive headlines becomes even more important to professional success.

DIRECTOR'S NOTES

» Create your headline, a one-sentence vision statement for your company, product, or service. The most effective headlines are concise (140 characters maximum), are specific, and offer a personal benefit.

» Consistently repeat the headline in your conversations and marketing material: presentations, slides, brochures, collateral, press releases, website.

» Remember, your headline is a statement that offers your audience a vision of a better future. It's not about you. It's about them.

Draw a Road Map

Today we are introducing three revolutionary products.

—STEVE JOBS, REVEALING THE iPHONE

On January 9, 2007, thousands of Mac faithful watched as Steve Jobs delivered an electrifying announcement. "Today Apple reinvents the phone," Jobs said as he revealed the iPhone for the first time to the public.[1]

Before delivering that headline, however, Jobs added to the drama and suspense when he told the audience that Apple would introduce not one, but three revolutionary products. He identified the first one as a wide-screen iPod with touch controls. This met with a smattering of applause. Jobs said the second product would be a revolutionary mobile phone. The audience cheered that announcement. And the third, said Jobs, was a breakthrough Internet communications device. At this point, the audience members sat back and waited for what they thought would be further product descriptions and perhaps some demos of the three new devices—but the real thrill was yet to come. Jobs continued, "So, three things: a wide-screen iPod with touch controls, a revolutionary mobile phone, and a breakthrough Internet communications device. An iPod, a phone, and an Internet communicator. An iPod, a phone—are you getting it? These are not three separate devices. This is one device, and we are calling it iPhone." The audience went wild, and Jobs basked in the glow of nailing yet another product launch that would solidify Apple's role as one of the world's most innovative companies.

Jobs draws a verbal road map for his audience, a preview of coming attractions. Typically these road maps are outlined in groups of three—a presentation might be broken into "three acts," a product description into "three features," a demo into "three parts." Jobs's love of threes can be traced back at least as early as the original Macintosh introduction on January 24, 1984. Appearing at the Flint Center, in Cupertino, California, Jobs told the audience, "There have only been two milestone products in our industry: the Apple II in 1977 and the IBM PC in 1981. Today we are introducing the third industry milestone product, the Macintosh. And it has turned out insanely great!"[2]

Verbal guideposts serve as road maps, helping your listeners follow the story. When coaching clients to appear in the media, I always instruct them to create an easy-to-follow story by clearly outlining three or, at the most, four main points before filling in the details. When this technique is followed, reporters will often take extensive notes. If the spokesperson misses a point, reporters will ask, "Didn't you say you had three points? I heard only two." A verbal road map of three things will help your listeners keep their place. See Figure 5.1.

Figure 5.1 Jobs sticks to the rule of three in his presentations.

It is well established that we can hold only small amounts of information in short-term, or "active," memory. In 1956, Bell Labs research scientist George Miller published a classic paper titled "The Magical Number Seven, Plus or Minus Two." Miller cited studies that showed we have a hard time retaining more than seven to nine digits in short-term memory. Contemporary scientists have put the number of items we can easily recall closer to three or four. So, it should not be surprising that Jobs rarely offers more than three or four key message points. As for that, in a Steve Jobs presentation, the number three is much more common than four. Steve understands that the "rule of three" is one of the most powerful concepts in communication theory.

Why Goldilocks Didn't Encounter Four Bears

Listeners like lists. But how many points should you include in the list?

Three is the magic number.

Comedians know that three is funnier than two. Writers know that three is more dramatic than four. Jobs knows that three is more persuasive than five. Every great movie, book, play, or presentation has a three-act structure. There were three musketeers, not five. Goldilocks encountered three bears, not four. There were three stooges, not two. Legendary NFL coach Vince Lombardi told his players there were three important things in life: family, religion, and the Green Bay Packers. And the U.S. Declaration of Independence states that Americans have a right to "life, liberty, and the pursuit of happiness," not simply life and liberty. The rule of three is a fundamental principle in writing, in humor, and in a Steve Jobs presentation.

The U.S. Marine Corps has conducted extensive research into this subject and has concluded that three is more effective than two or four. Divisions within the marines are divided into three: a corporal commands a team of three; a sergeant

commands three rifle teams in a squad; a captain has three pla-
toons; and so on. If the marines were kind enough to study this
stuff, why should we reinvent the wheel? Go ahead and use it.
So few communicators incorporate the rule of three in their presentations that you will stand apart simply by doing so. The rule
of three—it works for the marines, it works for Jobs, and it will
work for you.

At the Apple Worldwide Developers Conference on June 6,
2005, Jobs announced the switch from IBM's PowerPC chips to
Intel microprocessors. "Let's talk about transitions," Jobs said.

> The Mac in its history has had two major transitions so far
> [begins to outline three points]. The *first* one, 68K to PowerPC.
> That transition happened about ten years ago in the mid-
> nineties. The PowerPC set Apple up for the next decade. It
> was a good move. The *second* major transition has been even

How the Rule of Three Can Improve Your Golf Game

During a break from writing this chapter, I took a golf lesson
from a local coach. Any golfer will tell you that the toughest
part of the game is remembering the dozens of small moves
that ultimately result in a fluid swing: posture, grip, takeaway,
balance, hinging, weight shift, follow-through, and other
variables. Problems occur when you think about too many
things at the same time. The marines have found that giving
directions in groups of three makes it easier for soldiers to follow the directions. So, I asked my instructor to give me three
directives, and three only, to improve my swing. "Fine," he said.
"Today you're going to focus on closing your hips, shifting
your weight to the right side on the backswing, and making a
full follow-through. So, think hips, shift, follow-through." *Hips,
shift, follow.* That's it. The instruction worked wonders, and
since that day, my golf game has improved considerably. The
rule of three—good for presentations and good for golf, too!

bigger. And that's the transition from OS 9 to OS X that we just finished a few years ago. This was a brain transplant. And although these operating systems vary in name by just one [digit], they are worlds apart in technology. OS X is the most advanced operating system on the planet, and it has set Apple up for the next twenty years. Today it's time to begin a *third* transition. We want to constantly be making the best computers for you and the rest of our users. It's time for a third transition. And yes, it's true. We are going to begin the transition from PowerPC to Intel processors [emphasis added].[3]

Revealing the narrative in groups of three provides direction for your audience. It shows people where you've been and where you're going. In the preceding excerpt, Jobs sets the theme of "transitions," and we assume there will be at least a third transition because, as Jobs explains, the Mac has already had two of them. He also builds the drama with each point. The first transition was a "good move." The second was "even bigger." By extension, the third must be bigger still.

Apple's Three-Legged Stool

At the Apple Worldwide Developers Conference in September 2008, Jobs displayed a slide of a stool with three legs. "As you know, there's three parts to Apple now," he said. "The first part, of course, is the Mac. The second part is our music businesses, the iPod and iTunes. And the third part is now the iPhone." Jobs introduced the executives who would speak about the Mac and the iPod business. Jobs would take the iPhone portion himself.

As he launched into the iPhone discussion, Jobs once again provided a road map for his listeners—this time, a road map in *four* parts: "In a few weeks, it's going to be the iPhone's first birthday. We shipped our first iPhone on June 29. It was an amazing introduction, the most amazing one we've ever had. iPhone has had tremendous critical acclaim. It's the phone that has changed phones forever. But we have mountains to climb to reach the next level. What are these challenges? The first,

The *USA Today* Method

Journalists are trained to distill complex ideas into specific points, or takeaways. Read *USA Today*, America's most popular newspaper, and you will find that most articles condense main points into groups of three. When Intel rolled out a faster chip called Centrino 2, Michelle Kessler covered it for the newspaper. Kessler outlined three specific benefits and explained why each was important—why they matter:

» **Battery life.** "The best laptop in the world isn't worth much when its battery dies. Intel's new chip features an ultra low power processor and other energy-saving tools."
» **Graphics.** "Laptops traditionally use low-end graphics chips. But now 26 percent have powerful stand-alone graphics chips and more people watch movies, play games, and use graphics-intensive programs."
» **Wireless Internet.** "Intel's new chip line features the latest version of Wi-Fi, known as 802.11n. Later this year it plans to roll out chips using a new wireless Internet standard, WiMax, which can send a signal over several miles."[4]

Kessler proves that you can take the most complex technology —or idea—and describe it in three concise points.

Ed Baig also writes for *USA Today*, reviewing some of the latest technology products. After testing Microsoft's new operating system (Windows 7) in its beta, or test mode, Baig focused on three highlights:

» **Getting around.** "Icons on the task bar are bigger and you can arrange them in any way you choose."
» **Security.** "Windows 7 won't constantly bog you down with annoying security messages every time you try to load programs or change settings."
» **Compatibility.** "Even as a beta, Windows 7 recognized my printer and digital camera."[5]

Baig, Kessler, and other top reporters write their material in manageable chunks to make it easier to read. So does Jobs. He writes the content of his presentation just as a *USA Today* reporter would review a product: headline, introduction, three points, conclusion.

3G networking—faster networking. Second, enterprise support. Third, third-party application support. And fourth, we need to sell iPhone in more countries."

After providing that verbal preview of the four points he would discuss in more detail, Jobs returned to the first point: "So, as we arrive at iPhone's first birthday, we're going to take it to the next level, and today we're introducing the iPhone 3G."[6] This is a remarkably consistent technique in Jobs's presentations. He outlines three or four points, returns to the first point, explains each one in more depth, and then summarizes each point. This is a simple recipe for ensuring your audience will retain the information you are sharing.

Jobs and Ballmer Share a Love of Threes

In January 2009, Microsoft CEO Steve Ballmer opened the Consumer Electronics Show in Las Vegas. It was his first keynote speech at the conference, replacing Bill Gates, who had moved on to his philanthropic pursuits. Over fifteen years, it had become a tradition for Microsoft to open the conference, and Gates had delivered nearly every keynote. As a presenter, Ballmer was much different from Gates. He exuded passion, energy, and excitement. He stripped his talk of esoteric jargon and technical buzzwords. Ballmer also understood the value of the rule of three in providing a verbal road map for his listeners.

How the Rule of Three Helped DuPont Face an Economic Meltdown

In his book *Leadership in the Era of Economic Uncertainty*, management guru Ram Charan wrote about the global giant DuPont and how it aggressively responded to the economic meltdown in 2008. Chief executive Chad Holliday met with the company's top leaders and economists, formulating a crisis plan that was implemented within ten days. DuPont had sixty thousand employees at the time. Every employee met with a manager who explained in plain English what the company had to accomplish. Employees were then asked to identify three things that they could do immediately to conserve cash and reduce costs. The company had decided that if employees felt overwhelmed, they wouldn't take any action. Three, however, was a manageable and meaningful number that would spark employees to take action.

The groups of three just kept coming. Here are a few examples from his keynote:

» "I want to spend time with you talking about the economy, our industry, and the work that we are doing at Microsoft."
» "When I think about opportunities, in my mind I frame it in three key areas. The first is the convergence of the three screens people use every day: the PC, the phone, and the TV . . . The second major area is how you will interact with your computer and other devices in a more natural way . . . and the last area of opportunity is what I call connected experiences."
» "Looking back, there were three things that made Windows and the PC successful. First, the PC enabled the best applications and let them work together. Second, the PC enabled more choice in hardware. And, third, the Windows experience helped us all work together."

» "We're on track to deliver the best version of Windows ever. We're putting in all the right ingredients—simplicity, reliability, and speed."[7]

Ballmer used groups of three no fewer than five times in one presentation, making his speech much easier to follow than any of Gates's keynotes. Although there's no love lost between Apple and Microsoft, both Ballmer and Jobs understand that explaining complex technology in language that's easy to follow is the first step to creating excitement among their existing and future customers.

The Road Map as an Agenda

Jobs kicked off Macworld 2008 with the verbal equivalent of an agenda (there are no agenda slides in a Steve Jobs presentation, just verbal road maps). "I've got four things I'd like to talk to you about today, so let's get started," he said.

The *first* one is Leopard. I'm thrilled to report that we have delivered over five million copies of Leopard in the first ninety days. Unbelievable. It's the most successful release of Mac OS X ever . . . Number *two* is about the iPhone. Today happens to be the two hundreth day that the iPhone went on sale. I'm extraordinarily pleased that we have sold four million iPhones to date . . . OK, number *three*. This is a good one, too. Number three is about iTunes. I'm really pleased to report that last week we sold our four billionth song. Isn't that great? On Christmas Day we set a new record, twenty million songs in one day. Isn't that amazing? That's our new one-day record . . . So, that brings us to number *four*. There is something in the air. What is it? Well, as you know, Apple makes the best notebooks in the business: the MacBook and the MacBook Pro. Well, today we're introducing a third kind of notebook. It's called the MacBook Air . . ."[8]

What the World's Greatest Speechwriters Know

Ted Sorensen, John F. Kennedy's speechwriter, believed that speeches should be written for the ear and not for the eye. His speeches would list goals and accomplishments in a numbered sequence to make it easier for listeners. Kennedy's speech to a joint session of Congress on May 25, 1961, offers a perfect example of Sorensen's technique. In calling for a major commitment to explore space, Kennedy said:

> First, I believe that this nation should commit itself to achieving the goal, before this decade is out, of landing a man on the moon and returning him safely to earth. No single space project in this period will be more impressive to mankind, or more important for the long-range exploration of space . . . Secondly, an additional twenty-three million dollars, together with the seven million already available, will accelerate development of the Rover nuclear rocket . . . Third, an additional fifty million dollars will make the most of our present leadership, by accelerating the use of space satellites for worldwide communications. Fourth, an additional seventy-five million dollars will help give us at the earliest possible time a satellite system for worldwide weather observation. Let it be clear that I am asking the Congress and the country to accept a firm commitment to a new course of action, a course which will last for many years and carry heavy costs . . . If we are to go only halfway, or reduce our sights in the face of difficulty, in my judgment it would be better not to go at all.[9]

U.S. president Barack Obama, a fan of Kennedy's speeches, adopted some of Sorensen's rules to make his own speeches more impactful. Here are some samples from Obama's speeches that follow the rule of three, beginning with the speech that put him on the map, his keynote address at the 2004 Democratic National Convention:

I believe that we can give our middle class relief and
provide working families with a road to opportunity
. . . I believe we can provide jobs to the jobless, homes
to the homeless, and reclaim young people in cities
across America from violence and despair . . . I believe
that we have a righteous wind at our backs and that as
we stand on the crossroads of history, we can make the
right choices and meet the challenges that face us.[10]

As illustrated in this excerpt, Obama not only breaks up his
speeches into paragraphs of three sentences but also often
delivers three points within sentences.

When Obama took the oath of office to become America's
forty-fourth president on Tuesday, January 20, 2009, he
delivered a historical address to some two million people who
gathered to watch the speech in person and millions more
on television around the world. Obama made frequent use of
threes in the speech:

» "I stand here today humbled by the task before us, grateful for
the trust you have bestowed, mindful of the sacrifices born by
our ancestors."
» "Homes have been lost, jobs shed, businesses shuttered."
» "Our health care is too costly, our schools fail too many, and
each day brings further evidence that the ways we use energy
strengthen our adversaries and threaten our planet."
» "Today I say to you that the challenges we face are real, they
are serious, and they are many."
» "Our workers are no less productive than when this crisis
began, our minds no less inventive, our goods and services
no less needed than they were last month or last year."[11]

Every time Jobs announced a numeral, his slide contained
just one image—the number itself (1, 2, 3, and 4). We will
explore the simplicity of Jobs's slide design more thoroughly in
Scene 8, but for now keep in mind that your slides should mirror
your narrative. There is no need to make the slides complicated.

Jobs not only breaks up his presentations into groups but also describes features in lists of three or four items. "There are *three* major breakthroughs in iPod," Jobs said in 2005. "The *first* one is, it's ultraportable" [5 GB, one thousand songs in your pocket]. "*Second*, we've built in Firewire" [Jobs explained how Firewire enabled a download of an entire CD in five to ten seconds, versus five to ten minutes via a USB connection]. "*Third*, it has extraordinary battery life," Jobs said.[12] He then described how the iPod provided ten hours of battery life, ten hours of continuous music.

This chapter could easily have become the longest in the book, because every Steve Jobs presentation contains verbal road maps with the rule of three playing a prominent role. Even when he's not using slides in a traditional keynote presentation, Jobs is speaking in threes. Jobs kicked off his now famous Stanford commencement address by saying, "Today I want to tell you *three* stories from my life."[13] His speech followed the outline. He told three personal stories from his life, explained what they taught him, and turned those stories into lessons for the graduates.

Applying the Rule of Three

As we've learned, business leaders often prepare for major television interviews or keynote presentations by structuring their message around three or four key points. I know, because I train them to do so! Here is how I would apply the advice from Scenes 4 and 5 to prepare for an interview on the topic of this book. First, I would create a headline of no more than 140 characters: "Deliver a presentation like Steve Jobs." Next, I would write three big ideas: (1) Create the story, (2) Deliver the experience, and (3) Package the material. Under each of the three ideas, I would include rhetorical devices to enhance the narrative: stories, examples, and facts. Following is an example of how an abbreviated interview might unfold:

REPORTER: Carmine, tell us more about this book.

CARMINE: *The Presentation Secrets of Steve Jobs* reveals, for the first time, how to do deliver a presentation like Steve Jobs. The Apple CEO is considered one of the most electrifying speakers in the world today. This book walks you through the very steps he uses to sell his ideas. Best of all, anyone can learn these techniques to improve his or her very next presentation.

REPORTER: OK, so where would we start?

CARMINE: You can deliver a presentation like Steve Jobs [repeat the headline at least twice in a conversation] if you follow these three steps: First, create the story. Second, deliver the experience. And third, package the material. Let's talk about the first step, creating the story . . .

Jimmy V's Famous Speech

On March 4, 1993, college basketball coach Jimmy Valvano gave one of the most emotional speeches in recent sports history. Valvano had led North Carolina State to the NCAA championship in 1983. Ten years later, dying of cancer, Valvano accepted the Arthur Ashe Courage & Humanitarian Award. Valvano's use of the rule of three provided the two most poignant moments of the speech (emphasis added):

> To me, there are *three* things we all should do every day. We should do this every day of our lives. *Number one* is laugh. You should laugh every day. *Number two* is think. You should spend some time in thought. And *number three* is, you should have your emotions moved to tears—could be happiness or joy. But think about it. If you laugh, you think, and you cry, that's a full day . . . Cancer can take away all my physical ability. It cannot touch my mind; it cannot touch my heart; and it cannot touch my soul. And those three things are going to carry on forever. I thank you and God bless all of you.[14]

As you can tell in this example, providing a road map of three parts creates an outline for a short interview, a much longer interview, or an entire presentation.

Your listeners' brains are working overtime. They're consuming words, images, and sensory experiences, not to mention conducting their own internal dialogues. Make it easy for them to follow your narrative.

DIRECTOR'S NOTES

» Create a list of all the key points you want your audience to know about your product, service, company, or initiative.

» Categorize the list until you are left with only three major message points. This group of three will provide the verbal road map for your pitch or presentation.

» Under each of your three key messages, add rhetorical devices to enhance the narrative. These could include some or all of the following: personal stories, facts, examples, analogies, metaphors, and third-party endorsements.

Introduce the Antagonist

Will Big Blue dominate the entire computer industry? Was George Orwell right?

—STEVE JOBS

n every classic story, the hero fights the villain. The same storytelling outline applies to world-class presentations. Steve Jobs establishes the foundation of a persuasive story by introducing his audience to an antagonist, an enemy, a problem in need of a solution. In 1984, the enemy was "Big Blue."

Apple is behind one of the most influential television ads in history and one in which we begin to see the hero-villain scenario playing out in Jobs's approach to messaging. The television ad, 1984, introduced Macintosh to the world. It ran only once, during the January 22 Super Bowl that same year. The Los Angeles Raiders were crushing the Washington Redskins, but more people remember the spot than the score.

Ridley Scott, of *Alien* fame, directed the Apple ad, which begins with shaven-headed drones listening to their leader (Big Brother) on a giant screen. An athletic blonde, dressed in skimpy eighties-style workout clothes, is running with a sledgehammer. Chased by helmeted storm troopers, the girl throws the hammer into the screen, which explodes in a blinding light as the drones sit with their mouths wide open. The spot ends with a somber announcer saying, "On January 24, Apple Computer will introduce Macintosh and you'll see why 1984 won't be like *1984*."[1]

Apple's board members had unanimously disliked the commercial and were reluctant to run it. Jobs, of course, supported it, because he understood the emotional power behind the classic story structure of the hero and villain. He realized every protagonist needs an enemy. In the case of the historic 1984 television ad, IBM represented the villain. IBM, a mainframe computer maker at the time, had made the decision to build a competitor to the world's first mass-market home computer, the Apple II. Jobs explained the ad in a 1983 keynote presentation to a select group of Apple salespeople who previewed the sixty-second television spot.

"It is now 1984," said Jobs. "It appears IBM wants it all. Apple is perceived to be the only hope to offer IBM a run for its money . . . IBM wants it all and is aiming its guns on its last obstacle to industry control: Apple. Will Big Blue dominate the entire computer industry? The entire information age? Was George Orwell right?"[2]

With that introduction, Jobs stepped aside as the assembled salespeople became the first public audience to see the commercial. The audience erupted into a thunderous cheer. For another sixty seconds, Steve remained onstage basking in the adulation, his smile a mile wide. His posture, body language, and facial expression said it all—*I nailed it!*

Problem + Solution = Classic Jobs

Introducing the antagonist (the problem) rallies the audience around the hero (the solution). Jobs structures his most exciting presentations around this classic storytelling device. For example, thirty minutes into one of his most triumphant presentations, the launch of the iPhone at Macworld 2007, he spent three minutes explaining why the iPhone is a product whose time has come. The villains in this case included all the current smartphones on the market, which, Jobs would argue, weren't very smart. Listed in the left column of Table 6.1 are excerpts from the actual presentation; the right column shows the words or describes the images on the accompanying slides.[3] Pay attention to how the slides act as a complement to the speaker.

TABLE 6.1 JOBS'S iPHONE KEYNOTE PRESENTATION

STEVE'S WORDS	STEVE'S SLIDES
"The most advanced phones are called 'smartphones,' so they say."	Smartphone
"They typically combine a phone plus e-mail plus a baby Internet."	Smartphone Phone + Email + Internet
"The problem is they are not so smart and they are not so easy to use. They're really complicated. What we want to do is make a leapfrog product that is way smarter than any mobile device has ever been."	Smartphone Not so smart. Not so easy to use.
"So, we're going to reinvent the phone. We're going to start with a revolutionary user interface."	Revolutionary UI
"It is the result of years of research and development."	Revolutionary UI Years of research & development
"Why do we need a revolutionary user interface? Here are four smartphones: the Motorola Q, BlackBerry, Palm Treo, Nokia E62—the usual suspects."	Image of four existing smartphones: Motorola Q, BlackBerry, Palm Treo, and Nokia E62
"What's wrong with their user interface? The problem with them is in the bottom forty. It's this stuff right there [points to keyboards on the phones]. They all have these keyboards that are there whether you need them or not. And they all have these control	The top half of each image fades away, leaving just the bottom half—the keyboard

continued

TABLE 6.1 JOBS'S iPHONE KEYNOTE PRESENTATION (continued)

STEVE'S WORDS	STEVE'S SLIDES
buttons that are fixed in plastic and are the same for every application. Well, every application wants a slightly different user interface, a slightly optimized set of buttons just for it. And what happens if you think of a great idea six months from now? You can't add a button to these things. They're already shipped. So, what do you do?"	
"What we're going to do is get rid of all these buttons and just make a giant screen."	Image of iPhone
"How are we going to communicate with this? We don't want to carry around a mouse. So, what are we going to do? A stylus, right? We're going to use a stylus."	Image of iPhone on its side; a stylus fades in
"No [laughs]. Who wants a stylus? You have to get them out, put them away—you lose them. Yuck. Nobody wants a stylus."	Words appear next to image: Who wants a stylus?
"So, let's not use a stylus. We're going to use the best pointing device in the world—a pointing device that we're all born with. We're born with ten of them. We'll use our fingers."	Stylus fades out of frame as image of index finger appears next to iPhone
"We have invented a new technology called 'multi-touch,' which is phenomenal."	Finger fades out, and words appear: Multi-Touch
"It works like magic. You don't need a stylus. It's far more accurate than any touch display that's ever been shipped. It ignores unintended touches. It's supersmart. You can do multi-finger gestures on it, and boy have we patented it!" [laughter]	Words reveal upper right: Works like magic No stylus Far more accurate Ignores unintended touches Multi-finger gestures Patented

Make note of how Jobs asks rhetorical questions to advance the story. "Why do we need a revolutionary user interface?" he asked before introducing the problem. He even raises problems to his own solution. When he introduced the concept of replacing the keyboard with a touch screen, he rhetorically asked, "How are we going to communicate with this?" His ready answer was, "We're going to use the best pointing device in the world . . . our fingers."

Nobody really cares about your product or Apple's products or Microsoft's or any other company's, for that matter. What people care about is solving problems and making their lives a little better. As in the smartphone example in Table 6.1, Jobs describes the pain they're feeling, gives them a reason for their pain (usually caused by competitors), and, as you will learn in Scene 7, offers a cure.

Making His Case to CNBC

"Why in the world would Apple want to jump into the handset market with so much competition and so many players?" asked CNBC's Jim Goldman in one of the few interviews Jobs granted immediately after the iPhone announcement. Jobs answered the question by posing a problem in need of a solution: "We used all the handsets out there, and boy is it frustrating. It's a category that needs to be reinvented. Handsets need to be more powerful and much easier to use. We thought we could contribute something. We don't mind if there are other companies making products. The fact is there were one billion handsets sold in 2006. If we just got 1 percent market share, that's ten million units. We've reinvented the phone and completely changed the expectations for what you can carry in your pocket."

"What message is this sending to your competitors?" asked Goldman.

"We're a product company. We love great products. In order to explain what our product is, we have to contrast it to what products are out there right now and what people use," said Jobs.[4] This last sentence reveals Jobs's approach to crafting a persuasive story. Explanations of new products or services require context, a relevance to a problem in your customer's life that is causing that person "pain." Once the pain is established, your listener will be much more receptive to a product or service that will alleviate that pain.

The Apple Religion

In his book *Buyology*, marketing guru Martin Lindstrom equates Apple's message with the same powerful ideas that propel widespread religions. Both appeal to a common vision and a specific enemy.

"Most religions have a clear vision," writes Lindstrom. "By that I mean they are unambiguous in their missions, whether it's to achieve a certain state of grace or achieve a spiritual goal. And, of course, most companies have unambiguous missions as well. Steve Jobs's vision dates back to the mid-1980s when he said, 'Man is the creator of change in this world. As such he should be above systems and structures, and not subordinate to them.' Twenty years and a few million iPods later, the company still pursues this vision."[5]

According to Lindstrom, who spent years studying the common traits of lasting brands, religions and brands such as Apple have another quality in common: the idea of conquering a shared enemy. "Having an identifiable enemy gives us the chance not only to articulate and showcase our faith, but also to unite ourselves with our fellow believers . . . this us-versus-them strategy attracts fans, incites controversy, creates loyalty, and gets us thinking—and arguing—and, of course, buying."[6]

Will It Eat Me?

Establishing the antagonist early is critical to persuasion, because our brains needs a bucket—a category—in which to place a new idea. Think about it this way: your brain craves meaning before details. According to scientist John Medina, our brains were formed to see the big picture. Medina says that when primitive man saw a saber-toothed tiger, he asked himself, "Will it eat me?" and not "How many teeth does it have?"

The antagonist gives your audience the big picture. "Don't start with the details. Start with the key ideas and, in a hierarchical fashion, form the details around these larger notions," writes Medina in his book *Brain Rules*.[7] In presentations, start with the big picture—the problem—before filling in the details (your solution).

Apple unveiled the Safari Web browser during Macworld 2003, designating it the fastest browser on the Mac. Safari would join several other browsers vying for attention in the face of Microsoft's juggernaut—Internet Explorer. At his persuasive best, Jobs set up the problem—introducing the antagonist—simply by asking a rhetorical question: "Why do we need our own browser?"[8] Before demonstrating the new features—filling in the details—he needed to establish a reason for the product's existence.

Jobs told the audience that there were two areas in which competitors such as Internet Explorer, Netscape, and others fell short: speed and innovation. In terms of speed, Jobs said Safari would load pages three times faster than Internet Explorer on the Mac. In the area of innovation, Jobs discussed the limitations of current browsers, including the fact that Google search was not provided in the main toolbar and that organizing bookmarks left a lot to be desired. "What we found in our research is that people don't use bookmarks. They don't use favorites very much because this stuff is complicated and nobody has figured out how to use it," Jobs said. Safari would fix the problems by incorporating Google search into the main toolbar and adding features that would allow users to more easily navigate back to previous sites or favorite Web pages.

One simple sentence is all you need to introduce the antagonist: "Why do you need this?" This one question allows Jobs to review the current state of the industry (whether it be browsers, operating systems, digital music, or any other facet) and to set the stage for the next step in his presentation, offering the solution.

The $3,000-a-Minute Pitch

During one week in September, dozens of entrepreneurs pitch their start-ups to influential groups of media, experts, and investors at two separate venues—TechCrunch 50 in San Francisco and DEMO in San Diego. For start-up founders, these high-stakes presentations mean the difference between success and obsolescence. TechCrunch organizers believe that eight minutes is the ideal amount of time in which to communicate an idea. If you cannot express your idea in eight minutes, the thinking the goes, you need to refine your idea. DEMO gives its presenters even less time—six minutes. DEMO also charges an $18,500 fee to present, or $3,000 per minute. If you had to pay $3,000 a minute to pitch your idea, how would you approach it?

The consensus among venture capitalists who attend the presentations is that most entrepreneurs fail to create an intriguing story line because they jump right into their product without explaining the problem. One investor told me, "You need to create a new space in my brain to hold the information you're about to deliver. It turns me off when entrepreneurs offer a solution without setting up the problem. They have a pot of coffee—their idea—without a cup to pour it in." Your listeners' brains have only so much room to absorb new information. It's as if most presenters try to squeeze 2 MB of data into a pipe that carries 128 KB. It's simply too much.

A company called TravelMuse had one of the most outstanding pitches in DEMO 2008. Founder Kevin Fleiss opened his pitch this way: "The largest and most mature online retail segment is travel, totaling more than $90 billion in the United States alone [establishes category]. We all know how to book a trip online. But booking is the last 5 percent of the process [begins to introduce problem]. The 95 percent that comes before booking—deciding where to go, building a plan—is where all the heavy lifting happens. At TravelMuse we make planning easy by seamlessly integrating content with trip-planning tools to provide a complete experience [offers solution]."[9] By introducing the category and the problem before introducing the solution, Fleiss created the cup to pour the coffee into.

Investors are buying a stake in ideas. As such, they want to know what pervasive problem the company's product addresses. A solution in search of a problem carries far less appeal. Once the problem and solution are established, investors feel comfortable moving on to questions regarding the size of the market, the competition, and the business model.

The Ultimate Elevator Pitch

The problem need not take long to establish. Jobs generally takes just a few minutes to introduce the antagonist. You can do so in as little as thirty seconds. Simply create a one-sentence answer for the following four questions: (1) What do you do? (2) What problem do you solve? (3) How are you different? (4) Why should I care?

When I worked with executives at LanguageLine, in Monterey, California, we crafted an elevator pitch based on answers to the four questions. If we did our job successfully, the following pitch should tell you a lot about the company: "LanguageLine is the world's largest provider of phone interpretation services for companies who want to connect with their non-English-speaking customers [what it does]. Every twenty-three seconds, someone who doesn't speak English enters this country [the problem]. When he or she calls a hospital, a bank, an insurance company, or 911, it's likely that a LanguageLine interpreter is on the other end [how it's different]. We help you talk to your customers, patients, or sales prospects in 150 languages [why you should care]."

The Antagonist: A Convenient Storytelling Tool

Steve Jobs and former U.S. vice president turned global warming expert Al Gore share three things in common: a commitment to the environment, a love for Apple (Al Gore sits on Apple's board), and an engaging presentation style.

Al Gore's award-winning documentary, *An Inconvenient Truth*, is a presentation designed with Apple's storytelling devices in mind. Gore gives his audience a reason to listen by establishing a problem everyone can agree on (critics may differ on the solution, but the problem is generally accepted).

Gore begins his presentation—his story—by setting the stage for his argument. In a series of colorful images of Earth taken from various space missions, he not only gets audiences to appreciate the beauty of our planet but also introduces the problem. Gore opens with a famous photograph called "Earthrise," the first look at Earth from the moon's surface. Then Gore reveals a series of photographs in later years showing signs of global warming such as melting ice caps, receding shorelines, and hurricanes. "The ice has a story to tell us," he says. Gore then describes the villain in more explicit terms: the burning of fossil fuels such as coal, gas, and oil has dramatically increased the amount of carbon dioxide in the earth's atmosphere, causing global temperatures to rise.

In one of the most memorable scenes of the documentary, Gore explains the problem by showing two colored lines (red and blue) representing levels of carbon dioxide and average temperatures going back six hundred thousand years. According to Gore, "When there is more carbon dioxide, the temperature gets warmer." He then reveals a slide that shows the graph climbing to the highest level of carbon dioxide in our planet's history—which represents where the level is today. "Now if you'll bear with me, I want to really emphasize this next point," Gore says as he climbs onto a mechanical lift. He presses a button, and the lift carries him what appears to be at least five feet. He is now parallel with the point on the graph representing current CO_2 emissions. This elicits a small laugh from his audience. It's funny but insightful at the same time. "In less than fifty years," he goes on to say, "it's going to continue to go up. When some of these children who are here are my age, here's where it's going to be." At this point, Gore presses the button again, and the lift carries him higher for about ten seconds. As he's tracking the graph upward, he turns to the audience and says, "You've heard of 'off the charts'? Well, here's where we're going to be in less than fifty years."[10] It's funny, memorable, and powerful at the same time. Gore takes facts, figures, and statistics and brings them to life.

Gore uses many of the same presentation and rhetorical techniques that we see in a Steve Jobs presentation. Among them are the introduction of the enemy, or the antagonist. Both men introduce an antagonist early, rallying the audience around a common purpose. In a Jobs presentation, once the villain is clearly established, it's time to open the curtain to reveal the character who will save the day . . . the conquering hero.

DIRECTOR'S NOTES

» Introduce the antagonist early in your presentation. Always establish the problem before revealing your solution. You can do so by painting a vivid picture of your customers' pain point. Set up the problem by asking, "Why do we need this?"

» Spend some time describing the problem in detail. Make it tangible. Build the pain.

» Create an elevator pitch for your product using the four-step method described in this chapter. Pay particular attention to question number 2, "What problem do you solve?" Remember, nobody cares about your product. People care about solving their problems.

Reveal the Conquering Hero

**The only problem with Microsoft is they
just have no taste. And I don't mean that in
a small way. I mean that in a big way.**

—STEVE JOBS

Steve Jobs is a master at creating villains—the more treacherous, the better. Once Jobs introduces the antagonist of the moment (the limitation to current products), he introduces the hero, revealing the solution that will make your life easier and more enjoyable. In other words, an Apple product arrives in time to save the day. IBM played the antagonist in the 1984 television ad, as discussed in Scene 6. Jobs revealed the ad for the first time to a group of internal salespeople at an event in the fall of 1983.

Before showing the ad, Jobs spent several minutes painting "Big Blue" into a character bent on world domination. (It helped that IBM was known as Big Blue at the time. The similar ring to Big Brother was not lost on Jobs.) Jobs made Big Blue look more menacing than Hannibal Lecter:

It is 1958. IBM passes up the chance to a buy a new, fledgling company that has invented a new technology called xerography. Two years later, Xerox is born, and IBM has been kicking itself ever since. It is ten years later. The late sixties. Digital Equipment, DEC, and others invent the minicomputer. IBM

dismisses the minicomputer as too small to do serious computing and therefore unimportant to their business. DEC
grows to become a multihundred-million-dollar corporation, while IBM finally enters the minicomputer market. It
is now ten years later. The late seventies. In 1977, Apple, a
young, fledgling company on the West Coast, invents the
Apple II, the first personal computer as we know it today
[introduces the hero]. IBM dismisses the personal computer
as too small to do serious computing and unimportant to
their business [the villain overlooking the hero's qualities].
The early eighties. In 1981, Apple II has become the world's
most popular computer, and Apple has grown into a $300
million company, becoming the fastest-growing corporation
in American business history. With over fifty competitors
vying for a share, IBM enters the personal computer market
in November 1981, with the IBM PC. 1983. Apple and IBM
emerge as the industry's strongest competitors, each selling
over $1 billion in personal computers in 1983 [David has
now matched Goliath]. The shakeout is in full swing. The
first major firm goes bankrupt, with others teetering on the
brink. It is now 1984. It appears IBM wants it all [the hero
is about to spring into action]. Apple is perceived to be the
only hope to offer IBM a run for its money. Dealers initially
welcoming IBM with open arms now fear an IBM-dominated
and -controlled future. They are increasingly and desperately
turning back to Apple as the only force that will ensure their
future freedom.[1]

The audience broke out into wild cheers as Jobs created a classic
showdown. Jobs played his best James Bond. Just as the villain
is about to destroy the world, Bond—or Jobs—enters the scene
and calmly saves the day. Ian Fleming would be proud.

The Hero's Mission

The hero's mission in a Steve Jobs presentation is not nec-
essarily to slay the bad guy, but to make our lives better. The

introduction of the iPod on October 23, 2001, demonstrates this subtle but important difference.

It helps to understand the state of the digital music industry at the time. People were carrying portable CD players that looked monstrous compared with today's tiny iPods. The few existing digital music players were big and clunky or simply not that useful due to a small storage capacity that allowed only a few dozen songs. Some products, such as the Nomad Jukebox, were based on a 2.5-inch hard drive and, while portable, were heavy and were painfully slow to transfer songs from a PC. Battery life was so short that the devices were pretty much useless. Recognizing a problem in need of a solution, Jobs entered as the conquering hero.

"Why music?" Jobs asked rhetorically.

"We love music. And it's always good to do something you love. More importantly, music is a part of everyone's life. Music has been around forever. It will always be around. This is not a speculative market. And because it's a part of everyone's life, it's a very large target market all around the world. But interestingly enough, in this whole new digital-music revolution, there is no market leader. No one has found a recipe for digital music. We found the recipe."

Once Jobs whetted the audience's appetite by announcing that Apple had found the recipe, he had set the stage. His next step would be to introduce the antagonist. He did so by taking his audience on a tour of the current landscape of portable music players. Jobs explained that if you wanted to listen to music on the go, you could buy a CD player that held ten to fifteen songs, a flash player, an MP3 player, or a hard-drive device such as the Jukebox. "Let's look at each one," Jobs said.

A CD player costs about $75 and holds about ten to fifteen songs on a CD. That's about $5 a song. You can buy a flash player for $150. It holds about ten to fifteen songs, or about $10 a song. You can go buy an MP3 CD player that costs $150, and you can burn up to 150 songs, so you get down to a dollar a song. Or you can buy a hard-drive Jukebox player for $300. It holds about one thousand songs and costs thirty cents a song. We studied all these, and that's where we want to be [points to "hard drive" category on slide]. We are introducing a product today that takes us exactly there, and that product is called iPod.

With that, Jobs introduced the hero, the iPod. The iPod, he said, is an MP3 music player that plays CD-quality music. "But the biggest thing about iPod is that it holds a thousand songs. This is a quantum leap because for most people, it's their entire music library. This is huge. How many times have you gone on the road and realized you didn't bring the CD you wanted to listen to? But the coolest thing about iPod is your entire music library fits in your pocket. This was never possible before."[2] By reinforcing the fact that one's entire music library could fit in a pocket, Jobs reinforces the hero's (iPod) most innovative quality, reminding the audience that this was never possible until Apple appeared to save the day.

After the iPod's introduction, Knight-Ridder columnist Mike Langberg wrote an article in which he pointed out that Creative (the maker of the original Nomad Jukebox) saw the opportunity in portable music players before Apple and unveiled a 6 GB hard-drive player in September 2000; Apple followed with its first iPod a year later. "But," he noted, "Creative lacks Apple's not-so-secret weapon: founder, chairman, and chief evangelist, Steve Jobs."[3]

"I'm a Mac." "I'm a PC."

The "Get a Mac" advertising campaign kicked off in 2006 and quickly became one of the most celebrated and recognizable television campaigns in recent corporate history. Comedian John Hodgman plays "the PC," while actor Justin Long plays the "Mac guy." Both are standing against a stark white background, and the ads typically revolve around a story line in which the PC character is stuffy, slow, and frustrated, whereas the Mac has a friendly, easygoing personality. The ads play out the villain (PC) and hero (Mac) plot in thirty-second vignettes.

In one early ad (Angel/Devil), the Mac character gives PC an iPhoto book. An "angel" and a "devil" appear (the PC character dressed in a white suit and a red suit). The angel encourages PC to compliment Mac, while the devil prods PC to rip the book in half. The metaphor is clear. I'm a Mac/I'm a PC could be titled "I'm the good guy/I'm the bad guy."[4]

Once the hero is established, the benefit must be made clear. The one question that matters to people—Why should I care?—must be answered immediately. In an ad titled Out of the Box, both characters pop out of boxes. The conversation goes like this:

MAC: Ready to get started?

PC: Not quite. I've got a lot to do. What's your big plan?

MAC: Maybe make a home movie, create a website, try out my built-in camera. I can do it all right out of the box. What about you?

PC: First, I've got to download those new drivers, I have to erase the trial software that came on my hard drive, and I've got a lot of manuals to read.

MAC: Sounds like you've got a lot of stuff to do before you do any stuff. I'm going to get started, because I'm kind of excited. Let me know when you're ready. [Jumps out of box]

PC: Actually, the rest of me is in some other boxes. I'll meet up with you later.

Some observers have criticized Apple's campaign, saying it smacked of smug superiority. Whether you like the ads or hate them, there is no question they are effective, if only to keep people talking about Apple. In fact, the ads were so successful that Microsoft countered with an ad campaign of its own showing famous and not-so-famous people in all walks of life proudly proclaiming, "I'm a PC." But Apple had landed the first punch, painting the PC as nerdy and Apple as the cool kid you really want to be like. The Microsoft ads are fun to watch but lack the emotional punch of Apple's ads, for one reason—there's no villain.

Problem and Solution in Thirty Seconds

With more than ten thousand applications available for the iPhone, the App Store has been a resounding success for Apple. The company features some individual apps in television and print ads for the iPhone and iPod Touch. The television ads are effective because in thirty seconds they paint a picture of a problem and offer a solution.

For example, in one ad for an app called Shazam, a narrator says, "You know when you don't know what song is playing and it's driving you crazy? [introduces problem] With the Shazam app, you just hold up your iPhone to the song, and within seconds you will know who sings it and how to get it."[5] The taglines are always the same: "That's the iPhone. Solving life's dilemmas one app at a time."

In thirty seconds, the commercials succeed in raising a problem and solving those problems one app at a time. The ads prove that establishing problems and offering solutions need not be time consuming. Don't spend too much time getting to the punch line.

Jobs Doesn't Sell Computers; He Sells an Experience

After identifying the villain and introducing the hero, the next step in the Apple narrative is to show how the hero clearly offers the victim—the consumer—an escape from the villain's grip. The solution must be simple and free of jargon. Visit the Apple site, for instance, and you will find the top reasons "why you'll love a Mac."[6] The list includes specific benefits and largely avoids complicated technical language. As a case in point, instead of saying that a MacBook Pro comes with an Intel Core 2 Duo 2.4 GHz, 2 GB, 1,066 MHz, DDR3 SDRAM, and a 250 GB Serial ATA 5,400 rpm, the site lists direct benefits to the customer: "It's gorgeous inside and out; it does what a PC does, only better; it has the world's most advanced operating system, and then some; it's a pleasure to buy and own." You see, your target customers are not buying a 2.4 GHz multicore processor. They are buying the *experience* the processor provides.

Unlike his competitors, Jobs largely avoids mind-numbing data, stats, and jargon in his presentations. During Macworld 2006, Jobs added his famous "One more thing" signature phrase near the end of the presentation. The one more thing turned out to be the new MacBook Pro with an Intel Core 2 microprocessor, marking the first Intel chips in Mac notebooks. Jobs took a few minutes to clearly outline the problem and introduce the hero's tangible benefits, in plain and simple language.

"There's been this pesky little problem in the PowerBooks," Jobs said.

"It's not a secret that we've been trying to shoehorn a G5 [IBM microprocessor] into the PowerBook and have been unable to do so because of its power consumption. It's unrealistic in such a small package. We've done everything possible engineeringwise. We've consulted every possible higher authority [shows a slide with a photograph of the pope, drawing a huge laugh]."

Replacing the existing microprocessor with an Intel Core Duo, Jobs explained, yielded much better performance in a smaller package.

> Today we are introducing a new notebook computer we are calling the MacBook Pro. It has an Intel Core Duo chip in it, the same as we're putting in the new iMac, which means there will be dual processors in every MacBook Pro. What does this yield? It's four to five times faster than the PowerBookG4. These things are screamers . . . The new MacBook Pro is the fastest Mac notebook ever. It's also the thinnest. It's got some amazing new features. It has a 15.4-inch wide-screen display that is as bright as our cinema displays. It's a gorgeous display. It's got an iSight camera built in. Now you can have videoconferencing right out of the box on the go. It's great. Videoconferencing to go. This is heaven.[7]

You may or may not agree that a portable webcam is "heaven," but Jobs knows his audience and voices what is, to those present, a serious problem in need of a solution.

This skill, the ability to create a villain and sell the benefit behind the hero's solution, is a Steve Jobs messaging technique that appears in nearly every presentation and interview he gives. When Jobs agreed to be interviewed for Smithsonian's oral and video history series, he said that perseverance separates the successful entrepreneurs from the nonsuccessful ones. Perseverance, he said, comes from passion. "Unless you have a lot of passion about this, you're not going to survive. You're going to give it up. So, you've got to have an idea or a problem or a wrong that you want to right that you're passionate about. Otherwise, you're not going to have the perseverance to stick it through. I think that's half the battle right there."[8]

Jobs is the Indiana Jones of business. Just as great movie characters vanquish the villain, Jobs identifies a common enemy, conquers that enemy, and wins over the hearts and minds of his audience as he walks off into the sunset, leaving the world a better place.

DIRECTOR'S NOTES

» Describe the state of the industry (or product category) as it currently stands, followed by your vision of where it could be.

» Once you have established the antagonist—your customers' pain point—describe in plain English how your company, product, or service offers a cure for that pain.

» Remember, Steve Jobs believes that unless you're passionate about a problem that you want to make right, you won't have the perseverance to stick it out.

Obey the Ten-Minute Rule

Your audience checks out after ten minutes. Not in eleven minutes, but ten. We know this valuable fact thanks to new research into cognitive functioning. Simply put, the brain gets bored. According to molecular biologist John Medina, "The brain seems to be making choices according to some stubborn timing pattern, undoubtedly influenced by both culture and gene."[1] Medina says peer-reviewed studies confirm the ten-minute rule, as do his own observations. In every college course Medina teaches, he asks the same question: "Given a class of medium interest, not too boring and not too exciting, when do you start glancing at the clock, wondering when the class will be over?" The answer is always exactly the same—ten minutes.

Steve Jobs does not give the brain time to get bored. In a thirty-minute period, his presentations include demonstrations, a second or even third speaker, and video clips. Jobs is well aware that even his gifts of persuasion are no match for a tired brain constantly seeking new stimuli.

Exactly ten minutes into his presentation at Macworld 2007— and not a second more—Jobs revealed a new Apple television commercial for iTunes and iPods (the one with a dark silhouette of people dancing in front of brightly colored backgrounds— the silhouettes are holding iPods, and the stark white earphones noticeably stick out). "Isn't that great?" Jobs said as the commercial ended.[2] Jobs essentially provided an "intermission" between the first act of his presentation (music) and the second (the launch of Apple TV, a product designed to play iTunes content on a widescreen TV).

Obey the ten-minute rule and give your listeners' brains a break. Here we go . . . on to Act 2: delivering the experience.

ACT 2

Deliver the
Experience

Steve Jobs does not deliver a presentation. He offers an experience. Imagine visiting New York City to watch an award-winning play on Broadway. You would expect to see multiple characters, elaborate stage props, stunning visual backgrounds, and one glorious moment when you knew that the money you spent on the ticket was well worth it. In Act 2, you will discover that a Steve Jobs presentation contains each of these elements, helping Jobs create a strong emotional connection between himself and his audience.

Just as in Act 1, each scene will be followed by a summary of specific and tangible lessons you can easily apply today. Following is a short description of each scene in this act:

» **SCENE 8: "Channel Their Inner Zen."** Simplification is a key feature in all of Apple's designs. Jobs applies the same approach to the way he creates his slides. Every slide is simple, visual, and engaging.

» **SCENE 9: "Dress Up Your Numbers."** Data is meaningless without context. Jobs makes statistics come alive and, most important, discusses numbers in a context that is relevant to his audience.

» **SCENE 10: "Use 'Amazingly Zippy' Words."** The "mere mortals" who experience an "unbelievable" Steve Jobs presentation find it "cool," "amazing," and "awesome." These are just some of the zippy words Jobs uses frequently. Find out why Jobs uses the words he does and why they work.

» **SCENE 11: "Share the Stage."** Apple is a rare company whose fortunes are closely tied to its cofounder. Despite the fact that Apple has a deep bench of brilliant leaders, many observers say Apple is a one-man show. Perhaps. But Jobs treats presentations as a symphony.

» **SCENE 12: "Stage Your Presentation with Props."** Demonstrations play a very important supporting role in every Jobs presentation. Learn how to deliver demos with pizzazz.

» **SCENE 13: "Reveal a 'Holy Shit' Moment."** From his earliest presentations, Jobs had a flair for the dramatic. Just when you think you have seen all there is to see or heard all there is to hear, Jobs springs a surprise. The moment is planned and scripted for maximum impact.

Channel Their Inner Zen

Simplicity is the ultimate sophistication.

—STEVE JOBS, QUOTING LEONARDO DA VINCI

Simplicity is one of the most important concepts in all Apple designs—from computers, to music players, to phones, and even to the retail store experience. "As technology becomes more complex, Apple's core strength of knowing how to make very sophisticated technology comprehensible to mere mortals is in ever greater demand,"[1] Jobs told a *New York Times* columnist writing a piece about the iPod in 2003.

Apple's design guru, Jony Ive, was interviewed for the same *New York Times* article and noted that Jobs wanted to keep the original iPod free of clutter and complexity. What the team removed from the device was just as important as what they kept in. "What's interesting is that out of that simplicity, and almost that unashamed sense of simplicity, and expressing it, came a very different product. But difference wasn't the goal. It's actually very easy to create a different thing. What was exciting is starting to realize that its difference was really a consequence of this quest to make it a very simple thing,"[2] Ive said. According to Ive, complexity would have meant the iPod's demise.

Jobs makes products easy to use by eliminating features and clutter. This process of simplification translates to the way Jobs designs his slides as well. "It's laziness on the presenter's part to put everything on one slide," writes Nancy Duarte.[3] Where most presenters add as many words as possible to a slide, Jobs removes and removes and removes.

A Steve Jobs presentation is strikingly simple, visual, and devoid of bullet points. That's right—no bullet points. Ever. Of course, this raises the question, would a PowerPoint presentation without bullets still be a PowerPoint presentation? The answer is yes, and a much more interesting one. New research into cognitive functioning—how the brain works—proves that bullet points are the *least* effective way to deliver important information. Neuroscientists are finding that what passes as a typical presentation is usually the worst way to engage your audience.

"The brain is fundamentally a lazy piece of meat," writes Dr. Gregory Berns in *Iconoclast*.[4] In other words, the brain doesn't like to waste energy; it has evolved to be as efficient as possible. Presentation software such as PowerPoint makes it far too easy to overload the brain, causing it to work *way* too hard. Open PowerPoint, and the standard slide template has room for a title and subtitles, or bullets. If you are like most presenters, you write a title to the slide and add a bullet, a subbullet, and often a sub-subbullet. The result looks like the sample slide in Figure 8.1.

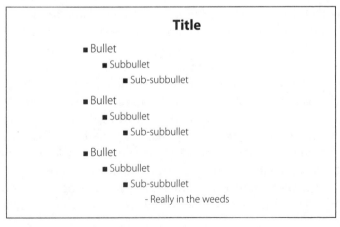

Figure 8.1 A typical, boring PowerPoint template.

This slide format gives me the willies. It should scare the heck out of you, too. Designer Garr Reynolds calls these creations "slideuments," an attempt to merge documents with slides. "People think they are being efficient and simplifying things," according to Reynolds. "A kind of kill-two-birds-with-one-stone approach. Unfortunately, the only thing 'killed' is effective communication."[5] Reynolds argues that PowerPoint, used effectively, can complement and enhance a presentation. He is not in favor of ditching PowerPoint. He is, however, in favor of ditching the use of "ubiquitous" bulleted-list templates found in both PowerPoint and Keynote. "And it's long past time that we realized that putting the same information on a slide in text form that is coming out of our mouths usually does not help—in fact, it hurts our message."[6]

Creating Steve Jobs–like slides will make you stand out in a big way, if only because so few people create slides the way he does. Your audience will be shocked and pleased, quite simply because nobody else does it. Before we look at *how* he does it, though, let's explore *why* he does it. Steve practices Zen Buddhism. According to biographers Jeffrey Young and William Simon, Jobs began studying Zen in 1976.[7] A Zen Buddhist monk even officiated at his wedding to Lauren Powell in 1991.

A central principle of Zen is a concept called *kanso*, or simplicity. According to Reynolds, "The Japanese Zen arts teach us that it is possible to express great beauty and convey powerful messages through simplification."[8] Simplicity and the elimination

No More Pencils

We've been trained since youth to replace paying attention with taking notes. That's a shame. Your actions should demand attention. (Hint: bullets demand note taking. The minute you put bullets on the screen you are announcing, "Write this down, but don't really pay attention to it now.") People don't take notes when they go to the opera.[9]

—SETH GODIN, SETH'S BLOG

of clutter is a design component that Jobs incorporates into his products and slides. In fact, most everything about his approach to life is all-out Zen.

In 1982, photographer Diana Walker took a portrait of Jobs in the living room of his house. The room was huge, with a fireplace and ceiling-to-floor windows. Jobs sat on a small rug on a wooden floor. A lamp stood next to Jobs. Behind him were a record player and several albums, some of which were strewn on the floor. Now, Jobs could surely have afforded some furniture. He was, after all, worth more than $100 million when the photograph was taken. Jobs brings the same minimalist aesthetic to Apple's products. "One of the most important parts of Apple's design process is simplification," writes Leander Kahney in *Inside Steve's Brain*.[10]

"Jobs," says Kahney, "is never interested in technology for technology's sake. He never loads up on bells and whistles, cramming features into a product because they're easy to add. Just the opposite. Jobs pares back the complexity of his products until they are as simple and as easy to use as possible."[11]

When Apple first started in the 1970s, the company's ads had to stimulate demand for computers among ordinary consumers who, frankly, didn't quite see the need for these new devices. According to Kahney, "The ads were written in simple, easy-to-understand language with none of the technical jargon that dominates competitors' ads, who, after all, were trying to appeal to a completely different market—hobbyists."[12] Jobs has kept his messages simple ever since.

The influential German painter Hans Hofmann once said, "The ability to simplify means to eliminate the unnecessary so that the necessary may speak." By removing clutter—extraneous information—from his products and presentations, Jobs achieves the ultimate goal: ease of use and clarity.

Macworld 2008: The Art of Simplicity

To gain a fuller appreciation of Jobs's simple slide creations, I have constructed a table of excerpts from his Macworld 2008 keynote presentation. The column on the left in Table 8.1

contains his actual words, and the column on the right contains the text on the accompanying slides.[13]

In four slides, Jobs's presentation contained fewer words by far than what most other presenters cram onto one slide alone. Cognitive researchers like John Medina at the University of Washington have discovered that the average PowerPoint slide contains forty words. Jobs's first four slides have a grand total of seven words, three numbers, one date, and no bullet points.

Let's Rock

On September 9, 2008, Jobs revealed new features for the iTunes music store and released new iPod models for the holiday season. Prior to the event—dubbed "Let's Rock"—observers speculated

TABLE 8.1 EXCERPTS FROM JOBS'S MACWORLD 2008 KEYNOTE

STEVE'S WORDS	STEVE'S SLIDES
"I just want to take a moment and look back to 2007. Two thousand seven was an extraordinary year for Apple. Some incredible new products: the amazing new iMac, the awesome new iPods, and of course the revolutionary iPhone. On top of that, Leopard and all of the other great software we shipped in 2007."	2007
"It was an extraordinary year for Apple, and I want to just take a moment to say thank you. We have had tremendous support by all of our customers, and we really, really appreciate it. So, thank you for an extraordinary 2007."	Thank you.
"I've got four things I'd like to talk to you about today, so let's get started. The first one is Leopard."	1
"I'm thrilled to report that we have delivered over five million copies of Leopard in the first ninety days. Unbelievable. It's the most successful release of Mac OS X ever."	5,000,000 copies delivered in first 3 months

that Jobs might be in ill health, given his gaunt appearance. (In January 2009, Apple revealed that Jobs was losing weight due to a hormone imbalance and would take a leave of absence for treatment.) Jobs addressed the rumor as soon as he stepped onstage. He did so without saying a word about it. He let a slide do the talking (see Table 8.2).[14] It was simple and unexpected. It generated cheers and deflected the tension. The rest of the introduction was equally as compelling for its simplicity.

Make note of the words and figures on the slides in the table. The words on the slide match the exact words that Jobs uses to deliver his message. When Jobs says, "We're going to talk about music," the only word the audience sees is "Music." The words act as a complement.

If you deliver a point and your slide has too many words— and words that do not match what you say—your audience will have a hard time focusing on both you and the slide. In short, wordy slides detract from the experience. Simple slides keep the focus where it belongs—on you, the speaker.

Empirical Evidence

Empirical studies based on hard data, not opinions, prove that keeping your slides simple and free of extraneous information is the best way to engage your audience. Dr. Richard Mayer teaches educational psychology at the University of California, Santa Barbara, and has been studying multimedia learning since 1991. His theories are based on solid, empirical studies published in peer-reviewed journals. In a study titled "A Cognitive Theory of Multimedia Learning," Mayer outlined fundamental principles of multimedia design based on what scientists know about cognitive functioning. Steve Jobs's slides adhere to each of Mayer's principles:

MULTIMEDIA REPRESENTATION PRINCIPLE

"It is better to present an explanation in words and pictures than solely in words," writes Mayer.[15] According to Mayer, learners can

TABLE 8.2 EXCERPTS FROM JOBS'S 2008 "LET'S ROCK" PRESENTATION

STEVE'S WORDS	STEVE'S SLIDES
"Good morning. Thank you for coming this morning. We have some really exciting stuff to share with you. Before we do, I just wanted to mention this [gestures toward screen]."	The reports of my death are greatly exaggerated.
"Enough said. So, let's get on with the real topic of this morning, which is music. We're going to talk about music today, and we've got a lot of fun, new offerings."	Music
"So, let's start with iTunes."	iTunes
"iTunes, of course, is the ubiquitous music and video player married with the largest online content store in the world."	Image of iTunes home page
"iTunes now offers over eight and a half million songs. It's amazing. We started with two hundred thousand. We now have over eight and a half million songs."	8,500,000 songs
"Over one hundred and twenty-five thousand podcasts."	125,000 podcasts
"Over thirty thousand episodes of TV shows."	30,000 episodes of 1,000 TV shows
"Twenty-six hundred Hollywood movies."	2,600 Hollywood movies
"And, as of very recently, we now offer over three thousand applications for iPhone and iPod Touch."	3,000 applications for iPhone & iPod Touch
"And over the years, we've built up a great customer base. We're very pleased to announce that we've got over sixty-five million accounts in iTunes now. It's fantastic: sixty-five million customers."	65,000,000 accounts with credit cards

Two-Minute Warning

> *The task of leaders is to simplify. You should be able to explain where you have to go in two minutes.*[16]
>
> —JEROEN VAN DER VEER, CEO, ROYAL DUTCH SHELL

more easily understand material when it is presented in both words *and* pictures. In Mayer's experiments, groups that were exposed to multisensory environments—texts and pictures, animation, and video—always had much more accurate recall of the information, in some cases up to twenty years later!

CONTIGUITY PRINCIPLE

"When giving a multimedia explanation, present corresponding words and pictures contiguously rather than separately," Mayer advises.[17] In Mayer's experiments, he exposed students to certain types of information and then tested them on what they had learned. Those students who had read a text containing captioned illustrations near the corresponding words performed 65 percent better than those students who had read only plain text. Mayer says this principle is not surprising if you know how the brain works. When the brain is allowed to build two mental representations of an explanation—a verbal model and a visual model—the mental connections are that much stronger.

SPLIT-ATTENTION PRINCIPLE

Mayer also advises, "When giving a multimedia explanation, present words as auditory narration rather than visual on-screen text."[18] When presenting information, words delivered orally have greater impact than words read by your audience on a slide. Having too many words to process overloads the brain.

COHERENCE PRINCIPLE

"When giving a multimedia explanation," writes Mayer, "use few rather than many extraneous words and pictures."[19] Shorter presentations with more relevant information are more consistent with cognitive-learning theories. In sum, adding redundant or irrelevant information will impede, rather than aid, learning.

Mayer says an ideal slide would contain an image along with a simple line drawing directing the eye to the area that you want the viewer to see. This is called "signaling," and it is based on the scientific premise that your audience should not have to waste cognitive resources trying to find their place on the screen. Now, keep this in mind as we return to the "Let's Rock" event. About six minutes into the presentation, Jobs described a new feature available on iTunes—Genius (see Table 8.3).[20]

What could be easier to follow than simple line arrows pointing to the relevant area of a slide? Line drawings, few words, and a rich library of colorful images and photographs make up the majority of Jobs's slides. Simplicity—the elimination of clutter—is the theme that ties them all together.

The "McPresentation"

Critics once derided *USA Today* as "McPaper" for its short, easy-to-read stories. They're not laughing now. *USA Today* boasts the largest circulation of any newspaper in the United States. Readers love the colorful and bold graphics, charts, and photographs. After *USA Today* launched in 1982, many daily newspapers had no choice but to follow with shorter stories, splashes of color, and more photographs.

USA Today became famous for its "snapshots," stand-alone charts carried on the lower left of the main sections (i.e., News, Sports, Money, Life). They are easy-to-read statistical graphics that present information on various issues and trends in a visually appealing way. These graphics are among the best learning tools to create more visual slides. Study them. You'll see Richard Mayer's theory in action. Statistics share the slide with images, making the information more memorable. For an index of *USA Today* "snapshots," visit usatoday.com/snapshot/news/snapndex.htm.

TABLE 8.3 MORE EXCERPTS FROM JOBS'S 2008 "LET'S ROCK" PRESENTATION

STEVE'S WORDS	STEVE'S SLIDES
"We're introducing a new feature called Genius. Genius is pretty cool."	Genius
"What Genius does is automatically allow you to make playlists from songs in your music library that go great together, with just one click. It helps you rediscover music from your own music library and make great playlists that you probably wouldn't think of making any other way, and it really works well with just one click."	Automatically make playlists from songs in your library that go great together—with just one click
"So, that's what Genius is. Here's what it looks like. Let's say you're listening to a song—in my case, a Bob Dylan song."	Image of an iTunes library screen shot with a song highlighted
"There's a Genius button down here in the corner. You push that, and voilà—you've made a Genius playlist. In addition, you can bring up the Genius sidebar that makes recommendations from the iTunes store of music you might want to buy."	Animated circle appears and surrounds small Genius logo at bottom right of screen
"So, how does all this work? Well, we've got the iTunes store in the cloud, and we've added Genius algorithms to it."	Simple cloud line drawing with Genius logo inside
"So, you've got your music library. If you turn on Genius, it's going to send up information about your music library to iTunes so we can learn about your musical tastes. This information is sent completely anonymously."	Image of iTunes music library; arrow appears moving up from iTunes to cloud
"But it's not just information from you, because we are going to combine your information with the knowledge of millions of iTunes users as well."	Many images of iTunes music libraries appear alongside original
"And so, you're going to send your information up, and so are they."	Arrow up from original image to cloud, followed by more than a dozen arrows from other images

STEVE'S WORDS	STEVE'S SLIDES
"And as that happens, Genius just gets smarter, and smarter, and smarter."	Genius logo in cloud replaced with word "Smarter"
"Everybody benefits. When we send back down Genius results to you, they are tailored to your music library."	Arrow appears moving downward from cloud to iTunes library image
"So, automatically make playlists from songs in your library that go great together, with just one click. That's what Genius is about." [moves to demo]	

White Space

According to Garr Reynolds, there is a clear Zen aesthetic to Jobs's slides. "In Jobs's slides, you can see evidence of restraint, simplicity, and powerful yet subtle use of empty space."[21] Top designers such as Reynolds say the biggest mistake business professionals make is filling up every centimeter of the slide.

Nancy Duarte describes white space as giving your slides visual breathing room. "Visible elements of a slide often receive the most focus. But you need to pay equal attention to how much space you leave open . . . It's OK to have clear space—clutter is a failure of design."[22] Duarte says it's "laziness" on the part of the presenter to put everything on one slide.

Dense information and clutter requires too much effort for your audience. Simplicity is powerful. Empty space implies elegance, quality, and clarity. To see examples of how designers use space, visit some slide design contest winners at Slideshare.net (slideshare.net/contest/results-2008).

Picture Superiority Effect

By now I hope you have decided to gather up your current slides, especially those with bullet points, and burn them. At least burn them digitally by deleting them and emptying your recycle bin so you can never retrieve those slides again. The argument for the visual representation of ideas is such a powerful concept that psychologists have a term for it: the picture superiority effect (PSE).[23] Researchers have discovered that visual and verbal information are processed differently along multiple "channels" in your brain. What this means for you and your next presentation is simple: your ideas are much more likely to be remembered if they are presented as pictures instead of words.

Scientists who have advanced the PSE theory believe it represents a powerful way of learning information. According to John Medina, a molecular biologist at the University of Washington School of Medicine, "Text and oral presentations are not just less efficient than pictures for retaining certain types of information; they are *way* less efficient. If information is presented orally, people remember about 10 percent, tested seventy-two hours after exposure. That figure goes up to 65 percent if you add a picture."[24]

Pictures work better than text because the brain sees words as several tiny pictures. According to Medina, "My text chokes you, not because my text is not enough like pictures but because my text is too much like pictures. To our cortex, unnervingly, there is no such thing as words."[25]

Steve's Love of Photos

On June 9, 2008, Steve Jobs announced the introduction of the iPhone 3G at the WWDC. He used eleven slides to do so, employing the concept of PSE to its fullest. Only one slide contained words ("iPhone 3G"). The others were all photographs. Take a look at Table 8.4.[26]

Given the same information, a mediocre presenter would have crammed all of it onto one slide. It would have looked something like the slide in Figure 8.2. Which do you find more memorable: Jobs's eleven slides or the one slide with a bulleted list of features?

When Steve Jobs introduced the MacBook Air as "the world's thinnest notebook," one slide showed a photograph of the new

TABLE 8.4 JOBS'S WWDC 2008 KEYNOTE

STEVE'S WORDS	STEVE'S SLIDES
"As we arrive at iPhone's first birthday, we're going to take it to the next level."	Photo of birthday cake, with white frosting, strawberries, and one candle in the middle
"Today we're introducing the iPhone 3G. We've learned so much with the first iPhone. We've taken everything we've learned and more, and we've created the iPhone 3G. And it's beautiful."	iPhone 3G
"This is what it looks like [turns and gestures toward screen; audience laughs]. It's even thinner at the edges. It's really beautiful."	Side view of iPhone, so slim that it's hard to see on the slide and takes up very little space—an example of using empty space to communicate an idea
"It's got a full plastic back. It's really nice."	Full-screen view of the back
"Solid metal buttons."	Another side view of the device, where buttons are visible
"The same gorgeous 3.5-inch display."	Photo of front, showing display
"Camera."	Close-up photo of camera
"Flush headphone jack so you can use any headphones you like."	Close-up of headphone jack
"Improved audio. Dramatically improved audio."	Another photo from top of the device
"It's really, really great. And it feels even better in your hand, if you can believe it."	Returns to first side-view photo
"It's really quite wonderful. The iPhone 3G."	iPhone 3G

---

iPhone 3G

- Thinner at the edges
- Full plastic back
- Solid metal buttons
- 3.5-inch display
- Built-in camera
- Flush headphone jack
- Improved audio

Figure 8.2 Dull slides have no images and too many words.

computer on top of an envelope, which was even larger than the computer itself. That's it. No words, no text boxes, no graphs, just the photo. How much more powerful can you get? The picture says it all. For illustrative purposes, I created the slide in Figure 8.3 as an example of a typical slide that a mediocre presenter would have created to describe a technical product. (Believe it or not, this mock slide is gorgeous compared with many slides I have actually seen in technical presentations delivered by sub-par presenters.) It's a mishmash of fonts, styling, and text. Not memorable and truly awful.

In contrast, Figure 8.4 shows one of Jobs's slides from the Macbook Air presentation. The majority of his slides for this presentation looked very similar, featuring mostly photographs. He referred customers to the Apple website for more technical information; visuals dominated the keynote. Clearly, presenting a technical product in such a way as Jobs did for the Macbook Air is far more effective.

It takes confidence to deliver your ideas with photographs instead of words. Since you can't rely on the slides' text as a crutch, you must have your message down cold. But that's the difference between Jobs and millions of average communicators in business today. Jobs delivers his ideas simply, clearly, and confidently.

Simplify Everything

Simplicity applies to Jobs's slides as well as the words he carefully chooses to describe products. Just as Jobs's slides are free

MACBOOK AIR

Display

13.3 inch LED-backlit glossy widescreen display
- Support for millions of colors
- Supported resolutions:
- -1280 by 800 (native)
- -1024 by 768 (pixels)
- -4:3 (aspect ratio)

Size & Weight
- ✓ Height: 0.16–0.76 inch (0.4–1.94 cm)
- ✓ Width: 12.8 inches (32.5 cm)
- ✓ Depth: 8.94 inches (22.7 cm)
- ✓ Weight: 3.0 pounds (1.36 kg)

Storage
120 GB hard disk drive
or
128GB solid-state drive

Battery Power
- Integrated 37-watt hour lithium-polymer
- 45W MagSafe power adapter
- MagSafe power port
- 4.5 hours of wireless productivity

Processor & Memory
- 1.6ghz processor
  - 6MB shared L2 cashe
- 1066 MHz frontside bus
- 2GB of 1066 MHz DDR 3 SDRAM

Figure 8.3 An ugly slide with too much information, too many different fonts, and inconsistent styling.

Figure 8.4 Jobs's slides are strikingly simple and visually engaging.

TONY AVELAR/AFP/Getty Images

Einstein's Theory of Simplicity

If you can't explain it simply, you don't understand it well enough.

—ALBERT EINSTEIN

from extraneous text, so are his words. For example, in October 2008, Apple unveiled a new line of environmentally friendly MacBook computers. There are two principal ways Jobs could have described the computers. The column on the left in Table 8.5 is technically accurate but wordy; the text in the column on the right is what Jobs actually said.[27]

Jobs replaces lengthy sentences with descriptions that could fit in a Twitter post (see Scene 4). Simple sentences are simply easier to recall. Table 8.6 shows other examples of how Jobs *could* have described a new product, compared with what he actually said.

Plain English Campaign

If you need help writing crisp, clear sentences, the Plain English Campaign can help. Since 1979, this UK-based organization has been leading the fight to get governments and corporations to simplify their communications. The site is updated weekly with examples of the most complex, unintelligible business language submitted by readers around the world. The organizers define plain English as writing that the intended audience can read,

TABLE 8.5 DESCRIBING THE ENVIRONMENTALLY
FRIENDLY MACBOOK

WHAT STEVE COULD HAVE SAID	WHAT STEVE ACTUALLY SAID
The new MacBook family meets the most stringent Energy Star standards and contains no brominated flame retardants. It uses only PVC-free internal cables and components and features energy-efficient LED-backlit displays that are mercury free.	"They are the industry's greenest notebooks."

TABLE 8.6 POSSIBLE VERSUS ACTUAL DESCRIPTIONS IN
JOBS'S PRESENTATIONS

WHAT STEVE COULD HAVE SAID	WHAT STEVE ACTUALLY SAID
MacBook Air measures 0.16 inch at its thinnest point, with a maximum height of 0.76 inch.	"It's the world's thinnest notebook."
Time Capsule is an appliance combining an 802.11n base station with a server-grade hard disk that automatically backs up everything on one or more Macs running Leopard, the latest release of the Mac OS X operating system.	"With Time Capsule, plug it in, click a few buttons, and voilà—all the Macs in your house are backed up automatically."
Mac OS X features memory protection, pre-emptive multitasking, and symmetric multi-processing. It includes Apple's new Quartz 2D graphics engine based on the Internet-standard portable document format.	"Mac OS X is the most technically advanced personal computer operating system ever."

understand, and act upon the first time they read (or hear) it. The website has free guides on how to write in plain English as well as marvelous before-and-after examples, such as the ones in Table 8.7.[28]

Nearly everything you say in any memo, e-mail, or presentation can be edited for conciseness and simplicity. Remember that simplicity applies not just to the words on the slides but also to the words that come out of your mouth.

Author and advertising expert Paul Arden says that people go to a presentation to see you, not to read your words. He offers this tip: "Instead of giving people the benefit of your wit and wisdom (words), try painting them a picture. The more strikingly visual your presentation is, the more people will remember it."[29]

Leonardo da Vinci stated, "Simplicity is the ultimate sophistication." One of the most celebrated painters in history, he understood the real power of simplicity, as does Steve Jobs. When you discover this concept for yourself, your ideas will become far more persuasive than you could ever imagine.

TABLE 8.7 BEFORE-AND-AFTER EXAMPLES FROM THE PLAIN ENGLISH CAMPAIGN

BEFORE	AFTER
If there are any points on which you require explanation or further particulars we shall be glad to furnish such additional details as may be required by telephone.	If you have any questions, please call.
High-quality learning environments are a necessary precondition for facilitation and enhancement of the ongoing learning process.	Children need good schools to learn properly.
It is important that you shall read the notes, advice and information detailed opposite then complete the form overleaf (all sections) prior to its immediate return to the Council by way of the envelope provided.	Please read the notes before you fill in the form. Then send it back to us as soon as possible in the envelope provided.

DIRECTOR'S NOTES

» Avoid bullet points. Always. Well, almost always. Bullet points are perfectly acceptable on pages intended to be read by your audience, like books, documents, and e-mails. In fact, they break up the text quite nicely. Bullet points on presentation slides should be avoided. Pictures are superior.

» Focus on one theme per slide, and complement that theme with a photograph or image.

» Learn to create visually aesthetic slides. Above all, keep in mind that you do not have to be an artist to build slides rich in imagery. Visit carminegallo.com for a list of resources.

Dress Up
Your Numbers

We have sold four million iPhones to date. If you divide four million by two hundred days, that's twenty thousand iPhones every day on average.

—STEVE JOBS

On October 23, 2001, Apple launched a digital music player that would revolutionize the entire music industry—the iPod. At $399, however, it was an expensive gadget. The iPod stored songs on a five-gigabyte drive, but the number itself—5 GB—meant very little to the average music lover. In his keynote presentation, Jobs made that number more meaningful by saying that 5 GB provided enough storage for one thousand songs. While that sounds more impressive, it still did not provide a compelling value, since competitors were offering devices containing more storage at a lower price. But wait, Jobs assured his audience, there's more. Jobs said the new iPod weighed 6.5 ounces and was so small that it could "fit in your pocket." When Jobs pulled one out of his own pocket, it immediately clicked with the audience. The iPod's slogan said it all: "1,000 songs in your pocket."[1]

Rarely do numbers resonate with people until those numbers are placed in a context that people can understand, and the best way to help them understand is to make those numbers relevant to something with which they are already familiar. Five gigabytes may mean nothing to you, but one thousand songs in your pocket opens up an entirely new way for you to enjoy music.

Jobs dresses up numbers to make them more interesting. *Rolling Stone* reporter Jeff Goodell once asked Jobs what he thought about Apple's market share's being "stuck" at 5 percent in the United States. (The interview took place in 2003. As of this writing, Apple's market share of the computer industry is 10 percent.) The average reader might consider a 5 percent market share to be tiny. Jobs put the number in perspective when he described it this way: "Our market share is greater than BMW or Mercedes in the car industry. And yet, no one thinks BMW or Mercedes are going away and no one thinks they're at a tremendous disadvantage because of their market share. As a matter of fact, they're both highly desirable products and brands."[2] A 5 percent market share sounded low but became much more interesting when Jobs put it into context using the automobile analogy. Comparing Apple's market share to that of two admired brands told the story behind the numbers.

Twice as Fast at Half the Price

Data transfers on the original iPhone were often painfully slow on AT&T's standard cellular network (EDGE). Apple solved the problem with the launch of iPhone 3G on June 9, 2008. In the presentation, Jobs said the new iPhone was 2.8 times faster than EDGE, but he didn't stop there. Jobs put the figure into a context that normal Web surfers would understand and appreciate. He showed two images back to back—a National Geographic website loading on the EDGE network and also on the new 3G high-speed network. The EDGE site took fifty-nine seconds to fully load. The 3G site took only twenty-one seconds.[3] Further, Apple offered customers a bonus by lowering the price.

According to Jobs, consumers would be getting a phone that was twice as fast at half the price. Average presenters spew numbers with no context, assuming their audience will share their excitement. Jobs knows that numbers might have meaning to the most ardent fans but are largely meaningless to the majority of potential customers. Jobs makes his numbers specific, relevant, and contextual.

Specific. Relevant. Contextual.

Let's take a look at two other examples in which Jobs made numbers specific, relevant, and contextual. On February 23, 2005, Apple added a new iPod to its lineup. The iPod featured 30 GB of storage. Now, most consumers could not tell you what 30 GB means to them. They know it's "better" than 8 GB, but that's about it. Jobs would never announce a number that big without context, so he broke it down in language his audience could understand. He said 30 GB of storage is enough memory for 7,500 songs, 25,000 photos, or up to 75 hours of video. The description was specific (7,500 songs, versus "thousands" of songs), relevant to the lives of his audience (people who want mobile access to songs, photos, and video), and contextual because he chose to highlight numbers that his core audience of consumers would care about most.

In a second example, Jobs chose Macworld 2008 to hold a two-hundreth-day birthday celebration for the iPhone. Jobs said, "I'm extraordinarily pleased that we have sold four million iPhones to date." He could have stopped there (and most presenters would have done just that), but Jobs being Jobs, he continued: "If you divide four million by two hundred days, that's twenty thousand iPhones every day on average." Jobs could have stopped there as well, but he kept going, adding that the iPhone had captured nearly 20 percent of the market in that short period. OK, you might be saying, surely Jobs would have stopped there. He didn't.

"What does this mean in terms of the overall market?" he asked.[4] He then showed a slide of the U.S. smartphone market share with competitors RIM, Palm, Nokia, and Motorola. RIM's BlackBerry had the highest market share at 39 percent. The iPhone came in second at 19.5 percent. Jobs then compared iPhone's market share to that of all of the other remaining competitors. Jobs concluded that the iPhone matched the combined market share of the remaining three competitors—in the first ninety days of shipments. The numbers, of course, were very specific, relevant to the category, and, above all, contextual (Jobs was addressing investors). By comparing the iPhone against well-established competitors, Jobs made this achievement—selling four million units in the first quarter—far more remarkable.

Dress Up Numbers with Analogies

When I worked with SanDisk executives to prepare them for a major announcement at the 2008 Consumer Electronics Show in Las Vegas, we took a page from the Steve Jobs playbook. The maker of flash memory cards was introducing a card small enough to fit into a cell phone's micro SD slot. That's very tiny. Even bigger news was that it held 12 GB of storage in that small form factor. Now, only gadget geeks would find 12 GB exciting. So, we had to dress up the numbers à la Steve Jobs. Our final announcement went something like this:

"Today we're announcing the first 12 GB memory card for cell phones. It has fifty billion transistors. Think of each transistor as an ant: if you were to put fifty billion end to end, they would circle the globe twice. What does this mean to you? Enough memory to store six hours of movies. Enough memory to listen to music while traveling to the moon . . . and back!"

The number 12 GB is largely uninteresting unless you truly understand the implications of the achievement and what it means to you. When SanDisk compared fifty billion transistors to the number of ants that could circle the globe, the company was using an analogy to jazz up the numbers. Analogies point out similar features between two separate things. Sometimes, analogies are the best way to put numbers into a context that people can understand.

The more complex the idea, the more important it is to use rhetorical devices such as analogies to facilitate understanding. For example, on November 17, 2008, Intel released a powerful new microprocessor named the Core i7. The new chip represented a significant leap in technology, packing 730 million transistors on a single piece of silicon. Engineers described the technology as "breathtaking." But that's because they're engineers. How could the average consumer and investors appreciate the profound achievement? Intel's testing chief, John Barton, found the answer.

In an interview with the *New York Times*, Barton said an Intel processor created twenty-seven years ago had 29,000 transistors; the i7 boasted 730 million transistors on a chip the same size. He equated the two by comparing the city of Ithaca, New York (population 29,000), with the continent of Europe (population 730 million). "Ithaca is quite complex in its own right, if you think about all that goes on. If we scale up the population to 730 million, we come to Europe at about the right size. Now take Europe and shrink it until it all fits in the same land mass as Ithaca."[5]

Number Smiths

Every industry has numbers, and nearly every presenter in every industry fails to make numbers interesting and meaningful. For the rest of this scene, let's examine several examples of individuals and companies who have accomplished what Jobs does in every presentation—make numbers meaningful.

DEFINING ONE THOUSAND TRILLION

On June 9, 2008, IBM issued a press release touting a superfast supercomputer. As its name suggests, Roadrunner is one really quick system. It operates at one petaflop per second. What's a petaflop? Glad you asked. It's one thousand trillion calculations per second. IBM realized that the number would be meaningless to the vast majority of readers, so it added the following description:

> How fast is a petaflop? Lots of laptops. That's roughly equivalent to the combined computing power of 100,000 of today's fastest laptop computers. You would need a stack of laptops 1.5 miles high to equal Roadrunner's performance.

It would take the entire population of the earth—about six billion—each of us working a handheld calculator at the rate of one second per calculation, more than 46 years to do what Roadrunner can do in one day.

If it were possible for cars to improve their gas mileage over the past decade at the same rate that supercomputers have improved their cost and efficiency, we'd be getting 200,000 miles to the gallon today.[6]

The comparisons were compelling and caught the attention of the media. Conduct a Google search for "IBM + Roadrunner + 1.5 miles" and the search returns nearly twenty thousand links to articles that use IBM's comparison word for word from the press release. The analogy works.

$700 BILLION BAILOUT

The bigger the number, the more important it is to place the number into a context that makes sense to your audience. For example, in October 2008, the U.S. government bailed out banks and financial institutions to the tune of $700 billion. That's the numeral 7 followed by eleven zeros, a number so large that few of us can get our minds around it. *San Jose Mercury News* reporter Scott Harris put the number into a context his Silicon Valley readers could understand: $700 billion is twenty-five times the combined wealth of the Google guys. It is the equivalent of 350 billion venti lattes at Starbucks or 3.5 billion iPhones. The government could write checks for $2,300 to every man, woman, and child in America or provide free education for twenty-three million college students. Few people can grasp the concept of 700 billion, but they know lattes and college tuitions. Those numbers are specific and relevant.[7]

CHIPPING DOWN $13 TRILLION

Environmental groups go to great lengths to make numbers more meaningful. They must if they hope to persuade individuals to break deeply ingrained habits and routines that might contribute to damaging climate change. The numbers are simply too big (and seemingly irrelevant) without connecting the dots. For example, try telling someone that in 2006 alone, the United States produced thirteen trillion pounds of carbon dioxide (CO_2). It sounds like a humongous number, but what does it mean? There is no context. Thirteen trillion could be small or large in comparison with other countries. And frankly, what would it mean to the average person? The number itself won't persuade people to change their habits.

Al Gore's website, ClimateCrisis.org, breaks the number down further, claiming the average American is responsible for 44,000 pounds of CO_2 emissions per year, while the world average is 9,600 pounds per individual.[8] That's specific and contextual. The site then makes the number even more relevant by telling its readers what might happen if that number doesn't come down: heat waves will be more frequent and intense, droughts and wildfires will occur more often, and more than a million species could be driven to extinction in the next fifty years.

Scientists at NOAA (National Oceanic and Atmospheric Administration) are also catching on. Senior scientist Susan Solomon once told the *New York Times* that if the burning of fossil fuels continues at its present rate, carbon dioxide emissions could reach 450 parts per million. What does that figure mean? According to Solomon, at 450 parts per million, rising seas will threaten coastal areas around the world, and western Australia could expect 10 percent less rainfall. "Ten percent may not seem like a high number," said Solomon, "but it is the kind of number that has been seen in major droughts in the past, like the Dust Bowl."[9]

Whether or not you believe in global warming, climate change experts such as Al Gore and Susan Solomon are masters at making large numbers meaningful, and by doing so, they hope to persuade governments and individuals to take the action they deem necessary to solve the problem.

CHANGE YOUR DIET OR PAY THE ULTIMATE PRICE

What if you knew nothing about blood pressure and a doctor told you your blood pressure was 220 over 140? Would you be motivated to change your diet and exercise habits? Perhaps not until those numbers are put into context that makes sense to you. One doctor I know once told a patient, "Your blood pressure is 220 over 140. We consider 120 over 80 to be normal. Your blood pressure is severely high. That means you have a much higher risk of having a heart attack, kidney disease, and stroke. In fact, with numbers this high, you could drop dead at any minute by blowing your gourd. The arteries in your brain will literally burst." By being specific, relevant, and contextual, the doctor made his point and motivated his patient to make changes right away!

Regardless of what industry you're in, the numbers you throw around will have little impact on your audience unless and until you make them meaningful. Numbers out of context are simply unimpressive. Whether you're presenting the data behind a new technology or a particular medical condition, comparing the number to something your listeners can relate to will make your message far more interesting, impactful, and ultimately persuasive.

DIRECTOR'S NOTES

» Use data to support the key theme of your presentation. As you do, consider carefully the figures you want to present. Don't overwhelm your audience with too many numbers.

» Make your data specific, relevant, and contextual. In other words, put the numbers into a context that is relevant to the lives of your listeners.

» Use rhetorical devices such as analogies to dress up your numbers.

Use "Amazingly Zippy" Words

Plug it in. Wirrrrrr. Done.

—STEVE JOBS, DESCRIBING THE SONG TRANSFER FEATURE
OF THE FIRST IPOD, *FORTUNE*, NOVEMBER 2001

Steve Jobs introduced an upgrade to the iPhone at Apple's Worldwide Developers Conference on June 9, 2008. The iPhone 3G was twice as fast as the original model, supporting the speedier third-generation AT&T data network. A 3G network has a potential transfer speed of 3 Mbps, versus 144 Kbps on a slower, 2G (second-generation) network. Simply put, 3G is better for accessing the Internet and downloading large multimedia files on a mobile phone. Jobs made it even simpler. "It's amazingly zippy," he said.[1]

Jobs speaks in simple, clear, and direct language, free of the jargon and complexity so common in business communications. Jobs is one of the few business leaders who could confidently call a product "amazingly zippy." In an interview for *Fortune* magazine, he was asked to describe the interface of Apple's new OS X operating system. "We made the buttons on the screen look so good, you'll want to lick them," he said.[2] Even if you think Jobs is grandstanding from time to time, his choice of words puts a smile on your face. He chooses words that are fun, tangible, and uncommon in most professional business presentations.

Jobs, Gates, and the Plain English Test

Seattle Post Intelligencer tech reporter Todd Bishop wrote a clever piece at the urging of his readers. He ran the transcripts from four presentations in 2007 and 2008 (Steve Jobs's Macworld keynotes and Bill Gates's Consumer Electronics Show presentations) through a software tool that analyzes language. In general, the lower the numerical score, the more understandable the language.

Bishop used an online software tool provided by UsingEnglish .com.[3] The tool analyzes language based on four criteria:

1. Average number of words per sentence.
2. Lexical density—how easy or difficult a text is to read. Text with "lower density" is more easily understood. In this case, a lower percentage is better.
3. Hard words—average number of words in a sentence that contain more than three syllables. In this case, a higher percentage is worse because it implies that are more "hard words" in the text that are generally less understood by the average reader.
4. Fog index—the number of years of education a reader theoretically would require to understand the text. For example, the *New York Times* has a fog rating of 11 or 12, while some academic documents have a fog rating of 18. The fog index simply means that short sentences written in plain English receive a better score than sentences written in complicated language.

It should be no surprise that Jobs did noticeably better than Gates when their language was put to the test. Table 10.1 compares the results for both 2007 and 2008.[4]

In each case, Jobs performs significantly better than Gates when it comes to using terms and language people can easily understand. Jobs's words are simpler, his phrases are less abstract, and he uses fewer words per sentence.

TABLE 10.1 LANGUAGE COMPLEXITY: STEVE JOBS VERSUS BILL GATES

PRESENTER/EVENT	STEVE JOBS, MACWORLD	BILL GATES, INTERNATIONAL CONSUMER ELECTRONICS SHOW
Jobs's 2007 Macworld Keynote and Gates's 2007 CES Keynote		
Average words/ sentence	10.5	21.6
Lexical density	16.5%	21.0%
Hard words	2.9%	5.11%
Fog index	5.5	10.7
Jobs's 2008 Macworld Keynote and Gates's 2008 CES Keynote		
Average words/ sentence	13.79	18.23
Lexical density	15.76%	24.52%
Hard words	3.18%	5.2%
Fog index	6.79	9.37

Table 10.2 compares some exact phrases from the 2007 presentations. Excerpts from Bill Gates's remarks are in the right column.[5] The left column contains excerpts from Steve Jobs.[6]

Where Gates is obtuse, Jobs is clear. Where Gates is abstract, Jobs is tangible. Where Gates is complex, Jobs is simple.

Now, I can hear you saying, "Bill Gates might not speak as simply as Jobs, but he's the richest guy in the world, so he must have done something right." You're correct. He did. Gates invented Windows, the operating system installed in 90 percent of the world's computers. You, however, did not. Your audience will not let you get away with language they'll accept

TABLE 10.2 VERBIAGE IN GATES'S 2007 CES KEYNOTE VERSUS JOBS'S 2007 MACWORLD KEYNOTE

STEVE JOBS, 2007 MACWORLD	BILL GATES, 2007 INTERNATIONAL CONSUMER ELECTRONICS SHOW
"You know, it was just a year ago that I was up here and announced that we were going to switch to Intel processors. It was a huge heart transplant to Intel microprocessors. And I said that we would do it over the coming twelve months. We did it in seven months, and it's been the smoothest and most successful transition that we've ever seen in the history of our industry."	"The processors are now opening the memory capability up to 64-bit, and that's a transition we're making without a lot of incompatibility, without paying a lot of extra money. Software, the old 32-bit software, can run, but if you need to get more space, it's just there."
"Now I'd like to tell you a few things about iTunes that are pretty exciting . . . We are selling over five million songs a day now. Isn't that unbelievable? That's fifty-eight songs every second of every minute of every hour of every day."	"The process we've been through over this year—there was a beta 2—got out to over two million people. The release candidate, which was our last chance for feedback, got out to over five million. We had a lot of in-depth things where we went in and sat and interviewed people using Windows Vista in family situations. We did that in seven different countries. We did incredible performance simulation, getting over sixty years equivalent of performance testing with all the common mix of applications that were out there."
"We've got awesome TV shows on iTunes. As a matter of fact, we have over 350 TV shows that you can buy episodes from on iTunes. And I'm very pleased to report that we have now sold fifty million TV shows on iTunes. Isn't that incredible?"	"Microsoft Office has got a new user interface; it's got new ways of connecting up to Office Live services and SharePoint, but the discoverability of the richness is advanced dramatically by that user interface."

from Gates. If your presentations are confusing, convoluted, and full of jargon, you will miss an opportunity to engage and excite your listeners. Strive for understanding. Avoid lexical density.

You might have noticed that many of Jobs's favorite words are the type of words most people use in everyday watercooler conversation: "amazing, incredible, gorgeous." Most presenters change their language for a pitch or presentation. Jobs speaks the same way onstage as he does offstage. He has confidence in his brand and has fun with the words he chooses. Some critics might say his language borders on hyperbole, but Jobs echoes the sentiments shared by millions of his customers.

Of course, you should use words that authentically represent your service, brand, or product. A financial adviser recommending a mutual fund to a client would appear insincere (and probably dishonest) if he or she said, "This new mutual fund will revolutionize the financial industry as we know it. It's amazing, and you need to invest your money in it right now." Instead, the financial adviser could say, "Mutual funds are amazing products that will help your money grow while lowering your risk. There are thousands of funds available, but I'm especially excited about a new one. Let me tell you more about it . . ." In the latter statement, our financial adviser has chosen words that are simple and emotional while still maintaining his or her professionalism and integrity.

Don't be afraid of using simple words and descriptive adjectives. If you genuinely find a product "amazing," go ahead and say so. After all, if you're not excited about it, how do you expect the rest of us to be?

Avoid Jargon Creep

Jargon rarely creeps into Jobs's language. His words are conversational and simple. Jargon—language that is specific to a particular industry—creates a roadblock to the free and easy exchange of ideas. I have attended countless meetings in which two people who work for different divisions of the same company cannot understand the jargon used by the other. Jargon and buzzwords are meaningless and empty and will most certainly make you *less* understandable and therefore less persuasive.

Mission statements are the worst culprits of jargon creep. Mission statements typically are long, convoluted, jargon-laden paragraphs created in multiple committee meetings and destined to be forgotten. They are replete with jargon and murky words you will rarely hear from Jobs, such as "synergy," "principle-centered," and "best of breed." These expressions are nonsense, yet on any given day, employees in companies around the world are sitting in committee meetings to see just how many such words can be crammed into a single sentence.

Apple's mission statement, on the other hand, is simple, clear, and impactful. It's full of emotive words and tangible examples. It reads (emphasis added):

> Apple *ignited* the personal computer revolution in the 1970s with the Apple II and *reinvented* the personal computer with the Macintosh. Today, Apple continues to *lead* the industry in *innovation* with its award-winning computers, OS X operating system, and iLife and professional applications. Apple is also *spearheading* the digital media revolution with its iPod portable music and video players and iTunes online store, and has entered the mobile phone market with its *revolutionary* iPhone.[7]

The words Jobs chooses to announce a new product have three characteristics: they are simple, concrete, and emotionally charged.

» **Simple.** Free of jargon and with few syllables.
» **Concrete.** Very specific phrases. Short, tangible descriptions instead of long, abstract discussions.
» **Emotional.** Descriptive adjectives.

Examples of each of these three characteristics appear in Jobs's introduction of the MacBook Air: "This is the MacBook Air. You can get a feel for how thin it is [concrete]. It has a full-size keyboard and display [simple]. Isn't it amazing [emotional]? This is what it looks

A Guru Who Keeps It Simple

It was hard to miss financial guru Suze Orman in 2008 and 2009 when the global financial markets were collapsing. In addition to appearing on her own CNBC show, the bestselling author was a frequent guest on shows such as "Oprah" and "Larry King Live." Banks and financial companies were also using her in advertisements meant to alleviate their customers' fears. I interviewed Orman several times and found her to be surprisingly candid about the secret to her success as a communicator.

"How do you make complicated financial topics easy to understand?" I once asked.

"Too many people want to impress others with the information they have so others think the speaker is intelligent," Orman responded.[8]

"But Suze," I said, "If your message is too simple, don't you risk not being taken seriously?"

I don't care what people think about it. All I care about is that the information I'm imparting empowers the listener or reader of my material . . . If your intention is to impart a message that will create change for the person listening, then if you ask me, it is respectful to that person to make the message as simple as possible. For example, if I gave you directions to how to get to my house, you would want me to give you the simplest directions to get there. If I made it more complicated, you would not be better off. You might get aggravated and give up. If it were simple, chances are you will get in your car and try to get to my house rather than giving up and saying it's not worth it. Others criticize simplicity because they need to feel that it's more complicated. If everything were so simple, they think their jobs could be eliminated. It's our fear of extinction, our fear of elimination, our fear of not being important that leads us to communicate things in a more complex way than we need to."[9]

like. Isn't it incredible [emotional]? It's the world's thinnest notebook [simple]. It has a gorgeous 13.3-inch wide-screen display and a phenomenal full-sized keyboard [emotional and concrete]. I'm stunned our engineering team could pull this off [emotional]."[10]

Table 10.3 lists even more examples of specific, concrete, and emotional phrases from the Jobs repertoire of language. This is just a small sample. Every Jobs presentation contains similar language.

Jargon: A Sure Way to Upset Jack Welch

Jack Welch made the observation, "Insecure managers create complexity." During his twenty years as GE's top executive, the conglomerate grew from $13 billion in revenue to $500 billion. Welch was on a mission to "declutter" everything about the company, from its management processes to its communication. He despised long, convoluted memos, meetings, and presentations.

In his book *Jack: Straight from the Gut*, Welch describes meetings that left him "underwhelmed." If you wanted to upset the new CEO, all you had to do was talk over his head. Welch would say, "Let's pretend we're in high school . . . take me through the basics." He recounts his first meeting with one of his insurance leaders. Welch asked some simple questions about terms he was unfamiliar with. He writes, "So I interrupted him to ask: 'What's the difference between facultative and treaty insurance?' After fumbling through a long answer for several minutes, an answer I wasn't getting, he finally blurted out in exasperation, 'How do you expect me to teach you in five minutes what it has taken me twenty-five years to learn!' Needless to say, he didn't last long."[11]

Speaking in jargon carries penalties in a society that values speech free from esoteric, incomprehensible bullshit. Speaking over people's heads may cost you a job or prevent you from advancing as far as your capabilities might take you otherwise.

TABLE 10.3 SPECIFIC, CONCRETE, AND EMOTIONAL PHRASES IN JOBS'S PRESENTATIONS

EVENT	PHRASE
Apple Music Event, 2001	"The coolest thing about iPod is your entire music library fits in your pocket."[12]
Introduction of the world's first seventeen-inch widescreen notebook, Macworld 2003	"I asked you to buckle up. Now I want you to put on your shoulder harness."[13]
Referencing the current Titanium PowerBook, Macworld 2003	"The number one lust object."[14]
Describing the new seventeen-inch PowerBook, Macworld 2003	"It's stunning. It is the most incredible product we have ever made. Look at that screen. It's amazing. Look at how thin it is. Isn't that incredible? When it's closed, it's only one inch think. It's beautiful, too. This is clearly the most advanced notebook computer ever made on the planet. Our competitors haven't even caught up with what we introduced two years ago; I don't know what they're going to do about this."[15]
Jobs's description of the original Macintosh	"Insanely great."
Persuading PepsiCo president John Sculley to become Apple's CEO	"Do you want to spend the rest of your life selling sugared water or do you want a chance to change the world?"
Quote in *Triumph of the Nerds*	"We're here to put a dent in the universe."[16]
Discussing CEO Gil Amelio's reign at Apple	"The products suck! There's no sex in them anymore!"[17]
Jobs creating a new word for the launch of a new iPod, September 2008	"iPod Touch is the funnest iPod we've ever created."[18]
Unveiling the first seventeen-inch notebook computer, January 7, 2003	"A giant leap beyond PC notebooks. Miraculously engineered."[19]

Some people will look at the language in this table and say Jobs is a master of hype. Well, hype is hype only if there's no "there" there. It would be hard to argue with Jobs that the Macintosh (the first easy-to-use computer with a graphical interface and mouse) wasn't "insanely great" or that products like the MacBook Air aren't "stunningly" thin.

Jobs isn't a hype-master as much as he's the master of the catchphrase. The folks at Apple think long and hard about the words used to describe a product. Language is intended to stir up excitement and create a "must-have" experience for Apple's customers. There's nothing wrong with that. Keep in mind that the majority of business language is gobbledygook—dull, abstract, and meaningless. Steve Jobs is anything but dull. Inject some zip into your words.

It's Like This . . .

Another way to add zip to your language is to create analogies, comparing an idea or a product to a concept or product familiar to your audience. When Steve Jobs shakes up a market category with the introduction of an entirely new product, he goes out of his way to compare the product to something that is widely understood, commonly used, and well known. Here are some examples:

- » "Apple TV is like a DVD player for the twenty-first century" (Introduction of Apple TV, January 9, 2007)
- » "iPod Shuffle is smaller and lighter than a pack of gum" (Introduction of iPod Shuffle, January 2005)
- » "iPod is the size of a deck of cards" (Introduction of iPod, October 2001)

When you find an analogy that works, stick with it. The more you repeat it, the more likely your customers are to remember it. If you do a Google search for articles about the products just mentioned, you will find thousands of links with the exact comparisons that Jobs himself used. Following are the three

A Cure for Bad Pitches

Don't sell solutions; create stories instead. The *New York Times* columnist David Pogue loves a good pitch. He says the majority of his columns come from pitches. What he doesn't want to hear is jargon. Surprisingly, PR professionals are among the worst offenders (surpassed only by bureaucrats, senior managers, and IBM consultants). Pogue argues that buzzwords (terminology such as "integrated," "best of breed," "B2B," and "consumer-centric") are unnecessary. The ideal pitch is a short paragraph telling Pogue exactly what the product is and does. For example, one company wrote Pogue and said it had a new laptop that could be dropped from six feet, could be dunked in water, and could survive three-hundred-degree heat and still work. This clever description was enough to grab Pogue's attention.

The Bad Pitch blog is a must-read for PR, marketing, and sales professionals. The site carries actual pitches from PR professionals who should know better than to issue impenetrable jargon masking as a press release.

Here's an example: "Hope you're well. I'd like to introduce you to _____ , a new, place-based out-of-home digital network that delivers relevant, localized media within the rhythm of consumers' daily rituals, like afternoon coffee or sandwiches at lunch." This particular pitch came from a company that puts video billboards in delis. Why couldn't they just say that? It's too simple, that's why. People are afraid of simplicity. This is not an isolated example. The site is updated daily with pitches from large and small PR agencies as well as small and large corporations. Apple pitches rarely make the site, because the company's press releases tell a story in the same conversational language that Jobs uses in his presentations.

As the site's mantra explains, "A good pitch disappears and turns into the story; a bad pitch becomes the story." Follow the blog posts at http://badpitch.blogspot.com.

analogies just reviewed (in the format of a search phrase) and the number of links to articles using those phrases:

> » Apple TV + DVD player for twenty-first century: 40,000 links
> » iPod Shuffle + pack of gum: 46,500 links
> » iPod + deck of cards: 227,000 links

Your listeners and viewers are attempting to categorize a product—they need to place the concept in a mental bucket. Create the mental bucket for them. If you don't, you are making their brains work too hard. According to Emory University psychology professor Dr. Gregory Berns, the brain wants to consume the least amount of energy. That means it doesn't want to work too hard to figure out what people are trying to say. "The efficiency principle has major ramifications," he states. "It means the brain takes shortcuts whenever it can."[20] Analogies are shortcuts.

Nothing will destroy the power of your pitch more thoroughly than the use of buzzwords and complexity. You're not impressing anyone with your "best-of-breed, leading-edge, agile solutions." Instead, you are putting people to sleep, losing their business, and setting back your career. Clear, concise, and "zippy" language will help transform your prospects into customers and customers into evangelists. Delight your customers with the words you choose—stroke their brains' dopamine receptors with words that cause them to feel good whenever they think of you and your product. People cannot follow your vision or share your enthusiasm if they get lost in the fog.

Word Fun with Titles

Your customers are your most potent evangelists. I recall a conversation with one of my clients, Cranium founder Richard Tait, who said he sold one million games with no advertising, all word of mouth. "Never forget that your customers are your sales force," he told me.

His customers—he calls them "Craniacs"—want to have fun. Since fun was the name of the game, so to speak, Tait decided that every facet of the company should have some whimsy associated with it. He started with job titles. Cranium employees are allowed to make up their own titles. For example, Tait is not Cranium's CEO. He is the Grand Poo-Bah. No kidding. It's on his business card.

You might think it's silly, but I'll tell you that when I first walked into the company's Seattle headquarters, I was hit with a wave of fun, enthusiasm, and engagement the likes of which I had never seen before and I have never seen since.

DIRECTOR'S NOTES

» Unclutter your copy. Eliminate redundant language, buzzwords, and jargon. Edit, edit, and edit some more.
» Run your paragraphs through the UsingEnglish tool to see just how "dense" it is.
» Have fun with words. It's OK to express enthusiasm for your product through superlatives or descriptive adjectives. Jobs thought the buttons on the Macintosh screen looked so good that you would want to "lick" them. That's confidence.

Share the Stage

Don't be encumbered by history. Go out and create something wonderful.

—ROBERT NOYCE, INTEL COFOUNDER

A t Macworld on January 10, 2006, Jobs announced that the new iMac would be the first Apple computer with an Intel processor inside. Earlier the previous year, Jobs had announced that the "brain transplant" would begin in June 2006. On January 10, he told the audience that he wanted to give everyone an update on the schedule. As he began, dry-ice-created smoke wafted upward in the middle of the stage. A man walked out wearing the famous bunny suit worn in Intel's ultrasterile microprocessor manufacturing plants. The man was carrying a wafer, one of the thin, round slices of silicon from which chips are made. He walked over to Jobs and shook hands. As the lights came up, it became obvious that the person in the bunny suit was none other than Intel CEO Paul Otellini.

"Steve, I wanted to report that Intel is ready," Otellini said as he handed Jobs the wafer. "Apple is ready, too," said Jobs. "We started a partnership less than a year ago to make this happen," Jobs told the audience. "Our teams have worked hard together to make this happen in record time. It's been incredible to see how our engineers have bonded and how well this has gone."[1] Otellini credited the Apple team in return. The two men talked about the achievement, they shook hands again, and Otellini left the stage. Jobs then turned to the audience and revealed the surprise: Apple would be rolling out the first Mac with Intel processors, not in June as originally announced, but *today*. See Figure 11.1.

Few companies are more closely associated with their founders than Apple is with Jobs. Regardless, Jobs himself is more than happy to share the spotlight with employees and partners onstage. A Jobs presentation is rarely a one-man play. He features supporting characters who perform key roles in the narrative.

Microsoft founder Bill Gates was one of the most unexpected partners to share the stage with Jobs. In 1997, at the Macworld Expo in Boston, Jobs, who had recently returned to Apple as interim CEO, told the audience that in order to restore Apple to health, some relationships had to be revisited. He announced that Microsoft's Internet Explorer would be the default browser on the Macintosh and that Microsoft would make a strategic investment of $150 million in the company. On that note, he introduced a "special guest," live via satellite. When Bill Gates appeared, you could hear some cheering, along with a lot of boos. Gates spoke for a few minutes and graciously expressed his admiration for what Apple had accomplished.

Figure 11.1 Steve Jobs sharing the stage with Intel CEO Paul Otellini.
Photo by Justin Sullivan/Getty Images

Jobs returned to the stage and, knowing that many people would be unhappy, sounded like a stern father as he admonished the audience to embrace the relationship. "If we want to move forward and see Apple happy and prospering, we have to let go of this notion that for Apple to win, Microsoft has to lose," Jobs said. "If we screw up, it's not somebody else's fault; it's our fault . . . If we want Microsoft Office on the Mac, we'd better treat the company that puts it out with a little bit of gratitude."[2]

Great actors are often said to be "giving"; they help other actors in the scene give better performances. When Jobs introduces another person onstage—an employee, a partner, or a former nemesis such as Gates—he's the most giving of performers. Everyone needs to shine for the good of the show.

The Brain Craves Variety

The brain doesn't pay attention to boring things. Not that Jobs is boring. Far from it. However, our brains crave variety. No one, no matter how smooth and polished, can carry an audience for long before his or her listeners start to glance at their watches. Great speechwriters have known this for years. Speeches written for John F. Kennedy, Ronald Reagan, and Barack Obama were scripted to last no longer than twenty minutes. A Jobs keynote presentation lasts much longer, of course, closer to 1.5 hours, but Jobs keeps it interesting by incorporating demonstrations, video clips, and—very important—guest speakers.

Know What You Don't Know

In October 2008, Apple introduced new MacBook laptops crafted from single blocks of aluminum. The design breakthrough allowed Apple to build mobile computers that were lighter and stronger than previous designs. "Let's talk about notebooks. We want to talk about some technologies and discoveries that we've made that help us build notebooks in some new ways," Jobs said.[3] However, instead of describing the new process himself, Jobs introduced Jony Ive, Apple's senior vice president of design.

Ive walked onstage, Jobs took a seat, and Ive gave the audience a six-minute crash course on notebook design. He explained how the new process allowed Apple to start with a 2.5-pound slab of aluminum and carve it out until the final frame weighed just one-quarter of a pound. The result was a stronger, thinner, and lighter computer. Jobs retook the stage and concluded the segment by thanking Ive and reaffirming the headline of the segment: "A new way to build notebooks." Jobs may have his hands all over Apple, but he knows what he doesn't know. Jobs shares the spotlight with other actors, who add credibility and excitement to the plot.

Your Best Sales Tool

When Apple launched an online movie-rental service, Jobs announced the list of studios that would make films available for online rentals via iTunes. The list included all the heavyweights—Touchstone, Sony, Universal, MGM, Walt Disney, and others. Still, Apple faced skepticism. The company was launching a movie-rental service in a field with established competitors such as Blockbuster and Netflix. Apple was betting that people would want the choice of watching their movies on their computers, iPods, iPhones, or wide-screen television sets via Apple TV. Jobs added credibility to the initiative by sharing the stage with one of Apple's key partners.

"We have support from every major studio," said Jobs. "The first studio to sign up was Twentieth Century Fox. We've developed a really great working relationship with Fox. It's my pleasure to introduce the chairman and CEO of Twentieth Century Fox, Jim Gianopulos."

An enthusiastic Gianopulos bounded onto the stage and talked about what people want: great movies; easy access; convenience; control over where, when, and how they watch movies; and the ability to take the movie with them wherever they go. "When Steve came to us with the idea, it was a no-brainer. It was the most exciting, coolest thing we've ever heard," Gianopulos said. "Video rentals are not a new thing. But there was music and then iPod. There was the phone and then iPhone. Apple does things in an intuitive, insightful, and innovative way. It will be a transformative version of the rental model, and we're incredibly excited about it. We couldn't be happier and prouder of our partnership."[4]

Gianopulos had provided Jobs with a company's best sales tool—a customer's endorsement. Best of all, the two men appeared side by side. A reference is good. A customer or partner physically sharing the stage is even better.

Number One Reason People Buy

Your customers are always mindful of budgets, but in tough economic times they are even more so, casting a critical eye on every last dollar. Prospects do not want to act as a beta group. Your product must deliver what it promises—saving your customers money, making them money, or providing the tools to make more efficient use of the money they have. Testimonials and endorsements are persuasive because, as discussed earlier, word of mouth is the number one influencer of purchasing decisions.

Successful companies know that a pool of reputable and satisfied customers is critical for sales success. In fact, some companies even have specific employees whose job it is to gather case studies and distribute them to their prospects. Most small business owners do not have the resources to designate a "case study" specialist, but they can easily adopt some of the techniques used by the world's most successful companies. One proven strategy is to steal a page from the Apple playbook and invite your customers to share the spotlight, either in person, on video, or, at the very least, through quotes.

Don't forget the media. Sharing the stage with publications that rave about your product will bolster your message. Jobs has a love-hate relationship with the media, but for presentation purposes, there's a lot of love in the room. In the first few minutes of his Macworld 2008 keynote address, Jobs announced that Leopard (the latest version of the OS X operating system) had sold five million copies in its first ninety days,

Twenty-First-Century Case Study

The case study remains an important marketing tool. Most of us are familiar with white papers or simple case studies featured on a company's website, but as video and audio become much less expensive to create and distribute online, some innovative companies are tapping into the power of YouTube to deliver customer evidence. Buying a $200 Flip video recorder, creating an inexpensive video of a customer testimonial, and posting it on YouTube carries as much weight as a slick marketing production. Posting video and audio testimonials on your site and incorporating them into your presentations will add another valuable layer of authenticity and credibility to your story.

If you are a business owner or an entrepreneur, it is important to develop a list of customers you can use as references. In fact, a customer who offers a testimonial is worth more than one who doesn't. Look for customers who will help you win new customers. Then, give them a *reason* to offer a reference. This could be as simple as offering a deeper relationship with your company, such as providing more access to you or your staff when your customer has questions. Other benefits might include access to product teams, input into new designs or products, and visibility.

Give your partners a reason to participate, and once they do, incorporate them into your presentations. Most customers will not be available for your presentation, but try the next best thing: insert a video testimonial into your presentation. It might not have the same impact as Paul Otellini appearing onstage with Jobs, but it might give you a step up on your competitors.

marking the most successful release of OS X. He also made sure that everyone knew that Leopard had been a hit with the media. "The press has been very kind. It's been a critical success as well as a commercial success," said Jobs.[5] As Jobs read reviews from major technology influencers, a slide appeared with their quotes. Here are the endorsements, along with their sources:

» "In my view, Leopard is better and faster than Vista."—Walt Mossberg, *Wall Street Journal*
» "Leopard is powerful, polished, and carefully conceived." —David Pogue, *New York Times*
» "With Leopard, Apple's operating system widens its lead esthetically and technologically."—Ed Baig, *USA Today*
» "It's by far the best operating system ever written for the vast majority of consumers."—Ed Mendelson, *PC* magazine

The last quote drew laughs. The irony of *PC* magazine's favorably reviewing a Mac gave the audience a chuckle. Reading favorable reviews is a common technique in a Steve Jobs presentation. Although Americans rate journalists among the least trustworthy professionals (only one step above politicians), a favorable endorsement from a top-tier media outlet or blogger still carries weight, giving buyers confidence that they are making a wise choice.

Successful companies that launch a splashy new product usually have tested it with a group of partners who have agreed to endorse it publicly or distribute review copies to the media and influencers. This arrangement gives those companies instant references, endorsements, and testimonials. Your customers need a reason to believe in you, and they want to minimize the risk associated with a new product or service. Having experts, customers, or partners testify to the effectiveness of your product will help you overcome the psychological barrier to participation.

Give Credit Where Credit's Due

Employees also get top billing in a Steve Jobs presentation. At the conclusion of Macworld 2007, Jobs said, "I want to highlight the folks who worked on these products. Would all of the folks who worked on today's products please stand up? Let's give them a round of applause. Thank you so much. I also can't leave without thanking the families. They haven't seen a lot of us in the last six months. Without the support of our families, we couldn't do what we do. We get to do this amazing work. They understand when we're not home for dinner on time because we've got to be in the lab, working on something because the intro is coming up. You don't know how much we need you and appreciate you. So, thank you."[6]

It's very easy to make the presentation all about you and your product. Don't forget to credit the people who make it possible. It shows your customers that you are a person of integrity, and, by praising your employees or colleagues publicly, you inspire them to work harder for you.

Finally, Jobs shares the stage with his audience, his customers, often thanking them profusely. He kicked off Macworld 2008 by recapping the previous year. "I just want to take a moment to say thank you. We have had tremendous support from all of our customers, and we really, really appreciate it. So, thank you for an extraordinary 2007."[7] Jobs built a rapport with his audience by acknowledging the people who matter—the people who build the products and the people who buy them.

Jobs Even Shares the Stage . . . with Himself!

Steve Jobs is the only person who can invite another Steve Jobs onstage. In 1999, "ER" star Noah Wyle traded in his scrubs for blue jeans, playing Jobs in the TV movie *Pirates of Silicon Valley*. In a practical joke at the 1999 Macworld Expo in New York, Wyle appeared onstage to kick off the keynote. At first glance (and to people seated far away), he looked like Jobs—blue jeans, black mock, and running shoes. Wyle had the same mannerisms and even used some of Jobs's famous phrases. "This is going to be a great Macworld," he said. "There's something happening here. The resurgence of Apple. You're going to see great new products today. Some insanely great new products. Some really, totally, wildly, insanely great new products!" The audience went crazy when the real Jobs showed up.

Jobs had a ton of fun with Wyle, telling the actor that he was blowing the impression. Jobs showed Wyle how he should act, talk, and walk if he really wanted to nail the impersonation.

Jobs told the audience, "I invited Noah here to see how I really act and because he's a better me than me!"

"Thank you. I'm just glad you're not mad about the movie," said Wyle.

"What? Me upset? It's just a movie," said Jobs. "But if you do want to make things right, you could get me a part on 'ER.' "[8]

The exchange generated a huge laugh and the bit showed that Jobs could poke some fun at himself. I still haven't seen any other presenter who could share the stage with himself!

DIRECTOR'S NOTES

» Upon release of a new product or service, make sure you have customers who tested the product and are available to back your claims. Media reviews are also helpful, especially from highly reputable publications or popular blogs.

» Incorporate testimonials into your presentation. The easiest way is to videotape your customer talking about your product, edit the tape to no more than two minutes in length, and insert it into your presentation.

» Publicly thank employees, partners, and customers. And do it often.

Stage Your Presentation with Props

Jobs has turned his keynote speeches at Macworld into massive media events. They are marketing theater, staged for the world's press.

—LEANDER KAHNEY

ndustry observers credit Apple for redefining notebook computer design with its MacBook family of computers unveiled on October 14, 2008. As described in the preceding chapter, Jobs had solicited Apple designer Jony Ive to explain the process of making the computer. The new MacBooks were built with a frame (unibody enclosure) crafted from a single block of aluminum. It doesn't sound impressive, but it represented a feat of engineering that produced thinner, lighter, more rugged notebooks that looked a lot cooler than their predecessors. About twenty-five minutes into the October presentation, Jobs discussed the new aluminum frame. He could have talked about it and perhaps shown a photograph or two, but Jobs being Jobs, he went above and beyond. He turned the presentation into a kinesthetic experience, letting the audience of analysts and reporters see and touch the frame for themselves.

"This is what the unibody looks like. It's especially beautiful," Jobs said as he held up a sample frame.

"It's a much more rigid, stronger construction. It's so cool, I'd like you to see it. If we can get the lights up, I'd actually like to pass one of these around so you can see how beautiful and high-tech this is."

At this point, Apple representatives who had been positioned at the end of each row handed audience members samples of the aluminum frames to pass around. As people touched and examined the frames for themselves, Jobs joked, "We need them back," eliciting a laugh from the audience. For the next sixty seconds, Jobs did not say a word. He let the product speak for itself.

Jobs then channeled his inner John Madden and provided color commentary as the audience members continued to examine the frames: "Teams of hundreds of people have worked on this for many, many months to figure out how to design these things and manufacture them economically. This is a tour de force of engineering."

Jobs remained silent for the next thirty seconds until everyone had a chance to handle the frames. "OK. A precision unibody enclosure. You're the first to get your hands on one," Jobs said as he closed the section and moved on to another feature of the new notebooks.[1] Using props, Jobs had transformed what could have been a boring explanation into an interesting, multisensory experience.

Kawasaki Method

Jobs introduces stage props in every presentation, usually during demonstrations. In *The Macintosh Way*, Guy Kawasaki writes that master communicators give good demo. "The right demo doesn't cost much," he points out, "but it can counteract your competitors' marketing and advertising. A great demo informs the audience about your product, communicates the benefits of owning your product, and inspires the audience to take action."[2] Kawasaki describes the five qualities of an outstanding demonstration. According to Kawasaki, good demos are as follows:

» **Short.** A good demo does not suck the wind out of your audience.
» **Simple.** A good demo is simple and easy to follow. "It should communicate no more than one or two key messages. The goal is to show the audience enough to get them tantalized but not so much that they get bewildered."[3]
» **Sweet.** A good demo "shows the hottest features and differentiates your product from the competition's." There's more: "You have to show real functionality, though. Imagine that every time you show a feature someone shouts, 'So what?' "[4]
» **Swift.** A good demo is fast paced. "Never do anything in a demo that lasts more than fifteen seconds."[5]
» **Substantial.** A good demo clearly demonstrates how your product offers a solution to a real-world problem your audience is experiencing. "Customers want to do things with your product, so they want to know how the product works."[6]

As noted in Scene 9, Jobs nailed all of Kawasaki's conditions for a good demo when he launched the iPhone 3G at the WWDC in October 2008. The phone ran on the faster, 3G cellular networks, an upgrade to the second-generation (2G) wireless data networks. Jobs's words from the presentation are listed in the left column of Table 12.1, and the right column describes the corresponding slides.[7]

In a brief demo, Jobs had met Kawasaki's criteria for a great demo.

» **It's short.** The EDGE-versus-3G demo lasted less than two minutes.
» **It's simple.** What could be more simple than showing two websites loading on a smartphone? That was as complicated as it got.
» **It's sweet.** Jobs placed the 3G network in a head-to-head face-off with its primary competitor, the EDGE network.
» **It's swift.** Jobs keeps the demo moving but remains silent at critical points to build the drama.
» **It's substantial.** The demo resolves a real-world problem: waiting an excruciatingly long time for graphically rich sites to load.

TABLE 12.1 JOBS'S GREAT DEMO AT THE 2008 WWDC

STEVE'S WORDS	STEVE'S SLIDES
"Why do you want 3G? Well, you want it for faster data downloads. And there's nowhere you want faster data downloads than the browser and downloading e-mail attachments."	Photographs of two icons: one represents the Internet, and the second represents e-mail
"So, let's take a look at the browser. We've taken an iPhone 3G and, at the same place and same location, we've downloaded a website on the EDGE network and one using 3G."	Animated image of two iPhones loading a website simultaneously: the same National Geographic website begins loading on each; the left iPhone is on the EDGE network, and the one on the right is using the new iPhone 3G network
"Let's see how we do." [Jobs remains silent as both images continue to load on the screen; it's a site with a lot of images and a complex layout]	Website loading on both iPhone images
"Twenty-one seconds on 3G; [waits silently for an additional thirty seconds, crossing his hands in front of his body, smiling, watching the audience— elicits laughs] fifty-nine seconds on EDGE. Same phone, same location: 3G is 2.8 times faster. It's approaching Wi-Fi speeds. It's amazingly zippy!"	3G site has completely loaded, while EDGE phone is still loading

History-Making Demo

Demonstrations and props play a role in every Steve Jobs presentation, some of which are more history-making than others. "We're going to make some history today," Steve Jobs said as he kicked off Macworld 2007. The history-making event was the introduction of the iPhone:

"We want to reinvent the phone," Jobs said. "I want to show you four things: the phone app, photos, calendar, and SMS text messaging [texting between two cell phones]—the kind of things you would find on a typical phone—in a very untypical way. So, let's go ahead and take a look." As he always does, Jobs walked to stage right (the audience's left) to sit down and conduct the demo, giving the audience a clear view of the screen.

"You see that icon in the lower-left corner of the phone? I just push it, and boom, I have the phone. Now I'm in Contacts. How do I move around Contacts? I just scroll through them. Let's say I want to place a call to Jony Ive. I just push here, and I see Jony Ive's contact with all his information. If I want to call Jony, all I do is push his number. I'll call his mobile number right now." The phone rings, and Ive picks up to say hello.

Jobs continued, "It's been two and a half years, and I can't tell you how thrilled I am to make the first public phone call with iPhone." At this point in the demo, Apple's VP of corporate marketing, Phil Schiller, calls in. Jobs places Ive on hold and conferences in the two callers to demonstrate one-click conferencing. Jobs proceeds to demonstrate the SMS texting function, followed by the photo package that came standard in the iPhone. "We have the coolest photo management app ever—certainly on a mobile device, but I think maybe ever." Jobs then shows off the capabilities of the photo gallery, using his fingers to widen, pinch, and manipulate the images. "Pretty cool," he says. "Isn't this awesome?"[8] Jobs appeared genuinely thrilled with the new features and, as he often does when demonstrating new products, looked like a kid in a candy store.

Having Fun with Demos

Don't forget to have fun with demos. Jobs certainly does. He concluded the iPhone demonstration by showing how to put Google Maps to work on the device. He searched for a Starbucks in San Francisco near Moscone West, the site of the conference. A list of Starbucks stores appeared on the phone, and Jobs said, "Let's give them a call." A Starbucks employee picked up and said, "Good morning. Starbucks. How can I help you?"

"Yes," said Jobs. "I'd like to order four thousand lattes to go, please. No, just kidding. Wrong number. Good-bye."[9] This

Props Galore for an Italian TV Host

I'm always looking for communicators who, like Jobs, push the envelope and create exciting ways to engage an audience. I've rarely seen anyone use more props than a young Italian entrepreneur and television host, Marco Montemagno.

Montemagno frequently speaks on the topic of Internet culture, showing Italians why the Internet should be embraced and not feared. He presents to groups as large as three thousand people in places such as Rome, Milan, and Venice. Since the majority of people in his audience are Web novices, he uses language that everyone can understand (well, assuming you know Italian). His slides are very simple and visual; he often employs just photographs, animation, and video. But what truly differentiates Montemagno from the majority of presenters is his unbelievable number of props and demonstrations. Here are three guidelines he follows to create dynamic moments:

1. **Give your audience something to do.** Montemagno's audience members get a pen and paper before taking their seats. During the presentation, he asks them to turn to the person next to them and, in thirty seconds, sketch the person's portrait. After that, he asks them to write the title of their favorite song, movie, and so forth. They then pass the paper around, continuing until each paper has changed hands up to five times. Everyone eventually takes home a piece of paper that once belonged to someone else. The exercise is intended to demonstrate how information is shared among individuals across networks.

2. **Ask someone to share the stage.** In other parts of his presentation, Montemagno will ask for volunteers to join him onstage. In one exercise, he asks them to fold a T-shirt. Most people will take about twenty seconds and fold the shirt in a conventional way. When they're done, he shows a popular YouTube video of someone demonstrating how to fold a shirt in five seconds. Montemagno then duplicates the feat as the audience cheers. His point is that the

Internet can instruct on a deep, intellectual level, but it can also make the most mundane tasks easier.

3. **Make use of your skills onstage.** Montemagno is a former world-ranked table tennis player and works that unique skill into his presentations. He invites another professional player onstage, and the two hit the ball back and forth quickly and effortlessly. As they do, Montemagno, speaking into a wireless headset, compares table tennis to the Internet.

Steve Jobs has elevated presentations to an art form, but few of us will ever introduce a product as world-changing as a revolutionary new computer. This fact is all the more reason to find new, exciting ways to engage your audience. To see video clips of Montemagno in action, visit his site: http://mon temagno.typepad.com.

exchange elicited a huge laugh. Jobs had literally crank-called a Starbucks as part of the demo. Jobs has so much fun showing off new products that his enthusiasm leaps off the stage and rubs off on everyone in attendance. It is precisely because he has fun that people enjoy watching him.

In another prime example of having fun with demos, Jobs took some quirky photographs of himself while introducing a feature called Photo Booth on October 12, 2005. Photo Booth is a software application for using a Web camera to take photographs and video.

"Now I want to show you Photo Booth," said Jobs. "This is an incredible way to have some fun. I can just go ahead and take my picture." Jobs looked into the built-in Web camera on the computer and smiled for a few seconds as his photograph was snapped and appeared on-screen. He said, "Isn't that great? Let me show you some pretty cool effects." Jobs proceeded to snap comical photographs of himself using features such as Thermal, X-Ray, and Andy Warhol. "But it gets even better," Jobs said as he smiled and rubbed his hand together. "We decided to put in the teenage effects."[10] Jobs snapped more photographs of himself as the software distorted his face into funny shapes—squeezing it, widening it, and otherwise contorting the images. The audience roared as Jobs relished the moment.

Focus on the One Thing

Each new Apple product or application contains numerous benefits and features, but Jobs will often highlight just one. Think of it like a movie trailer that teases the audience by revealing only the best parts. If people want the full experience, they'll have to watch the movie.

At WWDC in October 2007, Jobs spent most of the keynote presentation discussing OS X Leopard, but, as he often does, he had "one more thing" for the audience. Jobs introduced Safari for Windows, the "most innovative browser in the world and now the fastest browser on Windows." After telling the audience that he would like to show them the new browser, he walked to stage right, took his seat behind a computer, and started the

Add Pizzazz to Online Meetings

Seventy new Web meetings are launched every minute on software platforms such as WebEx, according to Cisco, which purchased the online meeting service. Today popular online "webinar" and collaboration tools, including WebEx, Citrix GoToMeeting, Adobe Connect, and Microsoft Office Live Meeting, allow you to add some high-tech pizzazz to demos. For example, you can create polls and receive instant feedback. Sales professionals can conduct a live demonstration of a product from a computer—drawing, highlighting, and pointing to areas right on the screen. Better yet, those same sales professionals can turn over mouse control to the client or prospect, letting the customer on the other end see, touch, and "feel" the product. Demonstrations are important elements in any presentation, offline or online.

demo. He told the audience that what he really wanted to show off was Safari's speed compared with Internet Explorer (IE 7).

The demo screen showed both browsers side by side. Jobs loaded a series of websites simultaneously on both. Safari accomplished the task in 6.64 seconds, while IE 7 took 13.56 seconds to accomplish the same task. "Safari is the fastest browser on Windows," Jobs concluded.[11] The entire demo took less than three minutes. It could have lasted much longer, but Jobs chose to focus on one feature and one feature only. Jobs doesn't overwhelm his audience. Just as he eliminates clutter on slides, his demos are likewise free of extraneous messages.

In 2006, Apple added a podcast studio to GarageBand, a tool bundled into the iLife suite of applications intended to make it easy for users to create and distribute multimedia content. "We've added a lot of great stuff to GarageBand," said Jobs, "but I'm going to focus on *one thing* to demo today, and that is we have added a podcast studio to GarageBand. We think GarageBand is now going to be the best tool in the world to create podcasts. It's pretty great. Let me go ahead and give you a demo."

Jobs walked to stage right, sat down, and created a short podcast in four steps. First, Jobs recorded the audio track and had loads of fun with it. He even stopped the first recording and started over because the audience caused him to laugh so hard. Jobs recorded the following: "Hi, I'm Steve. Welcome to my weekly podcast, 'Supersecret Apple Rumors,' featuring the hottest rumors about our favorite company. I have some pretty good sources inside Apple, and this is what I'm hearing: the next iPod will be *huge*, an eight-pounder with a ten-inch screen! Well, that's all for today. See you next week."

After making the playful recording, Jobs walked through the next three steps, showing the audience how to add artwork and background music. Once done, he played the podcast and said, "Pretty cool, huh? That is the podcast studio, which is now built into GarageBand."[12]

Although Jobs did a nice demonstration of the podcast studio, it could not compete with the first release of GarageBand in 2005: "Today we're announcing something so cool: a fifth app that will be part of the iLife family. It's name is GarageBand. What is

GarageBand? GarageBand is a major new pro music tool. But it's for everyone. I'm not a musician, so to help me demo GarageBand, we asked a friend, John Mayer, to help us."[13] Jobs took a seat behind a computer, and Mayer sat down at a mini keyboard hooked to the Mac. As Mayer played, Jobs manipulated the sound to make the piano resemble a bass, a choir, a guitar, and other instruments. Jobs then laid down multiple tracks, creating a bandlike sound. He took care to explain what he was doing at every step, to show the audience just how easy it was to create a studio-like experience.

Jobs must have rehearsed the demo for hours, because he looked like an expert musician. Nevertheless, Jobs knows what he doesn't know, and sometimes, as in the case of GarageBand, it makes more sense to bring in an outsider who speaks directly to the intended audience.

Element of Surprise

Jobs stunned developers when he announced a transition that had been rumored but largely dismissed—the transition from IBM/Motorola PowerPC chips to Intel processors. During the 2005 WWDC, where he made the announcement, Jobs acknowledged that one of the major challenges would be to make sure

The Next-Best Thing to John Mayer

Of course, you're not going to persuade John Mayer to perform at your next event, but do think about creative ways to reach your target audience. I watched an entrepreneur pitching his new Web service to venture capitalists in San Francisco. The service was geared to the teenage market, so it didn't make sense for a forty-something entrepreneur to demonstrate it. Instead, the founder introduced the company and then passed the demo off to two teens (a boy and a girl), who talked about their experience with the site and what they especially loved about it. The demo was different, engaging, and ultimately successful.

OS X would run efficiently on Intel chips. Having some fun with the audience, he said that the OS X had been "living a double life" for five years, secretly being developed to run on both PowerPC and Intel processors "just in case." The result, said Jobs, was that Mac OS X is "singing on Intel processors."

He then hit the audience with the unexpected: "As a matter of fact, this system I've been using . . ." His voice trails off, he flashes a knowing smile, and the audience laughs when it sinks

Connect with Three Types of Learners

Demonstrations help speakers make an emotional connection with every type of learner in the audience: visual, auditory, and kinesthetic.

» **Visual learners.** About 40 percent of us are visual learners, people who learn through seeing. This group retains information that is highly visual. To reach visual learners, avoid cramming too much text onto the screen. Build slides that have few words and plenty of pictures. Remember: individuals are more likely to act on information they have a connection with, but they cannot connect with anything that they have not internalized. Visual learners connect through seeing.

» **Auditory learners.** These people learn through listening. Auditory learners represent about 20 to 30 percent of your audience. Individuals who learn through listening benefit from verbal and rhetorical techniques that are featured in Act 3. Tell personal stories or use vivid examples to support your key messages.

» **Kinesthetic learners.** These people learn by doing, moving, and touching. In short, they are "hands-on." They get bored listening for long periods. So, include activities in your presentation to keep kinesthetic learners engaged: pass around objects as Jobs did with the aluminum frame, conduct writing exercises, or have them participate in demonstrations.

in that the system is running on new Intel processors. "Let's have a look," Jobs says as he walks to the side of the stage. He sits down and begins exploring many of the conventional computer tasks, such as calendar functions, e-mail, photographs, browsing, and movies, loading and working quickly and effortlessly. He concluded the two-minute demo by saying, "This is Mac OS X running on Intel."[14]

The CEO Sidekick

Cisco's Jim Grubb plays the sidekick to CEO John Chambers. Grubb's title is, literally, Chief Demonstration Officer. Nearly every Chambers presentation involves a demonstration, and Grubb is Chambers's go-to guy for some sixty events a year. The demonstrations are unique and truly remarkable. Cisco replicates a scenario onstage complete with furniture and props: it could be an office, a retail store, or rooms of a house. In a demonstration at the 2009 Consumer Electronics Show in Las Vegas, Chambers and Grubb called a doctor in a remote location thousands of miles away and, using Cisco's TelePresence technology, which lets you see a person as though he or she is right in front of you, held a medical evaluation over the network.

Chambers enjoys needling Grubb with lines such as "Are you nervous, Jim? You seem a little tense," or "It's OK if you mess up. I'll just fire you." Most of the jokes between the two men are scripted but are still funny as Grubb just smiles, laughs it off, and continues with the demonstration—the perfect straight man. Grubb studied music and theater in college. His polished performance reflects his training. Although it appears effortless, he and his staff spend countless hours in the lab testing and practicing, not only to simplify complicated networking technology so it's easy to understand in a fifteen-minute demonstration but also to make sure it works, so his boss doesn't get mad!

The launch of the iPhone in 2007 also provided Jobs with a memorable prop. He showed the audience how they could listen to their favorite music by playing one of his favorite songs from the Red Hot Chili Peppers. A phone call interrupted the music and a photo of Apple's VP of Marketing, Phil Schiller, appeared on the phone. Jobs answered it and talked to Schiller who was standing in the audience on another phone. Schiller requested a photograph; Jobs retrieved it and e-mailed it, and went back to listening to his song. Jobs is a showman, incorporating just the right amount of theater to make features come alive.

DIRECTOR'S NOTES

» Build in a product demo during the planning phase of your presentation. Keep the demo short, sweet, and substantial. If you can introduce another person on your team to participate in the demonstration, do so.

» Commit to the demo. Comedians say a joke works only if you commit to it. In the same way, commit to your demo, especially if your product has any entertainment value at all. Have fun with it.

» Provide something for every type of learner in your audience: visual, auditory, and kinesthetic.

Reveal a "Holy Shit" Moment

People will forget what you said, people will forget what you did, but people will never forget how you made them feel.

—MAYA ANGELOU

Every office worker has seen a manila envelope. But where most people see a manila envelope as a means of distributing documents, Steve Jobs sees a memorable moment that will leave his audience in awe.

"This is the MacBook Air," he said in January 2008, "so thin it even fits inside one of those envelopes you see floating around the office." With that, Jobs walked to the side of the stage, picked up one such envelope, and pulled out a notebook computer. The audience went wild as the sound of hundreds of cameras clicking and flashing filled the auditorium. Like a proud parent showing off a newborn, Jobs held the computer head-high for all to see. "You can get a feel for how thin it is. It has a full-size keyboard and full-size display. Isn't it amazing? It's the world's thinnest notebook," said Jobs.[1]

The photo of Jobs pulling the computer from the envelope proved to be the most popular of the event and was carried by major newspapers, magazines, and websites. The dramatic introduction even sparked an entrepreneur to build a carrying sleeve for the MacBook Air that looked like, you guessed it, a manila envelope. See Figure 13.1.

Figure 13.1 Jobs holding up the MacBook Air after dramatically removing it from an office-sized manila envelope.

TONY AVELAR/AFP/Getty Images

When Jobs slipped the computer out of the envelope, you could hear the gasps in the room. You knew most people in the audience that day were thinking, "Holy shit. That's thin!" ABC News declared, "The MacBook Air has the potential to reshape the laptop industry. The laptop fits inside a standard office manila envelope, which is how Jobs presented it as the showstopper of this year's conference of all things Apple."[2] The "showstopper" had been planned all along. Well before Jobs enacted the stunt in front of an audience, press releases had been written, images created for the website, and ads developed showing a hand pulling the notebook from a manila envelope. The "holy shit" moment had been scripted to elicit an emotional response; the presentation as theater.

Raising a Product Launch to an Art Form

On January 24, 2009, Macintosh celebrated its twenty-fifth anniversary. Apple's Macintosh had reinvented the personal computer industry in the eighties. A computer with a mouse and graphical user interface was a major transformation from the old command-line interfaces prevalent then. The Mac was much easier to use than anything IBM had at the time. The Mac's introduction was also one of the most spellbinding product launches of its day. The unveiling took place a quarter-century earlier during the Apple shareholders meeting, held at the Flint Center at De Anza College, near the Apple campus. All 2,571 seats were filled as employees, analysts, shareholders, and media representatives buzzed with anticipation.

Jobs (dressed in gray slacks, a double-breasted jacket, and bow tie) kicked off the presentation with a quote by his favorite musician, Bob Dylan. After describing the features of the new computer, Jobs said, "All of this power fits into a box that is one-third the size and weight of an IBM PC. You've just seen pictures of Macintosh. Now I'd like to show you Macintosh in person. All of the images you are about to see on the large screen are being generated by what's in that bag." He pointed to a canvas bag in the center of the stage. After a pause, he walked to center stage and pulled the Macintosh computer out of the bag. He plugged it in, inserted a floppy disk, and stood aside. The lights darkened, the Vangelis theme from *Chariots of Fire* began to play, and a series of images scrolled across the screen (MacWrite and MacPaint, which came free with the Mac). As the music faded, Jobs said, "Now, we've done a lot of talking about Macintosh recently, but today for the first time ever, I'd like to let Macintosh speak for itself." On that cue, Macintosh spoke in a digitized voice:

"Hello, I am Macintosh. It sure is great to get out of that bag. Unaccustomed as I am to public speaking, I'd like to share with you a maxim I thought of the first time I met an IBM mainframe: Never trust a computer you can't lift. Obviously, I can talk right now, but I'd like to sit back and listen. So, it is with considerable pride that I introduce a man who has been like a father to me: Steve Jobs."[3] The crowd went wild, standing, cheering, hollering.

Letting Macintosh speak for itself was a brilliant technique to garner the most buzz and publicity. Twenty-five years later, the

YouTube video clip from that portion of the announcement has been viewed half a million times. Jobs had created a memorable moment that people would talk about for decades. A genuine showstopper.

One Theme

The secret to creating a memorable moment is to identify the one thing—the one theme—that you want your audience to remember after leaving the room. Your listeners should not need to review notes, slides, or transcripts of the presentation to recall the *one thing*. They will forget many of the details, but they will remember 100 percent of what they *feel*. Think about the one thing Apple wanted you to know about MacBook Air: it's the world's thinnest notebook. That's it. A customer could learn more by visiting the website or an Apple store; the presentation was meant to create an experience and to bring the headline to life. It struck an emotional connection with the listener.

Jobs had one key message that he wanted to deliver about the first iPod: it fits one thousand songs in your pocket. The message

The Mental Post-it Note

"The brain doesn't pay attention to boring things," writes scientist John Medina. It does pay attention to an "emotionally charged event," as Medina explains: "The amygdala is chock-full of the neurotransmitter dopamine . . . When the brain detects an emotionally charged event, the amygdala releases dopamine into the system. Because dopamine greatly aids memory and information processing, you could say the Post-it note reads 'Remember this!' "[4]

According to Medina, if you can get the brain to put what amounts to a chemical Post-it note on an idea or a piece of information, the item will be more "robustly processed" and easily remembered. As you could imagine, this concept applies to business professionals as well as teachers and parents!

was simple and consistent in presentations, press releases, and the Apple website. However, it remained a tagline until Jobs brought it to life in October 2001.

Just as a playwright sets the stage early and reveals the plot over time, Jobs never gives away the big moment right out of the gate. He builds the drama. Jobs took the stage to introduce the iPod and, slowly, added layers to the message until he hit the big note.

"The biggest thing about iPod is that it holds a thousand songs," Jobs said.

"To have your whole music library with you at all times is a quantum leap in listening to music." (A device that carried a thousand songs wasn't unique at the time; what came next was the big news.) "But the coolest thing about iPod is your entire music library fits in your pocket. It's ultraportable. iPod is the size of a deck of cards." Jobs's slide showed a photograph of a card deck. "It is 2.4 inches wide. It is four inches tall. And barely three-quarters of an inch thick. This is tiny. It also only weighs 6.5 ounces, lighter than most of the cell phones you have in your pockets right now. This is what's so remarkable about iPod. It is ultraportable. This is what it looks like." Jobs showed a series of photographs. He still hadn't shown the actual device. "In fact, I happen to have one right here in my pocket!" Jobs then took a device out of his pocket and held it up high, as the audience cheered. He had his photo opp. He concluded, "This amazing little device holds a thousand songs and goes right in my pocket."[5]

The headline in the *New York Times* read: "1,000 Songs in Your Pocket." Jobs could not have written a better headline. Actually, he did write it! He also created an emotionally charged event that planted the headline into the dopamine-dumping frontal cortex of his listeners' brains.

Dropping a Welcome Bombshell

Jobs returned to Apple as the interim CEO in 1997. He dropped the "interim" from his title two and half years later. Instead of

Deliver Memorable Stories

A memorable moment need not be a major new product announcement. (After all, few of us will announce breakthrough products like iPod.) Something as simple as a personal story can be memorable.

I once worked with a major grower of organic produce. The executives were preparing a presentation and filled it with mind-numbing statistics to prove that organic was better than conventionally grown fruits and vegetables. The statistics provided supporting points, but there was no emotionally charged event, until a farmer turned to me and told me the following story: "Carmine, when I worked for a conventional farm, I would come home and my kids would want to hug me, but they couldn't. Daddy had to take a shower first, and my clothes had to be washed and disinfected. Today I can walk right off the lettuce field and into the waiting arms of my kids, because there is nothing toxic on my body to harm them." Several years later, I cannot recall any of the statistics this company presented, but I remember the story. The story became the emotionally charged highlight of the presentation.

simply announcing that news via a press release as most CEOs would do, Jobs created an experience out of it.

At the end of two-hour presentation on January 5, 2000, Jobs said, almost as an aside, "There is one more thing." But he did not break the news immediately. He built the anticipation. Jobs first acknowledged the people at Apple who had been working on the Internet strategy he had just described in the presentation, asking them to stand for applause. He publicly thanked his graphics and advertising agencies as well. Then he dropped the news.

"Everyone at Apple has been working extra hard these two and a half years. And during this time, I've been the interim CEO. I have another job at Pixar as the CEO, which I love. I hope that after two and a half years, we've been able to prove to our shareholders at Pixar that maybe we can pull this interim CEO thing off. So, I'm not changing any of my duties at either Pixar or Apple, but I'm pleased to announce today that I'm dropping the 'interim' title." The audience went nuts; people leaped from their seats, yelling, hollering, and cheering. Jobs was humbled and made it clear that he did not deserve all the credit for Apple's resurgence. "You're making me feel funny, because I get to come to work every day and work with the most talented people on the planet. I accept your thanks on the part of everyone at Apple," Jobs concluded.[6]

Revolutionary Product That Changes Everything

Twenty-six minutes into his Macworld 2007 keynote presentation, Jobs had just finished a discussion of Apple TV. He took a swig of water and slowly walked to the center of the stage, not saying a word for twelve seconds. He then told a story that would lead to one of the greatest product announcements in corporate history. We've discussed several elements of this presentation, including Jobs's use of headlines and the rule of three. For this discussion, let's examine a longer section of the segment. As you can see from the excerpt in Table 13.1, Jobs took his time to reveal the news that would rattle the industry and change the way millions of people access the Internet on the go.[7]

Once the laughter subsided, Jobs spent the rest of the presentation explaining the current limitations of existing smartphones, unveiling the actual iPhone, and reviewing its key features. Anyone who saw the entire presentation will most likely tell you that the three-minute introduction described in the table was *the* most memorable part of the entire keynote.

Take note of how Jobs heightened anticipation to create the experience. He could easily have said: "The next product we would like to introduce is called iPhone. It's Apple's first entry into the smartphone market. Here's what it looks like. Now let

TABLE 13.1 EXCERPT FROM JOBS'S MACWORLD 2007 PRESENTATION

STEVE'S WORDS	STEVE'S SLIDES
"This is a day I've been looking forward to for two and a half years. Every once in a while, a revolutionary product comes along that changes everything. One is very fortunate if you get to work on just one of these in your career. Apple has been very fortunate. It's been able to introduce a few of these into the world."	Image of Apple logo
"In 1984, we introduced the Macintosh. It didn't just change Apple; it changed the whole computer industry."	Full-screen photo of Macintosh; the date "1984" appears at the upper left next to the image
"In 2001, we introduced the first iPod. It didn't just change the way we all listen to music; it changed the entire music industry."	Full-screen photo of the original iPod; the date "2001" appears at the upper left
"Well, today we are introducing three revolutionary products of this class."	Back to image of Apple logo
"The first one is a wide-screen iPod with touch controls."	Only image on slide is an artistic rendering of iPod; words beneath the image: "Widescreen iPod with touch controls"
"The second is a revolutionary mobile phone."	Single artistic rendering of a phone, with the words "Revolutionary mobile phone"
"And the third is a breakthrough Internet communications device."	Single rendering of a compass, with the words "Breakthrough Internet communicator"

STEVE'S WORDS	STEVE'S SLIDES
"So, three things: a wide-screen iPod with touch controls, a revolutionary mobile phone, and a breakthrough Internet communications device."	The three images appear on the same slide, with the words "iPod, Phone, Internet"
"An iPod, a phone, and an Internet communicator. An iPod, a phone—are you getting it? These are not three separate devices."	Three images rotate
"This is one device, and we are calling it iPhone."	Text only, centered on slide: "iPhone"
"Today Apple is going to reinvent the phone!"	Text only: "Apple reinvents the phone"
"And here it is." [laughter]	A gag image appears: it's a photo of iPod, but instead of a scroll wheel, an artist had put an old-fashioned rotary dial on the MP3 player

me tell you more about it." Not very memorable, is it? By contrast, the actual introduction whetted the audience's appetite with every sentence. After Jobs outlined the revolutionary products of the past, a listener could be thinking, "I wonder what this third revolutionary product will be. Oh, I see: Jobs is going to announce three new products of this class. Cool. Wait. Is it three? Oh my gosh, he's talking about one product! All of those features in one product. This I've got to see!"

Every Steve Jobs presentation—major product announcements and minor ones—is scripted to have one moment that will leave everyone talking. The product takes center stage, but Jobs plays the role of director. Jobs is the Steven Spielberg of corporate presentations. What do you remember most from Spielberg's movies? Spielberg always has one scene that sticks in your memory for years: Indiana Jones pulling a pistol to kill the swordsman in *Raiders of the Lost Ark*, the opening scene of *Jaws*, or E.T. asking to phone home. In the same way, Jobs creates one moment that will define the experience.

Jobs has changed many things about his presentation style over the past thirty years, including his wardrobe, slides, and style. Through it all, one thing has remained consistent—his love of drama.

DIRECTOR'S NOTES

» Plan a "holy shit" moment. It need not be a break-through announcement. Something as simple as telling a personal story, revealing some new and unexpected information, or delivering a demonstration can help create a memorable moment for your audience. Movie directors such as Steven Spielberg look for those emotions that uplift people, make them laugh, or make them think. People crave beautiful, memorable moments. Build them into your presentation. The more unexpected, the better.

» Script the moment. Build up to the big moment before laying it on your audience. Just as a great novel doesn't give away the entire plot on the first page, the drama should build in your presentation. Did you see the movie *The Sixth Sense*, with Bruce Willis? The key scene was at the end of the movie—one twist that the majority of viewers didn't see coming. Think about ways to add the element of surprise to your presentations. Create at least one memorable moment that will amaze your audience and have them talking well after your presentation is over.

» Rehearse the big moment. Do not make the mistake of creating a memorable experience and having it bomb because you failed to practice. It must come off crisp, polished, and effortless. Make sure demos work and slides appear when they're supposed to.

Schiller Learns from the Best

P hil Schiller had some mighty big shoes to fill on January 6, 2009. Schiller, Apple's vice president of worldwide product marketing, replaced Steve Jobs as the keynote presenter at Macworld. (Apple had earlier announced that this would be the company's last year of participation in the event.) Schiller had the unfortunate role of being compared with his boss, who had more than thirty years of experience on the big stage. Schiller was smart, however, and delivered a product launch that contained the best elements of a typical Steve Jobs presentation. Following are seven of Schiller's techniques that Jobs himself would surely have used had he given the keynote:[1]

» **Create Twitter-like headlines.** Schiller set the theme of the day right up front. "Today is all about the Mac," he told the audience. This opening is reminiscent of how Jobs opened the two preceding Macworld shows. Jobs told the 2008 audience that something was in the air, foreshadowing the MacBook Air announcement, and in 2007, Jobs said that Apple was going to make history that day. It sure did when Jobs later introduced the iPhone.

» **Draw a road map.** Schiller verbally outlined a simple agenda at the beginning of his presentation and provided verbal reminders along the way. Just as Jobs uses the rule of three to describe products, Schiller also introduced the presentation as three separate categories. "I have three new things to tell you about today," he said (accompanying slide read: "3 New Things"). The first was a new version of iLife. The second product he discussed was a new version of iWork. Finally, the third was a new MacBook seventeen-inch Pro notebook computer.

» **Dress up numbers.** As his boss does, Schiller added meaning to numbers. He told the audience that 3.4 million customers visit an Apple store every week. To give his audience a relevant perspective, Schiller said, "That's one hundred Macworlds each and every week."

» **Stage the presentation with props.** Demonstrations play a prominent role in every Steve Jobs presentation. Schiller also used the technique smoothly and effectively. As Jobs likely would have done had he given the presentation, Schiller sat down at a computer on the stage and demonstrated several new features that come standard in '09 versions of iLife and iWork. My favorite demo was the new Keynote '09, which comes closer than ever to letting everyday users create Jobs-like slides without an expertise in graphic design.

» **Share the stage.** Schiller did not hog the spotlight. He shared the stage with employees who had more experience in areas that were relevant to the new products he introduced. For a demo of iMovie '09, a new version of the video-editing software, Schiller deferred to an Apple engineer who actually created the tool. When Schiller revealed the new seventeen-inch MacBook Pro, he said the battery was the most innovative feature of the notebook computer. To explain further, Schiller showed a video that featured three Apple employees describing how they were able to build a battery that lasted eight hours on a single charge without adding to the notebook's size, weight, or price.

» **Create visual slides.** There are very few words on a Steve Jobs slide, and there were few on Schiller's slides as well. The first few slides had no words at all, simply photographs. Schiller started by giving the audience a tour of some of the new Apple stores that had opened around the world the past year. There were no bullet points on Schiller's slides. When Schiller did present a list of features, he used the fewest words possible and often paired the words with an image. You can view the slide set yourself by watching the actual keynote presentation on the Apple website or visiting Slideshare.net.[2]

» **Deliver a "holy shit" moment.** In true Steve Jobs fashion, Schiller surprised the audience by announcing "just one more thing" to close his presentation. He applied the rule of three as he had done earlier, but this time to iTunes. He said there were three new things for iTunes in 2009: a change to the pricing structure, the ability of iPhone customers to download and buy songs on their 3G cellular network, and the fact that all iTunes songs would be DRM free (i.e., without copy protection). Schiller received a big round of applause when he announced that eight million songs would be DRM free "starting today" and got an even bigger round of applause when he said that all ten million songs on iTunes would be DRM free by the end of the quarter. Schiller knew that DRM-free songs in iTunes would be the big headline of the day, and he saved it for last. The announcement did, indeed, dominate the news coverage that followed.

ACT 3

Refine and Rehearse

So far, we've learned how Steve Jobs plans his presentations. We've talked about how he supports the narrative through his words and slides. We've discussed how he assembles the cast, creates demos, and wows his audience with one dynamic moment that leaves everyone in awe. Finally, you'll learn how Jobs refines and rehearses his presentation to make an emotional connection with the audience. This final step is essential for anyone who wants to talk, walk, and look like a leader. Let's preview the scenes in this act:

» **SCENE 14: "Master Stage Presence."** *How* you say something is as important as *what* you say, if not more so. Body language and verbal delivery account for 63 to 90 percent of the impression you leave on your audience, depending upon which study you cite. Steve Jobs's delivery matches the power of his words.

» **SCENE 15: "Make It *Look* Effortless."** Few speakers rehearse more than Steve Jobs. His preparation time is legendary among the people closest to him. Researchers have discovered exactly how many hours of practice it takes to achieve mastery in a given skill. In this chapter, you'll learn how Jobs confirms these theories and how you can apply them to improve your own presentation skills.

» **SCENE 16: "Wear the Appropriate Costume."** Jobs has the easiest wardrobe selection in the world: it's the same for all of his presentations. His attire is so well known that even "Saturday Night Live" and "30 Rock" poked some good-natured fun at him. Learn why it's OK for Jobs to dress the way he does but it could mean career suicide if you follow his lead.

» **SCENE 17: "Toss the Script."** Jobs talks to the audience, not to his slides. He makes strong eye contact because he has practiced effectively. This chapter will teach you how to practice the right way so you, too, can toss the script.

» **SCENE 18: "Have Fun."** Despite the extensive preparation that goes into a Steve Jobs presentation, things don't always go according to plan. Nothing rattles Jobs, because his first goal is to have fun!

Master Stage Presence

I was hooked by Steve's energy and enthusiasm.

—GIL AMELIO

Steve Jobs has a commanding presence. His voice, gestures, and body language communicate authority, confidence, and energy. Jobs's enthusiasm was on full display at Macworld 2003. Table 14.1 shows his actual words as well as the gestures he used to introduce the Titanium PowerBook.[1] The words he verbally emphasized in his presentation are in italics.

The words Jobs uses to describe a product are obviously important, but so is the *style* in which he delivers the words. He punches key words in every paragraph, adding extra emphasis to the most important words in the sentence. He makes expansive gestures to complement his vocal delivery. We'll examine his body language and vocal delivery more closely later in the chapter, but for now, the best way to appreciate his skill is to call on a guest speaker who pales in comparison.

"Who's Mr. Note Card?"

During the iPhone introduction at Macworld 2007, Jobs invited Cingular/AT&T CEO Stan Sigman to join him onstage and to share a few words about the partnership. Sigman took the floor and sucked the energy right out of the room. He immediately

TABLE 14.1 JOBS'S MACWORLD 2003 PRESENTATION

STEVE'S WORDS	STEVE'S GESTURES
"Two years ago, we introduced a *landmark product* for Apple. The Titanium PowerBook *instantly* became the best notebook in the industry. The number *one lust object.*"	Raises index finger
"Every review said so."	Pulls hands apart, palms up
"And you know what? Nobody has caught up with it in *two years.*"	Holds up two fingers on right hand
"Almost every reviewer today *still* says it is the number one notebook in the industry. No one is even *close.*"	Chops air with left hand
"This is important for Apple because we believe that someday *notebooks* are even going to outsell *desktops* . . . We want to replace even *more* desktops with notebooks."	Makes an expansive gesture with both hands
"So, how do we do this? What's next? Well, the Titanium PowerBook is a milestone product, and it's not going away. But we're going to step it up a notch to attract even *more* people from a desktop to a notebook."	Gestures, moving hand in a broad stroke from right to left
"And how do we do that? We do that with *this.*"	Pauses
"The new *seventeen-inch PowerBook*. A seventeen-inch landscape screen."	Another expansive gesture, hands pulled apart, palms up
"It's *stunning.*"	Pauses
"And when you close it, it is only *one inch* thick."	Makes thin gesture with left hand
"The *thinnest* PowerBook *ever*. Let me go ahead and show you one. I happen to have one right here."	Walks to stage right while maintaining eye contact with audience

STEVE'S WORDS	STEVE'S GESTURES
"It is the most incredible product we have ever made."	Picks up computer and opens it
"The new seventeen-inch PowerBook. It's amazing. Look at that screen."	Holds up computer to show screen
"Look at how *thin* it is. Isn't it incredible? It's beautiful, too."	Shuts computer and holds it up
"This is clearly the most advanced notebook computer ever made *on the planet*. Our competitors haven't even caught up with what we introduced two years ago; I don't know what they're going to do about *this*."	Smiles and looks directly at audience

put his hands into his pockets and proceeded to deliver his comments in a low-key monotone. Worst of all, he pulled note cards out of his jacket pocket and started reading from them word for word. As a result, Sigman's delivery became more halting, and he lost all eye contact with the audience. He continued for six long minutes that seemed like thirty. Observers were fidgeting, waiting for Jobs to return.

A post on CNN's international blog read: "Sigman . . . read stiffly from a script, pausing awkwardly to consult notes. By contrast, the silver-tongued Jobs wore his trademark black turtleneck and faded blue jeans . . . Jobs is one of the best showmen in corporate America, rarely glancing at scripts and quick with off-the-cuff jokes." Bloggers were relentless during Sigman's talk. Among the comments: "Who's Mr. Note Card?"; "Blah, blah, blah, and blah"; "Painfully bad"; and "A snoozer."

Sigman left AT&T that same year. Macworld.com wrote: "Sigman is perhaps best remembered by Apple fans as *completely negating* Jobs's Reality Distortion Field in an incident which left almost half of the entire keynote audience sound asleep. He has been sentenced to a cruel afterlife of being the butt of roughly 99 percent of Scott Bourne's jokes [Bourne is a Mac pundit and podcaster] . . . And what will Stan do in retirement? Word is he's thinking of giving public speaking workshops to underprivileged youth."[2]

Sigman spent forty-two years at AT&T, rising from the lowest rungs in the company to running its wireless division. Yet, to many people unfamiliar with his leadership, Sigman's appearance at Macworld will be his lasting legacy. It wasn't Sigman's fault. He had to follow the master. And, unfortunately, this book wasn't out yet to help him prepare!

Three Techniques to Improve Body Language

Steve Jobs resigned from Apple in 1985 after losing a boardroom battle for control of the company in a power struggle with then CEO John Sculley. He would remain away for eleven years, returning triumphantly when Gil Amelio, Apple's CEO in 1996, announced that Apple was going to buy Jobs's NeXT for $427 million. "I was hooked by Steve's energy and enthusiasm," Amelio wrote in *On the Firing Line: My Five Hundred Days at Apple*. "I do remember how animated he is on his feet, how his full mental abilities materialize when he's up and moving, how he becomes more expressive."[3]

Jobs comes alive when he is up and moving onstage. He has seemingly boundless energy. When he's at his best, Jobs does three things anyone can, and should, do to enhance one's speaking and presentation skills: he makes eye contact, maintains an open posture, and uses frequent hand gestures.

EYE CONTACT

Great communicators such as Jobs make appreciably more eye contact with the audience than average presenters. They rarely read from slides or notes. Jobs doesn't eliminate notes entirely. He often has some notes tucked out of view during demonstrations. Apple's presentation software, Keynote, also makes it easy for speakers to see speaker's notes while the audience sees the slides displayed on the projector. If Jobs is reading, nobody can tell. He maintains eye contact with his audience nearly all the time. He glances at a slide and immediately turns his attention back to where it belongs—on those watching.

Most presenters spend too much time reading every word of text on a slide. During demonstrations, mediocre presenters will break eye contact completely. Research has discovered that eye contact is associated with honesty, trustworthiness, sincerity, and confidence. Avoiding eye contact is most often associated with a lack of confidence and leadership ability. Breaking eye contact is a surefire way to lose your connection with your audience.

Jobs can make solid eye contact with his listeners because he practices his presentations for weeks ahead of time (see Scene 15). He knows exactly what's on each slide and what he's going to say when the slide appears. The more Jobs rehearses, the more he has internalized the content, and the easier it is for him to connect with his listeners. The majority of presenters fail to practice, and it shows.

The second reason why Jobs can make solid eye contact is that his slides are highly visual. More often than not, there are no words at all on a slide—just photographs (see Scene 8 and Scene 17). When there are words, they are few—sometimes just one word on a slide. Visual slides force the speaker to deliver the information to those whom the message is intended to reach—the audience.

OPEN POSTURE

Jobs rarely crosses his arms or stands behind a lectern. His posture is "open." An open posture simply means he has placed nothing between himself and his audience. During demos, Jobs sits parallel to the computer so nothing blocks his view of the audience or the audience's view of him. He performs a function on the computer and immediately turns to the audience to explain what he just did, rarely breaking eye contact for a long stretch of time. In Jobs's early presentations, most notably the 1984 Macintosh introduction, he stood behind a lectern. He abandoned the lectern soon after and has never used one since (with the exception of his 2005 Stanford commencement address). See Figure 14.1.

HAND GESTURES

Jobs emphasizes nearly every sentence with a gesture that complements his words. Some old-fashioned speaking coaches still instruct clients to keep their hands at their sides. I'm not sure where this started, but it's the kiss of death for any speaker hoping to captivate an audience. Keeping your hands at your sides will make you look stiff, formal, and, frankly, a little weird. Extraordinary communicators such as Jobs use *more* gestures than the average speaker, not fewer. There's even research to back up this observation.

Dr. David McNeill, at the University of Chicago, is known for his exhaustive research in the area of hand gestures. He's made it his passion since 1980. His research has shown that gestures and language are intimately connected. In fact, the *use* of gestures can help presenters speak better by clearing up their thought process. Yes, he says, it actually takes concentrated effort *not* to

Figure 14.1 Steve Jobs engages his audience with strong eye contact, hand gestures, and an open posture.

JOHN G. MABANGLO/AFP/Getty Images

use gestures. McNeill has found that very disciplined, rigorous, and confident thinkers use hand gestures that reflect the clarity of their thinking—it's like a window to their thought process.

Use hand gestures to emphasize your point. Be careful, however, that your hand gestures do not become robotic or overrehearsed. In other words, don't copy Jobs and his mannerisms. Be yourself. Be authentic.

Say It with Style

Steve Jobs uses his voice as effectively as his gestures. His content, slides, and demos create excitement, but his delivery ties the package together. When he introduced the iPhone in January 2007, he told a magnificently woven story, and his vocal expression provided just the right amount of drama. We reviewed the announcement and its slides in previous chapters. Now let's focus on *how* Jobs said what he said. It is a package

Is That a CEO or a Preacher?

Few among us have the public-speaking confidence to rival Cisco CEO John Chambers. People are often shocked the first time they watch him give a presentation. Like a preacher, Chambers roams among the audience. He spends only a minute or two onstage at the beginning of his presentation before stepping into the crowd. Chambers walks right up to people, looks them in the eye, calls some by name, even places his hand on someone's shoulder. Very few people have the confidence to pull this off.

I know as a fact that Chambers's confidence is the result of hours of relentless practice. He knows every word on each of his slides, and he knows exactly what he's going to say next. Observers have said watching a Chambers presentation is an "astonishing" experience. Be astonishing. Rehearse your presentation, and pay close attention to your body language and verbal delivery.

deal, after all. Great slides mean little without a great delivery. A great story will fall flat if delivered poorly.

Table 14.2 illustrates Jobs's vocal delivery. It's from the same iPhone presentation featured in Scene 13, with a focus on his actual delivery. The words Jobs chose to emphasize are italicized in the first column; the second column lists notes on his delivery, including the moments when he pauses right after a phrase or sentence.[4] Pay particular attention to pacing, pausing, and volume.

Jobs varied his delivery to create suspense, enthusiasm, and excitement. Nothing will do more to destroy all of the work you put into crafting a spectacular presentation than to deliver it in a boring monotone, which Jobs most certainly does not.

Jobs's voice complemented the drama of the plot. He uses similar devices in every presentation. This section details four related techniques that Jobs uses to keep his listeners engaged: inflection, pauses, volume, and rate.

INFLECTION

Jobs changes his inflection by raising or lowering the pitch of his voice. Think about how flat the iPhone launch would have sounded if all of his words had been delivered with exactly the same tone. Instead, Jobs raised his pitch when he said, "Are you getting it?" and "This is one device." Jobs has some favorite descriptors that find their way into many of his presentations: *unbelievable*, *awesome*, *cool*, and *huge*. These words would not carry the same impact if the tone in which they are delivered sounds exactly like the rest of the sentence. Jobs modifies his tone frequently, keeping his listeners on the edge of their seats.

PAUSES

Nothing is more dramatic than a well-placed pause. "Today we're introducing a third kind of notebook," Jobs told the Macworld audience in January 2008. Then he paused a few beats before saying, "It's called the MacBook Air." He paused again before the delivering the headline: "It's the world's thinnest notebook."[5]

Jobs does not rush his presentation. He lets it breathe. He will often remain quiet for several seconds as he lets a key point

TABLE 14.2 JOBS'S 2007 iPHONE PRESENTATION

STEVE'S WORDS	STEVE'S DELIVERY
"This is a day I've been looking forward to for two and a half years."	Pause
"Every once in a while, a revolutionary product comes along that *changes everything*."	Pause
"Apple has been very fortunate. It's been able to introduce a few of these into the world. In 1984, we introduced *Macintosh*. It didn't just change Apple; it changed the whole computer industry."	Pause
"In 2001, we introduced the first *iPod*."	Pause
"It didn't just change the way we all listen to music; it changed the entire *music* industry."	Pause
"Well, today we're introducing *three* revolutionary products of this class. The *first* one"	Pause
"is a wide-screen iPod with touch controls. The *second*"	Pause
"is a *revolutionary mobile phone*."	Voice grows louder
"And the *third*"	Pause
"is a *breakthrough* Internet communications device. So, three things: a wide-screen iPod with touch controls, a revolutionary mobile phone, and a breakthrough Internet communications device."	Pause
"An iPod, a phone, and an Internet communciator."	Voice grows louder
"An iPod, a phone—are you getting it?"	Speaks faster, voice grows louder
"These are not three separate devices. This is *one* device,"	Voice grows louder still
"and we are calling it *iPhone*."	Voice gets even louder
"Today Apple is going to *reinvent* the *phone*!"	Loudest volume of the presentation

sink in. Most presenters sound as though they are trying to rush through the material. In many ways, they are, because they scripted more material than the time allows. Jobs never hurries. His presentation is carefully rehearsed to give him plenty of time to slow down, pause, and let his message take hold.

VOLUME

Jobs will lower and raise his voice to add drama. He typically does this when introducing a hot new product. He often lowers his voice as he builds up to the announcement and then raises his volume to hit the big note. He'll do the opposite as well. When he introduced the first iPod, he raised his voice and said, "To have your whole music library with you at all times is a *quantum leap* in listening to music." He then lowered his voice and delivered the knockout: "But the coolest thing about iPod is your entire music library fits in your pocket."[6] Just as inflections and pauses keep your audience riveted to your every word, so does the volume of your voice.

RATE

Jobs speeds up the delivery of some sentences and slows down for others. Demonstrations are typically delivered at his normal rate of speech, but he slows down considerably when he delivers the headline or key message that he wants everyone to remember. When Jobs introduced the iPod for the first time, he lowered his voice nearly to a whisper to emphasize the key takeaway. He also slowed the tempo of his sentences to build the drama. Table 14.3 offers highlights.[7]

Act Like the Leader You Want to Be

Do not make the mistake of believing body language and vocal delivery are unimportant, "soft skills." UCLA research scientist Albert Mehrabian studied expression and communication for his book *Silent Messages*.[8] He discovered that nonverbal cues carry the most impact in a conversation. Tone of voice—vocal expression—was the second most influential factor. The third, and least important, were the actual words spoken.

TABLE 14.3 EXCERPT FROM JOBS INTRODUCING THE iPOD, WITH DELIVERY NOTES

STEVE'S WORDS	STEVE'S DELIVERY
"Now, you might be saying, 'This is cool, but I've got a hard disk in my portable computer, my iBook. I'm running iTunes. I'm really happy. I don't get ten hours of battery life on my iBook, but iBook has better battery life than any other consumer portable.'"	Slows down rate of speech
"'So, what's so special about iPod here?'"	Pauses and lowers volume
"It's ultraportable. An iBook is portable, but this is *ultra*portable. Let me show you what I mean."	Speeds up rate of speech
"iPod is the size of a deck of cards. It is 2.4 inches wide. It is four inches tall. And barely three-quarters of an inch thick. This is tiny. It also only weighs 6.5 ounces, lighter than most of the cell phones you have in your pockets right now. This is what's so remarkable about iPod."	Slows down and lowers voice
"It is ultraportable."	Almost at a whisper

To a large extent, how Steve Jobs speaks and carries himself leaves his audience with a sense of awe and confidence in him as a leader. U.S. president Barack Obama once said the most valuable lesson he learned as he worked himself up from a community organizer to the most powerful person on the planet was to "always act confident."

People are making judgments about you all the time, but especially in the first ninety seconds of meeting you. How you deliver your words and what your body language says about you will leave your listeners disillusioned or inspired. Steve Jobs is an electrifying communicator because he is expressive in both voice and gesture.

Bueller? Bueller?

Ben Stein provides us with one of the best examples of a horribly dull, monotone vocal delivery. In the 1986 movie *Ferris Bueller's Day Off*, Ben Stein played a boring economics teacher. Stein's most famous line in the movie occurred when he was taking attendance and Bueller (the Matthew Broderick character) was nowhere to be found. In the driest monotone on film, Stein asked, "Bueller . . . ? Bueller . . . ? Bueller . . . ?" as the camera flashed to an empty chair. In another scene, Stein discussed the Hawley-Smoot Tariff Act and voodoo economics. The looks on the students' faces are hilarious. One kid has his head on the desk as drool is coming out of the side of his mouth. Stein's character is so boring, it's funny.

If Stein were to read a transcript of a Steve Jobs presentation in the same manner in which he played the teacher, it would surely be one of the longest, dullest presentations in the history of corporate America. This proves once again that words matter, but an effective delivery makes the difference.

DIRECTOR'S NOTES

» Pay attention to your body language. Maintain eye contact, have an open posture, and use hand gestures when appropriate. Don't be afraid of using your hands. Research has shown that gestures reflect complex thinking and give the listener confidence in the speaker.

» Vary your vocal delivery by adding inflection to your voice, raising or lowering your volume, as well as speeding up and slowing down. Also, let your content breathe. Pause. Nothing is as dramatic as a well-placed pause.

» Record yourself. Watch your body language, and listen to your vocal delivery. Watching yourself on video is the best way to improve your presentation skills.

Make It *Look* Effortless

Practice isn't the thing you do once you're good. It's the thing you do that makes you good.

—MALCOLM GLADWELL

Steve Jobs is a master showman, working the stage with precision. Every move, demo, image, and slide is in sync. He appears comfortable, confident, and remarkably effortless. At least, it *looks* effortless to the audience. Here's his presentation secret: Jobs rehearses for hours. To be more precise: many, many hours over many, many days.

"Jobs unveils Apple's latest products as if he were a particularly hip and plugged-in friend showing off inventions in your living room. Truth is, the sense of informality comes only after grueling hours of practice," observed a *BusinessWeek* reporter. "One retail executive recalls going to a Macworld rehearsal at Jobs's behest and then waiting four hours before Jobs came off the stage to conduct an interview. Jobs considers his keynotes a competitive weapon. Marissa Mayer, a Google executive who plays a central role in launching the search giant's innovations, insists that up-and-coming product marketers attend Jobs's keynotes. 'Steve Jobs is the best at launching new products,' she says. 'They have to see how he does it.'"[1]

How does he do it? The *BusinessWeek* reporter provided the answer in the article: Steve Jobs puts in *hours of grueling practice*. When was the last time you could say that you devoted hours of grueling practice to prepare for a presentation? The honest answer is probably "never." If you really want to talk the way Jobs does, plan on spending more time rehearsing every portion of your presentation.

Glimpse Behind the Magic Curtain

In an article published in the *Guardian* on January 5, 2006, former Apple employee Mike Evangelist wrote about his personal experience rehearsing a portion of a demonstration for a Jobs keynote: "To a casual observer these presentations appear to be just a guy in a black shirt and blue jeans talking about some new technology products. But they are in fact an incredibly complex and sophisticated blend of sales pitch, product demonstration, and corporate cheerleading, with a dash of religious revival thrown in for good measure. They represent weeks of work, precise orchestration, and intense pressure for scores of people who collectively make up the 'man behind the curtain.' "[2]

According to Evangelist's first-person account, Jobs begins his preparation weeks in advance, reviewing products and technologies he is going to talk about. Evangelist had been tapped to demo the new iDVD, Apple's DVD-burning software, for Macworld 2001. Evangelist said his team spent hundreds of hours preparing for a segment that lasted five minutes. That's not a typo: *hundreds* of hours for a five-minute demo.

Evangelist said Jobs rehearsed for two full days before the presentation, asking for feedback from the product managers in the room. Jobs spends a lot of time on slides, personally writing and designing much of the content, along with some help from the design team. "On the day before show time, things get much more structured, with at least one and sometimes two complete dress rehearsals. Throughout it all Steve is extremely focused. While we were in that room, all his energy was directed at making this keynote the perfect embodiment of Apple's messages."[3]

In the weeks before the keynote, Evangelist saw the full range of Steve's emotions from disappointment to elation. "I believe it is one of the most important aspects of Steve Jobs's impact on Apple: he has little or no patience for anything but excellence from himself or others," Evangelist concluded.[4]

In October 1999, *Time* magazine reporter Michael Krantz was interviewing Jobs one day before the introduction of a line of multicolored iMacs. Jobs was rehearsing the big moment when he would announce, "Say hello to the new iMacs." The computers were then supposed to glide out from behind a dark curtain, but according to Krantz, Jobs was unhappy with the lighting. He wanted the lights to be brighter and to come up sooner. "Let's keep doing it till we get it right, OK?" said Jobs.[5] The show's lighting folks practiced again and again as Jobs grew increasingly frustrated.

"Finally," Krantz reports, "they get it right, the five impeccably lighted iMacs gleaming as they glide forward smoothly on the giant screen. 'Oh! Right there! That's great!' Jobs yells, elated at the very notion of a universe capable of producing these insanely beautiful machines. 'That's perfect!' he bellows, his voice booming across the empty auditorium. 'Wooh!' And you know what? He's right. The iMacs do look better when the lights come on earlier."[6] The scene that Krantz described could be interpreted in one of two ways: either Jobs is a micromanager or, as one of Jobs's friends observed in the article, "he is single-minded, almost manic, in his pursuit of quality and excellence."

What Steve Jobs, Michael Jordan, and Winston Churchill Have in Common

Psychology professor Dr. K. Anders Ericsson has studied top athletes such as Michael Jordan as well as superachievers in other walks of life: chess players, golfers, doctors, even dart throwers! Ericsson discovered that star performers refine their skills through *deliberative practice*. In other words, they do not just do the same thing over and over, hoping to get better. Instead, they set specific goals, ask for feedback, and continually strive to improve over the long run. From Ericsson's research, we have learned that star performers practice specific skills again and again over many, many years.

Ordinary speakers become extraordinary because they practice. Winston Churchill was one of the foremost communicators of the twentieth century. He was a master of persuasion, influence, and motivation. Churchill, too, deliberately practiced the skills required to inspire millions of British during the darkest days of World War II. "He would prepare in the days before a big parliamentary speech, practicing quips or parries against any number of possible interjections. Churchill practiced so thoroughly that he seemed to be speaking extemporaneously . . . he held his audience spellbound," wrote Churchill's granddaughter Celia Sandys and coauthor Jonathan Littman in *We Shall Not Fail*. "The lesson is simple but requires lots of hard work. Practice is essential, particularly if you want to sound spontaneous."[7] The world's greatest communicators have always known that "spontaneity" is the result of planned practice.

You *can* speak the way Jobs does, but it takes practice. Jobs makes an elaborate presentation look easy because he puts in the time. In *The Second Coming of Steve Jobs*, Paul Vais, a NeXT executive, was quoted as saying, "Every slide was written like a piece of poetry. We spent hours on what most people would consider low-level detail. Steve would labor over the presentation. We'd try to orchestrate and choreograph everything and make it more alive than it really is."[8] Making your presentation "more alive" takes practice. Once you accept this simple principle, your presentations will stand out in a sea of mediocrity.

Ten Thousand Hours to Mastery

There are no "naturals." Steve Jobs is an extraordinary presenter because he works at it. According to Malcolm Gladwell in *Outliers*, "Research suggests that once a musician has enough ability to get into a top music school, the thing that distinguishes one performer from another is how hard he or she works.

That's it. And what's more, the people at the very top don't work just harder or even much harder than everyone else. They work much, *much* harder."[9] Although the observation Gladwell makes in *Outliers* applies specifically to musicians, the vast amount of research on the subject of peak performance shows that practice is the common thread among all individuals who excel at a particular task. Neuroscientist and musician Daniel Levitin believes that the magic number is ten thousand.

"The emerging picture of such studies is that ten thousand hours of practice is required to achieve the level of mastery associated with being a world-class expert—in anything . . . In study after study, of composers, basketball players, fiction writers, ice-skaters, concert pianists, chess players, master criminals, and what have you, this number comes up again and again. Of course, this doesn't address why some people don't seem to get anywhere when they practice, and why some people seem to get more out of their practice sessions than others, but no one has yet found a case in which true world-class expertise was accomplished in less time. It seems that it takes the brain this long to assimilate all that it needs to know to achieve true mastery."[10]

The ten-thousand-hours theory is consistent with what we know about how the brain learns, according to Levitin and Gladwell. They say that learning requires consolidation in neural tissue; the more experiences we have with a particular action, the stronger those connections become.

Now let's do the math. Ten thousand hours is equivalent to roughly three hours a day, or twenty hours a week, over a period of ten years. To substantiate this theory, Gladwell tells the story of the Beatles, who performed together in Hamburg over a long period before they hit it big. According to Gladwell, before the Beatles enjoyed their first success in 1964, they had performed live together some twelve hundred times, sometimes for eight hours at a stretch. This is an extraordinary feat, because most groups don't perform that often in their entire careers. The band members became better and more confident the longer they played together. "Incidentally," writes Gladwell, "the time that elapsed between their founding and their arguably greatest artistic achievements—*Sgt. Pepper's Lonely Hearts Club Band* and *The Beatles* [White Album]—is ten years."[11]

With the ten-thousand-hours theory in mind, let's turn our attention once again to Jobs. Although Apple was founded in 1976, Jobs and friend-cofounder Steve Wozniak started attending meetings of the Homebrew Computer Club in 1974. Homebrew was an early computer-hobbyist club in Silicon Valley, California. It was at Homebrew that Jobs began tinkering and talking about how computers could change the world. Exactly ten years later, Jobs gave an outstanding presentation—the introduction of the Macintosh in 1984. Most people who saw that presentation consider it to be a magnificent achievement, packed with suspense, drama, and excitement. But remarkably, Jobs continued to practice, refine, and improve his presentation style.

A decade later, in 1997, Jobs had returned to Apple and was onstage at Boston's Macworld to discuss the steps he had taken to restore Apple to health. Everything about his performance that day was more polished and natural than it had been in previous years. He had lost the lectern, walking comfortably across the stage, and had started creating more visually engaging slides.

Flash forward another ten years to Macworld 2007, which, in my opinion, is Jobs's greatest presentation to date if you take into account every element of the keynote from start to finish. He hits home runs in every presentation, but he hit a bases-loaded homer in 2007. Everything clicked. Several sections of the presentation have been discussed throughout this book. The overall presentation was smooth and polished, with dramatic highs and lows, confident body language, captivating verbal delivery, and gorgeous slides. The iPhone announcement had even overshadowed every product at the vastly larger Consumer Electronics Show, held the same week in Las Vegas.

The chief misconception about Jobs is that he is a natural presenter, that he was born with the charisma that he exhibits onstage. Not true. As research has shown, nobody is a natural. You can achieve the same level of proficiency of the world's greatest communicators if you work at it much, *much* harder than everyone else.

Flushing Away $25,000

I once saw the executive of a major publicly traded company give a keynote presentation to a large audience of customers, press, and analysts. I later learned that the company had spent upwards of $25,000 for professional designers to create slick, animated slides. That figure did not account for the lighting, audio, and venue. The most creative slides will fail to impress your audience unless you practice your delivery; this guy did not practice, and it showed. Since he had not practiced coordinating his words to the animation, the slides were off, and he lost his place numerous times. He stumbled through most of the presentation and at one point threw up his hands in exasperation! If you spend money and time on a presentation—and time is money—you owe it to yourself to practice, practice, and practice some more!

Make Video Your Best Friend

Nearly every year, I'm asked to work with CEOs who give major presentations at the Consumer Electronics Show in Las Vegas. The conference is usually scheduled for the first full week in January, which means we're rehearsing over the holidays, often while the rest of the company's employees are off. Regardless, CEOs will show up for practice, because they know how important it is.

In one particular year, after several days of rehearsals, one of my CEO clients took the stage in Vegas but had trouble with the slides. The clicker had failed, and the slides were not advancing. Most amateur speakers who don't spend enough time practicing would have frozen, calling even more attention to the problem. Not this guy. He was so well prepared that he casually motioned to an assistant to advance the slides for him (we rehearse contingency plans). He didn't miss a step and kept talking. It didn't end there: something was wrong with the computer; it had locked and would have to be rebooted for the slide show to continue. The assistant simply shook his head, but the CEO stayed the course. He continued to deliver the rest of the presentation with no slides. He did so effortlessly and confidently.

He later told me that without practice (which I had urged him to do), he would have lost his confidence and floundered in front of employees, analysts, investors, customers, and the media. When I asked employees after the presentation what they had thought, none of them realized that anything had gone wrong.

VIDEO TRAINING TIPS

We had used a video camera during rehearsals. Very few presenters watch themselves on camera, even though perfectly appropriate camcorders are available for less than $300. I know that watching yourself on TV, especially a wide-screen, is not the most pleasant experience, but take my word for it: it's essential. Record your presentation and play it back. If possible, find objective friends and colleagues who will offer honest feedback. Use an external, clip-on microphone instead of the built-in microphone standard on all camcorders. Your voice will sound louder, clearer, and more resonant.

As you watch the video, pay close attention to these five areas:

» **Eye contact.** Commit most of your presentation to memory to avoid reading from notes. Your slides should act as your cue. Public-speaking expert Andrew Carnegie observed that notes destroy the intimacy between speaker and audience and make the speaker appear less powerful and confident. Notice that I didn't tell you to give the presentation "completely" without notes. Steve Jobs keeps notes out of his audience's sight. Only a careful observer would spot him glancing at them. He refers to notes during demonstrations, but since the audience's attention is on the demo itself, his notes do not detract from the presentation. The notes he does keep onstage are also unobtrusive and simple. He just needs to glance at them to find his place. Although it's easier in Keynote than PowerPoint to have a notes page for the speaker's view, you should still strive to deliver most of your presentation with no notes at all.

» **Body language.** Is your body language strong, confident, and commanding? Are your arms crossed or open? Are you keeping your hands in your pockets instead of keeping an open posture? Do you fidget, rock, or have other distracting habits? Are your gestures natural and purposeful or stiff and wooden? Remember that body language and verbal delivery account for the majority of the impression you leave on your listeners. Your body language should reflect the confidence of your words.

» **Filler words.** Are you constantly using "um," "ah," and "you know" to fill the space between thoughts? Just as text shouldn't fill every inch of your slide, your words shouldn't fill every pause between sentences. Reviewing your performance is the best way to eliminate these often distracting fillers. Once you catch yourself a few times, you will be more aware of the habit next time. Awareness is more than 90 percent of the solution!

» **Vocal delivery.** Vary the volume and inflection of your voice to keep the attention of your audience riveted on your words. Raise and lower your volume at different points in your presentation. Change your cadence. Varying the speed at which you talk will keep your presentation from sounding monotone. Speed up at certain points and then slow down. Pause for impact. Again, nothing is as dramatic as a well-placed pause. Don't sound rushed. Let the presentation breathe.

» **Energy.** Do you look as if you rolled out of bed on a Sunday morning, or do you appear vibrant, enthusiastic, and genuinely thrilled to be sharing your story with the audience? We all enjoy being around people with energy. They inspire us. They are stimulating, fun, and uplifting. An energetic person has passion in his voice, a bounce in his step, and a smile on his face. Energy makes a person likable, and likability is a key ingredient in persuasive communications. Many business professionals underestimate the energy level required to generate enthusiasm among their listeners. Electrifying speakers such as Jobs bring it. Jobs always has more energy than most other speakers who share the stage with him.

LEAVE YOUR COMFORT ZONE

Most business professionals could use an energy boost. But how do you project the right level of vigor without seeming over the top? By weighing yourself on an energy scale. And on this scale, more is better.

I often ask clients, "On a scale of one to ten—one being fast asleep and ten being wildly pumped up like motivational speaker Tony Robbins—tell me where you are right now."

"A three," most of my clients reply.

"OK," I say, "what would it feel like to be a seven, eight, or nine? Give it a try."

If they're being honest, most presenters place themselves at a three to six on the energy scale. That means there is plenty of room to raise their energy level.

Energy is hard to describe, but you know it when you see it. Television host Rachael Ray has it. President Barack Obama and Tony Robbins have it as well. These three individuals have different styles, but they speak with energy.

Try this exercise—practice leaving your comfort zone: Record several minutes of your presentation as you would normally deliver it. Play it back, preferably with someone else watching. Ask yourself and the observer, "Where am I on the energy scale?" Now try it again. This time, break out of your comfort zone. Ham it up. Raise your voice. Use broad gestures. Put a big smile on your face. Get to a point where you would feel slightly awkward and uncomfortable if you actually delivered the presentation that way. Now watch it again. Odds are your energy will be just right. You see, most people underestimate how little energy they actually have during a presentation. When they are asked to go "over the top" and to leave their comfort zone, they hit the right note.

Five Steps to Rehearsing "Off-the-Cuff" Remarks

With the economy plunging deeper into a recession, 2009 was a tough year to introduce a new car, but automobile companies

Caroline Kennedy's, ah, um, You Know, Performance

Filler words such as "ah," "um," and "you know" should not disqualify someone from public office, nor should they limit a person's effectiveness as a business leader. All too often, though, fillers will diminish your influence in the eyes of others. In early 2009, Caroline Kennedy had expressed interest in the New York Senate seat vacated by Hillary Rodham Clinton, who became U.S. secretary of state. The media skewered Kennedy's performance because of her verbal tendency to pack her remarks with, um, you know, like, fillers. Kennedy said "you know" more than thirty times in a two-minute interview. Listening for her filler words became sport among bloggers and radio talk-show hosts. She soon withdrew her name from consideration.

Here are three ways to eliminate fillers from your remarks before they detract from your message:

» **Ask for feedback.** Most of your colleagues are afraid of offending you. When someone asks me for advice and I see some real areas for improvement, I will be tough. At the same time, as is true of most other people, I hesitate to offer unsolicited advice even when I'm dying to say something that can improve someone's presentation skills. Likewise, since most of your family, friends, and peers avoid critiques for fear of "insulting" you, they will not voluntarily tell you that your mannerisms are annoying! Perhaps if Kennedy had asked for honest feedback, someone may have said, "Caroline, before you pitch yourself to the governor as the next New York senator, we need to work on how you answer the inevitable questions. Your answers must be specific, inspiring, and free from the filler words you use in everyday conversation."

» **Tap the glass.** I came across this technique entirely by chance, and it worked out extremely well. I was helping a woman rehearse a presentation and noticed that every other word was "ah" or "um." It became very distracting, so I told her I would tap a water glass with a spoon every time she used a filler word. My tapping became frequent—and irritating—prompting her to eliminate the fillers almost immediately. I've used it a few times since with equal success. Of course, this technique requires a second person to watch you and to tap the glass during your presentation rehearsal.

» **Record yourself, and play it back in the presence of others.** If you are serious about improving your presentation skills, record yourself on video, and replay it with someone else in the room. You don't have to tape your entire presentation, just the first five minutes. That should give you all the information you need to make some adjustments. You might be floored to hear how many filler words you use. For most people, simply watching themselves on video is enough to overcome some issues. Video feedback is even more effective in the presence of others who can pick up on some verbal mannerisms you might overlook.

A few "um"s and "ah"s from time to time will not detract from your ability to persuade an audience, but a steady stream of fillers can damage your efforts. The good news is that once you are made aware of the problem, you can easily follow the suggestions here to reduce or eliminate them.

can't put the brakes on designs and plans set in motion years ago. In January, I spoke to a group of auto executives who were designated spokespeople for new car models arriving soon to showrooms in North America. They were looking for advice on how to answer tough questions from the media. The same day, U.S. secretary of state–designate Hillary Clinton was fielding questions from the Senate Foreign Relations Committee in a confirmation hearing. The Associated Press called her performance "smooth," and NBC's Tom Brokaw said Clinton is known for her "legendary" preparation. I told the auto execs to prepare for tough questions in the same way that Clinton had probably prepared for her five-hour appearance.

It's a technique I call the "bucket method," and it is used in one form or another by CEOs, politicians, and, yes, Steve Jobs, who seems to have ready answers to any question. You can use it to prepare for presentations, pitches, sales calls, or any other situation in which you anticipate difficult or sensitive questions.

1. Identify the most common questions likely to be raised. Clinton expected a question about her husband's international foundation and its list of donors. Critics had widely publicized the issue, saying her appointment would be a conflict of interest. She also knew that each of the world's hot spots at the time would be fair game: Gaza, Iran, Iraq, Pakistan, and others. For the car executives, the most common question would be along the lines, "How do you expect to sell cars in this economy?" Or, "Will 2009 only get worse for the auto industry?"

2. Place the questions into "buckets," or categories. There might be only one question in a bucket, as in the case of the Clinton Foundation, or there might be several, as in the case of the carmakers and the economy. The point is to reduce the number of questions for which you must prepare. It's uncanny, but in my experience training thousands of speakers, the majority of questions will fall into about seven categories.

3. Create the best answer you have for the category. And this is critical—the answer must make sense regardless of *how* the question is phrased. You must avoid getting pulled into a detailed discussion based on the wording of the question. For example, here is Clinton's answer about her husband's fund-raising efforts: "I am very proud to be the president-elect's nominee for secretary of state, and I am very proud of what my husband and the Clinton Foundation and the associated efforts he's undertaken have accomplished, as well."[12] She would have said exactly the same thing regardless of how pointed the question from Republican senators was.

4. Listen carefully to the question, and identify a key word—a trigger—that will help you isolate the correct bucket from which to pull to your answer.

5. Look the person in the eye and respond with confidence.

"Well-prepared" speakers do not memorize answers to hundreds of potential questions. Instead, they prepare answers to *categories* of questions. The *way* a question is phrased is secondary. Think about it this way: your goal is to launch a minipresentation within a presentation.

You can use the bucket method to reframe the question in your favor. Let's assume that your company's product is more expensive than a similar offering by one of your competitors. Let's also assume that there is a good reason behind the higher price. The way the question is phrased is not as important as the answer you have created for the category, which is "price." A conversation might sound like this:

CUSTOMER: Why are you charging 10 percent more for the same product that I can get from company X?

YOU: You're asking about price. [Here, "charging more" is the trigger for the answer that you prepared on "price." Although the wording the customer chose is different from the term you chose, it triggers your prepared response on the subject.] We believe our product is priced competitively, especially for a product that improves the bottom line for our clients by 30 percent on average. It's important to remember that we have the best service team in the industry. That means when you need support, you'll get it. Our team is available to you 24-7. None of our competitors can say that.

I know the CEO of a large publicly traded company who uses this method very effectively. For example, during one tough meeting, an analyst asked him to respond to some unfavorable comments made by his largest competitor. "Competition" was his trigger word. This CEO smiled and confidently maintained the high road by saying, "Our view on competition is different from many others. Our view is that you play with class. We compete by giving our customers superior service and sharing our vision for where we see this industry going. As we get more successful, we see more competitors entering the market. It's part of the process of being a leader." With this one response, the CEO deflected his competitor's comments and reframed the issue to focus on his company's leadership.

When former secretary of state Henry Kissinger was asked how he handled media questions, he said, "What questions do you have for my answers?" He had his answers already prepared. The media is a tough audience, and these days so are your customers. Don't let uncomfortable questions throw you off your game.

Best Antidote to Nerves

Relentless preparation is the single best way to overcome stage fright: know what you're going to say, when you're going to say it, and how you're going to say it. Too many people focus inward during their presentations, creating even more anxiety for themselves. They'll ask themselves, "Is my shirt wrinkled? What is that person in the third row thinking?" In other words, it's all about you. Instead, go from "me" to "we." Shift the focus to what your product or service means to the lives of your listeners, and be confident in your preparation. I have worked with several executives who are worth millions (in some cases, billions) of dollars. Guess what? They get nervous speaking in front of groups. Funny thing about nerves, though—the more you practice, the less nervous you will be.

I know a world-famous business leader who gets very nervous before major presentations. He gets over it by preparing to the extreme. He knows the content on every slide and exactly what he is going to say. He arrives early to the venue so that he can test the audio and projector and advance through his slides. This particular executive even knows where the lights are in the room, so he is never in shadow. That's preparation! He might get nervous, but his routine makes him feel much more confident, and he is considered one of the best speakers in corporate America.

Golfer Vijay Singh hits thousands of balls a day to prepare for a tournament. Olympic gold-medal winner Michael Phelps swims fifty miles a week to prepare for a competition, and Steve Jobs spends hours of grueling practice before a keynote presentation. Superstar performers in all fields leave nothing to chance. If you want to thrill any audience, steal a page from the Jobs playbook and start practicing!

DIRECTOR'S NOTES

» Practice, practice, and practice some more. Don't take anything for granted. Review every slide, every demo, and every key message. You should know exactly what you're going to say, when you're going to say it, and how you're going to say it.

» Record your presentation. Spend a couple of hundred bucks on a camcorder and record yourself. You don't need to record the entire presentation. The first five minutes should give you plenty of information. Look for distracting body language and verbal tics, or fillers. When possible, review the video with someone else.

» Use the bucket method to prepare for tough questions. You will find that most lines of questions will fall into one of seven categories.

SCENE 16

Wear the Appropriate Costume

It is hard to think that a $2 billion company with 4,300-plus people couldn't compete with six people in blue jeans.

—STEVE JOBS, RESPONDING TO AN APPLE LAWSUIT AGAINST HIM
AFTER HE RESIGNED TO FORM NeXT

Steve Jobs is the anti-Cher. In her Vegas concert, Cher and her dancers had 140 costume changes; Jobs has one costume for every performance. For presentations, Jobs *always* wears a black mock turtleneck, faded blue jeans, and white sneakers. If you want to get more specific, he wears a *St. Croix* sweater, *Levi's 501* blue jeans, and *New Balance* running shoes. Not that it matters much, because you're not going to dress like him. He can get away with it because he's Steve Jobs and you're not. Seriously. When you're a business legend who is credited with reinventing the entire computer industry, you can show up in pretty much anything you want.

Although most people are familiar with Jobs's black shirt and blue jeans attire (even "The Simpsons" cartoon creators dressed the Jobs character in jeans and a black mock for an episode in 2008), Jobs did not always dress this way. When Jobs was a young man trying to be taken seriously by investors and the public, he dressed much more conservatively. The Jobs of

1984 looked a lot different from the Jobs of 2009. The first cover of *Macworld* magazine in January 1984 showed Jobs standing behind a desk with three of the original Macintosh computers. He was wearing a brown pin-striped suit, brown tie, and white shirt. Yes, Jobs once donned pinstripes. He wore an even more conservative outfit for the actual presentation when he unveiled the Macintosh, appearing in a white shirt, gray slacks, a dark blue double-breasted blazer, and a green bow tie. Imagine, Jobs in a bow tie! It's true.

Jobs is smart. His wardrobe always reflected the leader he wanted to become. He was well aware of the impression clothes could leave on people. While Jobs was away from Apple, he pitched his new company, NeXT, to Bank of America. Dan'l Lewin, NeXT's marketing executive, showed up at Jobs's house in blue jeans to accompany him to the meeting. Jobs walked out wearing an expensive Brioni suit from Wilkes Bashford. "Hey," Jobs said, "we're going to the bank today."[1] For Jobs, jeans were appropriate for the office, but not the bank. Now you might be confused. Jobs wore a suit to the bank and jeans in the office. What lesson does this hold for the rest of us? A true military hero, former U.S. Army ranger Matt Eversmann, once gave me the best piece of wardrobe advice I'd ever heard. Eversmann led troops in a fierce battle in Mogadishu, Somalia, in October 1993. The battle was turned into a movie called *Black Hawk Down*. I met Eversmann at a business conference and asked him for some leadership advice I could share with my readers. Eversmann told me that great leaders dress a little better than everyone else. He said that when he would meet a subordinate for the first time, his shoes were shinier, his whites were whiter, and his pants were better pressed.

I never forgot that piece of advice. I later interviewed George Zimmer, the founder of the Men's Wearhouse clothing chain. Zimmer agreed with Eversmann but added, "appropriate for the culture." It makes sense: you wouldn't show up for the company picnic in the same attire that you wear to the office. Also, different companies have different cultures. Apple is rebellious, creative, and committed to "think different." It's OK for an

Apple employee to wear more informal attire than a Wall Street executive.

Once you invent a product that changes the world, we can talk about dressing down. For now, here's the best wardrobe advice you'll ever hear: always dress a little better than everyone else, but appropriate for the culture.

DIRECTOR'S NOTES

» Dress like the leader you want to become, not for the position you currently have. Great leaders dress a little better than everyone else in the room. Remember, when Jobs was looking for funding at the bank, he dressed in an expensive suit.

» Wear clothes that are appropriate for the culture. Steve Jobs can get away with a black mock, blue jeans, and running shoes because everything about his brand is built on the concept of disrupting the status quo.

» If you're going to dress like a rebel, dress like a well-off rebel. Jobs wears St. Croix sweaters. It might look like a black T-shirt—but at least he spends money on it.

Toss the Script

**Be a yardstick of quality. Some people aren't used
to an environment where excellence is expected.**

—STEVE JOBS

S teve Jobs is the consummate presenter for twenty-first-century audiences who want to engage in conversations, not lectures. Jobs has a casual speaking style, an informality that, as discussed in the preceding chapter, comes from hours of practice. Practice allows him to work largely without a script. During demonstrations, Jobs conceals notes discreetly from the audience but never reads them word for word. The notes serve only as cue cards for the next step in the demonstration. Jobs performs largely without notes for the majority of his presentation.

As suggested in Scene 8, most presenters create "slideuments": documents masking as slides. Slideuments act as a crutch for mediocre presenters who read every word on the slide, often turning their backs to the audience to do so. Jobs does have a script—largely in his head. His slides, which are highly visual, act as a prompter. Each slide has one key idea and one idea only.

After Jobs pulled the new MacBook Air from a manila envelope in the "holy shit" moment at Macworld 2008, he explored the new computer in more detail. As you can see in Table 17.1, his slides contained very few words but contained just enough information to act as a prompter for one idea—one theme per slide.[1]

Jobs went on to explain that MacBook Air had the same processor used in all of Apple's other notebooks and iMacs. He marveled at the fact that Intel could step up to the challenge,

TABLE 17.1   ONE THEME PER SLIDE AT JOBS'S MACWORLD
2008 PRESENTATION

STEVE'S WORDS	STEVE'S SLIDES
"It's the world's thinnest notebook."	Text only: "World's thinnest notebook"
"Open it up and it has a magnetic latch; no hooks to catch on your clothing."	Photo of computer with the words "Magnetic latch" on left side of screen
"It's a got a full-size, 13.3-inch wide-screen display."	Photo of computer with the words "13.3 inch widescreen" in the middle of a black display
"The display is gorgeous. It has an LED-backlit display. It saves power, it's bright, and it's instant on the minute you open it."	Photo of computer with the words "LED backlight " on left side of screen
"On top of the display is a built-in iSight camera for videoconferencing right out of the box."	Photo of computer fades, revealing iSight camera on top of display
"Flip it down and there is a full-size keyboard. This is perhaps the best notebook keyboard we've ever shipped. It's a phenomenal keyboard."	Photo of keyboard with the words "Full size keyboard" on left side of screen
"We've got a very generous track pad, which is great. We've also built in multi-touch gesture support."	Photo of computer's track pad with the words "Multi-touch gestures" on left side of screen
"Again, you can see how beautiful and thin this product is. Now, how did we fit a Mac in here? I'm still stunned that our engineering team could pull this off."	Photo of computer from its side with the words "How did we fit a Mac in here?"
"The real magic is in the electronics. This is a complete Mac on a board. What's so special about that? This is how big the board is [does not mention pencil; let's the visual speak for itself]. It's really tiny. To fit an entire Mac on this thing was an amazing feat of engineering."	Photo of motherboard with image of a pencil alongside it—the board is smaller than the length of the pencil

STEVE'S WORDS	**STEVE'S SLIDES**
"We didn't compromise on performance. MacBook Air has the Intel Core 2 Duo. This is a really speedy processor . . . a 'screamer.'"	Photo of Intel Core 2 Duo microprocessor

creating a chip with the same power but in a package that was 60 percent smaller. Jobs then introduced Intel CEO Paul Otellini, who gave Jobs a sample processor. The chip was barely visible to anyone sitting past the front row, but Jobs lit up the auditorium with his smile. "This is awesome technology," he said, making no attempt to conceal his enthusiasm. See Figure 17.1.

Figure 17.1 Jobs shows genuine enthusiasm as he holds up the tiny Intel processor from the MacBook Air.

TONY AVELAR/AFP/Getty Images

Five Steps to Tossing the Script

Great actors rehearse for months before opening night. The audience would walk out if an actor appeared onstage with a script in hand. We expect actors to speak naturally, not as though they had memorized lines, even though that is exactly what they did. Your audience expects the same—a conversational speaker who, instead of rambling, hits each mark precisely. Following are five steps that will help you memorize your script while making you appear as natural as a gifted actor or a gifted presenter such as Steve Jobs:

1. **Write your script in full sentences in the "notes" section of PowerPoint.** This is not the time for extensive editing. Simply write your ideas in complete sentences. Do try, however, to keep your ideas to no more than four or five sentences.

2. **Highlight or underline the key word from each sentence, and practice your presentation.** Run through your script without worrying about stumbling or forgetting a point. Glance at the key words to jog your memory.

3. **Delete extraneous words from your scripted sentences, leaving only the key words.** Practice your presentation again, this time using only the key words as reminders.

4. **Memorize the *one* key idea per slide.** Ask yourself, "What is the one thing I want my audience to take away from the slide?" The visual on the slide should complement the one theme. In this case, the visual becomes your prompter. For example, when Jobs talked about the Intel Core 2 Duo as the standard processor built into the MacBook Air, his slide showed only a photo of the processor. The "one thing" he wanted the audience to know was that Apple had built an ultrathin computer with no compromise in performance.

5. **Practice the entire presentation without notes, simply using the slides as your prompter.** By the time you execute these five steps, you will have rehearsed each slide four times, which is much more time than the average speaker commits to practicing a presentation.

Now let's put the five-step method into practice. I came across an ad for Vanguard no-load mutual funds.[2] It showed two glasses of water; the glass on the left contained a small amount of water, and the glass on the right was completely full. The headline read: "The lower the cost, the more you keep." Ads such as this one provide excellent examples of how to create compelling visual slides. Assume the ad is one slide: Table 17.2 shows what a hypothetical script written with the five steps in

TABLE 17.2 APPLYING THE FIVE-STEP METHOD TO TOSSING THE SCRIPT

STEP	PRESENTATION SCRIPT
1	How much your investment costs is very important and could have an impact on how much money you make over the long run. In general, the lower the cost, the more you keep. Many investment firms say they are low cost, but the fact is they charge six times more than we do. This can cost you thousands of dollars. For example, if you invest $10,000 for twenty years at an 8 percent return, you would keep $58,000 more with our fund versus the industry average.
2	Your *investment costs* are very *important* and could have an impact on how much money you make over the long run. In general, *the lower the cost, the more you keep.* Many investment firms say they are low cost, but the fact is they charge *six times more* than we do. This can cost you thousands of dollars. For example, if you invest $10,000 for twenty years at an 8 percent return, you would *keep $58,000 more* with our fund versus the industry average.
3	Investment costs important Lower the cost, the more you keep Six times more Keep $58,000 more
4	The lower the cost, the more you keep.
5	Rehearse presentation with no notes. The slide of two water glasses—one empty, one full—should be enough to prompt you to deliver the information: the four bullets in step 3.

mind might look like. (I created the content based on information in Vanguard's marketing material.)

When you're actually delivering the final presentation, if the notes give you peace of mind, by all means, keep them available. A major benefit of Apple's Keynote presentation software is that it allows the speaker to see notes on the computer screen while the audience sees the slide on the projector. This is harder, but not impossible, to do with PowerPoint. However, regardless of the software you use, if you practice enough, you will find that you don't need to rely on your notes at all.

How to Use Notes When Notes Are a Must

Notes are not inherently bad. In a rare glimpse at how Jobs actually does use notes, a blogger took a photograph of Jobs's demo

How Joel Osteen Inspires Millions

Joel Osteen is the hugely popular pastor of Houston's Lakewood Church. He preaches to some forty-seven thousand people a week who show up to see him in person and to millions of others on television. Osteen speaks in a natural, conversational style and rarely misses a beat, despite creating thirty minutes of content every week. How does he do it? First, he commits. Osteen begins working on sermons on the Wednesday prior to his appearance and spends the better part of four days practicing. Second, he uses notes but glances at them very discreetly. He places notes on a lectern but never stands behind the lectern. This approach lets him keep eye contact with the audience and maintain an open posture. He never reads a full sentence from his notes. Instead, he walks behind the lectern, glances at his notes, and keeps walking to the opposite side, delivering his messages directly to worshippers.

notes at Macworld 2007, famous for the release of the iPhone. The notes were neatly bound, and color-coded tabs separated the sections. The blogger's photo showed the booklet opened to the page where Jobs demonstrated the Internet capabilities of iPhone. Four categories were clearly marked in bold and a larger font: Mail, Safari, Widgets, and Maps.[3] Under each main category, there were two to five supporting points. Let's take one in particular, the Maps section. Here is exactly what was printed on the page:

MAPS

» Moscone West
» Starbucks order 4,000 lattes to go
» Washington Monument
» Show satellite
» Eiffel Tower, Colosseum

That's it. These notes were all the prompting Jobs needed to walk his audience through a particular section of the demo.

Jobs began by telling his audience that he wanted to show them something "truly remarkable," Google Maps on iPhone. First, he opened up the application and zoomed in to a street-level view of San Francisco and Moscone West, the site of Macworld.

The second thing he did was to type "Starbucks" to search for a nearby coffee shop. He then called Starbucks on the iPhone and played the prank discussed in Scene 12, ordering four thousand lattes to go. (I had no idea that the lattes gag was scripted until I saw the photograph of Jobs's notes on the stage. He played it off as if it was a spontaneous moment, showing, once again, that Jobs takes nothing for granted.)

The third thing he did was visit the Washington Monument, double-tapping the screen to bring the map closer. Fourth, he selected the option to replace the map with satellite photographs. He brought up a live image of the Washington Monument. "Isn't that incredible, right on my phone?" he said. Finally, he visited the Eiffel Tower and Roman Colosseum and showed both in the satellite view. He concluded by saying, "Satellite imagery right on our phone. Unbelievable. Isn't that incredible?"[4] Jobs did rely on his script for the demo, but it had been written and rehearsed extensively so that only a few key words were all he needed to prompt him.

Yes, Steve Jobs appears conversational, but by now you should know that being "conversational" requires a lot of practice. And *how* you practice makes all the difference. Use the slides as your teleprompter, sticking to one theme per slide and several supporting points. If you forget some of your supporting points, you will at least have hit the main theme. Above all, toss the script. Notes will interfere with the emotional connection you need to establish with your audience, detracting from the presentation experience. Theatrics can turn an average presentation into an extraordinary event. A script gets in the way.

DIRECTOR'S NOTES

» Don't read from notes except in special circumstances in which you must follow a step-by-step process, such as a demonstration.

» When you must read from notes, create no more than three or four large-font bullet points on one note card or sheet of paper. Create one note card per slide. If you're using speaker's notes in Keynote or PowerPoint presentation software, keep your bullet points to no more than three or four. One is even better.

» Use the visuals on your slide to prompt you to deliver just one key theme—one main message—per slide. Think "one theme per slide."

SCENE 18

Have Fun

**Everyone wants a MacBook Pro
because they are so bitchin'.**

—STEVE JOBS

n 2002, the Mac OS X was brand new, and Apple was striving to get customers and developers to embrace it. Jobs decided to put the issue to rest, literally, at the Worldwide Developers Conference.

As the presentation began, Jobs was not onstage. Instead, white smoke surrounded a casket. Gloomy pipe-organ music played in the background. Jobs finally emerged from behind a curtain, walked to the casket, lifted the lid, and pulled out a large-scale copy of OS 9, Apple's previous operating system. The audience got the joke immediately and started laughing and applauding.

Jobs was committed to the joke and took it further. With a copy of OS 9 lying in the casket, Jobs pulled out a sheet of paper and eulogized the software. "Mac OS 9 was a friend to us all," he started.

He worked tirelessly on our behalf, always posting our applications, never refusing a command, always at our beck and call, except occasionally when he forgot who he was and needed to be restarted. He came into this world in October of 1998 . . . We are here today to mourn the passing of OS 9. He is in the great bit bucket in the sky, no doubt looking down upon this with that same smile he displayed every time he booted. Mac OS 9 is survived by his next generation, Mac

OS X . . . Please join me in a moment of silence as we remember our old friend, Mac OS 9."[1]

Jobs walked back to the casket, put the box back in, closed the lid, and gently laid a rose on the top. The audience ate it up. Jobs made his point, and he had a lot of fun doing it.

Jobs has fun, and it shows. Despite relentless planning and preparation, hours and hours of rehearsal, and near-fanatical devotion to getting every slide and every demo just right, sometimes things go wrong, but Jobs doesn't let the small stuff get to him. He's going to have fun, whether a demo works or not.

"Let's take a look at how big this market is," said Jobs as he described the market opportunity for the iPhone at Macworld 2007. Suddenly, his slides failed to advance. "My clicker's not working," he said. As he walked to the right of the stage to check the computer, the slide seemed to advance. "Oh, maybe it is working. No, it's not." Jobs picked up another clicker but it, too, failed to work. He smiled and said, "The clicker is not working. They're scrambling backstage right now."[2] The audience laughed, and after a few more seconds of trying to fix the clicker, Jobs simply paused, smiled, and told the following story:

> You know, this reminds me, when I was in high school, Steve Wozniak and I—mostly Steve—made this little device called a TV jammer. It was this little oscillator that put out frequencies that would screw up the TV. Woz would have it in his pocket. We would go out to a dorm at Berkeley, where he was going to school, and a bunch of folks would be watching "Star Trek." He would screw up the TV, someone would go to fix it, and just as they had their foot off the ground, he'd turn it back on, and then he'd screw up the TV again. Within five minutes, he'd have someone like this [contorts his body; see Figure 18.1] . . . OK, it looks like it's working now.[3]

In this one-minute story, Jobs revealed a side of his personality that few people get to see. It made him more human, engaging, and natural. He also never got flustered. I have seen even some experienced presenters get derailed over smaller problems.

A YouTube user posted a five-minute clip showing dozens of Jobs "bloopers."[4] The number of things that have gone wrong is surprising given the level of extraordinarily detailed practice that goes into a Steve Jobs keynote. This blooper reel proves that even the best-laid plans go awry from time to time: a slide may not advance, a wrong slide may come up, and a demo may not work. These things happen to even the best-prepared presenter, and they can, and probably will, happen to you at some point.

The difference between mediocre presenters and a true master such as Jobs is that when demonstrations do not turn out as planned, Jobs reacts with a cool confidence. The audience sees a showman in complete control of his material. If something fails to work, Jobs does not dwell on it or call undue attention to the

Figure 18.1 Jobs demonstrates a prank he and Apple cofounder Steve Wozniak would pull on unsuspecting college students.

David Paul Morris/Getty Images

issue. He smiles, has fun, explains to the audience what they should have seen, and moves on.

Don't Sweat the Small Stuff

During a demonstration of Apple TV at Macworld 2008, Jobs brought up a live connection to Flickr, a photo-sharing site. Jobs selected several categories to show the audience how photographs could be served from the site and displayed on a wide-screen television in a living room. Unfortunately, the screen went black. After about twenty seconds of trying to retrieve the images, Jobs simply turned to the audience, grinned, and said, "Well, I'm afraid Flickr isn't serving up photos on that one."[5]

Jobs doesn't let anything ruffle him onstage. Instead, he acknowledges the problem, continues the presentation, summarizes the material, and enjoys himself. He concluded the Apple TV demonstration by saying, "All of this from your wide-screen: movies, TV shows, music, podcasts, photos from dot-Mac and—when they're serving up photos—Flickr! So, that's what I wanted to show you today. Isn't that incredible?"[6] Jobs never loses his enthusiasm. The demo might not have gone perfectly, but that doesn't diminish the joy he has for the product.

No matter how much you prepare, something might, and probably will, go differently from how you had planned. Notice that I did not say something will go "wrong." It goes wrong only when you call attention to the issue or you let it ruin the rest of your presentation. People are there to hear you, to learn something new about a product, service, or initiative that could improve their lives.

When a demo fails to come off as smoothly as Jobs had rehearsed, he never loses his cool. He says something like, "Oops, that's not what I wanted" or "I need some help here, guys; this thing isn't working." He will take a few moments to get it working, and he will do so very calmly.

In one presentation, Jobs could not get a digital camera to work, so he had some fun with it, tossed it to an Apple employee in the front row, and said, "I need an expert to fix it. It's too technical for me. It's pretty awesome when it works."[7] That's it. *It's pretty awesome when it works.*

Think about watching an ice-skater perform an intricately choreographed routine. You know that the slightest mistake could land the skater on her butt. When it happens, you wince, but you hope the skater gets up to finish her routine on a high note. The same applies to your audience. Nobody expects perfection except you. Your audience will forgive a blooper as long as you get back on your feet.

During Jobs's leave of absence for a liver transplant, much had been written about what he revealed, how much he should have revealed, and whether he should have revealed it sooner. Jobs was clearly frustrated with the press, calling some reporters to chastise them about covering matters he wanted to keep private. While bloggers and reporters were scrambling to get the scoop on the exact nature of his illness, I was struck at how Jobs kept his trademark good humor.

In September 2008, Jobs walked onstage at the WWDC and said, "Good morning. Thank you for coming this morning. We have some really exciting stuff to share with you. Before we do, I just wanted to mention this." He pointed to the slide behind him, which had only one sentence: "The reports of my death are greatly exaggerated." "Enough said," Job told the audience, and he promptly continued with his presentation.[8] The audience laughed and cheered. The media and investors wanted more information, of course, but that's all that Jobs would give them at the moment, and he had fun with it at their expense.

Now, That's Infotainment!

Most business communicators lose sight of the fact that their audiences want to be informed *and* entertained. Jobs approaches presentations as infotainment; he teaches you something new and has fun doing it. It's the best of all worlds for his audience. Most business professionals do not smile nor relish the moment as much as they should. They get too caught up in "presentation mode" and lose the enthusiasm they really have about their company, product, or service. Jobs always walks onstage with a broad smile, an easy laugh, and a joke or two (often at Microsoft's expense).

On October 16, 2003, Jobs had finished the discussion of a new music alliance with AOL and an explanation of the new iTunes features. The audience thought he was done, but Jobs had "just one more feature" to talk about. He said it was a feature that "a lot of people thought we would never add till this happened." He pointed to the slide, which read: "Hell froze over." He said, "I'm here to report to you today that this has happened."[9] And with that introduction, Jobs announced iTunes for Windows. The audience laughed even harder when Jobs said, "iTunes for Windows is probably the best Windows app ever written!" The audience was thrilled, and Jobs himself was clearly enjoying the reaction.

Apple cofounder Steve Wozniak has said he and Jobs loved two things in common: electronics and pranks. From the early seventies when Jobs and "Woz" were building computers together in their parents' garages, Jobs had a passion for bringing personal computing to the masses. That "spirit" comes across in every Steve Jobs presentation. A Steve Jobs presentation is passionate, exciting, informative, and, above all, fun. In many ways, it comes naturally, because it's the way he has lived his life.

When Jobs took his leave of absence in 2009, Apple's shares plummeted on speculation over Jobs's health, a possible lack of new and exciting products, and potential management changes. Observers wondered, would Apple without Jobs be successful?

Richard the Fun-Hearted

I have no secret. There are no rules to follow in business. I just work hard and, as I always have done, believe I can do it. Most of all, though, I try to have fun.

—RICHARD BRANSON

One analyst, Shaw Wu, had a different take on all of it. Apple without Jobs would prosper, he argued, because his spirit had been "institutionalized." Wu said Apple had an uncanny ability to attract hardworking entrepreneurs who are looking to change the world.

PC World said that Jobs, a master showman, had raised new product presentations to an art form and wished him a "speedy return to health" so Jobs could head up the company again and take the stage once more.[10]

For more than three decades, Jobs has cast his spell on the world. And whether you're a "Mac" or a "PC," we all owe Jobs a debt of gratitude for a chance to join him on his "magic swirling ship," to quote his favorite musician, Bob Dylan.[11] It's been a magnificent ride, and if you pay close enough attention, Jobs can help you sell your ideas more successfully than you ever thought possible.

DIRECTOR'S NOTES

» Treat presentations as "infotainment." Your audience wants to be educated and entertained. Have fun. It'll show.

» Never apologize. You have little to gain from calling attention to a problem. If your presentation hits a glitch, acknowledge it, smile, and move on. If it was not obvious to anyone but you, do not call attention to it.

» Change your frame of reference. When something does not go exactly as planned, it did not "go wrong" unless you allow it to derail the rest of your presentation. Keep the big picture in mind, have fun, and let the small stuff roll off your back.

One More Thing

Stay hungry, stay foolish.

—STEVE JOBS

Steve Jobs keeps his audience guessing. Frequently, but not always, he will leave the audience with "just one more thing" before he ends a presentation. For example, Jobs announced that he would return as Apple's full-time CEO (dropping the "interim" from his title) as the "one more thing" at the conclusion of his Macworld presentation on January 5, 2000. It is the element of surprise that audiences have come to love and expect. Since his audience expects "one more thing," Jobs does not always deliver. A surprise would fail to surprise if everyone knows it's coming!

So, in true Steve Jobs fashion, I would like to add just "one more thing" to this discussion. On June 12, 2005, shortly after a bout with a rare, curable form of pancreatic cancer, Jobs gave the commencement address at Stanford University. It became an Internet sensation. It is one of the most popular commencement addresses on YouTube, far more popular than remarks of other famous commencement speakers such as Oprah; *The Last Lecture* author, Randy Pausch; or *Harry Potter*'s J. K. Rowling.

Jobs crafted the speech using many of the same techniques that make his presentations so electrifying. About the only thing absent that day were slides. The rest is classic Steve Jobs. I have excerpted sections to illustrate how he applied his extraordinary messaging and presentation skills to the now famous speech. I also urge you to watch the full speech on the Stanford website.[1]

Today I want to tell you three stories from my life. That's it.
No big deal. Just three stories.

We again see the rule of three (refer to Scene 5) playing a big
role in Jobs's message. He draws a road map for his listeners by
telling them to expect three stories—not one or four, but *three*.
The structure of the speech itself is strikingly simple: opening,
three stories, conclusion.

The first story is about connecting the dots.

Here Jobs tells the first of three personal anecdotes. This one is
about his dropping out of Reed College after six months. Jobs
said it was scary at first but ultimately worked out, because it
allowed him to continue to take courses he was interested in,
such as calligraphy. Ten years later, he incorporated calligraphy
fonts into the Macintosh, "connecting the dots."

It was beautiful, historical, artistically subtle in a way that
science can't capture, and I found it fascinating.

Jobs found his passion for simplicity and design at an early age.
He discovered his core purpose, a messianic zeal to change the
world, and never looked back. Share your passion for your subject, and your enthusiasm will be contagious.

My second story is about love and loss.

In this section, Jobs talks about falling in love with computers
at the age of twenty and sharing that passion with his friend
"Woz." He talked about building a $2 billion company in ten
years and then, at the age of thirty, being fired by Apple's board
of directors.

I'm convinced that the only thing that kept me going was
that I loved what I did. You've got to find what you love.

Again, passion is a central theme in Jobs's life. Jobs is convinced that he's successful because he followed his heart, his true passion. There's a lot of truth to it. Remember, none of his presentation techniques will work if you don't have genuine passion for your message. Find the one thing you love to do so much that you can't wait for the sun to rise to do it all over again. Once you do, you'll have found your true calling.

> My third story is about death.

This sentence begins the most poignant section of the speech. Jobs recalls the day doctors told him he had pancreatic cancer. He thought he had three to six months to live. The cancer turned out to be a very rare, curable form of the disease, but the experience left an indelible impression on Jobs.

> No one wants to die. Even people who want to go to heaven don't want to die to get there.

Jobs always has fun. He finds a way to inject humor into a morbid subject.

> Your time is limited, so don't waste it living someone else's life. Don't be trapped by dogma—which is living with the results of other people's thinking. Don't let the noise of others' opinions drown out your own inner voice.

This paragraph is an example of a powerful rhetorical device called anaphora, repetition of the same word(s) in consecutive sentences. Think of Martin Luther King's "I have a dream that . . . I have a dream . . . I have a dream today." Great political speakers from Churchill to King, from Reagan to Obama, have all used anaphora to structure strong arguments. As Jobs demonstrates, this classic sentence structure need not be reserved for political leaders. It is available to any person who wants to command an audience.

And most important, have the courage to follow your heart and intuition. They somehow already know what you truly want to become . . . stay hungry, stay foolish.

Jobs ends the speech with his headline, his key theme and advice—stay hungry, stay foolish. As we've discussed, Jobs repeated his key theme several times in a presentation. In this case, he repeats "stay hungry, stay foolish" three times in the concluding paragraph.

Jobs's speech reveals the secret to his success as a business leader and communicator: do what you love, view setbacks as opportunities, and dedicate yourself to the passionate pursuit of excellence. Whether it's designing a new computer, introducing new gadgets, running Apple, overseeing Pixar, or giving a presentation, Jobs believes in his life's work. This is the last and most important lesson Jobs can teach—the power of believing in yourself and your story. Jobs has followed his heart his whole life. Follow yours to captivate your audience. You'll be one step closer to delivering insanely great presentations.

Steve Jobs by the Book

It's technology married with liberal arts that makes our hearts sing.

—STEVE JOBS

Conduct an Internet search for the Apple iPad using the words *magical* and *revolutionary* and you will find more than two million links to articles containing the phrase. It's an interesting choice of words when you consider that before 10:00 A.M. on January 27, 2010, many observers were skeptical that consumers needed another electronic device to carry around. By 11:00 A.M. they were converts.

After the iPad launch, Steve Jobs would unveil more new devices in subsequent presentations, including the iPhone 4, the iPad2, and iCloud—not a device exactly, but a new service first introduced in June of 2011. Each presentation was classic Steve Jobs. Here's how he wowed his audience in each presentation and how you can use these techniques to sell your ideas and products the Steve Jobs way.

Introducing the iPad

It's so much more intimate than a laptop and so much more capable than a smartphone.

—STEVE JOBS

The iPad: January 27, 2010

A "Fox Business News" producer had asked me to appear on the morning show to preview the big announcement on the day Steve Jobs introduced the iPad at San Francisco's Yerba Buena Events Center. Prior to the launch there had been plenty of speculation about Apple's new "tablet," but no official announcement. The best I could do was go by the book and discuss *how* Steve Jobs would introduce the world to a new category of device. Sure enough, Jobs did stick to the playbook, chapter by chapter. Jobs used every single principle that you have just read. The presentation itself was a game changer for Apple, the technology industry, and corporate communicators in every field.

CREATE A TWITTER-FRIENDLY HEADLINE

Steve Jobs's first slide delivered the headline—or theme—of his presentation and previewed the iPad's tagline. "We want to kick off 2010 by introducing a truly magical and revolutionary product today,"[1] said Jobs. At the conclusion of the presentation Jobs summed up the iPad in one sentence:

> Our most advanced technology in a magical and revolutionary device.

Since Twitter allows 140 characters, Jobs could have posted this description on Twitter and still be left with plenty of room for people to retweet the post and add their comments.

Your brain craves meaning before detail. Deliver the big picture before filling in the details. If you can't describe your product or service in 140 characters or less, go back to the drawing board.

INTRODUCE AN ANTAGONIST

Every great book or movie has a hero and a villain. Consider a presentation in the same way—a theatrical event complete with a protagonist and antagonist. The role of the antagonist in the iPad presentation was played by a category of devices called

Netbooks, which were growing in popularity at the time. Before unveiling the iPad—the hero—Jobs spent two minutes discussing the role of the villain in his narrative:

> All of us use laptops and smartphones. And the question has arisen lately, is there room for a third category of device in the middle? Something that is in between a laptop and a smartphone? In order to create a new category of devices, those devices have to be far better at doing some key tasks. Better than a laptop. Better than a smartphone. What kind of tasks? Things like browsing the Web. That's a tall order. Something that's better at browsing the Web than a laptop? Doing e-mail. Enjoying and sharing photographs. Watching videos. Enjoying your music collection. Watching games. Reading e-books. If there's going to be a third category of device it has to be better at these types of tasks than either a laptop or a smartphone, otherwise it has no reason for being. Now, some people have thought that's a Netbook. The problem is that Netbooks aren't better at anything. They're slow. They have low quality displays and they run clunky old PC software. They're not better than a laptop at anything. They're just cheaper. They're just cheap laptops and we don't think they're a third category of device. But we think we've got something that is and we'd like to show it to you today for the first time, and we call it the iPad.²

By introducing an antagonist—a problem in need of a solution—Jobs answered the question that most people had on their mind: Why do I need a third device? Jobs tackled the question head-on and even used the rhetorical device of raising a question and providing the answer. Your audience is asking, "What's in it for me?" Don't leave them guessing. A villain can be a competitor, a category of competitors, or in many cases, a problem in need of a solution.

STICK TO THE RULE OF THREE

The human mind can only consume three points of information in short-term memory. Steve Jobs understands this and often presents his content as three chunks of information. Here are some examples in the iPad presentation.

» Steve Jobs kicked off the presentation with "three updates": iPod sales, retail store growth, and App Store popularity.

» When he talked about the fact that 250 million iPods had been sold to date, Jobs said that iPods had changed the way consumers "discover, purchase, and enjoy music."

» Jobs said Netbooks had three failings: slow, low-quality displays, "clunky" old PC software.

» When Jobs picked up the iPad and demonstrated its functionality he chose three features to focus on: Web browsing, e-mail, and photographs.

» Jobs introduced the new iBooks Store as rounding out the three areas where Apple now sells digital content: iTunes Store, App Store, and the iBooks Store.

» The iPad would be made available in three options: 16GB, 32GB, and 64GB models.

UNLEASH YOUR INNER ZEN

Steve Jobs's "inner zen" was on full display during the iPad presentation. The slides were impactful because they contained very few words and plenty of compelling visuals. The first three minutes' worth of slides contained fewer words than most presenters put on one slide (fourteen words, five photographs, and five numbers). Take a look at Table 1.

USE "AMAZINGLY ZIPPY" WORDS

Jobs avoids the jargon and dense language that is so common among business professionals. Instead he wears his passion on his sleeve. If Jobs thinks something is "cool," he'll tell you so. Here are some examples from the iPad launch:

» "It's pretty amazing."
» "It feels great."
» "It's an incredible phenomenon."

TABLE 1 VISUAL DISPLAY ACCOMPANYING STEVE'S WORDS IN THE iPAD PRESENTATION, JANUARY 27, 2010[3]

STEVE'S WORDS	STEVE'S SLIDES
"We want to kick off 2010 by introducing a truly magical and revolutionary product. But before we do that I have a few updates."	Apple logo
"The first is an update on iPods."	Photo of iPods
"A few weeks ago we sold our 250-millionth iPod. iPods have changed the way we purchase, discover, and enjoy music."	250,000,000
"The second update is about our retail stores."	Photo of Apple Store
"We now have 284 retail stores."	284 Apple Retail Stores
"And last quarter, the holiday quarter, we had over fifty million visitors to our stores."	50,000,000 visitors last quarter
"One of our newest stores is our fourth store in New York City. It's really beautiful. This is a shot of it before it opened. It won't look this good again. It is so wonderful to be putting these stores with their phenomenal buying experience right in the neighborhoods of our customers. It feels great."	Photos of Apple Store in New York City
"Next update, a store of another kind. The App Store."	Image of Apple "App" logo
"We now have over 140,000 applications in the App Store."	140,000 applications in the App Store
"And a few weeks ago we announced that a user downloaded the three-billionth application from the App Store."	3 billion applications downloaded

» "It's unbelievably great."
» "It's awesome."
» "It's a dream to type on."
» "It has a gorgeous display."
» "It screams."

I'm not asking you to copy these phrases, but if you are genuinely excited about your product, let your audience know it. They are giving you permission to express your passion.

STAGE YOUR PRESENTATION WITH PROPS

Steve Jobs staged the iPad presentation beautifully. Instead of simply showing slides and demonstrating the device, Jobs walked to the center of the stage where a comfy leather chair and small coffee table had been set up. He picked up the iPad from the table, settled into the chair and said, "It's so much more intimate than a laptop and so much more capable than a smartphone."

Don't always think about "props" as a physical set. A prop can be something as simple as reading from a letter (some people still write them), writing on a flip chart, or demonstrating a physical product. Think of a prop as almost anything that takes the attention away from the presentation deck. Give the audience a break from the slides. They will appreciate the diversion.

DON'T FORGET TO PRACTICE

The iPad presentation lasted about ninety minutes and included seven speakers. Each of the speakers had been given a set time to speak and had been asked to practice on stage in front of the folks at Apple to make sure their demonstrations worked well and that they stuck to their time, not a second more. It's not uncommon for one hundred hours of work and practice to go into preparing for a five-minute demo in an Apple presentation. How many hours did you practice for your last presentation? If it didn't go as smoothly as you would have liked, you might benefit from more rehearsal time.

HAVE FUN AND INSPIRE

Steve Jobs ended the iPad presentation by reinforcing his Twitter-friendly headline. "To sum it up," he said as his delivery slowed considerably, "The iPad is our most advanced technology in a magical and revolutionary device at an unbelievable price." He also gave his audience some insight into what makes Apple well, *Apple*. "The reason why Apple can create products like the iPad is because we've always tried to be at the intersection of technology and liberal arts. When you feel this much power and this much fun in your hands, you never want to go back. We hope you love the iPad as much as we do."[4]

When is the last time you heard the words "love" and "fun" in a presentation? That's the difference between Steve Jobs and average presenters—Jobs has the courage to express how he truly feels about the brand.

The iPhone 4: June 7, 2010

Steve Jobs introduced the iPhone 4 at Apple's Worldwide Developers Conference. The presentation itself made news because of a glitch in the demo—a rare event for an Apple launch. The way Jobs handled it, however, was a case study in preparation. The glitch and other notable moments are discussed here.

CREATE A TWITTER-FRIENDLY HEADLINE

According to Steve Jobs, the iPhone 4 would mark "The biggest leap since the original iPhone."[5] You could say this is more of a boast than a headline but if you conduct an Internet search for the phrase "biggest leap iPhone 4," it will show up in millions of links. Whether or not you agree with Jobs's description is beyond the point. This is the way Apple and Jobs *chose* to frame it. Jobs crafted the narrative for press, bloggers, and customers.

Launching the iPhone 4

This is beyond a doubt one of the most beautiful things we've ever made.

—STEVE JOBS

Jobs also spent time building up the story before introducing his headline. He could have simply said, "It's been three years since our original iPhone and we thought it was time for an update. Here it is." Instead Jobs spent a few minutes reviewing the history of the iPhone. Jobs said that in 2007 Apple reinvented the phone with the iPhone. He explained that in 2008 Apple added 3G networking and the hugely popular App Store. In 2009 the iPhone 3Gs was "twice as fast with cool features like video recording." And finally, in 2010, "We're going to take the biggest leap since the original iPhone." Where most presenters would simply deliver information about a new product, Jobs tells a story.

STICK TO THE RULE OF THREE

As in every presentation, Steve Jobs chose to focus the audience's attention on three chunks of information instead of overwhelming them with too much content. For example, Jobs divided the presentation into three parts. He told the audience that he had "three updates" to deliver: iPad, App Store, and iPhone (the update would be the release of iPhone 4). When he discussed the App Store, Jobs chose to demonstrate three new apps that would be made available on the App Store (Netflix, Farmville, and Guitar Hero).

Most presenters have more information than they can easily convey in a short amount of time. Don't try to squeeze in everything. Simplify your communications. Three pieces of information are easier to digest than thirteen, eighteen, or twenty-two. If you want to deliver a "Jobs-worthy" presentation, avoid content overload.

DRESS UP YOUR NUMBERS

In several instances Steve Jobs put large numbers into perspective. Here are some examples from the iPhone 4 presentation.[6]

» "We have sold over two million iPads in the first fifty-nine days. That's one every three seconds."

» "There are 8,500 native apps on the iPad and these apps have been downloaded thirty-five million times. If you divide that by those two million iPads, that's seventeen apps per iPad that have already been downloaded. That's a great number for us."

» "Users have downloaded over five million books on the iPad Bookstore. That's in the first sixty-five days. That's two-and-a-half books per iPad."

» "The iPhone 4 is nine millimeters thick. That's 24 percent thinner than the iPhone3Gs. A quarter thinner just when you didn't think it could get any thinner. It's the thinnest smartphone on the planet."

FOLLOW THE TEN-MINUTE RULE

The ten-minute rule simply states that your audience will lose attention after approximately ten minutes. Jobs understands this instinctively. He will rarely speak longer than ten minutes without introducing an alternative stimulus (e.g., video, another presenter, or a demo). Approximately four minutes into his iPhone 4 presentation—before he introduced the new phone—he showed the audience a video clip of the international coverage the iPad had generated in the first few months of sale. Exactly ten minutes after the video clip ended, Steve Jobs introduced another speaker—Netflix CEO Reed Hastings, who took the stage for a few minutes to discuss his company's new mobile app.

Try to avoid presenting for more than ten minutes at a time. At the ten-minute mark introduce a break in the action: video, stories, another speaker, a demo.

MAKE IT LOOK EFFORTLESS WITH PRACTICE

Now let's talk about "the glitch." Apple presentations are so finely tuned that when something goes wrong it makes news. Several news outlets called me immediately to get my reaction. Some reporters called it a "meltdown." Not quite. A true meltdown is what would have happened to most presenters. Steve Jobs wasn't pleased, by any means. But he recovered.

While attempting to demonstrate some of the new features of the iPhone 4, Jobs ran into a WiFi problem. As he was attempting to download the *New York Times* website, it failed to load. "Our networks in here are always unpredictable,"[7] Jobs said. "You can help me out. If you're on WiFi, if you can just get off I'd appreciate it," Jobs remarked with a smile. The smile quickly evaporated as it became clear the demo would not work. "We're having a problem here. I don't know what's wrong with our networks. I'm afraid there is a problem and I won't be able to show you much here today."

Most presenters would have completely frozen. Not Jobs. He knew where he wanted to go next and effortlessly showed the audience what he had intended to show later in the presentation, such as new photography capability on the phone. A few minutes later Jobs took control—not of the presentation, but the audience. "We figured out why my demo crashed," he said.

> There are 570 WiFi base stations in this room and hundreds of those MiFi bay stations. We can't deal with that. We have two choices. I have more demos that are really great that I'd really like to show you. Either you turn off all the stuff or we give up and I don't show you the demos. Would you like to see the demos? [Applause.] Here's the deal. Let's turn up the lights in the hall. All you bloggers turn off your bay stations, your WiFi, put notebooks on the floor. Shut off laptops and these MiFi bay stations. Police each other. I think bloggers have a right to blog but we're not going to see these demos unless we do this. . . . Go ahead, I've got time.

The glitch didn't hurt sales. AT&T temporarily suspended sales the next day because they were getting more orders than units available. Sales blew past the initial revenue for the original iPhone as consumers stood in line for hours to get their hands on the new device. Despite the technical snafu, Jobs had provided enough content to win over consumers.

Steve Jobs takes nothing for granted. He practices many, many hours over many, many weeks. Sometimes, despite the best plans, things can and do go wrong—even for Steve Jobs. The more you have internalized the content, the better prepared you'll be to handle the curve balls that come your way.

The iPad2: March 2, 2011

Steve Jobs shocked a packed audience at San Francisco's Yerba Buena Events Center on March 2, 2011, simply by showing up. Jobs had taken medical leave in January (his third health-related absence since 2004). Chief Operating Officer Tim Cook was running Apple in Jobs's absence and most observers expected Cook to give the presentation. The audience gave Jobs a standing ovation when he walked on stage. Jobs's passion was on full display when he said, "We've been working on this product for a while and I just didn't want to miss today."[8]

I found it remarkable that a leader who wasn't well enough to run his company day-to-day had the energy to carry a ninety-minute presentation. It speaks to his passion for the product and for the brand. Passion brings energy and Jobs wears his passion on his sleeve and the iPad2 presentation was no exception. The rest of the presentation was also vintage Steve Jobs.

ANSWER THE ONE QUESTION THAT MATTERS MOST

Remember, your customers are asking themselves one question—*why should I care?* Steve Jobs used the "Rule of Three" and created a "Twitter-friendly headline" to explain the benefit of the iPad2. "First, it's dramatically faster. Second, it's dramatically thinner. And it's lighter as well,"[9] Jobs said. In a sentence, the iPad2 was "thinner, lighter, and faster" than the original.

If you only know three things about the new device—thinner, lighter, faster—it tells you a lot. It's a clever headline and it's memorable. A reporter for the *San Francisco Chronicle* began his review with "Apple CEO Steve Jobs took a break from his medical leave Wednesday to unveil a sequel to the company's

Launching the iPad2

I just didn't want to miss today.

—STEVE JOBS

best-selling iPad—one that is thinner, lighter, and faster." *Good Housekeeping* ran this headline: "iPad2. Thinner, lighter, faster." The *Wall Street Journal* said the new device was thinner, lighter, and came with a faster processor. Jobs had crafted the narrative and the press ran with it.

Apple's Twitter headline is remarkably consistent for each product. On the day that Jobs introduced the iPad2, millions of Apple customers received an e-mail with the subject line, "iPad: thinner, lighter, faster." The Apple website displayed a photo of the iPad2 with the words thinner, lighter, faster. Once you craft the story line—or the narrative—behind your product, service, or cause, make sure it is consistently communicated across all marketing channels.

INTRODUCE THE VILLAIN AND THE HERO

Steve Jobs took the opportunity to discuss Apple's vision for the future of computing: a post-PC world. "A lot of folks in the tablet market are rushing in and they look at this category as the next PC. They are talking about speeds and feeds just like they did with PCs. Every bone in our body says this is not the right approach. These are post-PC devices that need to be even easier to use than a PC. More intuitive than a PC. The software, hardware, and apps need to intertwine in a more seamless way than in a PC."[10]

Apple's hero, of course, would be the iPad2. "It's in Apple's DNA that technology is not enough," said Jobs. "It's technology married with liberal arts that makes our hearts sing." In two paragraphs, Jobs had introduced a villain—an entire category of devices that his competitors were launching—and a hero, a company that wants to make easy, fun, and simple-to-use devices.

CREATE VISUAL SLIDES

Apple presentations are always magnificent displays of visual storytelling, but the iPad2 presentation took visual display to the next level. The average presentation slide contains forty words. Steve Jobs's slides included a grand total of thirty-three words in the first *five minutes'* worth of slides. You owe it to yourself to watch the first five minutes of the iPad2 keynote presentation. You'll notice that Jobs does not clutter the slides with extraneous content. Every slide has one theme (see Table 2). In these seven slides, Jobs's presentation contained far fewer words than most presenters display on just one slide.

Since the average PowerPoint slide contains forty words and you can't find forty words in the first ten slides of a Steve Jobs presentation, I've come up with the Ten-Forty Rule: your first ten slides should contain forty words or less. It's very difficult to follow, but your presentations will be far more effective for doing so.

DRESS UP YOUR NUMBERS

When Jobs introduced the iPad2 he said that the previous year had turned out be "the year of the iPad" with fifteen million

TABLE 2 VISUAL DISPLAY ACCOMPANYING STEVE'S WORDS
IN THE iPAD2 PRESENTATION, MARCH 2, 2011[11]

STEVE'S WORDS	STEVE'S SLIDES
"We have some updates for you. The first is iBooks."	iBooks (with image of the iBook Store)
"We launched the iBooks Store under a year ago and users have downloaded a hundred million books in less than a year from the iBook Store."	100 million books downloaded
"Another milestone is in the App Store. Developers have earned over two billion dollars from selling their Apps on the App Store."	Image of check with the number 2,000,000,000
"Today we're here to talk about Apple's third post-PC blockbuster product."	Apple's third post-PC blockbuster
"We started off in 2001 with the iPod."	Photo of iPod
"In 2007 we added the iPhone."	Photo of iPhone
"And in 2010 we added the iPad."	Photo of iPad

iPads sold in the first nine months of the product's release. Fifteen million sounds like a big number, but compared to what? Jobs put the statistic into context by adding, "That's more than every tablet PC ever sold."[12] He also mentioned that the iPad generated 9.5 billion dollars in revenue for Apple since its launch. "We've never had a product get off to such a fast start," he said. "Our competitors are flummoxed."

Again, don't let large numbers just hang out there. Put them into context.

OBEY THE TEN-MINUTE RULE

The iPad2 presentation proves, once again, that Steve Jobs doesn't speak more than ten minutes without changing the action. Exactly nine minutes after he started speaking, Jobs showed a video that Apple had created called "The Year of the iPad." The video interspersed clips of Apple employees talking about the iPad along with video of customers using the devices in places around the world.

HAVE FUN

Sometimes Steve Jobs likes to have fun at the expense of his competitors. After the video ran about iPads' popularity in 2010, Jobs said, "So what about 2011? *Everybody's* got a tablet. Is 2011 going to be the year of the copycats? None of these tablets are even catching up with the first iPad. But we're not going to rest on our laurels because in less than one year we're introducing iPad2, the second generation iPad. We think 2011 is going to be the year of the iPad2."

iCloud: June 6, 2011

Steve Jobs returned from medical leave on June 6, 2011, for a brief introduction to Apple's new cloud-storage service called iCloud. In typical Jobs fashion he said he had three announcements. First, he offered a preview of OS X Lion, the new operating system for Macs. Second, he unveiled the iOS5, the mobile operating system for iPhones and iPads. Finally, Jobs described Apple's new service that fit in to his

Introducing iCloud

> *You like everything so far? Well, I'll try not to blow it.*
>
> —STEVE JOBS

vision of a "post-PC" world: a world in which people will create, share, and access content from a variety of devices. The idea behind iCloud is simple and powerful. Here's how Jobs unveiled it.

INTRODUCE AN ANTAGONIST

As we've discussed, in nearly every product launch, Steve Jobs outlines the problem before offering a solution. Before describing iCloud, Jobs took a couple of minutes to discuss the problem that the new service would solve—a problem many people could relate to.

About ten years ago we had one of our most important insights. The PC would be the digital hub of our digital life. That's where you were going to put your digital photos, video, and music. It worked fine for the better part of ten years. But it's broken down in the last few years. Why? Because devices have changed. They now all have photos. They now all have music. They now all have video. If I acquire a song, I buy it on my iPhone, I want to get it to my other devices. I pick up my iPad and it doesn't have the other songs on it. So I have to sync my iPhone to my Mac to get those songs. Keeping these devices in sync is driving us crazy. We've got a great solution to this problem. We're going to demote the PC and the Mac to be a device. We're going to move the digital hub, the center of your digital life, to the cloud.[13]

CREATE A TWITTER-FRIENDLY HEADLINE

Steve Jobs followed up the problem statement with his one-sentence description that sold the benefit behind the service, made it simple for the audience to understand, and easily fit within a Twitter post: iCloud stores your content and wirelessly pushes it to all your devices (seventy-two characters).

Again, Apple kept the message consistent across all of its marketing, advertising, and communication channels. During the presentation, Steve Jobs displayed a slide that contained only the one-sentence headline. As soon as the presentation ended—not a minute later—the Apple website displayed the new iCloud icon along with the description: iCloud stores your content and wirelessly pushes it to all your devices. Sound familiar? The official Apple press release and in-store material all reflected the same headline. Make sure everyone on your team is speaking from the same playbook. Make the headline consistent across all communication channels.

DISPLAY VISUAL INFORMATION

The iCloud presentation is the most visual presentation of Steve Jobs's career. I can say that with confidence because just as I developed the Ten-Forty Rule, Jobs went one step further—no words in the first ten slides!

Each of the first ten slides in the iCloud presentation comprised device images and some subtle animation. No words. No bullet slides. No charts. No text. The first words appeared on slide eleven when Jobs introduced the Twitter-friendly headline. Steve Jobs is the storyteller. The slides *complement* the story but the slides are not the story.

The four case studies in this Postscript prove that Steve Jobs—a man considered the world's greatest corporate storyteller—uses the same techniques every time to deliver a presentation. The products might change, but the storytelling techniques remain the same.

You also have a story to tell. It might be the story behind a product, a company, a brand, a service, an initiative, or an idea. Is your presentation dull, confusing, and boring, or interesting, illuminating, and inspiring? Use this template to unleash your inner Steve Jobs. Your audience will love you for it.

NOTES

Prologue

1. Jon Fortt, "Steve Jobs, Tech's Last Celebrity CEO," *Fortune*, December 19, 2008, http://money.cnn.com/2008/12/19/technology/fortt_tech_ceos .fortune/?postversion=2008121915 (accessed January 30, 2009).
2. Wikipedia, "Charisma," includes Max Weber quote, http://en.wikipedia .org/wiki/charisma (accessed January 30, 2009).
3. Nancy Duarte, *Slide:ology* (Sebastopol, CA: O'Reilly Media, 2008), xviii.
4. Michael Hiltzik, "Apple's Condition Linked to Steve Jobs's Health," *Los Angeles Times*, January 5, 2009, latimes.com/business/la-fi-hiltzik5 -2009jan05,0,7305482.story (accessed January 30, 2009).
5. Stephen Wilbers, "Good Writing for Good Results: A Brief Guide for Busy Administrators," *The College Board Review*, no. 154 (1989–90), via Wilbers, wilbers.com/cbr%20article.htm.
6. "The Big Idea with Donny Deutsch," first aired on July 28, 2008, property of CNBC.
7. Wikipedia, "Steve Jobs," includes Jobs's quote, http://en.wikiquote.org/ wiki/steve_jobs (accessed January 30, 2009).
8. Alan Deutschman, *The Second Coming of Steve Jobs* (New York: Broadway Books, 2001), 127.

Scene 1: Plan in Analog

1. Garr Reynolds, *Presentation Zen* (Berkeley: New Riders, 2008), 45.
2. Nancy Duarte, *Slide:ology* (Sebastopol, CA: O'Reilly Media, 2008).
3. Cliff Atkinson, *Beyond Bullet Points* (Redmond, WA: Microsoft Press, 2005), 14.
4. Ibid., 15.
5. Apple, "Macworld San Francisco 2007 Keynote Address," Apple, apple .com/quicktime/qtv/mwsf07 (accessed January 30, 2009).
6. YouTube, "Steve Jobs, 'Computers Are Like a Bicycle for Our Minds,'" YouTube, youtube.com/watch?v=ob_GX50Za6c (accessed January 30, 2009).
7. John Paczkowski, "Apple CEO Steve Jobs," D5 Highlights from D: All Things Digital, May 30, 2007, http://d5.allthingsd.com/20070530/steve -jobs-ceo-of-apple (accessed January 30, 2009).
8. Apple, "WWDC 2008 Keynote Address," Apple, apple.com/quicktime/qtv/ wwdc08 (accessed January 30, 2009).
9. Leander Kahney, *Inside Steve's Brain* (New York: Penguin Group, 2008), 29.

Scene 2: Answer the One Question That Matters Most

1. YouTube, "The First iMac Introduction," YouTube, youtube.com/watch?v=0BHPtoTctDy (accessed January 30, 2009).
2. YouTube, "Apple WWDC 2005—The Intel Switch Revealed," YouTube, youtube.com/watch?v=ghdTqnYnFyg (accessed January 30, 2009).
3. Wikipedia, "Virtual Private Server," http://en.wikipedia.org/wiki/server_virtualization (accessed January 30, 2009).
4. Ashlee Vance, "Cisco Plans Big Push into Server Market," *New York Times*, January 19, 2009, nytimes.com/2009/01/20/technology/companies/20cisco.html?scp=1&sq=cisco%20+virtualization&st=search (accessed January 30, 2009).
5. YouTube, "Macworld 2003—The Keynote Introduction (Part 1)," YouTube, youtube.com/watch?v=ZZqYn77dT3s&feature=related (accessed January 30, 2009).
6. Apple, "Apple Introduces the New iPod Nano: World's Most Popular Digital Music Player Features New Aluminum Design in Five Colors and Twenty-Four-Hour Battery Life," Apple press release, September 12, 2006, apple.com/pr/library/2006/sep/12nano.html (accessed January 30, 2009).
7. Apple, "Apple Announces Time Capsule: Wireless Backup for All Your Macs," Apple press release, January 15, 2008, apple.com/pr/library/2008/01/15timecapsule.html (accessed January 30, 2009).
8. YouTube, "3G iPhone WWDC Keynote 6/9/08," YouTube, June 9, 2008, youtube.com/watch?v=mA9Jrk16Ki4 (accessed January 30, 2009).
9. YouTube, "Steve Jobs Announces iTunes 8 with Genius," YouTube, September 9, 2008, youtube.com/watch?v=6XsgEH5HMvI (accessed January, 2009).
10. YouTube, "Steve Jobs CNBC Interview: Macworld 2007," YouTube, CNBC reporter Jim Goldman, youtube.com/watch?v=0my4eis82jw&feature=playlist&p=0520CA6271486D5B&playnext=1&index=13 (accessed January 30, 2009).
11. Guy Kawasaki, *The Macintosh Way* (New York: HarperCollins, 1990), 100.

Scene 3: Develop a Messianic Sense of Purpose

1. John Sculley, *Odyssey* (New York: Harper & Row, 1987), 90.
2. Alan Deutschman, *Inside Steve's Brain* (New York: Penguin Group, 2008), 168.
3. Stanford University, "'You've Got to Find What You Love,' Jobs Says," *Stanford Report*, June 14, 2005, Steve Jobs commencement address, delivered on June 12, 2005, http://news-service.stanford.edu/news/2005/june15/jobs-061505.html (accessed January 30, 2009).

4. YouTube, "Macworld Boston 1997—Full Version," YouTube, youtube.com/watch?v=PEHNrqPkefl (accessed January 30, 2009).
5. Carmine Gallo, "From Homeless to Multimillionaire," *BusinessWeek*, July 23, 2007, businessweek.com/smallbiz/content/jul2007/sb20070723_608918.htm (accessed January 30, 2009).
6. Jim Collins and Jerry Porras, *Built to Last: Successful Habits of Visionary Companies* (New York: HarperBusiness, 1994), 48.
7. *Triumph of the Nerds*, PBS documentary written and hosted by Robert X. Cringely (1996: New York).
8. Wikipedia, "Steve Jobs," includes Jobs's quote, http://en.wikiquote.org/wiki/steve_jobs (accessed January 30, 2009).
9. Malcolm Gladwell, *Outliers* (New York: Little, Brown and Company, 2008), 64.
10. John Markoff, "The Passion of Steve Jobs," *New York Times*, January 15, 2008, http://bits.blogs.nytimes.com/2008/01/15/the-passion-of-steve-jobs (accessed January 30, 2009).
11. John Paczkowski, "Bill Gates and Steve Jobs," D5 Highlights from D: All Things Digital, May 30, 2007, http://d5.allthingsd.com/20070530/d5-gates-jobs-interview (accessed January 30, 2009).
12. "Oprah," first aired on October 23, 2008, property of Harpo Productions.
13. Marcus Buckingham, *The One Thing You Need to Know* (New York: Free Press, 2005), 59.
14. Ibid., 61–62.
15. John Sculley, *Odyssey* (New York: Harper & Row, 1987), 65.
16. Smithsonian Institution, "Oral History Interview with Steve Jobs," Smithsonian Institution Oral and Video Histories—Steve Jobs, April 20, 1995, http://americanhistory.si.edu/collections/comphist/sj1.html (accessed January 30, 2009).
17. *BusinessWeek*, "Steve Jobs: He Thinks Different," *BusinessWeek*, November 1, 2004, businessweek.com/magazine/content/04_44/b3906025_mz072.htm (accessed January 30, 2009).
18. Jeff Goodell, "Steve Jobs: The *Rolling Stone* Interview," *Rolling Stone*, December 3, 2003, rollingstone.com/news/story/5939600/steve_jobs_the_rolling_stone_interview/ (accessed January 30, 2009).
19. Jim Collins and Jerry Porras, *Built to Last: Successful Habits of Visionary Companies* (New York: HarperBusiness, 1994), 234.
20. *Triumph of the Nerds*, PBS documentary written and hosted by Robert X. Cringely (1996, New York).
21. Gary Wolf, "Steve Jobs: The Next Insanely Great Thing," *Wired*, 1996, via Wikipedia, wired.com/wired/archive//4.02/jobs_pr.html (accessed January 30, 2009).

22. Wikipedia, "Think Different," http://en.wikipedia.org/wiki/think_different (accessed January 30, 2009).

23. Alan Deutschman, *The Second Coming of Steve Jobs* (New York: Broadway Books, 2001), 242.

24. Apple, "Macworld San Francisco 2007 Keynote Address," Apple, apple .com/quicktime/qtv/mwsf07 (accessed January 30, 2009).

Scene 4: Create Twitter-Like Headlines

1. Apple, "Macworld 2008 Keynote Address," Apple, apple.com/quicktime/ qtv/mwsf08 (accessed January 30, 2009).

2. Ibid.

3. Ibid.

4. CNBC, "Steve Jobs Shows off Sleek Laptop," CNBC interview after 2008 Macworld keynote, http://video.nytimes.com/video/2008/01/15/ technology/1194817476407/steve-jobs-shows-off-sleek-laptop.html (accessed January 30, 2009).

5. Ibid.

6. Apple, "Apple Introduces MacBook Air—The World's Thinnest Notebook," Apple press release, January 15, 2008, apple.com/pr/ library/2008/01/15mbair.html (accessed January 30, 2009).

7. Ibid.

8. Apple, "Macworld San Francisco 2007 Keynote Address," Apple, apple .com/quicktime/qtv/mwsf07 (accessed January 30, 2009).

9. YouTube, "Steve Jobs Introduces GarageBand 1.0 (Assisted by John Mayer)," YouTube, youtube.com/watch?v=BVXWFgQvdlK (accessed January 30, 2009).

10. YouTube, "The First iMac Introduction," YouTube, youtube.com/ watch?v=0BHPtoTctDY (accessed January 30, 2009).

11. YouTube, "Apple Music Event 2001—The First Ever iPod Introduction," YouTube, youtube.com/watch?v=KN0SVBCJqLs&feature=related (accessed January 30, 2009).

12. Matthew Fordahl, "Apple's New iPod Player Puts '1,000 Songs in Your Pocket,'" Associated Press at seattlepi.com, November 1, 2001, http:// seattlepi.nwsource.com/business/44900_ipod01.shtml (accessed January 30, 2009).

13. YouTube, "Macworld 2003—The Keynote Introduction (Part 1)," YouTube, youtube.com/watch?v=ZZqYn77dT3s&feature=related (accessed January 30, 2009).

14. Apple, "Apple Unveils Keynote," Apple press release, January 7, 2003, apple.com/pr/library/2003/jan/07keynote.html (accessed January 9, 2009).

Scene 5: Draw a Road Map

1. Apple, "Macworld San Francisco 2007 Keynote Address," Apple, apple. com/quicktime/qtv/mwsf07 (accessed January 30, 2009).
2. YouTube, "The Lost 1984 Video (The Original 1984 Macintosh Introduction)," YouTube, youtube.com/watch?v=2B-XwPjn9YY (accessed January 30, 2009).
3. YouTube, "Apple WWDC 2005—The Intel Switch Revealed," YouTube, youtube.com/watch?v=ghdTqnYnFyg (accessed January 30, 2009).
4. Michelle Kessler, "Better Computer Chips Raise Laptops' Abilities," *USA Today*, usatoday.com/printedition/money/20080715/1b_chips15.art .htm?loc=interstitialskip (accessed January 30, 2009).
5. Edward Baig, "Windows 7 Gives Hope for Less-Bloated Operating System," *USA Today*, sec. 6B, January 22, 2009.
6. Apple, "WWDC 2008 Keynote Address," Apple, apple.com/quicktime/qtv/ wwdc08 (accessed January 30, 2009).
7. CESweb.org, "Steve Ballmer and Robbie Bach Keynote: International Consumer Electronics Show 2009," remarks by Steve Ballmer and Robbie Bach at International CES 2009, January 7, 2009, cesweb.org/docs/ microsoft-steveballmer-_robbiebach-transcript.pdf (accessed January 30, 2009).
8. Apple, "Macworld 2008 Keynote Address," Apple, apple.com/quicktime/ qtv/mwsf08 (accessed January 30, 2009).
9. John F. Kennedy Presidential Library and Museum, "Special Message to the Congress on Urgent National Needs Page 4," President John F. Kennedy speech, May 25, 1961, jfklibrary.org/historical+resources/ archives/reference+desk/speeches/jfk/urgent+national+needs+page+4 .htm (accessed January 30, 2009).
10. American Rhetoric, "Barack Obama 2004 Democratic National Convention Keynote Address: The Audacity of Hope," July 27, 2004, americanrhetoric.com/speeches/convention2004/barackobama2004dnc .htm (accessed January 30, 2009).
11. American Rhetoric, "Barack Obama Presidential Inaugural Address: What Is Required: The Price and Promise of Citizenship," January 20, 2009, americanrhetoric.com/speeches/barackobama/ barackobamainauguraladdress.htm (accessed January 30, 2009).
12. YouTube, "Apple Music Event 2001—The First Ever iPod Introduction," YouTube, youtube.com/watch?v=kN0SVBCJqLS&feature=related (accessed January 30, 2009).
13. Stanford University, " 'You've Got to Find What You Love,' Jobs Says," *Stanford Report*, June 14, 2005, Steve Jobs commencement address,

delivered on June 12, 2005, http://news-service.stanford.edu/news/2005/june15/jobs-061505.html (accessed January 30, 2009).

14. American Rhetoric, "Jim Valvano Arthur Ashe Courage & Humanitarian Award Acceptance Address," March 4, 1993, americanrhetoric.com/speeches/jimvalvanoespyaward.htm (accessed January 30, 2009).

Scene 6: Introduce the Antagonist

1. Wikipedia, "1984 (Advertisement)," http://en.wikipedia.org/wiki/1984_ad (accessed January 30, 2009).
2. YouTube, "1983 Apple Keynote—The '1984' Ad Introduction," YouTube, youtube.com/watch?v=lSiQA6KKyJo (accessed January 30, 2009).
3. YouTube, "Macworld 2007—Steve Jobs Introduces iPhone—Part 1," YouTube, youtube.com/watch?v=PZoPdBh8KUS&feature=related (accessed January 30, 2009).
4. YouTube, "Steve Jobs CNBC Interview: Macworld 2007," YouTube, youtube.com/watch?v=0mY4EIS82Jw (accessed January 30, 2009).
5. Martin Lindstrom, *Buyology* (New York: Doubleday, 2008), 107.
6. Ibid.
7. John Medina, *Brain Rules* (Seattle: Pear Press, 2008), 84.
8. YouTube, "Macworld SF 2003 Part 1," YouTube, youtube.com/watch?v=lSiQA6KKyJo (accessed January 30, 2009).
9. Demo.com, TravelMuse, Inc., pitch, DEMO 2008, demo.com/watchlisten/videolibrary.html?bcpid=1127798146&bclid=1774292996&bctid=1778578857 (accessed January 30, 2009).
10. *An Inconvenient Truth*, DVD, directed by Davis Guggengeim (Hollywood: Paramount Pictures, 2006).

Scene 7: Reveal the Conquering Hero

1. YouTube, "1983 Apple Keynote," YouTube, youtube.com/watch?v=lSiQA6KKyJo (accessed January 30, 2009).
2. YouTube, "Apple Music Event 2001—The First Ever iPod Introduction," YouTube, youtube.com/watch?v=kN0SVBCJqLs&feature=related (accessed January 30, 2009).
3. Mike Langberg, "Sweet & Low: Well-Designed iPod Upstarts Are Music for the Budget," *Seattle Times*, sec. C6, August 9, 2003.
4. Apple, "Out of the Box," 2006 television ad, Apple website, apple.com/getamac/ads (accessed January 30, 2009).
5. YouTube, "New iPhone Shazam Ad," YouTube, youtube.com/watch?v=P3NSsVKcrnY (accessed January 30, 2009).
6. Apple, "Why You'll Love a Mac," Get a Mac page, Apple website, apple.com/getamac/whymac (accessed January 30, 2009).

7. YouTube, "Macworld San Francisco 2006—The MacBook Pro Introduction," YouTube, youtube.com/watch?v=I6JWqllbhXE (accessed January 30, 2009).

8. Smithsonian Institution, "Oral History Interview with Steve Jobs," Smithsonian Institution Oral and Video Histories—Steve Jobs, April 20, 1995, http://americanhistory.si.edu/collections/comphist/sj1.html (accessed January 30, 2009).

Intermission 1: Obey the Ten-Minute Rule

1. John Medina, *Brain Rules* (Seattle: Pear Press, 2008), 74.

2. Apple, "Macworld San Francisco 2007 Keynote Address," Apple, apple.com/quicktime/qtv/mwsf07 (accessed January 30, 2009).

Scene 8: Channel Their Inner Zen

1. Rob Walker, "The Guts of a New Machine," *New York Times*, November 30, 2003, nytimes.com/2003/11/30/magazine/30ipod.html?pagewanted=1& ei=5007&en=750c9021e58923d5&ex=1386133200 (accessed January 30, 2009).

2. Ibid.

3. Nancy Duarte, *Slide:ology* (Sebastopol, CA: O'Reilly Media, 2008), 93.

4. Gregory Berns, *Iconoclast* (Boston: Harvard Business Press, 2008), 36.

5. Garr Reynolds, *Presentation Zen* (Berkeley: New Riders, 2008), 68.

6. Ibid., 12.

7. Carrie Kirby and Matthew Yi, "Apple Turns Thirty: The Man Behind the Mac," SF Gate, March 26, 2006, sfgate.com/cgi-bin/article.cgi?file=/c/a/2006/03/26/mng7ehueq51.dtl (accessed January 30, 2009).

8. Garr Reynolds, *Presentation Zen* (Berkeley: New Riders, 2008), 113.

9. Seth Godin's Blog, "Nine Steps to PowerPoint Magic," October 6, 2008, http://sethgodin.typepad.com/seths_blog/2008/10/nine-steps-to-p.html (accessed January 30, 2008).

10. Leander Kahney, *Inside Steve's Brain* (New York: Penguin Group, 2008), 61.

11. Ibid., 60.

12. Ibid., 131.

13. Apple, "Macworld 2008 Keynote Address," Apple, apple.com/quicktime/qtv/mwsf08 (accessed January 30, 2009).

14. Apple, "Apple Special Event September 2008," Apple Pre–Holiday Season Presentation, apple.com/quicktime/qtv/letsfrock (accessed January 30, 2009).

15. Richard Mayer and Roxana Moreno, "A Cognitive Theory of Multimedia Learning: Implications for Design Principles," University of California,

Santa Barbara, unm.edu/~moreno/pdfs/chi.pdf (accessed January 30, 2009).

16. *BusinessWeek*, "The Best Managers of 2008," BusinessWeek.com slide show, http://images.businessweek.com/ss/09/01/0108_best_worst/14 .htm (accessed January 30, 2009).

17. Richard Mayer and Roxana Moreno, "A Cognitive Theory of Multimedia Learning: Implications for Design Principles," University of California, Santa Barbara, unm.edu/~moreno/pdfs/chi.pdf (accessed January 30, 2009).

18. Ibid.

19. Ibid.

20. Apple, "Apple Special Event September 2008," Apple Pre–Holiday Season Presentation, apple.com/quicktime/qtv/letsfrock (accessed January 30, 2009).

21. Garr Reynolds, *Presentation Zen* (Berkeley: New Riders, 2008), 105.

22. Nancy Duarte, *Slide:ology* (Sebastopol, CA: O'Reilly Media, 2008), 106.

23. Wikipedia, "Picture Superiority Effect," http://en.wikipedia.org/wiki/picture_superiority_effect (accessed January 30, 2009).

24. John Medina, *Brain Rules* (Seattle: Pear Press, 2008), 234.

25. Ibid.

26. YouTube, "WWDC 2008 Steve Jobs Keynote—iPhone 3G," YouTube, youtube.com/watch?v=40YW7Lco0og (accessed January 30, 2009).

27. Apple, "WWDC 2008 Keynote Address," Apple, apple.com/quicktime/qtv/wwdc08 (accessed January 30, 2009).

28. Plain English Campaign, "Before and After," section of site with before-and-after examples, http://s190934979.websitehome.co.uk/examples/before_and_after.html (accessed January 30, 2009).

29. Paul Arden, *It's Not How Good You Are, It's How Good You Want to Be* (London: Phaidon Press, 2003), 68.

Scene 9: Dress Up Your Numbers

1. YouTube, "Apple Music Event 2001—The First Ever iPod Introduction," YouTube, youtube.com/watch?v=kN0SVBCJqLs&feature=related (accessed January 30, 2009).

2. Jeff Goodell, "Steve Jobs: The *Rolling Stone* Interview," *Rolling Stone*, December 3, 2003, rollingstone.com/news/story/5939600/steve_jobs _the_rolling_stone_interview (accessed January 30, 2009).

3. Apple, "WWDC 2008 Keynote Address," Apple, apple.com/quicktime/qtv/wwdc08 (accessed January 30, 2009).

4. Apple, "Macworld 2008 Keynote Address," Apple, apple.com/quicktime/qtv/mwsf08 (accessed January 30, 2009).

5. John Markoff, "Burned Once, Intel Prepares New Chip Fortified by Constant Tests," *New York Times*, November 16, 2008, nytimes. com/2008/11/17/technology/companies/17chip.html ?_r=1&scp=1&sq=barton%20+%20intel%20&st=cse (accessed January 30, 2009).

6. IBM, "Fact Sheet and Background: Roadrunner Smashes the Petaflop Barrier," IBM press release, June 9, 2008, -03.ibm.com/press/us/en/ pressrelease/24405.wss (accessed January 30, 2009).

7. Scott Duke Harris, "What Could You Buy for $700 Billion?" *San Jose Mercury News*, sec. E, October 5, 2008.

8. ClimateCrisis.org, "What Is Global Warming?" ClimateCrisis website, http://climatecrisis.org (accessed January 30, 2009).

9. Cornelia Dean, "Emissions Cut Won't Bring Quick Relief," *New York Times*, sec. A21, January 27, 2009.

Scene 10: Use "Amazingly Zippy" Words

1. Apple, "WWDC 2008 Keynote Address," Apple, apple.com/quicktime/qtv/ wwdc08 (accessed January 30, 2009).

2. Brent Schlender and Christine Chen, "Steve Jobs's Apple Gets Way Cooler," *Fortune*, January 24, 2000, http://money.cnn.com/magazines/ fortune/fortune_archive/2000/01/24/272281/index.htm (accessed January 30, 2009).

3. UsingEnglish.com, "Text Content Analysis Tool," usingenglish.com/ resources/text-statistics.php (accessed January 30, 2009).

4. Todd Bishop, "Bill Gates and Steve Jobs: Keynote Text Analysis," The Microsoft Blog, January 14, 2007, http://blog.seattlepi.nwsource.com/ microsoft/archives/110473.asp (accessed January 30, 2009).

5. Microsoft, "Bill Gates, Robbie Bach: 2007 International Consumer Electronics Show (CES)," Microsoft Corporation, CES, Las Vegas, January 7, 2007, microsoft.com/presspass/exec/billg/speeches/2007/01-07ces.mspx (accessed January 30, 2009).

6. Apple, "Macworld San Francisco 2007 Keynote Address," Apple, apple .com/quicktime/qtv/mwsf07 (accessed January 30, 2009).

7. Apple, "What Is Apple's Mission Statement?" Apple website: Investor Relations: FAQs: Apple Corporate Information, apple.com/investor (accessed January 30, 2009).

8. Carmine Gallo, *Ten Simple Secrets of the World's Greatest Business Communicators* (Naperville, IL: Sourcebooks, 2005), 116.

9. Ibid., 116–117.

10. Apple, "Macworld 2008 Keynote Address," Apple, apple.com/quicktime/ qtv/mwsf08 (accessed January 30, 2009).

11. Jack Welch, *Jack: Straight from the Gut* (New York: Warner Books, 2001), 70.
12. YouTube, "Apple Music Event 2001—The First Ever iPod Introduction," YouTube, youtube.com/watch?v=kN0SVBCJqLs&feature=related (accessed January 30, 2009).
13. YouTube, "Macworld San Francisco 2003—PowerBook 17" + 12" Intro (Pt. 1)," YouTube, youtube.com/watch?v=3iGTDE9XqJU (accessed January 30, 2009).
14. Ibid.
15. YouTube, "Macworld SF 2003 Part 1," YouTube, youtube.com/watch?v=Xac6NWT7EKY (accessed January 30, 2009).
16. *Triumph of the Nerds*, PBS documentary written and hosted by Robert X. Cringely (1996, New York).
17. *BusinessWeek*, February 6, 2006, businessweek.com/magazine/content/06_06/b3970001.htm (accessed January 30, 2009).
18. Apple, "Apple Introduces New iPod Touch," Apple press release, September 9, 2008, apple.com/pr/library/2008/09/09touch.html (accessed January 30, 2009).
19. YouTube, "Macworld San Francisco 2003—PowerBook 17" + 12" Intro (Pt. 1)," YouTube, youtube.com/watch?v=3iGTDE9XqJU (accessed January 30, 2009).
20. Gregory Berns, *Iconoclast* (Boston: Harvard Business Press, 2008), 36.

Scene 11: Share the Stage

1. YouTube, "Macworld San Francisco 2006—The MacBook Pro Introduction," YouTube, youtube.com/watch?v=I6JWqIlbhXE (accessed January 30, 2009).
2. YouTube, "Macworld Boston 1997—The Microsoft Deal," YouTube, youtube.com/watch?v=WxOp5mBY9IY (accessed January 30, 2009).
3. Apple, "Apple Special Event October 2008," Apple, apple.com/quicktime/qtv/specialevent1008 (accessed January 30, 2009).
4. Apple, "Macworld 2008 Keynote Address," Apple, apple.com/quicktime/qtv/mwsf08 (accessed January 30, 2009).
5. Ibid.
6. Apple, "Macworld San Francisco 2007 Keynote Address," Apple, apple.com/quicktime/qtv/mwsf07 (accessed January 30, 2009).
7. Apple, "Macworld 2008 Keynote Address," Apple, apple.com/quicktime/qtv/mwsf08 (accessed January 30, 2009).
8. YouTube, "Noah Wyle as Steve—EpicEmpire.com," YouTube, youtube.com/watch?v=_KRO5Hxv_No (accessed January 30, 2009).

Scene 12: Stage Your Presentation with Props

1. Apple, "Apple Special Event October 2008," Apple, apple.com/quicktime/qtv/specialevent1008 (accessed January 30, 2009).
2. Guy Kawasaki, *The Macintosh Way* (New York: HarperCollins, 1990), 149.
3. Ibid.
4. Ibid.
5. Ibid.
6. Ibid.
7. Apple, "WWDC 2008 Keynote Address," Apple, apple.com/quicktime/qtv/wwdc08 (accessed January 30, 2009).
8. YouTube, "Macworld 2007—Part 4—Steve Jobs Demos the iPhone (Video)," YouTube, http://macblips.dailyradar.com/video/macworld_2007_part_4_steve_jobs_demos_the_iphone (accessed January 30, 2009).
9. Apple, "Macworld San Francisco 2007 Keynote Address," Apple, apple.com/quicktime/qtv/mwsf07 (accessed January 30, 2009).
10. YouTube, "Demo of PhotoBooth (From All About Steve)," YouTube, youtube.com/watch?v=h4Al6Mt4jQc (accessed January 30, 2009).
11. YouTube, "Safari on Windows (WWDC 2007)," YouTube, youtube.com/watch?v=46DHMaCbdxc (accessed January 30, 2009).
12. YouTube, "Steve Jobs Demos GarageBand," YouTube, youtube.com/watch?v=E03Bj2R749c (accessed January 30, 2009).
13. YouTube, "Steve Jobs Introduces GarageBand 1.0 (Assisted by John Mayer)," YouTube, youtube.com/watch?v=BVXWFgQvdLK (accessed January 30, 2009).
14. YouTube, "Apple WWDC—The Intel Switch Revealed," YouTube, youtube.com/watch?v=ghdTqnYnFYg (accessed January 30, 2009).

Scene 13: Reveal a "Holy Shit" Moment

1. Apple, "Macworld 2008 Keynote Address," Apple, apple.com/quicktime/qtv/mwsf08 (accessed January 30, 2009).
2. Sasha Cavender, "Thinnest Laptop: Fits into Manila Envelope," ABC News, January 15, 2008, http://abcnews.go.com/print?id=4138633 (accessed January 30, 2009).
3. YouTube, "Steve Jobs Showcases Macintosh 24-Jan-1984," YouTube, youtube.com/watch?v=4KkENSYkMgs (accessed January 30, 2009).
4. John Medina, *Brain Rules* (Seattle: Pear Press, 2008), 81.
5. YouTube, "Apple Music Event 2001—The First Ever iPod Introduction," YouTube, youtube.com/watch?v=kN0SVBCJqLs&feature=related (accessed January 30, 2009).

6. YouTube, "Macworld San Francisco 2000, Steve Jobs Become iCEO of Apple," YouTube, January 5, 2000, youtube.com/watch?v=JgHtKFuY3be (accessed January 30, 2009).
7. Apple, "Macworld San Francisco 2007 Keynote Address," Apple, apple .com/quicktime/qtv/mwsf07 (accessed January 30, 2009).

Intermission 2: Schiller Learns from the Best
1. Apple, "Macworld 2009 Keynote Address," Apple, apple.com/quicktime/ qtv/macworld-san-francisco-2009 (accessed January 30, 2009).
2. Slideshare, "Phil Schiller's Mac World 2009 Keynote Address," Slideshare, slideshare.net/kangaro10a/phil-schillers-mac-world-2009-keynote -presentation (accessed January 30, 2009).

Scene 14: Master Stage Presence
1. YouTube, "Macworld SF 2003 Part 1," YouTube, youtube.com/ watch?v=Xac6NWT7EKY (accessed January 30, 2009).
2. Dan Moren, "Stan Sigman Says Sayonara," Macworld.com, October 12, 2007, http://iphone.macworld.com/2007/10/stan_sigman_says _sayonara.php (accessed January 30, 2009).
3. Gil Amelio, *On the Firing Line: My Five Hundred Days at Apple* (New York: Collins Business, 1999), 199.
4. Apple, "Macworld San Francisco 2007 Keynote Address," Apple, apple .com/quicktime/qtv/mwsf07 (accessed January 30, 2009).
5. Apple, "Macworld 2008 Keynote Address," Apple, apple.com/quicktime/ qtv/mwsf08 (accessed January 30, 2009).
6. YouTube, "Apple Music Event 2001—The First Ever iPod Introduction," YouTube, youtube.com/watch?v=kN0SVBCJqLs (accessed January 30, 2009).
7. Ibid.
8. Albert Mehrabian, *Silent Messages* (Stamford, CT: Wadsworth, 1980).

Scene 15: Make It *Look* Effortless
1. *BusinessWeek*, "Steve Jobs's Magic Kingdom," *BusinessWeek* cover story, February 6, 2006, businessweek.com/magazine/content/06_06/ b3970001.htm (accessed January 30, 2009).
2. Mike Evangelist, "Behind the Magic Curtain," *Guardian*, for Guardian .co.uk, January 5, 2006, guardian.co.uk/technology/2006/jan/05/ newmedia.media1 (accessed January 30, 2009).
3. Ibid.
4. Ibid.

5. Michael Krantz, "Steve's Two Jobs," *Time*, October 18, 1999, time.com/time/magazine/article/0,9171,992258-1,00.html (accessed January 30, 2009).

6. Ibid.

7. Celia Sandys and Jonathan Littman, *We Shall Not Fail* (New York: Penguin Group, 2003), 55.

8. Alan Deutschman, *The Second Coming of Steve Jobs* (New York: Broadway Books, 2001), 82.

9. Malcolm Gladwell, *Outliers* (New York: Little, Brown and Company, 2008), 39.

10. Daniel Levitin, *This Is Your Brain on Music* (New York: Plume-Penguin, 2007), 97.

11. Malcolm Gladwell, *Outliers* (New York: Little, Brown and Company, 2008), 48.

12. *New York Times*, "Senate Confirmation Hearing: Hillary Clinton," January 13, 2009, *New York Times* transcript, nytimes.com/2009/01/13/us/politics/13text-clinton.html?pagewanted=all (accessed January 30, 2009).

Scene 16: Wear the Appropriate Costume

1. Alan Deutschman, *The Second Coming of Steve Jobs* (New York: Broadway Books, 2001), 22.

Scene 17: Toss the Script

1. Apple, "Macworld 2008 Keynote Address," Apple, apple.com/quicktime/qtv/mwsf08 (accessed January 30, 2009).

2. Vanguard, ad on website, vanguard.com (accessed January 30, 2009).

3. Spymac, "Steve's Notes Closeup—Four Thousand Lattes to Go," Spymac, January 11, 2007, spymac.com/details/?1793780 (accessed January 30, 2009).

4. Apple, "Macworld San Francisco 2007 Keynote Address," Apple, apple.com/quicktime/qtv/mwsf07 (accessed January 30, 2009).

Scene 18: Have Fun

1. YouTube, "Apple WWDC 2002—The Death of Mac OS 9," YouTube, youtube.com/watch?v=Cl7xQ8i3fc0&feature=playlist&p=72CF29777B67F776&playnext=1&index=9 (accessed January 30, 2009).

2. YouTube, "Steve Jobs, TV Jammer Story," YouTube, youtube.com/watch?v=xiSBSXrQ8D0 (accessed January 30, 2009).

3. Ibid.

4. YouTube, "Apple Bloopers," YouTube, youtube.com/watch?v= AnVUvW42CUA (accessed January 30, 2009).

5. Apple, "Macworld 2008 Keynote Address," Apple, apple.com/quicktime/ qtv/mwsf08 (accessed January 30, 2009).

6. Ibid.

7. YouTube, "Apple Keynote Bloopers!!" YouTube, youtube.com/watch?v= KsKKQNZG3rE&feature=related (accessed January 30, 2009).

8. Apple, "WWDC 2008 Keynote Address," Apple, apple.com/quicktime/qtv/ wwdc08 (accessed January 30, 2009).

9. YouTube, "Apple Announces iTunes for Windows," YouTube, October 16, 2003, youtube.com/watch?v=-YtR-DKDKil (accessed January 30, 2009).

10. Nick Mediati, "Jobs Has Been an Extraordinary Spokesman," *PC World*, January 14, 2009, pcworld.com/article/157114/jobs_has_been_an _extraordinary_spokesman.html (accessed January 30, 2009).

11. Bob Dylan, "Mr. Tambourine Man," *Bringing It All Back Home*, Sony, 1965.

Encore: One More Thing

1. Stanford University, " 'You've Got to Find What You Love,' Jobs Says," *Stanford Report*, June 14, 2005, Steve Jobs commencement address, delivered on June 12, 2005, http://news-service.stanford.edu/news/2005/ june15/jobs-061505.html (accessed January 30, 2009).

Postscript: Steve Jobs by the Book

1. YouTube, "Apple iPad Event Part 2 of 10 (HD)," YouTube, http://www.you tube.com/watch?v=LK_VunL9rjY&feature=related (accessed June 6, 2011).

2. Ibid.

3. Ibid.

4. Ibid.

5. Apple, "Apple WWDC 2010 Keynote Address," Apple Events, June 7, 2010, http://www.apple.com/apple-events/wwdc-2010/ (accessed June 6, 2011).

6. Ibid.

7. Ibid.

8. YouTube, "Apple-Special Event-March 2, 2011," YouTube, http://www.you tube.com/watch?v=qQG0XfU-bFs (accessed June 6, 2011).

9. Ibid.

10. Ibid.

11. Ibid.

12. Ibid.

13. Apple, "Apple-Special Event," Apple Events, June 6, 2011, http://events.apple .com.edgesuite.net/11piubpwiqubf06/event/ (accessed June 6, 2011).

INDEX

corporate America. I find it amazing that Jobs has actually improved his presentation style in the twenty-five years since the launch. The 1984 presentation was tough to beat—one of the greatest presentations of our time. Still, Jobs's keynotes at the Macworld Expo in 2007 and 2008 were his best ever. Jobs's introduction of the iPad in 2010 and the iPad2 in 2011 also rival almost any presentation he has delivered. Both presentations are discussed and dissected in a brand-new "Postscript" at the end of this book. Everything that he had learned about connecting with audiences came together to create truly magnificent moments.

Now the bad news. Your presentations are being compared with those of Steve Jobs. He has transformed the typical, dull, technical, plodding slide show into a theatrical event complete with heroes, villains, a supporting cast, and stunning backdrops. People who witness a Steve Jobs presentation for the first time describe it as an extraordinary experience. In a *Los Angeles Times* article about Jobs's medical leave, Michael Hiltzik wrote: "No American CEO is more intimately identified with his company's success . . . Jobs is Apple's visionary and carnival barker. If you want a taste of the latter persona, watch the video of the original iPod launch event in October 2001. Jobs's dramatic command is astonishing. Viewing the event recently on YouTube, I was on the edge of my seat, even though I knew how the story came out."[4] Jobs is the Tiger Woods of business, raising the bar for the rest of us.

Now the good news. You can identify and adopt each of Jobs's techniques to keep your audience members at the edge of their seats. Tapping into his qualities will help you create your own magnificent presentations and give you the tools to sell your ideas far more persuasively than you have ever imagined.

Consider *The Presentation Secrets of Steve Jobs* your road map to presentation success. It's as close as you will ever get to having Jobs speak directly in your ear as you present the value behind your service, product, company, or cause. Whether you are a CEO launching a new product, an entrepreneur pitching investors, a sales professional closing a deal, or an educator trying to inspire a class, Jobs has something to teach you. Most business professionals give presentations to deliver information.

Moving On Up

> *As soon as you move one step up from the bottom, your effectiveness depends on your ability to reach others through the spoken and written word.* [5]
>
> —PETER DRUCKER

Not Jobs. A Steve Jobs presentation is intended to create an experience—"a reality distortion field"—that leaves his audience awed, inspired, and wildly excited.

Some of the most common terms used to describe Steve Jobs are "seductive," "magnetic," "captivating," and "charismatic." Other terms, typically related to his interpersonal traits, are less flattering. Jobs is a complicated man who creates extraordinary products, cultivates intense loyalty, and also scares the shit out of people. He is a passionate perfectionist and a visionary, two qualities that create a combustible combination when the way things are do not match the way Jobs believes they should be. This book is not intended to tackle everything about Steve Jobs. It is neither a biography of the man nor a history of Apple. This book is not about Jobs the boss, but about Jobs the communicator. One prominent industry analyst recomends that the book should be in every executive's library. It offers the most thorough breakdown of exactly how Jobs crafts and delivers the story behind the Apple brand. You will learn how Jobs does all of the following:

» Crafts messages
» Presents ideas
» Generates excitement for a product or feature
» Delivers a memorable experience
» Creates customer evangelists

The techniques will help you create your own "insanely great" presentations. The lessons are remarkably simple to learn, but applying them is up to you. Speaking the way Steve speaks requires work, but the benefit to your career, company, and personal success will be well worth your commitment.